Citizenship and Collective Identity
in Europe

D1611463

This book is the first monograph to systematically explore the relationship between citizenship and collective identity in the European Union, integrating two fields of research – citizenship and collective identity.

Karolewski argues that various types of citizenship correlate with differing collective identities and demonstrates the link between citizenship and collective identity. He constructs three generic models of citizenship including the republican, the liberal and the caesarean citizenship to which he ascribes types of collective identity. Using a multidisciplinary approach, the book integrates concepts, theories and empirical findings from sociology (in the field of citizenship research), social psychology (in the field of collective identity), legal studies (in the chapter on the European Charter of Fundamental Rights), security studies (in the chapter on the politics of insecurity) and philosophy (in the chapter on pathologies of deliberation) to examine the current trends of European citizenship and European identity politics.

This book will be of interest to students and scholars of European politics, political theory, political philosophy, sociology and social psychology.

Ireneusz Pawel Karolewski is Professor of Political Science in the Willy Brandt Centre for German and European Studies at the University of Wroclaw, Poland and Adjunct Professor in the Department of Political Science, University of Potsdam, Germany. His most recent publications include, as co-editor, *Nationalism and European Integration*; *Nationalism in Contemporary Europe* and *Nation and Nationalism: Political and Historical Studies*.

Routledge Advances in European Politics

Citizenship and Collective Identity in Europe

Ireneusz Pawel Karolewski

Routledge
Taylor & Francis Group

LONDON AND NEW YORK

First published 2010
by Routledge
2 Park Square, Milton Park, Abingdon, Oxon, OX14 4RN

Simultaneously published in the USA and Canada
by Routledge
711 Third Avenue, New York, NY 10017

Routledge is an imprint of the Taylor & Francis Group, an informa business

First issued in paperback 2011

© 2010 Ireneusz Pawel Karolewski

Typeset in Times New Roman by
HWA Text and Data Management, London

British Library Cataloguing in Publication Data
A catalogue record for this book is available from the British Library

Library of Congress Cataloging in Publication Data
Karolewski, Ireneusz Pawel.
  Citizenship and collective identity in Europe / Ireneusz Pawel Karolewski.
     p. cm.
  Includes bibliographical references and index.
  1. Citizenship – European Union countries. 2. Group identity – European
Union countries. 3. European Union. I. Title.
JN40.K38 2009
323.6094 – dc22   2009007480

ISBN13: 978-0-415-50276-4 (pbk)
ISBN13: 978-0-415-49658-2 (hbk)
ISBN13: 978-0-203-87226-0 (ebk)

For my son Adam

Contents

Acknowledgments

This book was originally written as a German professorial dissertation. It greatly profited from the support and intellectual input of friends and colleagues at the University of Potsdam, the University of Trento and the University of Cambridge. In particular, I would like to thank Klaus Goetz, Peter Wagner, David Lane and Dario Castiglione for their valuable comments on the dissertation. Most especially, I thank Viktoria Kaina, my dear friend and most appreciated colleague for her ongoing encouragement, critical input and professional advice. I also thank Andrzej Marcin Suszycki, my exceptional friend, for his private and professional support.

This book has been written during my final years as assistant professor at the Chair of Political Theory of the University of Potsdam in Germany. I would like to thank Heinz Kleger for all nine years of our cooperation and shared work at the Chair of Political Theory. The research and teaching on citizenship and identity that Heinz and I have been following for years helped crystallize the ideas for the book. In particular, I am grateful for the freedom of choice in my teaching that I enjoyed during my assistant professor years. Finally, I greatly appreciate the comments I received from the reviewers at Routledge.

Introduction

The issue of European citizenship has been subject to a heated debate in legal studies as well as in social sciences. The debate has covered several aspects. Originally, it began with the controversy of whether citizenship beyond the nation-state is possible at all.[1] Afterwards, some scholars focused on the limitations of European citizenship in comparison to national citizenship bemoaning the underdeveloped character of European citizenship,[2] whereas others highlighted the constructive potential of European citizenship for the future, grounding it in citizenship practice.[3] The constructive potential of European citizenship was discussed particularly with respect to the concept of constitutionalism against the background of the European constitutionalization process[4] and additionally as a specific form of social citizenship of the European Union.[5] Moreover, the debate on European citizenship has spawned a sub-debate on the very concept of European citizenship. It has proceeded on three tracks. The first track covered the rather abstract issue of optimal citizenship for the EU as well as the instrumental function of citizenship, both analyzed from the perspective of political economy.[6] The second track related to the issue of whether European citizenship is a mere derivative of the member states' citizenship. In this vein, some authors postulated extending European citizenship to cover European denizens (citizens of non-EU countries with residence in an EU member state), thus dislodging European citizenship from the national, which would make European citizenship an independent and recognizable construction. The third track referred to the controversy of whether citizenship indicates only legally institutionalized categories of rights and obligations or if it is also based on shared values and objectives.[7] Recently, the rejection of the draft constitutional treaty has led to a critical assessment of European citizenship.[8]

This account is by no means exhaustive, as we can observe a growing complexity of the European citizenship discourse. Despite this complexity one issue seems to be particularly neglected in all the debates on European citizenship. Although a wealth of research exists on the issue of citizenship and collective identity,[9] the link between the two phenomena in the European studies appears to be far from clarified.[10] This is also visible from the perspective of the collective identity, which appears in different research contexts such as the politics of recognition[11] or dilemmas of collective action.[12] Here, the link between collective identity and citizenship also remains highly controversial. In general, we can distinguish *three methods* of conceptualizing it.

Firstly, some scholars regard the conceptual link between citizenship and collective identity as non-coincidental and to be realized solely in the framework of the nation-state. In this case, citizenship becomes absorbed by nationality, and only thus it can be a basis for democratic politics, where majority decisions require a permanent integration into the context of the interests of the entire society. This perspective is relatively popular in the European studies, particularly concerning the democratic deficit of the EU.[13] Collective identity is viewed as a necessary condition for democratic decision-making and stability of political regimes. However, this position tends to utilize the model of collective identity characteristic for nation-states with regard to the EU. It assumes that polities draw their collective identity in the main from a common history and from the memory of their common past as well as through communication with each other in an integrated common public space.[14] Furthermore, it is frequently supposed to be not just any collective identity but a substantive, resilient feeling of commonness (in some cases even almost unconditional), which would not only cement the society in times of crisis but also make the political minority trust that the ruling majority would not exploit its privileged power position at the expense of the minority. The shortcoming of this approach consists in the fact that it is anchored in the model of nation-state, thus ignoring a variety of possible collective identities beyond the nation-state context. In this sense, it is semantically conservative and statist. While it negates the state character of the EU, it simultaneously requires from the EU the fulfilment of the main characteristics of the continental nation-states.

Moreover, this position tends to ignore the debate on the 'impending crisis of the hyphen' in the concept of the nation-state.[15] As a consequence of globalization ever fewer societies can be described as nation-states.[16] As the global economic dynamics transcend national borders and become less controllable for national governments, the autonomy and effectiveness of the nation-state is being increasingly questioned. This has implications for the nation-state ideology, which regards autonomous and homogeneous national cultures represented by distinct states as *natural* and *organic* entities. Although the ideology of homogeneous nations is always based on a myth, homogenization and the construction of national identity are at the core of every project of nation-building and nationalism. As national identities increasingly erode, not least as a result of the new waves of transnational migration, we face a spread of global values and a simultaneous reinvention of culture on sub-national levels. The new migration trend differs from historically similar phenomena in terms of quantities, global range and frequency. As a consequence, large numbers of migrants cannot be easily assimilated into the national population, since they come from increasingly distant regions and cultures.[17] In a nutshell, the erosion of national sovereignty (but not its obliteration) entails parting of the hitherto overlapping cultural and political spheres of the nation and the state. The invalidation of the Gellnerian principle of integration between culture and political authority within the modern nation-state has the consequence that citizenship and collective identity are at the level of citizenship practice no longer intertwined.[18] Therefore, today more than ever we might be confronted with citizenship without shared identity.[19] The issue is, however, a stochastic one, since citizenship without shared identity does not necessarily replace citizenship with collective identity. Therefore, the question would rather pertain to which types of citizenship (with what collective identity) will be dominant in a given empirical context.

Secondly, an opposite method of linking citizenship and identity attempts to completely decouple collective identity from citizenship and to construct citizenship as an independent rights regime, which circumvents the nation-state and renders it obsolete.[20] Arguments used in favour of this position are both empirical and normative. The former relate to the structural change in the global capitalist mode of production as well as to transnational migration, both of which put the nation-state and its territorial citizenship under increasing pressure. As a consequence, citizenship has to transform itself and to find a new form beyond the nation-state, liberating itself from the constraints of national identity.[21] Particularly against the background of globalization, new approaches are developed that conceptualize citizenship not only without reference to shared identity, but also without relating it to nation-states. For example, Seyla Benhabib pleads for a 'republican federalism', which is expected to enhance popular sovereignty by perpetuating cosmopolitan norms such as those pertaining to refugee, immigrant and asylum status across the local, the national and the global levels. At the same time, Benhabib acknowledges that these norms challenge the nation-state by escaping from its control.[22] Equally, in his account of European citizenship, Rainer Bauböck builds on a modification of Kant's model for a global confederation of republics, without recurring to collective identity. He focuses instead on institutional aspects of the architecture of citizenship such as the differentiation of citizenship statuses in Europe, the allocation of voting rights to these categories, and the rules for acquisition and loss of citizenship at various levels.[23] According to this position, European political community does not have to be based on a substantive and resilient collective identity, but rather on political rights reflecting universal moral entitlements. In the context of the European Union, this position finds its reflection to some extent in the doctrine of constitutional patriotism, which is deemed by its supporters an appropriate model for supranational political association in Europe. Consequently, the overlapping of citizenship and national identity is viewed as a contingent historical development, which can be overcome by the project of European constitution-making redirecting citizens' identities towards a new supranational polity. The European constitution-making is believed to remedy the democratic deficit of the EU, particularly its lack of demos, by establishing the terms and conditions for democratic negotiation and institutionalizing shared practices of law-making in the EU.[24]

However, the decoupling strategy also has its limitations. The concept of citizenship reduced to rights and law-making suffers from neglecting the political requirements of citizenship, mainly its connection to the political authority, without which rights cannot be guaranteed. By decoupling citizenship and collective identity, a growing social and cultural heterogeneity transforms citizenship beyond the nation-states into an asymmetric and variable mechanism for political negotiations among groups and individuals.[25] Consequently, citizenship ceases to be an integrative mechanism for equal membership in a political community aspiring to collective exercise of political power and becomes either an ephemeron (encompassing rights that are non-judiciable) or becomes a description of a status (expressing asymmetrical privileges), and therefore can be viewed as a proxy for group specific rights in diverse and heterogeneous societies.[26] Furthermore, citizenship loses its specific political nature, since (political) rights grow to be indistinguishable from human rights with their cosmopolitan appeal.[27]

Thirdly, a further strategy of conceptualizing citizenship and collective identity merges citizenship with individual or group identity. Here, subjective feelings of belonging are regarded as essential for citizenship, perhaps even more relevant than its legal dimension, thus leading us to the 'feeling of citizenship'.[28] In Christian Joppke's account, the citizenship becomes supplemented by identity politics, which endows citizenship with two possible meanings: the actual identity attitudes held by average citizens, and the official identity politics propagated by the government.[29] For Richard Bellamy, subjective feelings of belonging are regarded as essential for citizenship, sometimes even more than its legal framework, whereas Antje Wiener extends the meaning of formal citizenship into the concept of shared values and common belonging.[30] Consequently, European citizenship is also expected to integrate the notion of identity, which enables the members of the community of the EU to identify each other as members of the same community within the political processes of European integration. In this manner, European citizenship becomes contextualized, since it is sensitive to specific conditions of individual citizens.[31] This strategy, however, integrates two distinct concepts that need to be examined separately, even though they are connected to each other. It proceeds according to the same weakness as the first method, which merges nationalism with citizenship.[32] Thus, it dilutes the semantic core of citizenship amalgamating it with different phenomena such as attitudes, perceptions and feelings of the citizens.

Furthermore, some authors attempt to enrich the meaning of citizenship (while using the term 'formal citizenship' as an opposition, which suggests its incompleteness) to fit a broader notion of shared values.[33] But by making identity a component of citizenship and opening it additionally to values and attitudes we amalgamate citizenship semantics with social practice. If one incorporates 'belonging' into the concept of citizenship, a merger of two different phenomena is conducted, preventing an exploration of their relationship. Consequently, if citizenship *is* belonging, then we cannot discuss for instance the issue of whether citizenship causes a feeling of belonging or whether collective identity is in turn a prerequisite of citizenship. Moreover, a merger between citizenship and collective identity deforms the concept of equality of citizens into a tautological construction in which citizenship practice is more highlighted than judiciable aspects of rights and obligations, thus claiming that citizenship is what citizens actually make of it. This amalgamation of citizenship and collective identity is unhelpful in analyzing the phenomenon of European citizenship, since it dilutes the difference between citizenship as a judiciable institution of equality, and the actual political activity of concrete citizens stemming from citizenship. Driving this position to the extreme, European citizenship would also encompass hearings and conferences organized by the European Commission (although practically inaccessible for the majority of citizens, but with a participation of some citizens/officials), the Commission's green and white papers (although uninfluenced by average citizens) or the activity of interest groups, even when these opportunity structures for citizens' participation are highly informal. The political activity of citizens and their actual utilization of opportunity structures is, however, highly asymmetrical, as it is dependent on the uneven distribution of information and power resources among citizens.[34] However, if collective identity was regarded as analytically differentiable from citizenship, we shall assume that both variables find themselves in a correlative or associative, rather than in a mutually inclusive, relationship. In this perspective, collective identity remains an autonomous phenomenon, separable from citizenship, even though in some cases it is closely associated with it. For instance, macro-sociological theories such as the civilizing process of Norbert Elias conceptualize collective identity as a variable of social change, rather than a component of specific institutional settings such as citizenship. According to Elias, societies run through a process of increasing interdependence and functional differentiation, which require a growing degree of drive and emotion control. Therefore, in less differentiated societies, individuals are subject to extrinsic and sanction-based drive control (stronger collectivistic), whereas in highly differentiated societies individuals rely on an intrinsic drive and emotion regulation (less collectivistic).[35] In this sense, citizenship might entail cognitive and emotive aspects of belonging or identity. However, it is not the only device for establishing identity, nor is it always accompanied by collective identity. Consequently, a methodological disaggregation of citizenship and identity should be undertaken.[36]

The three methods of conceptualizing citizenship and collective identity discussed above are mutually exclusive. However, a possibility of transcending them exists and will be attempted in this book. As an underlying principle we would differentiate the semantic dimension of analysis from the social practice. As pointed out above, treating actual participation of citizens or their belonging as aspects of citizenship dilutes the difference between the semantics of citizenship and the social practice. The practice theory describes 'practice' as a routinized type of behaviour that consists of interconnected elements of bodily and mental activities, knowledge, emotions and motivations.[37] In contrast, semantics pertain to analytical categories, for instance in the form of ideal types, which are pragmatic, value-free constructs and non-existent in the empirical reality, since their main function is to highlight their differences from reality. They isolate certain characteristics of social reality without assuming that they are empirically present. Therefore, the methodological function of ideal types, pure types or generic models is not to find their correspondence vis-à-vis the empirical reality, but to demonstrate to what extent they correspond to reality in order to grasp it using these analytical tools.[38]

Against this background, the *first step* should be to determine the *semantic core* of citizenship irrespective of normative expectations, which would be of application in different empirical contexts. The localization of the semantic core of citizenship should allow it to be distinguished from other phenomena such as identification with the political community or the political process, even if belonging or identification appear to correlate with citizenship. The same applies to the notion of participation, which is regarded by some authors as a component of citizenship.[39] We would anchor participation in social practice, rather than in the semantic core of citizenship.

In the *second step*, we should generalize citizenship rather than contextualize it, thus escaping the idiosyncratic nature of specific feelings, perceptions and attitudes of citizens. Therefore, an analysis of citizenship has to escape the fallacies of the strategies discussed above: It cannot be locked up within the framework of the nation-state, and nor should it be indistinguishable from human rights by exhibiting its specific political character. The goal would be to develop an analytical framework that would shift the exploration of citizenship and collective identity beyond the semantic boundaries of nationalism and national identity and simultaneously regard the very notion of collective identity outside the nation-state as still applicable.

In the *third step*, citizenship has to be associated with collective identity, while these two phenomena are kept separate. Therefore, a more suitable approach would be to first examine various types of citizenship, before turning to the question of the corresponding collective identity. This would give us the opportunity to explore the relationship between different models of citizenship and various forms of collective identity. In other words, we would focus on variations of citizenship and their different configurations with collective identity.

In the *fourth step,* we can apply the semantic dimension of citizenship and collective identity to the social practice. The social practice of citizenship and collective identity refers to identity politics and identity technologies of political authorities such as governments or the European Union. As identity politics can be located in different policy fields, their choice appears to be essential. At the empirical level, a mismatch can arise between the expected identity and the identity technologies associated with a specific form of citizenship. If different types of citizenship are associated with diverse collective identities, ill-conceived identity politics would generate an expectations–outcome gap, rather than produce stable collective identity.

In sum, this book represents an attempt to elucidate the relationship between citizenship and collective identity in the European Union. In Chapter 1 I will explore the conceptual dimension of citizenship. I will begin by discussing the variety of citizenship conceptions. Afterwards I will offer a conception of citizenship as a relational setting by disaggregating citizenship into the three components of rights, obligations and compliance. Following this, I will explore the linkage between the components of citizenship and will focus on the nexus between citizenship and collective identity. Chapter 2 will examine functions of collective identity such as the cognitive function, self-esteem booster function and political functions of collective identity. The debate on European identity will be depicted and organized in Chapter 3 according to the functions of collective identity.

Against this background, in Chapter 4 I will frame my argument. First, I will explore limitations of the approaches to collective identity discussed above. Next, I will argue that various types of citizenship (semantic ideal types) correlate with differing collective identities, which are consequential for the social practice. I will therefore establish the link between citizenship and collective identity. The disaggregation of citizenship into rights, obligations and compliance will serve here as a point of departure for the generic models of citizenship. I will use each of these components of citizenship to construct generic models of citizenship, to which I will ascribe types of collective identity. These three generic models of citizenship include the republican, the liberal and the caesarean citizenship.

Against this theoretical background I will explore the social practice of citizenship and identity politics in the European Union in Chapter 5. After a brief discussion of the developments of the EU's politics of citizenship up to now, I will focus on current trends of European citizenship and European identity politics. Here I will illustrate the EU's attempts to engage in discursive ethics within the convention method as a case of republican citizenship, the liberal model of European citizenship with regard to the Charter of Fundamental Rights, and also current trends in the EU's caesarean citizenship regarding the development of the European Leviathan and the politics of insecurity. The concluding chapter will offer a recapitulation of the book's main findings and will propose final remarks.

1 The conceptual dimension of citizenship

Depending on the epistemological access to the notion of citizenship, scholars in general subscribe either to a normative account of citizenship or to the functionalist one.

Therefore, some scholars might be interested in an ideal of citizenship. Sometimes, this assumes a standard of citizenship referring to a lost ideal of Ancient Greece or the Roman Empire, where citizens were higher beings in ethical, ontological (Greek Polis) and legal terms (Roman Empire). Not only were they believed to make intelligent and purposive judgments, but also expected to pursue common goods. This view idealizes a specific historical form of citizenship by canonizing it into a universal standard of citizenship. It is usually accompanied by a critical stance towards contemporary types of citizenship bemoaning their liberal, thin or underdeveloped shape.[1] Further normative approaches to citizenship attempt to abstract from specific historical accounts of citizenship and anchor it in a system of liberty and equality. The realization of liberty and equality is therefore regarded as a prerequisite for citizenship in a democratic regime. Probably the most prominent thinker in this field was John Rawls, who viewed modern citizenship through a magnifying glass of societal justice. Against the background of the hypothetical veil of ignorance, a universal form of citizenship (attached to the principles of liberty and difference) is to be established. It is believed to reconcile conflicting interests and ideologies in a diverse society.[2]

In contrast, functional approaches to citizenship deal with the explanations of specific citizenship forms and their development as associated with functional requirements of societies such as military aspects of social life or the mode of economic activity. For instance, Max Weber explains the development of mass-based citizenship in medieval cities of the Western world as a result of the cities being organized as defence groups. Municipal communities had to rely on the participation of as many individuals as possible in the military activities of the city, thus having access to military training and being allowed to bear arms. In contrast, no participatory citizenship developed in the Eastern world of China, Egypt and India, since the survival of the local communities was dependent less on defence matters and more on the effectiveness of the irrigation system and water supply, which led to the rise of bureaucracy rather than citizenship. While in the Western world the ruler became dependent on the military capability of the individuals, in the Eastern world the individuals were dependent on the ruler in matters of water supply.[3]

In a similar functionalist vein, T. H. Marshall argues that the development of modern citizenship occurred in a three-tier process of expanding civil, political and social rights to large parts of modern society. However, the order of their expansion was not accidental. Civil rights were an epiphenomenon of industrialization and capitalism, since rights of free contracting are essential for a proper functioning of the capitalist economy. Consequently, social change is the reason why the original amalgamate of civil, political and social rights for a small group of citizens in ancient and medieval times became functionally dissolved and civil rights expanded territorially to encompass larger strata of the society.[4] Political rights have been introduced primarily as a functional requirement for participation of the masses in the warfare of the twentieth century.

Beyond the normative and functionalist accounts of citizenship we are confronted with a plethora of conceptions of citizenship such as civic citizenship, cosmopolitan citizenship, transnational citizenship, technological citizenship, sexual citizenship etc.[5] These conceptions attach different meanings to citizenship and espouse frequently diverging implications for the social practice. My aim is, however, to find a way of examining citizenship despite all the conceptual variety and despite the discursive wave of citizenships with adjectives that sometimes blur the distinction between citizenship and other social phenomena. Therefore, I will discuss the *semantic core* of the concept of citizenship, which could be applicable in different institutional settings and cultural contexts.

The semantic core of citizenship

Three clarifications are necessary before we turn to the exploration of the semantic core of citizenship. The *first clarification* is conceptual in nature. Since we need a working definition of citizenship, a minimal definition would delineate citizenship as a shared membership in a political community.[6] This definition is insensitive regarding the type of territoriality, since citizenship may be based in smaller territories of the cities or larger territories of nation-states or even federations.[7] In addition, this parsimonious definition does not tell us anything about the *substance* of citizenship, but relates it to the political authority and the relationship among citizens by stressing the political nature of the membership. Consequently, it leaves the question of who belongs to a polity unanswered by treating it as a variable.[8]

The *second clarification* is methodological in nature. We need to distinguish between the concept of citizenship (semantic core) and the practice of citizenship (social practice), as already noted in the introduction. By practice of citizenship I mean everyday social and political experience, developed by social and political actors, as distinguished from the analytical categories used by social analysts.[9] This reflects the approach of this book to first explore the semantic dimension of citizenship as well as the theoretical nexus between citizenship and collective identity. Only then will I analyze the social practice of citizenship and collective identity in the context of the European Union. Nonetheless, we should be aware that there is a close reciprocal connection and mutual influence between the concept of citizenship and the practice of citizenship. The ideal types stem from specific historical and social contexts, and they in turn are applied as instruments of the state-induced socialization upon individuals. The practice theory describes 'practice' as a patterned and repeated type of behaviour for the analysis of social reality and its feedback on the ideational constructs.[10] The anchoring of citizenship in specific historical, social and cultural practices indicates that we deal with a 'momentum concept' that unfolds under the influence of social actors. This leads to a dynamic understanding of citizenship with a high potential for change.[11] Sometimes, the distinction between the concept of citizenship and the practice of citizenship is shifted entirely into the empirical realm of analysis and denotes the difference between formal citizenship as stipulated legally and the so-called lived citizenship. In this case, we would move from the methodological distinction between the concept and the practice and are confronted with a rather activist understanding of citizenship as a lived experience, which not only cannot be divorced from its context, but also becomes a proxy for the everyday political activity of people who understand and negotiate rights, responsibilities and participation.[12]

The *third clarification* is theoretical in nature. Since citizenship relates the individual to a political collectivity, it is associated with collective identity of individuals. The type of collective identity strongly depends, however, on the form of citizenship at hand. To learn more about collective identity of individuals as members of a political community, we should ask about the type of citizenship. In this sense, citizenship is a regulative notion, which links an individual to the political community by both enabling and constraining him. As with every other institution, citizenship enables individuals by ascribing rights to them, and constrains them by requiring duties and compliance vis-à-vis the collectivity.[13] Based on rights, obligations and compliance we can identify different types of citizenship and their corresponding collective identity.

Citizenship as a relational setting

The relational perspective on citizenship disaggregates it into categories and reconfigures these categories into relational clusters in which individuals, organizations, political authority and power are positioned and examined. In this sense, citizenship can be analyzed as a relational setting.[14] A relational setting is a patterned matrix of relationships among citizenship components, among citizens and between citizens and political authority. Departing from a minimal definition of citizenship as a shared membership in a political community, we cannot explain the institutional specifics of citizenship, nor can we conclude on normatively proper courses of action. Consequently, in addition to citizenship as a reciprocal and horizontal relationship among citizens, it remains a relational phenomenon that is also determined through the relationship between the citizen and the political authority. This relational aspect does not explain much about the range of rights ascribed to citizens, nor does it say who is included into citizenship. It also ignores the allocation of territory vis-à-vis the citizens.[15] Charles Tilly describes the relational nature of citizenship primarily with regard to political authority:

> Citizenship designates a set of mutually enforceable claims relating categories of persons to agents of governments. Like relations between spouses, between co-authors, between workers and employers, citizenship has the character of a contract: variable in range, never completely specifiable, always depending on unstated assumptions about context, modified by practice, constrained by collective memory, yet ineluctably involving rights and obligations sufficiently defined that either party is likely to express indignation and take corrective action when the other fails to meet expectations built into the relationship.[16]

In sum, the relational perspective on citizenship is threefold. First, it delineates a relationship between citizens themselves, since they constitute a community as formally equal political actors. As mentioned above, this relationship links citizenship to collective identity. Second, it describes the relationship between each individual citizen and the political authority.[17] Third, the relational perspective pays attention to the relationship between the components of citizenship.

Citizenship components

We can map citizenship along the three criteria of rights, obligations and compliance. We identify these three criteria as components of citizenship. These components can assume different forms, different scope, different range as well as different degrees. In this sense, they are variables that can assume different values and should be viewed neither as constants nor as teleological categories that need to be fulfilled in order to claim the 'genuine' citizenship. The advantage of such a disaggregative and synthetic conception of citizenship is that by using rights, obligations and compliance we can examine any type of citizenship irrespective of its territorial range or its cultural background. Therefore, this approach is on the one hand synthetic, combining different aspects of citizenship as its components, and disaggregative on the other as we can examine the components of citizenship separately, thus disaggregating it along different analytical lines. Moreover, we can analyze the relation between the components as being, for instance, in tension with each other or strengthening one other. As the next step I will discuss the components of citizenship in more detail.

The rights component

Rights are an essential component of almost every conception of citizenship. Historically derived from the Roman concept of citizenship, in which citizenship was a legal status, rights are regarded as entitlements or privileges. In the legal sense, rights empower citizens to resolve their conflicts before courts. Therefore, citizenship protects from arbitrary political decisions and renders the citizens free. Citizens can sue in courts and involve a law that grants them rights. In the social sense, rights bestow a status or an honour, which associates citizenship with social esteem as a member of upper class vis-à-vis non-citizens.[18] This view reflects the paradigm of 'possessive individualism', according to which rights are possessions of individuals and therefore can be extended or reduced.[19]

In the modern version of citizenship, T. H. Marshall presents an apogee of the rights-accentuated citizenship. He argues that citizenship is a unified pool of various types of citizenship rights including civil, political and social rights.[20] These rights are sustained in an interactive relationship, in which the exercise of one type of citizenship rights requires other citizenship rights. Once the principle is grounded in one area, such as the civil sphere, it spills over into the political and social spheres. The rights-orientated conception of citizenship is underpinned by two principles. It is the principle of legality that allows for judiciability of rights in the case of their violation by political or social actors. The other underlying principle of citizenship is the equality of status, which means that citizens cannot be excluded from entitlements enjoyed by other citizens. Moreover, the equality principle of citizenship makes citizenship attractive and desirable. While many social inequalities and differences between individuals are impossible to annihilate, it is citizenship that equalizes individuals by bestowing the same entitlements upon them. Marshall's account of the development of citizenship in Britain entails the power of citizenship rights to mitigate class divisions.

Evidently, Marshall's conception of citizenship espouses a telos of citizenship, according to which a fully fledged citizenship requires all three elements of civil, political and social rights. The equality of status in citizenship means that all types of citizenship rights are connected or unified. However, it is not the equality of outcome, but rather the equality with regard to the rights of citizenship as entitlements. This amounts to legal equality and is closely linked to liberty.

However, the rights-accentuated approach to citizenship can take an alternative turn to Marshall's equality of status. The special group rights approach points in the opposite direction. They all argue in favour of recognition of differences in status for minority groups in diverse societies in order to achieve the equality of the outcome.[21] Since in their account equal treatment of individuals (in the sense of equal status) is 'difference-blind', it tends to perpetuate oppression or disadvantages.[22] In this perspective, the procedural equality of status does not result in the substantive equality of the outcome. This position holds that a more substantive equality cannot be achieved without recognizing and valuing differences alongside individual rights. Consequently, the pursuit of equality should involve according differential rights on the basis of group membership to reduce potential vulnerability and disadvantage from majorities.[23] Irrespective of the aim of the citizenship rights (equality of status or equality of outcome), rights are believed to be the central regulative instrument in achieving citizenship.

Traditionally, rights reflect the ontological priority of the individual, and link the individual to a political community. At the same time, rights exclude non-members from the community by not ascribing these rights to them.[24] Therefore, rights integrate members of the community and 'close' the community socially. However, within the debate on group rights they become attributes of collectivities that seem to question the ontological priority of the individual, since individuals require their rights not as individuals in the political community, but are 'receivers' of privileges due to their membership in groups. Consequently, Kymlicka's labelling of his minority rights citizenship as liberal might appear inconsistent, as he individualizes cultures not individuals.[25]

The obligations component

Next to rights we identify obligations as a further component of citizenship. The main thrust of the obligation-based component of citizenship is that civic virtues such as solidarity, loyalty or trust (moral resources) are necessary features of living in freedom.[26] This approach maintains that freedom is inextricably linked with political virtue and public service. It can assume at least two argumentative forms. There is an ethical understanding of citizenship as obligation and virtue. Its point of departure is frequently a critique of a liberal society and selfhood, which are supposed to be remedied with the Aristotelian conception of citizenship as civic friendship.[27] In this sense, 'genuine' citizens demonstrate altruistic features, since they are concerned with the welfare of their friends for their friends' sake, not merely for their own. The general bonds of civic friendship are a basis for a political community whose goal is to fulfil civic obligations towards each other.[28] Citizens who view one another as civic friends are likely to support a broad consensus on matters of public policy.[29]

Beyond this virtue-accentuated and ethical account of citizenship, we can discern a rather instrumental view of civic obligations. This position argues first and foremost that potential threats to citizens' welfare and democracy exist whenever low levels of participation, trust and solidarity occur, thus endangering the existence of the republic.[30] In addition, there exists an individually instrumental account of the obligation-accentuated approach to citizenship: individuals who neglect their civic duties face the risk of being marginalized by the political decision-making procedures, in which they tend to play an insignificant role.[31] This position reverts to the observation of Tocqueville that the central ideal of democracy, which is citizens' equality, becomes threatened by the limitation of their political activity to the election of representatives. An average citizen ceases, then, to play an essential role in the processes of governance, which results in the erosion of democratic equality and potentially in the tyranny of majority.[32]

In the obligations-centred approach to citizenship, deliberative norms assume a particularly outstanding position.[33] Most of the contemporary versions of obligation-based citizenship put an emphasis on deliberation processes and communicative norms, rather than demanding civic obligations in forms of the communal ethic of care or the obligation to participate fully in public life.[34] Meanwhile, these communicative norms are regarded as equally (or even more) relevant than many other conceptions of civic obligation, above all in their function as potential solutions to some of our most urgent contemporary political problems.[35] In this perspective, activating the deliberative capabilities of citizens becomes a political priority. Citizens must learn to give their fellow citizens (and expect to receive from them) reasonable accounts of their political preferences and be ready to accept the power of better argument relating to common goods. Communicative norms are therefore norms of truth- and consensus-seeking, transferable to any of the deliberative settings such as legislative sessions, court proceedings, and administrative hearings, as well as non-governmental associations.[36] These deliberative settings are rule-free, since the citizens' goal is not to exercise power *over* each other, but rather to exercise power *with* each. This discourse of ethics grounded in communicative norms can be derived from the Aristotelian concept of civic friendship, even though they can be practised, for instrumental reasons as well as normative ones.[37] Whatever the implications, the obligations-orientated component of citizenship highlights the necessity of an ethical underpinning of citizenship, be it for normative reasons or for instrumental ones. A mere status or rights limited citizenship is rejected, since such citizenship is not capable of guaranteeing stability and legitimacy of the political community.

The compliance component

Beyond the matrix of rights and obligations we identify a third component of citizenship, which is compliance. In this perspective, citizens are also defined as the subjects of political authority. This perspective merges the concept of the citizen as a free person and as the subject of political authority with an accentuation of the latter.[38] In this sense, the condition of liberty can only be reached when citizens are subject to political rule, which guarantees their survival in view of political conflicts.[39] However, it does not necessarily mean an arbitrary power or domination. Central to this understanding of citizenship is the relationship between the citizenship and the political authority, where the interventions of the political authority can be legitimate and reasonable. This legitimacy generates political rule according to collective interests of citizens, rather than to domination. In this perspective, citizens possess enough rationality to understand the necessity of compliance to political authority, without which there would be no civilized existence and therefore no citizenship. Citizens have the power to choose their leaders, and the leaders in turn are obligated to consider citizens' will. Therefore, the goal of citizenship for the citizens is to be ruled, otherwise societies will end up in chaos and anarchy, which would endanger the survival of the citizens. The focus of this component of citizenship shifts towards the notion of power sovereignty and away from individual rights and obligations of citizens. However, it does not mean that citizens degenerate into slaves, serfs or subjects of authoritarian power. The political ruler can possess democratic legitimacy, since he is either elected by the citizens or the political decisions are accepted by them. In this sense, discussing citizenship as compliance relates rather to a question of final political authority, which does not reside with individual citizens.[40]

In contemporary accounts of citizenship the compliance-orientated citizenship is discussed mainly with regard to three aspects. *First*, there is the hypothesis of Albert O. Hirschman referring to shifting involvements of the citizens. Hirschman argues that people easily become disappointed with engagement in public affairs, which constitutes civic activity, and subsequently become involved in private activity instead, only to find that also to be disappointing.[41] In this sense, we are confronted with cyclical shifts of political activity and political compliance of citizens. The former is associated with disappointment or boredom with politics, which leads to citizens' withdrawal and passivity with regard to political authority. If individuals are drawn to public activity it is because of expectations they have about the rewards of public service. However, if those expectations remain unfulfilled, they are likely to seek membership in organizations compatible with their private interests. However, this cycle has a useful function. Hirschman argues that there are phases in history where private activity is more useful than public activism.[42] In his account, the realization of the postulate of a politically hyperactive citizen whose priority is to constantly and actively exercise his rights for public activity is even undesirable. Communities have to rely on periods of political inactivity and compliance in order to be able to address common concerns of the citizens or to tackle collective problems. Particularly in complex differentiated societies, periods of citizen passivity and compliance gain even more significance, as opposed to other regimes or less complex societies.

A similar argument has been formulated by Almond and Verba in their famous study on civic culture as the cultural underpinning of democratic regimes. They stressed that both the active and the compliant/obedient features of citizen behaviour are significant in keeping democratic regimes at work.[43] A permanent mobilization of political actors is typical for totalitarian regimes, rather than for democratic regimes. Since democratic regimes have to cope by definition with contestation and participation, too much of them might be destructive for democracies. In this sense, citizens have to be able to shift between their passive and their active roles and compliance becomes a relevant aspect of citizenship. Consequently, Almond's and Verba's argument refers to the compliance component of citizenship as one of functional requirements for democracy.

Second, Peter Wagner's account emphasizes both liberty and discipline as regulative principles of modernity.[44] Both are aspects of modern statehood and by the same token of modern citizenship. Wagner's approach is socio-historical in nature, since it focuses on the organizational practices of the modern state in the nineteenth and twentieth centuries. Even though liberty and discipline appear to be in opposition, they become integrated within the modern statehood and citizenship. According to Wagner, the disciplining activity of the modern state occurred in the name of collectivity, which promised collective liberation, as individual liberty found its governance limitations. The spread of collectivization processes within the modern nation-states enabled individuals to partake in actions that could never be organized locally. However, this empowerment took place under the strict condition of following disciplined lines of behaviour.[45]

Therefore, the goal of discipline is to assure governance of modern states that are characterized by complexity and functional differentiation. Consequently, modern states apply both techniques of rule (liberty and discipline) to politically integrate modern societies. In emphasizing the disciplining function of citizenship, Barry Hindess demonstrates an apotheosis of citizenship as a mode of modern governance. Hindess highlights the compliance aspect of citizenship with regard to the functional necessity of rendering the global population governable by dividing it into sub-populations consisting of discrete, politically independent and competing states.[46] In this sense, citizenship becomes an instrument of social closure, whose architect and guarantor is the modern nation-state, which routinized, standardized, and normalized the relationship between citizenship and territory.[47]

Third, citizenship as compliance and citizen as the object of disciplinary policies becomes particularly relevant in the context of security-focused policies of the contemporary state. Inspired by the writings of Michel Foucault, surveillance practices of record-keeping and monitoring behaviour can be seen as defining features of modernity and citizenship.[48] Considering the emergence of 'disciplinary technologies', Foucault drew upon Jeremy Bentham's design of a prison (called panopticon), and used it as a model for his social analysis. The key element of panopticism is that citizens are never certain if they are being observed at any one particular moment by the state. Therefore, the rational citizen seeking to avoid punishment will act as if s/he were the object of constant surveillance.[49] This theoretical perspective has been reinvigorated particularly recently as a result of a growth in new communications technology and data processing systems.[50] It stresses that the state treats challenges to citizenship (defined through political freedom, equality and democratic accountability) posed by encroaching security measures as largely negligible in the face of indeterminable danger.[51]

However, this perspective cannot be simply described as a conspiracy of the state against its citizens. The growing acceptance and seeming inevitability of increased risk and uncertainty in social relationships helps to legitimize surveillance measures such as video monitoring, control of credit card transactions and email traffic. It results in the shift from the category of civil, political and social citizenship with their emphasis on rights and participation, to the citizenship of the risk society and to the neurotic citizen. The neurotic citizen becomes the object of government activity whose conduct is based not merely on calculating rationalities but also responds to the fears, anxieties and insecurities of citizens.[52]

The relationship between the components of citizenship

All three components of citizenship can be found in most scholarly accounts of citizenship. Rights-based approaches to citizenship, even though they do not necessarily highlight duties and responsibilities (being relatively modest such as obeying the law and paying taxes), implicitly acknowledge their relevance.[53] Similarly, obligation-based approaches tend to regard rights as the reward for civic commitment of citizens, and therefore recognize their validity, even if they grant moral primacy to obligations.[54] In this perspective, political life is superior to the private concerns of family and profession and therefore it should be placed in the centre of citizens' lives. Absence from public life renders citizens' existence incomplete. Consequently, rights tend to be viewed as a result of citizens' activity in the public sphere, and not necessarily as natural entitlements. Nevertheless, citizens are attached to a matrix of both duties and rights.[55]

Also, compliance-accentuated citizenship does not ignore rights and obligations. Even if it focuses on obedience and discipline, it does highlight certain types of rights (such as the right to security and physical intactness of citizens in view of risk and uncertainty) and obligations (societal cooperation for the sake of mutual security and survival). In this sense, citizenship is regarded as a function of 'risk society', which is associated with dangers of nuclear catastrophes such as Chernobyl, global warming, financial crises and terrorist attacks, rather than merely a strategy of nation-state elites to boost their legitimacy by projecting threat scenarios onto an incapacitated population.[56] As a consequence, compliance and obedience to authority are viewed as grounded in an enlightened and informed choice of citizens, rather than from state propaganda and manipulation. These three components of citizenship including rights, obligations and compliance can be examined with regard to their mutual relationship. We can identify equilibrium, incongruence, contradictions as well as a spill-over relationship between the citizenship components.

Equilibrium between citizenship components

First of all, we might assume equilibrium between all the citizenship components. Even though one of them dominates the others, the remaining two are strong enough to keep an extreme form of the dominating component at bay. If it is not the case, citizenship might assume extreme forms of clientelism, collectivism or paternalism. Clientelism not only occurs when the rights component of citizenship becomes dominating, but also when the obligation and compliance components cease to be capable of containing the excess of the rights component. The rights empower the citizens vis-à-vis the state, but they cease to reflect upon the necessity of common good and turn into clients paying taxes and expecting services from the state. Sometimes, it assumes an even more extreme form of political subordination in exchange for material benefits, which might lead to corruption of citizens by the state.[57] Therefore, political legitimacy of the state shifts to economic legitimacy of the firm, as the state is regarded in terms of material efficiency.[58] In contrast, collectivism occurs when the obligations begin dominating citizenship. The collectivist citizen is entirely determined by its functions vis-à-vis the political authority, which makes this extreme form of citizenship the opposite case of clientelism.[59] The citizens might still enjoy rights, but social expectations and political pressure are so high that the individual conceives himself mainly as a member of a political community, which becomes the dominating system of reference for a citizen's moral action such as loyalty, solidarity and trust. Sometimes, it can assume an even more extreme form of collective aggression towards other collectives.

In contrast, paternalism arises when the citizens willingly accept the disciplining, controlling and surveillance activity of the political authority.[60] Sometimes, it can assume an even more extreme form of citizen passivity, which leads to the state domination over society.[61]

Incongruence between citizenship components

In addition, we might identify incongruence between the components of citizenship that is exacerbated by external pressures. In the case of a territorial incongruence the components of citizenship cease to neatly map onto the terrain of the nation-state, as they come under pressure from globalization processes.[62] The globalization of the capital, the transnational migration and the development of supranational human rights regimes lead to a partial disaggregation of the state sovereignty and therefore to disintegration of the hitherto unified citizenship.[63]

Consequently, citizenship becomes fragmented and diversified, whereas nation-states become weak and unable to protect their citizens against global pressures and therefore, according to the most radical interpretation, ultimately irrelevant. Emerging supranational regimes and functional equivalents for the state such as the EU could be the remedy, since they are conducive to partial re-institutionalization of citizenship at a different level of governance.[64] For some authors it is the transnationalization of participation in the form of non-governmental organizations that aim at establishing a regulatory framework to constrain the operation of the transnational capital.[65] The objectives of transnational activists include the protection of the global goods, the erection of a transnational welfare net for the poor, the promotion of the agendas of vulnerable minorities as well as the creation of more adequate forms of governance at regional and global levels. This transnational political participation shifts the active and participatory component of citizenship into a new territorial framework, which transcends the border of the nation-state.

In this perspective, growing transnational activities and participation become associated with cosmopolitism as a transformative political project in respect of national citizenship by entrenching human rights, global democracy and cultural diversity in an age of globalization. Therefore, the disintegration of national citizenship is regarded as an opportunity to realize global principles of justice pertaining to the distribution of economic and social goods and to re-conceptualize the democratic process in the light of globalization that providentially severs the historically coincidental association between democracy and the nation-state.[66]

Furthermore, we might encounter a functional incongruence between the citizenship components. Departing from the thesis about the crisis of the nation-state, which loses its capacity for social integration, this perspective sees the hitherto integrated societies breaking apart into group particularisms along class, ethnic, religious, and regional lines. Thus, citizenship disintegrates into competing plurality of alternative forms of group membership that become increasingly politicized. Citizenship as a principle of commonality capable of integrating societies abdicates in favour of politics of conflict, which is characterized by permanent power struggles between diverse groups.[67] This is caused by the functional weakening of rights, obligations and compliance, which are incapable of integrating social identities of individuals. Individual citizen rights degenerate into claims to special group rights, whereas individuals withdraw from their community obligations and focus on duties towards other organizations or groups. Simultaneously, citizens lose incentives to obey the political authority representing shared citizenship, since the authority loses its legitimacy and becomes viewed in merely legal terms. This leads to what Claus Offe calls 'divided citizenship', since it arises from descriptive politics of difference, rather than from an equality-based rationale of integrated citizenship.[68] Such 'divided citizenship' includes an asymmetrical system of recognition claims and special group rights as well as a competition towards the politicization of difference. However, the problem of the divided citizenship is not necessarily its fragmentation, but its essentialism. While integrated citizenship transcends different social identities and roles, politicized group membership claims its minority status on the grounds of its essential characteristics, which are difficult to surrender, and strives for a fuller recognition. In this sense, minority groups tend to use essentialist arguments in order to validate their special recognition claims. However, essentialist group rights can be an impediment to the very freedom and self-determination of the group members, particularly when the cultural 'essence' of the group is oppressive in nature or when it entails an exemption from civic duties. In addition, it could mean that special rights and exemptions from duties promote free-riding, rather than shared citizenship, and are used strategically to legitimize the leadership of these groups, since acculturation undermines privileges of the group leadership. In this context, critics of essentialist group rights see an antagonism between group rights and individual rights of citizenship.[69]

Contradictions between citizenship components

Furthermore, the components of citizenship might exhibit contradictions with regard to each other. In particular, we can point to the implications of the citizenship components regarding the exclusion and inclusion mechanisms of citizenship.

Concerning the obligations component, only citizens fulfilling criteria of active, participative, responsible and deliberative citizenship are worthy to be deemed genuine citizens. For instance, a deliberative citizen is supposed to be highly informed, able to produce reflective judgments, espouse concerns for common goods as well as exhibit deliberative dispositions.[70] In this sense, citizens are not only expected to understand their own interests, however defined, and realize them in the political process, but also to be public spirited. However, this conception of citizenship, ambitious as it is, entails exclusionary effects, as most of the citizens' competences are anchored in a specific culture. The minimal prerequisite for citizenship is fluency in the language, which established itself as a standard medium of politics and public administration.[71] Fluency in the language is particularly essential in democratic regimes based on contestation and participation, as opposed to authoritarian regimes.[72] Even this minimal civic qualification appears problematic with regard to the growing wave of transnational migration, whereby increasingly numerous individuals with an immigrant background tend (or are encouraged) to settle in culturally distinct areas, thus perpetuating their lacking language proficiency. Consequently, they become excluded from citizenship on the grounds of their absent acculturation, even though they may possess formal citizenship.[73] However, the exclusionary nature of cultural prerequisites for citizenship becomes evident not only in societies confronted with migration, but also in established multicultural societies. Jeremy Waldron demonstrates how demanding the deliberative dispositions of citizens in multicultural society have to be to arrive at 'civic responsibility'.[74] Departing from the principle of equal dignity of citizens, he argues that in a political community every citizen's cultural identity is entitled to the same respect, since there should be no second-class citizens in a democratic, multicultural society. However, this means that cultural identities, as crucial for individual dignity, might be non-negotiable. Therefore, the task of finding common good, which is a touchstone of the obligation-accentuated citizenship, may become very difficult. In this context, even strongly deliberative dispositions of citizens are not necessarily helpful, since arguments pertaining to the common good are not allowed to touch upon the cultural authenticity of citizens, which may lead to deliberative stalemate and consequently a discursive hegemony of the dominant majority culture.[75]

In contrast, the rights-based component of citizenship is inclusive by nature.[76] Processes of denationalization can be conducive to the inclusiveness of the rights-based component of citizenship. Seyla Benhabib argues that the emergence of cosmopolitan norms such as those of universal human rights, crimes against humanity as well as refugee, immigrant and asylum status strengthens citizenship, rather than undermines it. While citizenship finds itself in a process of reconstitution, it shifts from national citizenship towards a citizenship of residency, pertaining to the multiple ties to locality, to the region, and to transnational institutions. In this respect, we are witnessing a universalistic extension of civil and social rights, and, in some cases, even of political participation rights (as in the context of the European Union).[77] This line of reasoning stresses that citizenship cannot be regarded as an aggregated bundle of all three components, since the integration of citizenship might be a historical coincidence, which occurred due to a very specific structure of society, in which nation overlaps with culture. What follows from that is the necessity of decomposition of the aggregated citizenship paradigm as a result of the external pressure on citizenship. Consequently, the revival of cosmopolitan accounts of citizenship considers the supranational extension of rights as normatively welcome, whereas obligation-based approaches regard citizenship as functioning under certain cultural conditions and therefore as exclusionary in nature. While the legal side of globalization can be understood as an opportunity for citizenship as a legal status, globalization leading to multiculturalism is regarded as a burden for the obligation component.

Spill-over between the citizenship components

In addition, a spill-over relationship between the components of citizenship can be conceptualized. In this perspective, there might exist a normative pressure (as opposed to the functional pressure of Marshall's conception of the expansion of rights in Great Britain), which links all three components of citizenship. This pressure arises when the components of citizenship are shaped asymmetrically. It would mean that citizen obligations are accepted merely against the background of rights expansion, as in the classical motto of the American War of Independence: "No taxation without representation". A similar normative claim could be laid with regard to the compliance component, which would not be accepted without citizen rights such as an effective control of government activity. Therefore, an asymmetrical distribution of rights, obligations and compliance might provoke a pressure towards more symmetry. In other words, we can conceptualize the relationship between the components of citizenship as an expansive one, regardless of the nature of causation.

The spill-over relationship pertains to asymmetrical types of citizenship representing an unequal contract between the citizen and the state. The bond is neither mutual nor consensual, since it is characterized by an inequitable distribution of rights, duties and compliance between the contracting parties. Legal-history literature describes examples of this type of citizenship, such as the Soviet citizenship in the 1930s. The citizenship under the long prevailing Soviet doctrine was regarded as a sort of bondage of the individual to the state that commenced at birth and terminated at death. In the course of this relationship the state could, at its option, divest itself of this 'property' if it proved to be too burdensome or perhaps unprofitable. For instance, to demonstrate its absolute dominion over its subjects, the Soviet state at one point prohibited its citizens from marrying foreigners.[78] However, this possession-oriented citizenship was eventually alleviated, as there was a growing resistance in the population against it. Although a complete liberalization of citizenship ensued only as an aftermath of the breakdown of the Soviet empire, we could assume a normative pressure between the citizenship components even under circumstances of totalitarian regimes.

In a similar vein, even though from a different angle, James Burk argues in favour of symmetry between civic duties and the necessity of the state to legitimize wars for their citizens. He criticizes the argument that citizens should take active responsibility for the defence of their political community and be willing to sacrifice their life to establish and protect a liberal democratic social order. He demonstrates that democratic societies vary in form and virtue and that it is necessary to explain when citizen soldiers will promote the establishment of one kind of democracy or another. Consequently, Burk ties the service of citizen soldiers during war to the quality of democratic society, which as a consequence gives the citizens the right to refuse military service.[79]

In a rather institutionalist vein, Margaret Somers argues that varying patterns of institutional relationships among communities, and political cultures were central factors in the expansion of modern citizenship rights. Focusing on regional variation in citizenship practices among eighteenth-century English working communities, she suggests that citizenship should be redefined as an 'instituted process' rather than a status. Consequently, research on citizenship and democratization should include a theory of relationships among public spheres, community associational life, and patterns of political culture highlighting the interactive character of citizenship components. By so doing, abstractions of state, citizenship, and social class can be replaced with the concept of contingent patterns of relationships and social practices. In this sense, Marshall's focus on rights-based citizenship should also be revised, since citizenship cannot be entirely explained by using the category of 'ready-made' rights granted by states. Instead, the focus must be on the presence of national universal laws and legal institutions, which under certain conditions of place, political culture, and participation could be transformed into rights.[80]

In sum, the aim of the relational perspective is to demonstrate that citizenship comprises three components and that there are interactions between them. Consequently, not only diverse configurations exist between the components, but the nature of the interactions between them strongly influences the form of citizenship. Whenever the citizenship components find themselves in dissonance, it encourages a dynamic between these components. The relation between the components of citizenship implies, however, that it is not only an abstract notion of relationship between categories, but a notion describing interactions between individuals and their identity. The following section will deal with the link between citizenship and collective identity.

Citizenship–collective identity nexus

The relational approach is inspired by Erving Goffman's interactional sociology in which he coined the term 'interaction order'. In this context, we can analyse citizenship as individual claims that are conceptualized on the basis of a matrix of interactional rights, accompanied by a set of obligations individuals are expected to honour. Additionally, this matrix of rights and obligations is mapped against the relationship between individuals and political authority, which is equally crucial in understanding interactions between individuals.[81] Goffman regards the interaction order as a distinct unit of analysis, composed of elements that 'fit together more closely than with elements beyond' it. The interaction order therefore operates to constrain and coordinate social interactions.[82] In this sense, citizenship is a form of an 'interaction order' of three citizenship components, which cause patterned behaviour of citizens. Rights, obligations and compliance are closely coupled with each other, whereas a 'loose coupling' exists between the interaction order and other social realms. Certainly, links exist between the interaction order and its environments, but neither can be reduced to the other. However, the autonomy of the interaction order implies neither that we can reduce citizenship to contextualism or situationalism nor that the interaction order has homogeneous effects. On the one hand, the interaction order has its sources in the institutionalized dimension of citizenship, which includes formal rights, obligations and compliance, as constructed, codified and perpetuated by political authority. But this institutionalized side of citizenship does not always account for the variance in citizens' behaviour acting under the same institutional circumstances. On the other hand, the patterns of citizens' behaviour observable in particular settings cannot always be generalized, since they partly reflect the prior experience of participants and their culturally specific framework of action. This indicates that we can conceptualize citizenship neither entirely as an autonomous institutionalized interaction order of formal rights, obligations and compliance, nor as an entirely local production of specific and contextualized character. Citizens are not only subject to the institutionalized order but they can change it as well. Nevertheless, citizenship is not solely what a citizen makes of it, but it is constrained or coordinated by formal institutions of citizenship.

Given the dynamics inherent in citizenship as an interaction order we can assume shifts and movements between rights, obligations and compliance. However, the dynamics are not only strategic or utilitarian in nature.[83] The interaction order contains a moral dimension, which is a powerful regulative of citizens' behaviour and is attached primarily to the obligations component of citizenship. It takes forms of self-confirming and self-condemning moral emotions (e.g. shame, pride, embarrassment, humiliation) as well as public confirming and public condemning triggering these moral emotions.[84] These moral emotions are largely responsible for the construction of citizens as moral beings who are governed by reciprocally held norms of good or proper conduct.[85] While Goffman in his account of social interactions focuses primarily on the face-to-face domain of interactions, which produce the interaction order locally, we can apply it in the larger context of citizenship.[86]

In contrast to local interaction orders, citizenship assumes a highly abstract form, which connects it to the notion of collective identity.[87] Even though the majority of citizens will never encounter each other, they assume that they belong to the same group as other citizens. It implies that citizenship impinges directly on individuals' sense of inclusion, leading us to the link between citizenship and collective identity. Therefore, citizenship as an interaction order shifts the focus of collective identity from the social to the political domain.[88] In this sense, citizenship relates to rights, obligations and compliance in the context of a polity, a political system and political decision-making. This associates citizenship with political collective identity, distinguishable from other social identities and social roles.[89]

However, the nature of the political collective identity frequently remains uncertain, as many authors speak vaguely of bonds between citizens or the feeling of we-ness without explaining the source of this feeling, its strength and its implications. In these accounts, collective identity repeatedly fluctuates between causing a community and constituting a community with an uncertain relationship to citizenship.[90] In other words, there exists no reliable theoretical perspective on citizenship and collective identity taking into account the varying nature of citizenship and its relationship to collective identity. Despite the vagueness of the link between citizenship and collective identity, a normative claim can be found in the literature on the subject at hand. Citizenship is frequently conceptualized as an integrative device, which bridges differences of a cultural and social nature. Such shared citizenship is expected to generate a collective identity that supersedes rival identities induced by cultural diversity and differences in social status. Such *citizenship identity* can assume different forms allowing for varying degrees of multiplicity (unitary vs. multiple) and bonding (individualist vs. collectivist).[91]

At the abstract level, the link between citizenship and collective identity can be conceptualized as a *three-tiered* one. *First*, collective identity facilitates the construction of citizenship as an abstract category and structures the non-face-to-face interactions on the basis of citizenship. Citizens assume that significantly more individuals belong to the same political group as they do and act upon this assumption. In other words, citizenship without collective identity would have to rely on situational and contextual ad hoc provision of collective identity based on the face-to-face experience. However, the situational context does not suffice to construct citizenship as a stable pattern of reciprocity and recognition as citizens. Therefore, reciprocity and recognition among participants in an interaction order requires a specific set of institutionalized values that can be provided by the institutions of citizenship.[92]

Second, the specific form of collective identity is generated by the relationship between the three components of citizenship that in turn generates three models of citizenship. The type of collective identity therefore results from the domination of one of the citizenship components over the others, thus suggesting whether we deal with rights-orientated, obligations-accentuated or compliance-focused citizenship. The right-orientated citizenship leads to the model of liberal citizenship; the obligation-accentuated citizenship spawns the republican model of citizenship and the compliance-focused citizenship produces the caesarean model of citizenship. These models of citizenship are coupled with differently strong and resilient collective identities. In other words, the models of citizenship are associated with specific collective identity.

Third, the very notion of citizenship as a membership in a political community implies a normative claim of collective identity as pointed out in the notion of citizenship identity. In this sense, collective identity pertains to the core of citizenship as delineating a community, of which individuals define themselves as members, in which they participate, and towards which they feel a sense of obligation.[93] Therefore, citizenship identity assumes special ties binding citizens in a community.[94] How strong and extensive these ties are is in turn an issue pertaining to the model of citizenship. These ties can relate to a thin collective identity found in a shared rationality, a thick collective identity stemming from mutual demanding obligations and specific responsibilities, or a specific collectivism of shared perception of threat and danger. At the same time, the notion of citizenship identity as implicating special ties is associated with an exclusion of non-citizens and relates to the issue of access to the political community and assimilation of the new citizens.[95] This, again, is the matter of the model of citizenship, as various models delineate different exclusion and assimilation mechanisms.

These preliminary considerations on the citizenship–collective identity nexus will be explored in more detail in Chapter 4, where I frame my main argument. The next four chapters will deal with conceptual and theoretical aspects of collective identity. Only against this background will we be able to discuss the citizenship–collective identity nexus in more depth.

2 Collective identity and its functions

Collective identity has been theorized upon in a plethora of contexts and meanings. Rogers Brubaker and Frederick Cooper stress that the concept of identity has been stretched to the point of semantic emptiness by a wide range of approaches within social science. They criticize the situation whereby 'strong' versions of identity, which point to a fundamental and durable sense of selfhood, have been replaced by 'weak' versions that emphasize fluidity, complexity and context sensitivity of identities rather than resilient and stable forms of identity, including collective identity.[1]

Fluidity and context sensitivity of identity are part of the terminology frequently used as a result of the so-called postmodern or cultural turn in social sciences, which describes a shift in methodological focus from the explanatory power of social structures to an analysis of discourse and cultural symbols. Recent research in this field highlights multiple or hybrid identities of individuals and it has become common to underline the process of making and claiming identities, in which identities are not attributes but rather resources that people use.[2] An example of that is the work of Zygmunt Bauman, in which individualization of identity is regarded against the background of 'liquid' modernity, in which the traditional collective identities lose their grip on individuals. However, individualization does not necessarily imply a shift towards self-centredness as opposed to collectivist identity, but rather a choice of identity or its permanent change depending on the context and necessity. The concept of liquid modernity suggests a rapidly changing social order that undermines all notions of durability. It implies a sense of 'rootlessness' and fluidity of identity.[3]

However, it is pointless to immerse ourselves here into the debate on modern versus postmodern variants of identity theories, since our interest is not in contributing to the debate on the fluidity of identity. In order to link citizenship to collective identity we would need to introduce some basic differentiations that would allow us to map collective identity, rather than question it. I will proceed with various *functions* of collective identity, which will demonstrate in what different perspectives collective identity is looked at. Despite various uses of the concept of collective identity, several distinct meanings can be discerned according to the expected function of collective identity. In addition, using different functional perspectives on collective identity will shed some light on the relationship between collective identity and citizenship. Therefore, while discussing functions of collective identity, I will do so through the prism of citizenship, since citizenship ties the individual to the political community qua collective identity. I differentiate between three main functions of collective identity: the cognitive function, the self-esteem booster function, and three political functions of collective identity (national community building, identity politics, and solution of collective dilemmas).

Cognitive function of collective identity

A plethora of psychological theories attribute cognitive functions to collective identity. This common cognitive perspective departs from the assumption that human social relations are arranged through the definition and elaboration of collective self-categories, through which individuals organize their social relations. Collective self-categorization indicates that individuals perceive themselves as members of groups.[4] This perception reduces social complexity for individuals by rendering it comprehensible. In addition, the reduction of perceived social complexity decreases social uncertainty.[5] In the cognitive perspective, collective self-categorization is regarded as crucial in determining individual self-concept (identity), since self-concepts reflect to a certain degree the categorization of the self as a group member. However, there exist (potentially) a number of group memberships for each individual, which provide multiple bases for self-categorization at any given time. According to the theory of self-categorization, a given self-definition is adopted at the moment at which the context-dependent collective identity becomes activated. Therefore the categorization of the self as a member of a social group depends on the *range* and the *salience* of stimuli that are present at the current moment.[6] It implies that alternative social categories can be present and salient in different situations.[7] Once self-categorization has occurred, the individual comes to perceive him or herself as indistinguishable from and interchangeable with other members of the category (and increasingly different from members of contrasting categories).[8] As a result of this depersonalization process, the importance of the individual's personal identity is diminished, and the importance of the person's social (collective) identity is increased.[9] Consequently, the boundaries between self and other in-group members become eclipsed by a higher salience of the boundaries between in-group and out-groups. In addition, the successes and failures of the in-group are incorporated into the self-concept and perceived as personal outcomes. By the same token, the attributes of the individual 'self' become assimilated to the holistic image of the in-group, highlighting the distinctive features of the group as opposed to other social categories, which leads to higher uniformity and cohesion within the group.[10] The consequence is self-stereotyping (and frequently xeno-stereotyping), during which the individual acquires the properties and characteristics of the group: the person assumes that the attributes stereotypic of the group (and also other more cohesive collectivities) are also characteristic of the self. The outcome of such context-dependent self-categorization is that one's self-perceptions can change depending on the particular self-categorization. The cognitive side of collective identity is associated with perception effects of depersonalization and the so-called entitativity.[11] While depersonalization delineates the inclination of a person to act as a member of a group, rather than as a unique individual, entitativity pertains to the nature of in-group and out-group impressions in terms of their perceived and expected unity.[12] In other words, the perception of the in-group unity depends on the perception of the out-group, meaning that group identification is a relational phenomenon depending on the mutual perception of groups.[13]

Citizenship in the cognitive perspective

There are at least *two* consequences of the cognitive function of collective identity and citizenship. *First*, if group identities and self-categorizations are fluid and context dependent, the self cannot be considered a completely stable and static mental structure.

Rather, the identity is an outcome of a process of activation and categorization, which includes social judgment and social recognition of identity claims. This perspective corresponds to the postmodern difference-accentuating conceptions of citizenship, which renounces the equality claim of citizenship in favour of fragmentation and contextuality of citizenship.[14] In this view, citizenship disintegrates into a number of separate groups that, depending on the context, lay political claims of public recognition and attempt to extract public resources as a result of these claims. Diverse social identities become politicized and depoliticized, leading to a contextual and fragmented citizenship of competing citizenship claims. However, the demarcation lines between groups are contextual and situational, as individuals belong to overlapping groups and exhibit a multitude of social roles and identities. Nonetheless, the question remains whether citizenship as an integrative meta-identity can still provide a sort of primary identity framework of reference, able to transcend all other social identities despite their politicization, or whether citizenship instead becomes permanently differentiated, fragmented and conflictive.[15]

For scholars postulating the new transnationalism, global mobility and multiethnic global cities, citizenship becomes denationalized, contextual and repositioned, as it is increasingly constructed in a new context of social interactions.[16] It also implies that legal, political, and social aspects of citizenship assume post-national or extra-national forms.[17] In this perspective, postmodern citizenship becomes located in multi-ethnic cities, where new ethnic and social boundaries are forged[18] and non-state forms of political belonging are constructed.[19] This conception of citizenship emphasizes the 'momentum' character, due to which it unfolds as a dynamic notion, subject to change and permanent struggle over its precise content and meaning.[20] Apart from the transborder mobility as a booster for transnationalism, recent technological inventions such as the Internet are also regarded as crucial for the development of alternative notions of citizenship transcending the nation-states. In this context, civil society is believed to play an important role by organizing itself at a transnational level. It is expected to deal with political and social issues beyond the boundaries of the nation-state and thus to allow citizens to engage with 'unbounded' issues and to create a transnational public sphere.[21]

However, the perspective of fluid and contextual identities of transnational or post-national citizenship does not only stress the freedom of choice and the establishment of new citizenship forms.[22] New identity conflicts emerge as identities clash with each other due to the new multi-ethnicity, which reproduces ethnic, religious and socio-economic cleavages.[23] Against this background, we can observe a shift in the academic discourse from the optimism of post-national citizenship to the pessimism of post-citizenship society.[24] In this vein, some authors argue that the globalization of the economy and human affairs has made individuals ontologically insecure and existentially uncertain. Therefore, we might expect as a response to such insecurity attempts to reaffirm the self-identity by approaching any collectivity that is expected to decrease insecurity and existential anxiety. Consequently, we should expect a rise of collectivism as an 'identity-signifier', particularly in forms of religion and nationalism as a reaction to ontological insecurity associated with cultural fluidity, mobility and contextuality.[25] This would suggest that despite the hopes for liquid modernity and the end of the nation-state, fluid identities might be prone to 'chronic' identities, which tend to freeze and become conflictive, rather than flexible, hybrid and multi-compatible. 'Chronic group identities' would always be potentially accessible; therefore they have an impact on the self-categorization of individuals across diverse social contexts, thus exhibiting a continual significance for the self-conception. Consequently, the collective identity of an individual would result from joint influences of contextual and chronic self-categorizations.[26]

However, the issue at hand is whether citizenship can generate such a chronic identity resistant to disintegration, which could be accessed and used as a resource in times of crises and at the same time be capable of bridging differences as an encompassing category. The cognitive perspective would suggest that the contextuality and the salience are the central features of collective identity, which points to fragmenting rather than integrating the effects of citizenship.

Second, the entitativity phenomenon indicates the out-group homogeneity effect that occurs when out-group members are perceived as similar to each other in comparison to in-group members, who are viewed as diverse. This effect is strengthened when there is a perception of an identity threat to the in-group. The threat makes the out-group appear more unitary or 'groupy' than the in-group and therefore more dangerous. Consequently, the dangerous out-group is perceived as more unitary and can be more easily categorized in pejorative terms, thus depersonalizing members of the given out-group.[27] Other groups can be viewed as threats to the own self-concept and be reacted to with bias and discrimination.[28] In this respect, discrimination of other groups mirrors not only favouritism towards the in-group, but also reflects the differences between the out-group and the in-group as a challenge to one's own position. Since the out-group is evaluated negatively, discrimination might ensue as a valid norm of behaviour towards the out-group.[29]

In the cognitive perspective, citizenship can thus be construed primarily as a boundary-drawing instrument, which makes collective self-categorization and categorization of others possible.[30] Citizenship establishes a categorization that distinguishes primarily between citizens and non-citizens. In an extreme form it can foster prejudice against non-citizens, particularly if citizenship rests on ascriptive and ethnic traits of group membership. In his seminal work on 'cognitive prejudice', Henri Tajfel indicated that the 'blood-and-guts model' of citizenship can lead to dehumanization of out-groups and as a consequence to aggression against them.[31] Therefore, depersonalization of the behaviour as a group member occurs at the levels of both the in-group and the out-group, since the out-group comes to be viewed as a depersonalized agglomerate of similar members.[32] Even though the modern citizenship conception is associated with the claim of citizen equality, most states discriminate within their citizenries, distinguishing at least between minors and adult citizens, prisoners and free citizens, naturalized and native citizens. As a rule even finer nuances exist, for instance by restricting voting rights or military service to male citizens, imposing property qualifications for certain rights such as the right to residence, or distinguishing between a variety of citizenship shades – from temporary residents, asylum seekers and applicants for citizenship to participants in all citizenship's rights and obligations.[33] In this sense, citizenship as a boundary-drawing instrument allows for self-categorization within the citizenry. Categorization as boundary-drawing is conceptualized in social psychology as a fundamental mental process.

However, it finds its reflection as a political project in everyday social and political practices. States categorize and classify people by assigning them to categories that are associated with consequential identities, for instance during censuses. In this respect, states congeal the salience of certain collective identities through political practices of categorization. Even if census categories might not overlap with self-understanding of the categorized social groups, they are frequently utilized by cultural and political actors and eventually redraw the boundaries of collective identity, which are conducive to fragmentation and discrimination, rather than integration and equality. In this sense, states impose ethnic or even racial categories on individuals, inscribing them in documents, which often entail political consequences for these identities such as discrimination by state authorities.[34]

The cognitive perspective suggests that ethnicities, nations, minorities groups etc. are mental and social constructs, which allow individuals to develop self-concepts as group members under circumstances of social complexity and uncertainty. Individuals can identify themselves, make sense of their problems and interests and adjust their actions along the lines of social categorization. Furthermore, the cognitive function of collective identity gives political authorities a tool for drawing boundaries in the society by recognizing and classifying people as group members. In this sense, states construct similarity as well as difference, which they use as templates for organizing perceptions and cognitions as well as frames for social comparisons.[35]

In conclusion, we can identify fluidity and multiplicity of social roles that become activated in a salient context as the key features of the cognitive perspective. Regarding citizenship, it can imply favouritism, discrimination and inequality, which are the opposite of the equality claim of the modern citizenship, rather than integration through citizenship and resilience of collective identity in crises. In this sense, the cognitive perspective cannot offer any reliable response to the search for integrative functions of citizenship that is expected to convey a common identity.

Self-esteem booster function

Social identity theory equally seeks to explain collective identity by focusing on the perceived similarities between members of the in-group as opposed to the out-group.[36] However, here the function of collective identity is not to reduce uncertainty and the perception of complexity by individuals, but rather to acquire a positive image from membership in a social group. The motivation for positive social identity that drives the process by which one's self-esteem is produced and maintained is created by comparing oneself favourably to the out-group.[37] Consequently, if one identifies with a negatively valued group, the self-stereotyping will create a negative impact on one's current level of self-esteem. Therefore, the underlying motivation for membership in groups (and also larger collectives) is the enhancement of self-esteem, whereby psychological gains are achieved through group identification and differentiation of one's own group from other groups in such a way that the in-group is favourably evaluated.[38] In this perspective, groups (and other larger and more cohesive collectivities) are social resources used by individuals for their psychological benefits; collective identity is therefore more strongly associated with a certain rationality of choice.[39] Whilst in the cognitive perspective collective identity is a result of salience of a given collective category, being structural in nature, the social identity approach stresses a strategic dimension of collective identity.

According to social identity theory, individuals have two fundamental strategies for their collective status improvement. On the one hand, an individual can attempt to leave the collectivity and become a member of a more positively evaluated group. The permeability of the group boundaries is a relevant criterion in this context, since some groups are difficult to abandon in light of their sanctioning mechanisms.[40] On the other hand, individuals may attempt to redefine the inter-group comparison process by selecting other reference points or standards of comparison.[41]

Following Marilynn B. Brewer, social identity theory distinguishes four types of social identity. Only one of them is labelled collective identity, the other three types being person-based social identities, relational social identities and group-based social identities. As opposed to person-based and relational social identities, collective identities are constructed not through face-to-face relationships between individuals, but are instead forged through common ties, experiences and interests. Furthermore, Brewer's conceptualization of collective identity integrates an active dimension of shaping and creating of a group image by its members (what the group represents and how it expects to be viewed by others), as opposed to the self-categorization theory stressing depersonalization processes. In this sense, collective identity results from common efforts of the members and is more interactive in terms of structure–agency relationships.[42]

Two aspects of collective identity are central in the social identity theory, which are the construction of the 'Other' and the establishment of a collective memory of the group. Collective identity is associated with demarcation and a juxtaposition of the in-group in relation to the 'Other', whereas the 'Other' frequently acquires a more durable image, that is, less contextual, less situational and less salience-based than the cognitive categorization processes.[43] Collective memory additionally provides a sense of group continuity, which makes collective identity even more resilient.

The 'Othering' as a device for collective identity formation has been thoroughly examined in nationalism studies. According to Michael Billig, nationalism tells 'us' who 'we' are by relating 'us' to 'them'.[44] Nationalism as a specific sort of collective identity therefore responds to the needs of societies to create and recreate its own 'Others'. Even though the category of 'Others' is more durable than collective identity formation in the self-categorization theory, it is also subject to dynamic processes of redefinition, since collective identity of nationalism has to constantly deliver a relevant psychological framework for new societal circumstances. In this sense, the construction of 'Others' reacts to the (changing) symbolic or affective needs of the nation members.[45] Particularly in times of crises, the significant Other becomes activated in the collective identity of individuals, since the binary construction of 'us' versus 'them' helps in overcoming the crises by using blaming and scapegoating strategies.[46] The significant Other unites the nation (or any other group or collectivity) in front of a common enemy by highlighting that the nation is different and unique. Therefore, what matters is not merely the image of the 'Other' as such, but the perceived attributes of the 'Other'. The initial and necessary step of 'Othering' includes the decision in favour of recognition of otherness or in favour of its negation. However, the nature of representing the 'Other' is also significant for the consequences of collective identity. First, there can be significant and insignificant Others, but only the significant Other becomes the relevant reference for collective identity formation. Consequently, the insignificant Other remains a cognitive category without affective implications. As Michael Billig argues, foreignness is subject to meticulous distinctions between different groups of Others, which are created in debates and controversies about similarities between various groups of foreigners to 'us'.[47] Second, if the Other is constructed as threatening qua an enemy-accentuating political rhetoric, it may produce xenophobia and (verbal and physical) violence against the Others. But the Other can also be constructed as inferior, which boosts the feeling of supremacy and grandeur of a given nation and might lead to stigmatization of Others, particularly if the Other can be found within the collectivity. Third, the Other can additionally assume positive attributes. In the context of nationalism studies, some authors indicate that there exist images of positive Others, which can be a minority group, living in the same political territory as the majority nation, but is not considered a threat to the identity and integrity of the majority. This positive image of Others can be forged by the consideration of the minority as legitimate but historically less favoured.[48]

A culturalist variant of 'Othering' can be found in social anthropology and sociology, particularly in association with the codes of collective identity.[49] The codes of collective identity are conceptualized as socially constructed boundaries that segregate group similarity against group strangeness.[50] In other words, the codes of collective identity are devices used in social practices to define and redefine group (or collectivity) membership.[51] Eisenstadt distinguishes primordial, civic and transcendental codes of collective identity, which are constructed and applied by political elites qua collective rituals, socialization, conjuration of similarity, and establishment of enemy images. Primordial codes are based on ascriptive traits such as gender, kinship, age, and language, whereby they refer to the social realm of natural order. In contrast, civic codes refer to traditions and social routines, whereas transcendent codes define collective identity as a difference between 'us' and 'them' in relation to the realm of the Sacred and the Sublime such as God or reason, thus relating to salvation, progress and rationality.[52] The codes of collective identity delineate how communities construct the images of the 'Other' and how they reflect a patterned boundary-making. Communities using primordial codes create the 'Others' through demonizing them. In this perspective, the 'Other' is perceived as threatening for the natural order of the community. Therefore, the contacts with the 'Others' have to be reduced and the community members are subject to cleansing rituals after they have had contact with the 'Others'. Since membership is a matter of belonging by default, the possibilities of passage from the outside world into the community in question are very limited. In contrast, transcendent (or universalistic) codes regard the 'Others' as potential members and attempt to include them by using proselytization and conversion pedagogy.[53] The non-members are considered inferior as long as they are not converted. However, due to a successful conversion they can find their genuine identity and therefore salvation, be it as believers in God or acolytes of Reason. In contrast, civic codes are based in rituals of commemoration and locality. The 'Others' are viewed as people with differing social traditions, experiences and history. In this sense, 'Others' become neither 'demons' nor are they potential subjects of conversion, as the community is preoccupied with its own practices of commemoration.

This leads us to the second aspect of social identity theory, which is collective memory. The collective memory is as equally central to the development of collective identities as 'Othering'. A sense of shared continuity and shared memories of the past give the individual the feeling of greater durability and meaning, without which the self-esteem through belonging to a group is difficult to establish. The significance of time and continuity in the processes of collective identity construction can be stressed with the argument that a collective memory of past experiences supplies a resource container from which a community derives a sense of uniqueness, unity, and continuity. This continuity is directed both at the past (represented in memories and routines), and at the future (represented in expectations and aspirations). The feeling of continuity generated by collective identity is one of the features attracting individuals to groups, since it can be conceptualized as an immortality strategy of individuals.[54]

The theme of collective memory is also present in the research on collective identity in social psychology. Marilynn Brewer points to the relevance of shared experiences and histories for the formation of collective identity. As a consequence of these attributes, collective identity in the context of social identity theory can be forged first and foremost against the background of common history.[55] However, the sociological perspective highlights not only the mere existence of common experiences, but equally (if not even more so) the relevance of commemorative rituals. Commemorative rituals effectuate a revitalization of a group's social heritage, cause a reaffirmation of its bonds and entail a reinforcement of the in-group solidarity.[56] As Barbara A. Misztal argues, collective memory is essentially social in nature and is located not in history itself, but in social rules, laws, routines and records. It is a strategic resource that can be transformed into a reliable source of collective identity for the present.[57] Periodic commemorations are significant for the renewal of the sentiment of unity by vitalizing social energy and arousing emotions by means of shared deliberation of a mythical past. Therefore, commemorative rituals and their symbolism become a condition for continuity of collective identity. In this sense, collective memory and commemorative rituals respond to the need of the community to resist change in the self-conception. Commemorative rituals function as 'mnemonic devices', used by communities to let emotions of unity act on their mind, the goal being to boost people's feeling of belonging.[58]

Citizenship and the self-esteem booster function

Let us now return to the issue of citizenship and collective identity as a self-esteem booster. The social identity school of thought offers some insights into the link between citizenship and collective identity.[59] We can distinguish three aspects of this link.

First, some studies in social identity theory view citizenship through the modernist prism of the nation-state. In this perspective, citizenship delineates either the differentiation between citizens and non-citizens or differentiation of various groups within citizenry. For some authors, the most worrisome aspect is the competitive nature of collective self-esteem, which implies that citizens feel better when their collectivity does better than others. This can lead to outright hostility, particularly when groups compete for resources and political power. In the context of citizenship as a national category, collective identity (as a source of self-esteem) might be viewed as a device that produces tensions between groups.[60] Once in-groups become larger and increasingly depersonalized, the rules, social routines and commemorative rituals that maintain in-group loyalty and solidarity acquire a character of moral authority. Consequently, if the citizenship becomes fragmented into a plethora of groups, each of them is likely to establish its own moral order that may be incompatible with a tolerance for difference. When out-groups within the citizenry do not subscribe to the same moral rules as the in-group, indifference can be replaced by deprecation and disrespect. As Marilynn Brewer argues, moral superiority provides justification or legitimization for domination or active subjugation of out-groups.[61]

Therefore, some theorists argue in favour of a cross-cutting collective supra-identity that would be capable of containing conflicting intra-citizenship group identities. The civic cross-cutting identity or citizenship identity would integrate all its citizens by rendering cultural matters a private concern, thus depoliticizing them.[62]

However, critics of this position argue that the civic nation or constitutional patriotism that would bring into being a civic citizenship, which is supposed to be based on a non-cultural form of belonging, is merely a normative claim and never to be applied in the political reality. The reason for this is that it is hard to even imagine how civic citizenship could be decoupled from any kind of cultural identity, since states are not mere containers of political practices, exercising culturally neutral citizenship politics. Instead, states (especially nation-states) as a rule support a biased interpretation of history and perpetuate commemorative practices endowed with specific cultural or religious meanings.[63] Against this background, the notion of cultural neutrality of the nation-state is to be regarded as wishful thinking at best, or a form of ideological domination at worst.

However, group identities are not always causes of the inter-group conflict, as conflicts are multivariate phenomena, whose explanation requires additional variables. John Turner argues that the probability of inter-group conflicts depends on the type of inter-group comparisons group members uphold. This applies particularly to the cases in which the in-group and out-group are not in a competitive relationship on a salient comparative dimension.[64] In this case, conflicts are less likely to occur. In addition, Mark Schafer argues that identity affects conflict behaviour but it is mediated by the degree of insecurity, implying that increased feelings of security correspond to more cooperative behaviour.[65] This would suggest that threats to identity might be one of the major conflicts with regard to citizenship.

In a similar vein, Tariq Modood advocates the so-called citizen hybridity that is anchored both in the political and the cultural dimension of citizenship. Modood argues that the political promotion of hyphenated identities of Indo-Canadians or Italo-Americans has inclusive consequences for citizens, rather than the freezing of particularistic identities that would run counter to the integrated concept of citizenship. In this context, the 'ethnicity paradox' delineates the phenomenon that participation in particular communal institutions fosters the involvement in wider society, whereas the feared communal conservatism of ethnic minorities develops instead under the circumstances of the ideology of mono-culturalism, which in turn promotes the feeling of rootlessness, powerlessness and insecurity on the part of minorities. Consequently, societal diversity does not necessarily lead to fragmentation of citizenship and permanent antagonisms between the majority culture and minority cultures (even though it certainly increases its likelihood). Against this background, Modood supports special participation channels for minorities as well as an official ideology of multiple identity, which would be integration-friendly in terms of citizenship, rather than forcible policies of integrative mono-culturalism.[66]

Second, a further implication for the collective identity beyond the possible fragmentation of citizenship is the 'Othering' of immigrants by the majority of citizens. If self-esteem can be boosted by lowering the perceived value of others, majorities in crises might be prone to finding scapegoats for their perceived misery, which can result not only in discrimination as a political category of asymmetry, but also in stigmatization or victimization as a cultural category. As Joanna Goodey argues, there is a visible tendency in some European nation-states for political or public stereotyping of migrants as 'undesirables' or as potential criminals. The populist criminalization of migrants is frequently based on the selective focus on some offences or crimes committed by migrants and on the simultaneous ignoring of the criminality of the majority group. Interestingly enough, a citizenship hierarchy exists with the national citizens of the EU member states at the top, followed by other EU nationals, and with non-EU nationals at the bottom of the ladder. Additionally, there is a hierarchy of non-EU nationals that seems to be based on colour more than the category of nationality.[67] This hierarchy can lead to stigmatization, which conveys a devalued social identity within the context of citizenship.[68] Consequently, the hierarchy of citizenship perpetuates a new variety of the 'Other' as a basis for collective identity.

On the one hand, the line between citizens and aliens is becoming less distinct as the latter gain increasing civil and social rights and as access to citizenship becomes liberalized.[69] Particularly in the context of the EU (but not only), it is argued that the policies of universal human rights endowed immigrants with virtually all the privileges associated with formal citizenship (even though largely with the exception of political rights).[70] Therefore, instead of a citizen–foreigner dichotomy, we should rather distinguish a membership continuum including citizens, residents, asylum seekers, etc. In this sense, as access to citizenship becomes less difficult, citizens are confronted with a perception of devalued citizenship, which might entail a stronger need for boundary-making vis-à-vis incomplete citizens. The incomplete citizens or non-citizen members might in turn react to stigmatization processes with anger, stress, aggression and isolation from the majority.

On the other hand, despite the liberalization and differentiation of citizenship, national governments increasingly demand affirmation of belonging and loyalty from non-citizens or naturalized citizens. They seek to restrict foreign, particularly diasporic, identities and to attach them to the core identity of the nation-state. While notions of fluidity, hybridity and multiplicity of identities are found in academic discourses on globalization, increasingly determined demands for exclusive loyalty and belonging to national cultures and polities make the unattached citizens and non-citizen residents appear suspect to national governments. In particular, citizens and residents of differing religions such as Islam are expected to conform to the core identity and to assert their commitments to the nation-state of their residence.[71] This return of assimilation policy is a sign of a shift from the previous focus on cultural difference, as was visible in the 1990s, to a focus on national collectivity, which stems from an uneasiness about possibly disintegrative impacts of cultural heterogeneity on civic integration.[72]

Third, the aspect of collective memory has implications for the collective identity of diverse societies. The bonds of collectivity are drawn primarily from historical memory of the community, which fosters ancestral forms of political obligation. Since the ancestors spilt their blood to build and defend the nation, citizens are believed to inherit an obligation to continue their work.[73] However, this conception of a commemoration-based citizenship fails to explain why immigrant citizens have political duties towards their citizens, since they should have obligations towards their communities of origin rather than their communities of residence. Therefore, a commemoration-based citizenship tends to isolate immigrants, rather than integrate them into the practices of citizenship. As Laura Andronache argues, ancestral conception of citizenship leaves open the possibility that the public culture of commemoration might be illiberal or unjust and hence prone to oppression towards minorities.[74]

To sum up the perspective on social identity/self-esteem and citizenship, we can conclude that it shares similar problems with the cognitive angle. Even though fluidity and contextuality are not the major problems here, the social identity/self-esteem perspective stresses excessively the instrumental side of collective identity. In this sense, citizens as other social beings are prone to acquire and to maintain a positive social identity (including citizenship identity), which is in conflict with the expectation that collective identity should have an integrative function, particularly when it comes to citizenship. While numerous authors highlight the link between collective identity and citizenship associating as a stable collective bond, social identity theory highlights the permeability of social boundaries, which allows individuals to utilize strategies to hold a collective identity, mainly derived from a positively perceived group. In this sense, collective identity becomes an individual resource, whereby group membership is utilized by individuals as a variable for the boosting of their self-esteem. Moreover, the positive group image is likely to be manipulated by the group itself, which can apply various strategies of 'Othering' and establish commemorative rituals in order to attract new members and keep old ones. However, this implies a top-down view of citizenship (despite the focus on individual motivation), which makes both citizenship and collective identity subject to identity politics using boundary-making instruments as the primary devices for the construction of collective identity, whereas citizens are 'receivers' of collective identity, selecting between different group memberships in accordance with their attractiveness. The voluntaristic and instrumental core of social identity theory, according to which citizens can change their collective identity at will, implies that heterogeneous societies in particular can be confronted with changing and fragmenting patterns of identity formation, rather than with the development of a resilient, stable and overarching collective identity for a political community.

Political functions of collective identity

Beyond the cognitive and social identity/self-esteem perspective, we can identify political functions of collective identity. Three political functions of collective identity can be distinguished, namely national community building, legitimacy of political authority, and solution of cooperation dilemmas.

National community building

Collective identity as national identity has been examined thoroughly in the sociology of nationalism. Nationalism as a criterion (as opposed to an ideology or an attitude) presumes that the nation is not only the empirically most common form of a modern political community, but also implies a normative value of nations. The probably most pronounced argument in favour of nation and nationalism has been offered by Liah Greenfeld, who associates the nation with popular sovereignty and equality, whereas nationalism becomes an engine of dignity provision for individuals in a modern society.[75] Nationalism is therefore regarded as a unique form of social consciousness that is historically anchored and hence not easily replaced.[76] In the same vein, authors such as David Miller or Yael Tamir argue that national identity is conducive to individual enrichment in the moral and political sense.[77] The collective bond of nationalism is supposed to deepen commitments and obligations between those who share it by providing an essential motivation behind civic commitments. Apart from obligations, nationalism is expected to produce social trust, drawn primarily from the cultural layer of the community, in which deep obligations stem from collective identity and relatedness. This argument is applied to the conditions of modern economy, which are regarded as requiring high levels of moral commitment in the form of mutual solidarity. Only against the background of a high level of social trust can democracy function in a sustainable manner, since redistributive measures cannot be otherwise justified.[78] A version of this argument is discussed in the debate on the democratic deficit of the European Union, which is believed to occur because majority decisions are not underpinned by a collective feeling of mutual trust and belonging to the same political community.[79]

In this perspective, national identity delivers trust and motivation for citizens to participate and deliberate on public matters. By identifying with the community, individuals become receptacles of collective will. However, citizenship occurs only in combination with nationality, since it does not assume any political meaning outside the context of the nation-state. Therefore, there cannot be any disaggregating between citizenship and nationality. On the contrary, the normative value of nationalism would suggest a necessary strengthening of the nation-state against the workings of globalization and fragmentation. It would include granting national independence to communities striving for such, as nation-states are not only the basic, but also the 'natural', organizational units for modern political communities.[80] Although associated mainly with functional requirements of modernity, nationalism has developed as a contingent consequence of unique events such as the invention of the print press. Benedict Anderson's analysis of nationalism traces the origins of nationalism back to the spread of 'print-capitalism', which made the modern nation-state possible by generating an 'imagined community' of nation.[81] National imagined community was produced in the process of dialect suppression while promoting one specific vernacular version of language, which integrated a diversity of vernacular speakers previously unable to communicate.[82] The notion of contingency of national communities does not exclude its functional indispensability in the context of modern statehood.[83] In this vein, Ernest Gellner stresses that nationalism is associated with the development of a homogeneous language facilitating communication, and therefore enables national sentiments to be constructed and preserved. This sort of unity and equality between members of the national community is viewed as a functional requirement for cognitive and material growth of modern capitalist societies. Therefore, nationalism is believed to be a functional corollary of industrialization.[84]

The main distinction between the social psychology of collective identity and the national perspective of collective identity is found in the specific nature of national identity. Even though most of the nationalism scholars admit the constructed and contingent character of nationalism, they also agree that nationalism is not easily replaced. Here we are confronted with the historical and macro-sociological argument with political consequences: the process of nation-building, which occurred most intensely in the nineteenth century, was possible only to the detriment of other identities. National, territorial and political integration had to be accompanied by the weakening of the local and regional ties in favour of the centre, making the nation-state the key factor of societal integration in modernity.[85]

Furthermore, national identity has become the dominant collective identity in modern human societies because it was associated first and foremost with the establishment of states as powerful identity-making agents. Therefore, even today other identities are significantly less institutionalized and have a less statist character, even in federal or multicultural states, compared with national identities.[86] More strongly than any other political organizations, nation-states are expected to pursue a policy of identity construction and reconstruction as the major agents of identity politics. Ernest Gellner argues that nation-states establish collective identity (the process called 'exo-socialization') via standardized education systems.[87] The standardization of language is one component of the process, while the production of a mythologized historiography is another.[88] This allows for a communicative centralization of a modern society despite its cultural variety and complexity.[89] At this point, nationalism theory applies similar notions as the social psychology does: identity politics of categorization is as relevant for the cognitive perspective on collective identity as mythology and commemoration are for the social identity theory. The major distinction relates to the conceptualization of the agents and bearers of identity politics. Whereas individuals and groups are in social identity theory the key agents of identity, nationalism research ascribes the identity-making capacity mainly to the states due to their ability to establish broad channels of communication and standardization.

Citizenship and nationalism

As noted above, citizenship and collective identity are merged within the framework of nationalism and national identity. On the one hand, citizenship is confined within boundaries of national political communities, since citizens' moral obligations towards each other end at the borders of the nation-states.[90] In this sense, a cosmopolitan citizenship is a contradiction in terms.[91] On the other hand, the effectiveness of citizenship is assumed to be only assured in the framework of the nation-state, since no central political authority that could guarantee civil rights exists beyond the nation-state. Only the monopoly of legitimate violence of a nation-state is supposed to close the gap between the equality claim of citizenship and its social reality. Compared to other territorial identities such as the regional or cosmopolitan, national identity is therefore expected to be more stable. According to this position, regional identity lacks the political dimension of citizenship that would congeal regional membership into a stable construction, making it difficult for citizens to assume new national or cosmopolitan identities. Here we can observe a tension between the nationalist perspective on citizenship and the primary explanation of social identity theory pertaining to positive group image. The nationalism perspective denotes national citizenship not only as generating 'chronic' identity in relation to other less stable and resilient identities, but also highlights its functionality with regard to modern industrialized societies. In this sense, national citizenship produces the dominant and structurally useful identity that is associated with the nation-state. In other words, as long as nation-states remain the major units of political organization, national identity remains the primary and chronic form of collective identity.

A further controversy relates to the differentiation between the liberal and nonliberal nationalism, with implications for citizenship. Nonliberal nationalism has played a prominent role not only in European history, but also in previously colonized nations of the Third World and recently in the former Yugoslavia, but its assessment by the majority of political theorists has not been favourable. It is believed that nonliberal nationalism is prone to be oppressive to minorities and marginalized members, since it views cultures as essentialist and static while rejecting the fundamental value of individual rights.[92] However, some authors attempt to defend the nonliberal nationalism of previously colonized nations by arguing that it can be justifiable, particularly if they are democratic. This communitarian argument constructs a moral agency of cultures, highlighting that even nonliberal cultures can hold emancipatory potential for individuals participating in the reconstruction of their national culture.[93]

In contrast, liberal nationalism highlights the significance of nationality for citizens and its role in the justification of liberal policies.[94] Liberal nationalists argue that national identity serves the basic individual needs of citizens and is not only compatible with postulates of equality and individuality, but should also be fostered for the liberal-democratic state to function. Therefore, the dark side of nationalism is believed to be exaggerated, as many nationalism scholars tend to focus on the few cases of nationalist aggression and oppression and neglect the majority of benign cases of nationalism. In addition, this controversy refers to the question of whether the doctrine of liberal nationalism points to the significance of democratic action or rather to the national sentiment. Some authors argue that civic ties between citizens engaging in the public domain have more relevance for addressing the functional requirements of liberal states than the bonds of national identity.[95] Other scholars argue that even the notion of ethnicity can be expressed in liberal terms, thus constituting a variant of the good life based on a synthesis of liberalism and ethnicity.[96]

Nonetheless, there are enough reasons for distrust towards nationalism. For instance, Andrew Vincent argues that there is a distinction to be made between pragmatic acceptance and a principled ethical esteem of nationalism. Nationalism can be pragmatically accepted with reluctance as a pervasive form of group loyalty, but one should not bestow any ethical significance upon it. Nationalism is more a currently inevitable form of allegiance, and the proponents of liberal nationalism simply transfer respect and dignity from individuals to nations, a procedure not only theoretically unsatisfactory, but also politically irresponsible.[97] In a similar vein, Sune Lægaard considers whether appeals to 'national values' in public discourse might be a form of nationalism. He argues that 'the nationalization of liberal values' exhibits, particularly in the context of immigration and Europeanization, 'boundary mechanisms' that are among the essential features of nationalism. In this sense, nationalized liberal values tend to be interpreted as organic; that is, as governed by a deterministic logic, which does not allow for the sort of voluntary choices emphasized by liberalism.[98] In this sense, the theoretical construction of liberal nationalism seems to be contradictory by nature.

Moreover, nationalism can entail negative and exclusionary impulses that would supersede the discriminatory categorization practices by the state implicit in the cognitive perspective on collective identity. This is the case since the chauvinistic impulses of nationalism can be regarded as symptoms of collective communities that are made victims by other communities and turn thereupon to political devices of revenge and resentment.[99] These chains of causes and effects lead to political action, which defines national and ethnic collectivities in socio-biological terms of survival. Consequently, solutions to violent identity clashes based on the right to national self-determination are likely to strengthen the divisions between those identities rather than contribute to their reconciliation. Even Gellner's functional theory of nationalism, which posits that the industrial mode of production of modernity demands national homogeneity, implies the sinister side of nationalism. Gellner ignores, however, that cultural homogeneity can often only be achieved brutally by forced integration, ethnic cleansing and genocide, even if it is only a communication-based and standardization-ridden homogenization. In this sense, nationalism can only be defended if it is kept at bay by strong liberal institutions of constitutional state, which guarantees minority rights.

From the perspective of nationalism, there are two implications for the collective identity in the post-national context. First, we might identify national identity as historically non-coincidental. In this case, national identity cannot be replaced or superseded at the post-national level. Although there might be collective identities beyond the nation-state, they will never assume a resilience and durability comparable to the national identity. In this perspective, the nation-state represents the end of history. Second, there might be post-national identities with similar strengths and stability as national identity. However, the construction of such an identity would need to follow the same path of state-building as nation-states. In other words, we would deal here with a new nation-state at a higher level, which would spawn a European nation. The development of a European nation would occur to the detriment of national identities, which would be diluted in the process. In addition, a European nation will be associated with European nationalism, involving its sinister side in forms of discrimination and even oppression, mostly with regard to non-European minorities. Even if European nationalism exhibited a weaker discriminatory potential than its nation-state protoplast, it would be based on exclusion and boundary-making.

Identity politics and the legitimacy of political authority

Every political system, irrespective of its form or institutional configuration, can be analyzed with regard to its legitimacy or, differently put, with regard to its source of acceptability. Legitimate political authorities are accepted by the citizens, even if material interests or normative preferences of individuals are not fully considered by a given political decision. A political system thereby maintains acceptability without guaranteeing that a given political decision will satisfy every single citizen.

The legitimacy function pertains to collective identity insomuch as it plays a decisive role in legitimizing political decisions, that is to say collectively binding decisions. In the case of political systems this legitimacy is nurtured from two sources. On one hand it is the legitimacy by output: the quality of the results of the political process. However, assessment of what is a good political decision depends on the expectations of the citizens and therefore their collective identity, which modulates expectations towards the results of the political decision-making process.[100] On the other hand it is the participation of citizens in the process of political decision-making, which is expected to result from a common will of the citizenry. This typology (although with only an implicit link to collective identity) was coined by Fritz Scharpf, who derived it (at least partially) from the legitimacy concept of David Easton.[101] Scharpf argues that the input dimension of legitimacy is covered by the effective participation of citizens in the decision-making system of the polity.[102] Moreover, he postulates that even democratic participatory systems, which draw their legitimacy primarily from the input, are also dependent in their legitimation on their problem-solving capacity. Therefore, mere input legitimacy cannot guarantee the long-term acceptability and hence the stability of the political system at hand. Even perfectly democratic systems have to be capable of generating government for the people; otherwise they are doomed to lose their legitimacy. Therefore, both dimensions have to be fulfilled in order to legitimize modern political systems. However, the ability to produce good governance (which is the ability of societies to provide an effective public policy) is likely to gain even more importance nowadays, as complex societies rely increasingly on the positive feedback from the citizenry.

The measurement of how far a political authority generates its legitimacy via input, output or both depends, however, on the collective identity. This relates to the question of whether political decisions, generated by the political authority, correspond to the collective will of the population as opposed to the will of the majority. In other words, one could take a look at the difference between the political preferences of an average citizen (for example the median voter) and a given political decision. This would provide for a relatively good account of whether popular preferences become translated into the decisional actions of the political system. In contrast, the legitimacy via output refers to the expectations and definitions of collective problems to be solved as well as the results of political actions related to them.

Furthermore, the legitimacy function of collective identity pertains to the so-called identity politics.[103] The notion of identity politics refers to political action and political measures using collective identity as a basis for political mobilization or a construction of collective identity by political authorities. Therefore, we can identify two types of collective identity. First, there is the bottom-up approach of strategic essentialism, which utilizes established and recognized identities as a support for their political claims. These existing and authentic identities become the basis for the political activity of the citizens. However, it also includes actions of (mostly minority) group leadership to gain recognition on the basis of the supposedly authentic group identity.[104] As Claus Offe argues, political claims of communal group leaders to preserve their specific group culture via special group rights can be motivated by the desire to prevent assimilation that could undermine the power and privilege of leadership. In other words, the political claim of collective identity has the function of power legitimating and power preservation.[105] Second, identity politics also pertains to a political strategy of political elites whose aim is to establish new collective identity in a top-down manner in order to legitimize their policies, which otherwise would not gain sufficient political support. This can include manipulation of cultural and political symbols, propaganda and collective brainwashing through mass media and political events designed to spur emotions and therefore to generate the feelings of commonness. Each of these approaches subordinates collective identity to political interests of the elites.[106]

From the perspective of the elites, collective identity is an instrument to achieve two fundamental principal goals. On the one hand they claim legitimacy (and hence monopoly) in representing the collective concerns of the group and on the other they control 'deviant' behaviour of their political opponents within the group by interpreting what collective identity is.[107] Identity politics relies on the fact that the majority of group members are unlikely to have any direct contact with each other.[108] Nonetheless, they draw on a horizontal feeling of belonging, which is expected to be sufficiently powerful to mobilize and legitimize political actions. This feeling of belonging is supported and stabilized by an ideology of 'we-ness', which holds that the defining characteristics of the group establish authentic boundaries towards other groups and at the same time generate a legitimate basis for laying political claims of either a special treatment or collective self-determination. In order to support their political claims, group leaders emphasize and manipulate shared myths, symbols and cultures associated with a particular territory or a particular way of good life as factors that help to consolidate and maintain collective identity. Since there is no face-to-face communication among the majority of the group members, collective identity is transported via images and representations such as the soccer team of eleven players whom most of the group members do not know.

However, collective identity can have illiberal consequences in this context as well. A construction of fraternization and a development of communitarian loyalty have a flip side of oppressive measures, in case an individual breaches the norms of loyalty. Ernest Gellner critically conceptualizes such communities as legitimizing 'tyranny of the cousins'.[109]

Furthermore, we can distinguish between an instrumentalist version and an ideological version of identity politics. An instrumentalist version is applied by political elites as a resource to address relative deprivation, whereas the ideological identity politics tries to mitigate social heterogeneity by constructing politics of confrontation between the 'Us' and the significant 'Other'.[110] This instrumentalist approach is associated with a general instrumentalist understanding of politics as dominated by the pragmatic, self-interested pursuit of material resources and political advantage. The instrumentalist perspective highlights that identity conflicts are activated when competing elites mobilize their political support along the lines of language, religion or race. In a multicultural context, this type of identity politics can be conceptualized as bargaining demands for access to state patronage. In contrast, the ideological version of identity politics promotes feelings of fear and distrust and engenders collectivist prejudicial stereotyping of the 'Other' fuelling permanent conflict, which cannot be resolved by a more favourable redistribution of material resources. Consequently, the ideological identity politics finds its fulfilment in the pursuit of moral certainty. For that purpose, myths of common ancestry for instance are employed because they have the capacity to modulate perceptions of self-interest, to modify collective identities, and to add a moral dimension to political conflict. As the identity conflict becomes one between the moral 'Us' and the immoral 'Other', it turns into an identity battle in which bargaining and redistribution of material resources have a secondary meaning.

Citizenship and identity politics

One of the controversies of identity politics is the possible scope of manipulation of citizens by political leaders. This is particularly evident in the debate on nationalism as a particular case of legitimacy-seeking identity politics. In contrast to modernists such as Ernest Gellner or Liah Greenfeld, primordialists represent the position that the rise of the modern nation is related to the ethnic communities of the ancient and medieval world, rather than the result of the making of modernity. For instance, Anthony D. Smith highlights how a nation's emphasis on its own unique culture leads to a sense of 'chosenness' of its people, which develops historically as a result of ethnic conflicts.[111] Consequently, national identities of citizens can be traced back to ethnic communities that spread to the detriment of other ethnic communities and, due to the emergence of a homogeneous language and its origin in the ethnic past, gave birth to the political identity of nationalism. It follows that political leaders cannot freely manipulate collective identity of citizens, since ethnicities are the raw material for identity politics and cannot be easily ignored.

In contrast, other scholars support the rather constructivist conception of identity politics as grounded in social interaction and voluntarism. In the sociological traditions of symbolic interactionism and its contemporary variant of 'social constructionism', collective identity develops against the background of social processes, which encompass interactions with others, and the symbolic exchanges of gestures and language, in which meanings are negotiated.[112] In this sense, collective identity is a dynamic result of our everyday social interaction among citizens. Being socially shaped, collective identities are products of social processes, meaning that they can change, but it does not mean that they are fluid.

The classical symbolic interactionism puts a particular emphasis on the interactions with 'significant others', who are emotionally important, parent-like figures, perceived as close. This perspective differs from the socio-psychological approach, in which 'Others' are external representations of out-groups essential for boundary-making and in-group identification, rather than for a positive identification with the 'significant others'.[113] In the framework of symbolic interactionism, 'significant others' are particularly powerful when they control emotional life, as parents do in early childhood. Therefore, identity politics frequently generates collective emotions in order to legitimize political claims of collectivities. In the process, collective identity of citizens becomes emotionally charged and relates to parental figures of political leaders (living or dead) or uses personification of the state as an emotional system of reference.[114]

A further aspect of identity politics relates to the so-called cultural 'tacit knowledge' that includes habits and unconscious social patterns of citizens' behaviour, established by cumulative repetition and social routinization. Against this background, identity politics is viewed as a long-term identity creating project of governing elites with the aim of formatting citizens or future citizens from their early childhood. Identity politics delivers patterns of interpreting the social environment and thus restricting possibilities of narrative identity building at the personal level. Usually, it involves interpretation matrices that are applied by citizens in the unconscious process of explanation of social reality. However, these matrices do not float freely, but are delivered by the political elites with the goal of fostering a certain collective interpretation of the community, relating both to its past and its future.[115] For this purpose, social and political events are not interpreted as such, but are intentionally adapted in a narrative manner retrospectively. They are integrated in an interpretative framework, which ascribes social events to specific semantic categories, thus organizing cognition, understanding and interpretation of these events.[116] In the process, social events become parts of a composite system of interpretation, which gives citizens a grasp both of the inside and outside world. Therefore, identity politics constructs matrices of interpretation pertaining also to the membership of citizens in a political collectivity, making collective identity of individuals/citizens a product of narrative creation.[117] Certainly, the most well-known methods of identity politics refer to the national identity construction perpetuated by nation-states, as they are in possession of institutionalized tools of official historiography, public education systems and mass media.[118] This kind of background process of identity construction was analyzed by Michael Billig, who coined the term 'banal nationalism' to describe this phenomenon with regard to national identity.[119] Billig observed that the everyday language used by the mass media, particularly in news and weather reporting, invokes 'us' and 'we' as a community on an everyday basis, thus establishing a largely unconscious interpretation matrix for citizens who regard themselves as belonging to the same collective category. In contrast to traditional nationalism research, Billig argues that national community is not forged on special occasions such as national holidays and international crises. Instead of being a form of temporary and situational sense of belonging, it occurs first and foremost as a certain ideological habit of thought that must be reproduced on a daily basis to be activated when needed. Only by a piecemeal and subconscious construction can a stable and legitimacy-providing collective identity therefore be developed.

To sum up, approaches to identity politics oscillate between voluntarism of authentic groups and the constructionism of citizens' collective identity by political elites. Both perspectives suffer from certain weaknesses. Oliver Zimmer proposes distinguishing between the mechanisms that social actors use for the reconstruction of the collective identity boundaries at a particular point in time and the symbolic resources upon which they draw in order to reconstruct these boundaries. Employing the Swiss example, Zimmer argues that the sole reliance on a voluntarist vision of the political community posed considerable problems for nation-building elites. According to nationalism's core doctrine, nations have to be 'natural' communities to be authentic. The national ideologues of multiethnic Switzerland were therefore at pains to demonstrate that their nation was organically determined rather than merely a product of human will.[120] In contrast, constructivism is criticized by some authors as a general weakness of contemporary sociological theory. It describes a methodological paradigm regarding ethno-cultural identities as constructed by individuals and groups from the cultural resources available to them in their social environment. However, the constructivist paradigm exaggerates the responsibility of individuals for their own identity and ignores the social and political constraints of ethnic choices. At the same time, it underplays the fact that many minority demands for justice are made through the group prism, rather than in individualist terms.[121]

Solution for collective action dilemmas

The third type of political function of collective identity relates to what is well-known in social sciences as dilemmas of collective action.[122] These dilemmas delineate types of social situations in which individual rationality of interdependent actors leads to collectively irrational outcomes. For instance, in a collective-good dilemma, each actor benefiting from the provision of a collective good such as pollution control does not have any incentive to contribute to the production of the good at hand, since they cannot be excluded from its consumption.[123]

A similar problem of free-riding can be found in collective action literature on political participation, since political protesters also aim for collective goods. As soon as such goods are produced, they are obtainable to everyone regardless of whether they participated in the protests that made the goods possible. Simultaneously, the production of collective goods is rarely determined by the contribution of a single person. Therefore, rational and socially unencumbered individuals would refrain from participating in political protest or production of other collective goods, as they can enjoy the benefits in any case. Further collective action dilemmas include the famous prisoner's dilemma, which, when played once, encourages collectively suboptimal outcomes of individually rational decisions. As a consequence, individuals that are interdependent in terms of their decisions are unlikely to cooperate with each other.[124] In other words, when cooperation occurs in a one-shot prisoner's dilemma or when free-riding is neglected, we would assume a behavioural anomaly.[125]

There is a variety of solutions to the collective action dilemmas, discussed in the debates on cooperation problems. For the prisoner's dilemma there exist among other things various models of game iteration[126] or models of information provision. Regarding the solution of the free-riding problems, models of threshold, selective incentives, critical mass concepts or social norms, among others, are proposed and examined.[127] However, collective identity of citizens is increasingly debated as one of the possible explanations to the anomaly of collective action.[128]

Citizenship and the collective dilemmas

There is growing evidence that rationality is too limited as a theoretical framework to account for participation, cooperation and other forms of collective action among citizens where there should be none. Particularly in sociology and social psychology is the concept of collective identity applied as a solution to dilemmas of collective action.

For instance, group identification is viewed as a significant factor in the explanation of citizens' participation in protest, whereby identification is expected to foster protest participation. Bert Klandermans argues that of three components of citizens' identity – cognitive, evaluative, and affective – the latter appears to be the most relevant for protest behaviour.[129] He includes an additional behavioural component pertaining to the citizens' membership in a group, and stresses that group identification becomes visible in organizations that encompass members of a specific social category. Therefore, both the affective and the behavioural components of identity appear to have an impact on the readiness of citizens to engage in protect actions. Klandermans argues that the relationship between identification and protest participation is a double-edged one, since identity promotes citizens' participation, and participation reinforces identification.[130]

Furthermore, social identity approaches to collective identity suggest that members of in-groups are likely to cooperate with other in-group members, rather than with out-group members, both in continuous and binary-choice versions of the prisoner's dilemma. Even though many social psychologists would agree that social identity has an impact on cooperation, they differ in their explanations of the mechanism of the influence. Brent Simpson argues, for instance, that social identity is likely to reduce actors' responses to the 'greed component' in the prisoner's dilemma (the motivation to 'free-ride' on others' cooperation), but it does not have an effect on the responses to the 'fear component' (the motivation to avoid being 'exploited').[131]

In addition, social movement literature highlights that collectively defined grievances can generate a sense of 'we-ness' that is directed at 'them', who are deemed responsible for the grievances in question. If political authorities become regarded by the citizens as the culprits in a given context, it will politicize collective identity leading to the overcoming of a collective action dilemma. This is particularly the case when political authorities are unresponsive or react in repressive ways. Citizens' collective identity produced in a social movement can even tip over to produce a revolutionary mobilization.[132] Consequently, the concept of collective identity in the literature on social movements primarily involves shared representations of the group based on common interests and experiences, but it also pertains to a process of shaping and creating an image of what the group stands for and how it wants to be viewed by others. In this sense, collective identity is conceptualized as an *achievement* of collective efforts.[133]

Other scholars examining social movements stress the cultural background of collective action, as actors pull elements from their cultural repertoire and adapt them to their movement's purposes. Consequently, collective grievances would not be the only source of collective identity, but rather the hitherto existent wider cultural repertoire of the given social movement. In this sense, collective identity is explained less as a consequence of individual rationality, but more strongly in a structuralist manner.[134]

A further argument pertaining to the solution of collective dilemmas through collective identity can be found in the neo-Marxist literature. For instance, Jon Elster highlights the Marxian class consciousness as the solution to the problem of collective action. If a class is able to overcome the free-rider problem in realizing class interests, we might speak of a collective identity at a class level.[135] However, the form of class consciousness differs depending on the relations of production. Therefore, interests, identities and organization of workers and capitalists will vary, particularly regarding their demands on the state.[136] Nonetheless, class consciousness leads to a class solidarity, which also allows for effective organization of class interests against the interest of the opposing class. This transforms the class 'in itself' into a 'class for itself'. The neo-Marxist account of collective identity is, however, divided regarding the issue of how collective identity comes about. Whereas Marx assumed a creation of class consciousness by default depending on the critical degree of exploitation, some of his apologists supported an active role for the Communist party in creating collective identity of the working class.[137]

In sum, political functions of collective identity pertain to a specific (in strength, resilience and durability) and irreplaceable (in character) bond of national identity, legitimacy of political authority with the particular reference to identity politics and the solution to collective action dilemmas. All three types of this political function are all-pervasive in the political science literature, but exhibit rather *implicit* links to the issue of citizenship. The integrative relationship between national identity and citizenship comes under pressure from globalization and transnationalization processes. As a result, increasingly fewer scholars defend the normative claim of citizenship within exclusive national boundaries. In addition, the subject of legitimacy of political systems through collective identity is strongly connected to identity politics. Even if identity politics is in principle not confined to the framework of the nation-state, the effectiveness of identity politics in light of the nation-state resources and identity technologies appears to be significantly higher than in other political contexts. This suggests that identity politics in a post-national context, such as the European Union, might be inclined to mimic identity politics of the nation-state. The focus on the nation-state and national identity is equally visible in the debate on the solution of collective dilemmas, which are frequently anchored in the context of the nation-state. All this poses certain problems for the theoretical and empirical uses of collective identity in the context of the EU. These problems will be addressed in Chapter 3.

Recapitulation

I argued throughout Chapter 2 that we can systematize research on collective identity according to *functions* of collective identity. Using different functional perspectives on collective identity sheds some light on the relationship between collective identity and citizenship. I differentiated between three main functions of collective identity: the cognitive function, the self-esteem booster function, and three political functions of collective identity (building of a national community, identity politics, and solution of collective dilemmas).

In the cognitive perspective, collective identity reduces social complexity for individuals by rendering it comprehensible. It also decreases perceived social complexity and thus social uncertainty. Here, citizenship can be construed primarily as a boundary-drawing instrument, which makes collective self-categorization and categorization of others possible. In this view, citizenship disintegrates into a number of separate groups that, depending on the context, lay political claims of public recognition and attempt to extract public resources as a result of these claims. Diverse social identities become politicized and depoliticized, leading to a contextual and fragmented citizenship of competing citizenship claims.

In the context of the self-esteem booster, the function of collective identity is to acquire a positive image from membership in a social group. The motivation for positive social identity that drives the process by which one's self-esteem is produced and maintained is created by comparing oneself favourably with the out-group. In this perspective, citizenship can delineate either the differentiation between citizens and non-citizens or the differentiation of various groups within citizenry. For some authors, the most worrisome aspect is the competitive nature of collective self-esteem, which implies that citizens feel better when their collectivity does better than others. This can lead to outright hostility, particularly when groups compete for resources and political power.

Beyond the cognitive and self-esteem perspective, we can identify political functions of collective identity. The national community building can go hand in hand with negative and exclusionary impulses. This is the case since the chauvinistic impulses of nationalism can be regarded as symptoms of collective communities that are made victims by other communities and turn thereupon to political devices of revenge and resentment. The identity politics refers to political action and political measures using collective identity for political mobilization or a construction of collective identity by political authorities with the goal of generating legitimacy. Approaches to identity politics oscillate between voluntarism of authentic groups and the constructionism of citizens' collective identity by political elites. Furthermore, collective identity is debated in the context of cooperation dilemmas. There is growing evidence that rationality is too limited as a theoretical framework to account for participation, cooperation and other forms of collective action among citizens where there should be none.

One common concern of all the discussed functions of collective identity is whether citizenship can generate such a stable or 'chronic' identity resistant to disintegration, one which could be accessed and used as a resource in times of crisis and at the same time be capable of bridging differences as an encompassing category. At the same time, there are concerns that attempts at generating collective identity in particular exhibit a tenuous relationship with citizenship by being close to manipulation and brainwashing.

3 The debate on European identity in the functional perspective

In the last chapter I systematized the research on collective identity on the basis of the functions of collective identity and discussed their implications for the concept of citizenship. In this chapter I want to narrow down the perspective on collective identity and citizenship to the European identity.

The heated debate on European identity, which we have been experiencing for the last fifteen years, has several roots. First, the empirical evidence highlights that citizens' distance from the European Union is increasing.[1] The so-called 'permissive consensus' of European integration (citizens' tacit agreement to the elite-driven integration project) can therefore no longer be taken for granted. However, if there is a growing distance between citizens and elites, it can be construed as connected to lacking identification with the EU. Although identification and collective identity is not the same thing, they appear to be closely connected. Whereas identification processes relate mostly to institutions, norms and values, collective identity is frequently referred to as a feeling of belonging (emotional aspect) or a perception of commonness (cognitive aspect) among individuals. Second, the EU's legitimacy shortfalls are increasingly explored with a diagnosis of legitimacy and democracy deficits. In this context, collective identity is viewed as an instrument of legitimization.[2] Third, the size of the European Union, with currently 27 member states, and its increased heterogeneity as a result of the recent enlargements to the East and South in 2004 and 2007 raises the issue of a multicultural, multinational and socially diverse EU. This in turn begs the question of common grounds for collective identity in the diverse EU. This becomes particularly vital regarding the expanding application of the majority decision rule under the circumstances of diversity and a simultaneous lack of thick collective identity.[3] The absence of collective identity can turn a majority rule into a tyranny of majority. Fourth, the EU is currently facing difficulties of problem-solving while lacking strong support among the citizens. Therefore, the question arises whether there can be any form of collective identity that would cement the crises-ridden European Union. If it *is* possible, what kind of collective identity is there or should be there to make the EU resist pressure and persist despite crises? In other words, what does it take to fortify the EU to endure in times of scarcity, internal conflict and growing societal cleavages? In this sense, European identity also pertains to the issue of identity politics. For instance, Bo Stråth remarked that the concept of European identity was introduced at the Copenhagen summit in 1973 in order to instrumentally consolidate the European Community (EC), since the oil price crisis undermined the very belief in the EC's political effectiveness.[4]

Seeking responses to these questions, a plethora of publications on European identity has emerged in recent years. A surge of studies on collective identity in Europe are dealing with features of the potential European identity, the prospects of a European identity as well as obstacles to a collective identity in the EU. This chapter reviews various approaches to European identity against the background of the functions of collective identity discussed previously. In addition, it discusses aspects of the debate on the European citizenship in the context of European identity. The chapter also shows that the notion of European identity is a complex one and that it is associated with many conceptual connotations and theoretical perspectives. This conceptual and theoretical variety is caused, on the one hand, by the fact that the phenomenon of collective identity is of an interdisciplinary nature. It was primarily anchored in psychology and sociology, but has successively become enriched by other disciplines such as philosophy and political science, which in turn shed light on it with their specific methods and questions. On the other hand, the concept of European collective identity frequently merges with adjacent terms of social science such as community, solidarity, trust and legitimacy in a way that makes it difficult to analytically isolate it and pin it down.

Cognitive function and European identity

As noted above, the cognitive function of collective identity relates to the function of psychological reduction of social complexity and the resulting decrease of social uncertainty. While collective identity reflects the categorization of the self as a group member, a number of potential group memberships provide multiple bases for the self-categorization of individuals.[5] In the context of debate on European identity we can identify three main connotations pointing to the cognitive perspective: salience and perception, fluidity and hybridity as well as the manipulation of symbols.

Salience and perception

European identity becomes increasingly associated with shared categories, images and frames, used by the citizens in their perception. These shared categories denote collective identity as a sphere of European social subjectivity and intersubjectivity.[6] As Juan Díez Medrano argues, German, Spanish and British citizens exhibit perception similarities of the EU, which could be conceptualized as a beginning of an imagined community at the European level. However, they also hold very different images and frames of the EU as a result of their specific national experiences and self-perceptions. Whereas Germans criticize the EU's democratic deficit and fear foreign competition in the labour market, Britons worry about losing their national identity as a result of the European integration. In contrast, Spaniards tend to categorize the EU positively with an opportunity to modernize and end their tradition of isolation in Europe.[7] In this sense, European identity boils down to shared images and common views of the EU, without answering the question of how stable these perceptions are and whether they can indeed be conceptualized as collective identity. This conflation of collective identity and shared perceptions can lead to a common fallacy, which uses support for European integration as a proxy for European identity. However, the mere support for the EU does not necessarily imply a sense of European identity, as it can be motivated by instrumental interests of political actors, such as the increase in the efficiency of political decisions through delegation of controversial policy fields to 'Brussels', stimulation of economic growth via additional investments in infrastructure or augmenting of external and legal security.

Furthermore, the cognitive perspective on European identity highlights certain perceptional effects such as entitativity.[8] For instance, Thomas Risse uses this concept to explain the differences in the intensity of collective identity in European political, economic and social elites as opposed to the average citizens, for whom the EU is rather a distant framework of reference. Since the salience of European policies appears to be low for average citizens, its 'identifiability' assumes also low figures. The perceptional 'fuzziness' of the EU for average citizens leads to a paradoxical situation, in which the citizens' interest in the activities of the EU remains low despite its real influence on people's lives. Thus, the perception of the 'realness' of the EU diverges from its actual realness. However, for the elites the EU assumes higher values regarding their perception of its 'realness'. It applies particularly to those elites who are main actors in the EU-wide social interactions and therefore may develop the 'in-group' bias, which denotes a positive evaluation of one's own community over the out-group.[9] As a consequence, the elites are prone to develop a community feeling towards the EU, whereas average citizens retain their national belonging as primary reference for their collective identity.

This leads us directly to the issue of identity technologies, which refers to the policies of constructing collective identities in accordance with the images of European elites and political authorities. Whereas the cognitive perspective highlights mainly self-categorization processes in individuals, we can relate it also to the categorization technologies used by political authorities of the European Union. As mentioned previously, political authorities categorize and classify people by assigning them to categories which are associated with consequential identities. Thus, they enhance and freeze the salience of certain collective identities through political practices of categorization.[10] Regarding the European Union, Elena Jileva shows how the extension of the EU's visa policy and the policy of free movement of labour to the Central and Eastern European countries (CEE) established categories of inequality. In the wake of EU accession, the applicant countries were required to adopt completely the EU's visa policy, even prior to their accession, although some EU old member states were granted substantial derogations. In contrast, the EU has introduced restrictive policies on the free movement of labour from the CEE countries by establishing transitional periods after their accession, while at the same time encouraging labour mobility of EU citizens. In this perspective, the EU generated two categories of citizens: complete citizens entitled to all rights (including exemptions from certain duties) and incomplete citizens, fully obligated but with restricted rights.[11]

This sort of categorization used as identity technology gains significance in respect of, for instance, the EU's asylum policy, which can be construed as an expansion of exclusion spheres in Europe.[12] By constructing Europeans as an exclusive and bounded category, European authorities attempt to invent the 'European people', which at the first glance is a cognitive category, which establishes a difference allowing primarily for a negative identification.[13] As a further category of identity technology we could consider the European passport policy, which in addition to the constructed external boundary has a goal of homogenizing the EU internally. Passports not only denote a categorization of citizens but also become linked to security issues, thus enhancing the salience of this category.[14] Both asylum policy and passport policy are accompanied by the EU border policy which supports the salience of the citizen/non-citizen categories and thus functions as a technology of identity by introducing a territorial dimension of collective identity similar to that of the nation-state.[15]

Moreover, when directed at out-groups, categorization frequently entails discriminatory consequences. For instance, Peo Hansen argues that the concept of European identity envisaged by the European Community has given the citizen/non-citizen of the EU categories increasingly ethno-cultural underpinning with implications for the European identity. As a result of ethno-cultural articulation, European citizenship became an instrument of exclusion towards the EU's non-white and non-Christian populations, thus fostering a collective identity in essentialist terms.[16] In other words, we could argue that the European integration with its inclusive developments strongly relied on the continued exclusion of outsiders, which renders the EU by no means a post-Westphalian polity, but rather territorial and replicating the identity-making mechanisms of the nation-state.[17] Regardless of the thesis on ethno-cultural substantiation of European citizenship, we might argue alongside the cognitive approach that citizenship as every socio-political and collective notion establishes a category designating its own opposition. In this sense, the category of citizenship establishes non-citizens as the antipodal reference for citizenship.[18]

Notwithstanding the substantial effects of European citizenship on European identity, the immigration-based, asylum-orientated and border-controls-accentuating emphasis on European identity entails two consequences. First, citizens with primary national identity (as opposed to European identity) would be less likely to support EU control over immigration policy than those citizens who rather exhibit European identity.[19] In other words, anti-immigration sentiments should positively influence the attitudinal support for European integration. In fact, de Vreese and Boomgaarden demonstrate in their statistical analysis that fear of immigration is one of the strongest predictors of both support for integration and citizens' inclination to vote in a referendum in favour of the enlargement of the EU.[20] Second, assuming the effectiveness of European identity technology, EU citizens should perceive the external migration in the EU differently from the internal migration. However, as Lauren M. McLaren shows, the EU was not successful in creating a strong and broad feeling of 'Europeanness', since most citizens in EU countries view external and internal migration identically. Therefore, the majority of the EU citizens fail to regard their EU fellow citizens as necessarily belonging to a different (and thus privileged) community, as compared to migrants from outside the EU. Nonetheless, a large minority of EU citizens is inclined to treat internal migrants more favourably than the external ones. This could warrant a conclusion that the EU identity technologies were capable of exerting a certain effect on the European identity.[21]

Fluidity and hybridity

As the cognitive perspective stresses fluidity and a recurrent reconstruction of collective identity, European identity tends to be conceptualized as a layer of multiple identities or as a component of a hybrid identity. Different layers or components of multiple identities can relate to each other in various configurations. As Matthias L. Maier and Thomas Risse argue, identities can be nested, cross-cutting, or like marble cake. Nesting suggests some hierarchy between a people's sense of belonging and loyalties, whereby the EU forms the outer boundary, and regions or nation-states constitute the core. In cross-cutting identities, members of one identity group are also members of another identity group, even though conflictual relationships between the group identities are not excluded. Finally, in the marble cake model of multiple identities, various components of an individual's identity cannot be clearly separated, but rather blend into one another.[22] Depending on the salience of the situation, individual citizens change their identity layers.[23] In this sense, European identity only becomes activated when there is a context relating directly to the EU and the individual becomes mobilized as an EU citizen. However, it is frequently argued that the EU is likely to have relatively little salience in the everyday citizenship practice, since it regulates solely policy fields of secondary significance to the average citizen.[24]

In this perspective, European identity is unlikely to replace other attachments, particularly the national ones. As the EU is characterized by cultural diversity, rather than unity, a cultural uniformization appears to be improbable. The fluidity, plurality and multiplicity of collective identities of the EU can be conceptualized as 'deep diversity', which denotes more than a mere cultural plurality.[25] John Erik Fossum applies this term introduced by Charles Taylor to describe the existence of cultural, national and ethnic structures of a society that in turn bring about different collective goals. These different collective goals are acknowledged by society and political authorities as legitimate, for instance via differentiated citizenship. In addition, this deep diversity is regarded as a wishful and legitimate state not subject to assimilating and acculturating policies.[26]

The idea of deep diversity is mirrored in the concepts of fragmented or diverse European citizenship. European citizenship is regarded as transcending the framework of nationality and constructed in practice particular to time, place, actors, and institutions. Since the EU is conceptualized as a political system sui generis,[27] the Union citizenship can be interpreted as a concomitant phenomenon of diversity or even its major aspect, which can be identified only in its own context.[28] First, Union citizenship is delineated as derivative and supplementary with regard to the national citizenship of the member states.[29] On one hand, it transcends the national citizenship as an indicator for the 'crises of the hyphen' in the term nation-state,[30] and on the other it remains parasitic concerning the citizenship of the member states. Second, European citizenship evolved as a fragmented citizenship establishing special rights for special groups of Europeans, and not for Europeans as a people. Whereas it encourages students and academics to move across the borders, other societal groups such as workers have limited opportunities. This strengthens boundaries among groups in the EU, rather than unifying the European citizenship.[31] Third, not only is the European citizenship fragmented, but it can be interpreted as a set of norms and practices in motion. As the EU is an open-ended and extending polity, European citizenship does not reflect a fixed set of rights and duties, but exhibits a high degree of fluidity.[32] Fourth, the EU citizenship establishes different degrees of citizenship such as full citizenship, partial citizenship (limited access to the labour market as a result of transition periods for new member states), denizenship (for third country residents in the EU) and the status of asylum-seeking 'helots'.[33] Fifth, even among the full citizens, there is a varying degree of access to political channels. An active citizenship practice in the context of the EU frequently requires a membership in lobbying organizations whose success depends on fast-changing and issue-specific alliances usually constructed on an ad hoc basis of 'policy coalitions'.[34]

Besides features of deep diversity, the cognitive perspective increasingly stresses the hybridity of collective identities in Europe. The notion of hybridity puts emphasis on the fusion of identities, which is a result of the increasingly interwoven and multicultural nature of modern societies. This is first and foremost due to the large-scale migration within the EU as well as from outer Europe into the EU.[35] The expansion of European borders and the consequent transnationalization of the European societies are expected to foster not only cultural diversity, but also cultural hybridity.[36] In this view, hybrid identities become the social tissue of European integration and correspond to the institutional hybridity of the EU itself.[37] Since identities in the EU are likely to become increasingly multiple and hybrid, a sense of belonging to a particular territory or a community can be upheld alongside a simultaneous attachment to supranational collectivities such as the EU. The socio-cultural dimension of the EU matches the notion of transnational syncretism,[38] whereas the political authorities of the EU promote 'the unity in diversity' by respecting the national identities of the member states. Therefore, the debate dichotomizing national and European identities is rejected by the proponents of multiplicity and fluidity in collective identities. In this perspective, not only are the citizens capable of having multi-layered and fluid identities, but these tend also to be inclusive and nested, rather than mutually exclusive. Moreover, this multiplicity and hybridity of identity corresponds perfectly to the notion of transnational citizenship. Transnational citizenship departs from multiplicity and fluidity of identity but anchors it within a territorial framework, although transcending the framework of the nation-state.[39]

In this vein, Gary Marks maps multiple identities along two dimensions: intensity of attachment to a particular territorial community, and exclusive versus multiple attachments across territorial levels. With the example of Catalonia, he shows that identity is not a zero-sum game, and that European identity may very well coexist with strong regional and national identities, even though this coexistence is not context-dependent.[40] Marks suggests that attachments can be mutually inclusive: attachment at one territorial level is associated with greater rather than less attachment at other levels. Additionally, an individual with a relatively high attachment to any one of these territorial levels is likely to have a relatively high attachment to other levels. Nonetheless, a more conflictual relationship between national, regional, and European identity may also develop. In cases of conflict or salience of conflictual issues, the primary or core identity is activated, since individuals tend to reduce the cognitive complexity of social reality. Against this background, European identity can stabilize and satisfy the individual need for reducing complexity, if the given individual strongly engages in social and cognitive networks at the European level. In this perspective, European identity would allow for much more efficient interpretation of social reality than the national identity.

This territorially multiple identity corresponds to the concept of nested citizenship. According to this conception, European citizenship is nested in various sites and levels: regional, state and supra-state forms of citizenship, which are not only complementary in terms of coexistence, but are also subject to mutual influence, constant revision and continuous development at all governance levels. Thus, rights associated with nested citizenship represent an enshrined system that interconnects and readapts various sites of regional, national and supranational governance. In this sense, it establishes a sort of a federative membership, which goes further than a multiple citizenship (implying a simple coexistence). Thomas Faist argues with regard to the social aspects of European citizenship that it is sited as a whole in various governance levels that interrelate interactively with each other, thus being a cumulative phenomenon, rather than a purely additive one. European regulations and rights in the realm of social policy have impact and entail feedback effects on other levels and vice versa.[41]

In the same social interactionist vein,[42] Daniel Fuss and Marita A. Grosser relate the construction of European identity to specifically European social interactions. In other words, European identity cannot develop unless individuals participate in social interactions related to the EU or Europe. Consequently, there are at least two conditions for the development of European identity. First, as Europe has to be salient in social interactions of individuals, citizens with only local and national horizons are unlikely to develop European identity. Second, European identity (as any other social identity) requires 'raw material' such as contacts with foreigners or a command of foreign languages. However, this raw material is unequally distributed within the population. Therefore, individuals develop European identity to differing extents. This conception of European identity purports an abstract feeling of belonging, but not necessarily in the emotional sense. The analysis of the survey data from the project 'Youth and European identity' reveals that European identity, as an abstract category, is a lower priority (in contrast to national identity) for most young people. However, the majority of respondents in the survey had either dual focus identification on their nation and on Europe or did not feel affiliated at all. The in-depth interviews suggest that European identity denotes a 'status identity' of Europeanness, difficult to explain by individuals holding it. This status identity does not necessarily entail any feelings of solidarity or obligation vis-à-vis fellow Europeans, which makes it neither stable nor crisis-proof.[43]

The cognitive perspective on European identity highlights the multiplicity and fluidity of collective identity, and salience can activate one or the other layer of multiple collective identities. However, this perspective does not explain what would happen when the salient context triggers not one but several identities, thus bringing them into conflict. One possibility is for the citizen to commit to one dominant group identification and subordinate all other affiliations, precisely as the notion of 'chronic identity' presupposes. This would mean that either national or European identity will have to take the upper hand. Consequently, citizens would identify with their fellow Europeans, mostly to the extent that European identity converges with national interests. However, this would render European identity meaningless.

A second approach would include ascribing different group identities to different domains. Thus, segregated multiple identities would not be mobilized simultaneously. European identity would therefore be adopted in the political context, for instance in relations between the EU and the USA or the EU and Asia, and ethnic identity would be maintained in the cultural domain. A third case would involve a situation in which identities can be neither subordinated to one chronic identity nor segregated. When two identities become salient at the same time, one can use the inclusive strategy of extending the in-group category to all members of the conflicting identity groups. For instance, when a German national identifies both with Europe and Germany and finds it conflictive, he might consider being German as a category of Europeanness, thus assuming an overlapping between Germany and Europe. In other words, every German would be European by definition. The alternative strategy would include a conjunction, in which the in-group is perceived as the intersection of several categories. For instance, only Western Germans would perceive themselves as genuine Europeans, since the EU was part of their social reality for the last fifty years, as opposed to the Eastern Germans. In this case, only Western German identity would overlap with the European identity, thus excluding the other Germans. While the additive strategy would increase the inclusiveness of an individual's collective identity, the conjunctive approach would narrow it down.[44]

Against this background, European citizenship is regarded by some authors as a tool for raising salience of the European category. By institutionalizing a particular European category of membership linked directly to citizens, the norms and practices of European citizenship are believed to impact on the salience of Europeanness and, by the same token, citizens' sense of belonging.[45] The understanding of European citizenship thus moves beyond the legal dimension of Union citizenship as defined by the treaties, and puts emphasis on the socio-cultural meaning of the European citizenship, which is expected to stimulate the emergence of a supranational collective identity with reference to the European Union.[46] Others are more sceptical about the impact of the European citizenship on the collective identity in the EU. First, it is contested whether European citizenship is capable of delivering a stable and thus effective framework for the construction of collective identity due to a plethora of contradictions and asymmetries (e.g. transition periods in access to the labour markets) in the European system of rights.[47] Second, there are serious doubts whether the rights-component of European citizenship is compatible with the EU's security policies. Some authors do not believe that these polices can be attuned with civil rights, in particular with the freedom of movement.[48] Third, the open-ended character of the EU (and consequently of its citizenship) as well as the polycentric nature of the political authority in the EU promote a diffuse concept of citizenship, rather than its salience in the eyes of the European public. As a consequence, instead of European collective identity we may expect 'alienage', which is a permanent and structural cognitive dissonance as a hallmark of Union citizenship.[49] Fourth, some authors are sceptical about the development of Union citizenship up to now and hence its potential. While there is a visible Europeanization of nation citizenship regimes in cosmopolitan forms of citizenship (anchored in particular in the 'thin identity' of human rights), it has also led to a deficit in the values of solidarity and social justice, which is viewed as a major crisis at the heart of the European project. In other words, not only is European citizenship deficient as compared to solidarity based forms of national citizenship, but the denationalization (Europeanization) of citizenship may be regarded as an indicator of crises, rather than a tool for constructing a supranational collective identity.[50]

Manipulation of symbols

The cognitive perspective follows the conceptualization of European citizenship as inducing a 'soft' collective identity (as a derivative of national identity) at best or as promoting fluid and fragmented identity – failing to establish any sense of collective continuity and integration – at worst. European cultural and political diversity is therefore viewed as undermining a solid sense of collective self and of social belonging. This understanding depicts the European citizenship identity through a prism of its limitations. For instance, Gerard Delanty suggests that European citizenship cannot rest on any culturally stable grounds similar to a common language, a shared history, religion, an educational system and mass media. Delanty's position stresses in particular the significance of cultural symbols for the construction and stability of European citizenship identity.[51] These cultural symbols are expected to pave the way for an emergence of collective identity based not only on exclusion (a Europeanness where the mere reference point is a non-European one), but also on identification allowing for a more 'thick' collective identity.

Against this background, other authors believe that the EU already practises manipulation of cultural symbols pertaining to collective identity in order to compensate for the 'weakness' of European citizenship in terms of its identity generating capacity. One of the cases of the EU's manipulation of cultural symbols is the introduction of the common currency in the EU.[52] The establishment of a tangible symbol of the euro and its iconography raises the salience of Europeanness without the necessity of homogenizing the European cultural diversity, since the euro allows for different iconographic connotations. At the same time, a common currency establishes a certain degree of commonality and therefore fosters new identity content.[53] This currency would be completely in tune with the fluid and multiple nature of European culture, since it is rather abstract and open to multiple interpretations, at the same time endowing the citizen with something to identify with, without surrendering their own subjective vision of European 'community'. This trend towards abstraction is also visible with regard to other collective symbols such as flags and anthems.[54]

In the same vein, Thomas Risse stresses the significance of the euro for the development of the collective identity in the European Union. Since money generally fulfils a role of a relevant symbolic marker in the processes of community building, the euro is also associated with collective identities. Risse argues that the introduction of the euro has a substantial impact on the citizens' identification with the EU and Europe, as the common currency enhances the 'realness' of Europe by providing a tangible link from the European level to the daily lives of the citizens.[55]

Further cases of manipulation of cultural symbols pertain to the EU's cultural policy. This encompasses symbolic initiatives such as the 'European Cities of Culture', with the goal of raising visibility and identifiablity of the EU. The EU increasingly promotes commonality symbols, while attempting to respect the realm of national cultures.[56] Thus, the EU tries to enhance its salience via the symbolic diffusion into the everyday life of citizens, but without relinquishing the symbolic ambiguity. However, it is argued that in the case of the EU ambiguity does not necessarily mean confusion, but rather is to be viewed as a response to the European cultural fluidity and multiplicity. The EU's symbolism serves as a tool for constructing a community in the specific context of the EU's multiple identities.[57]

In contrast to the aggregated view of cultural policy, Michael Bruter examines separate symbols and items pertaining to collective images and identity in Europe. According to his qualitative analysis of focus-group discussions in France, UK and the Netherlands, he argues that the majority of the participants' perceptions of Europe and their self-assessment of their European identity referred to predominantly 'civic' images, whereas a minority perceived the EU in 'cultural' terms. The images of 'cultural' Europe by the participants were associated with peace, harmony, the disappearing of historical divisions and cooperation between similar people. In contrast, the images of 'civic' Europe were linked to borderless-ness, circulation of citizens, and prosperity.[58] Even though Bruter's typology of civic and cultural images is not entirely convincing, his research highlights that the EU imitates nation-states by delivering national symbols in order to stimulate a European political community. These include, besides euro notes and coins, a flag, an anthem,[59] a national day, and until recently an attempt to introduce a constitution.[60] In other words, the EU manipulates symbols to construct European mass identity by mimicking technologies of national identity. The particular role of symbols in the development of collective identities seems to be particularly instructive for the technology of collective identity, since symbols apparently play an important role in the generation of collective identities. This could suggest that a more intense construction and application of symbols could stimulate a thicker and more stable identity than suggested by mere categorization processes.[61]

Furthermore, one could argue that attempts to personify the EU, for instance through the establishment of an office of Foreign Minister or President in the Lisbon Treaty, point in the same direction as the manipulation of symbols.[62] Personification techniques are frequently used by the nation-state elites to stimulate collective identity and hence loyalty. Since nation-states or political systems in general are abstract entities, they necessitate a more concrete embodiment for mass population to conceive of them and develop shared identity with reference to them. This embodiment can occur as personification, in which the state or in our case the European Union as a polity becomes associated with the most salient figure in the political system. Recent studies in political psychology confirm the hypothesis that personification of political systems facilitates 'stronger' attitudes and hence may be decisive in the formation of collective identities. As opposed to personification, embodying the political system as a parliamentary institution is likely to produce weaker attitudes, which leads to the conclusion that a widespread practice of personification of the political system has robust and potentially far-reaching attitudinal consequences.[63] For the EU, it could mean that the proposals made in the Lisbon Treaty implying personification techniques would be more effective in terms of collective identity than a public visibility of the European Parliament.

At this point, we should address the tension between the manipulation of symbols by European authorities and European citizenship. A construction of collective identity by political authorities corresponds to a collectivist and authoritarian understanding of citizenship. By manipulating symbols pertaining to citizenship, the EU makes use of citizenship as an order-creating cultural system and a conveyor of identity, but not as a basis for popular sovereignty.[64] In other words, manipulation of cultural symbols reflects the identity technology used by nation-states, which socialize their citizens into bearers of loyalty towards the state. However, as a supposedly post-national polity, the EU relies too strongly on technologies of nationalism, which highlight the claim of the state sovereignty to the detriment of popular sovereignty.[65] However, both claims are highly problematic in the EU, since the EU is neither a state nor is any European demos in sight.[66] Consequently, the identity construction qua manipulation of symbols might not be easily discernible from collective brainwashing, which contradicts the very notion of an autonomous citizenry. This collectivistic stimulation of citizens' identity responding to cultural manipulation exhibits a predilection for authoritarian politics, since it enhances the inequality between the rulers and the ruled, and thus increases the democratic deficit of the EU. Consequently, the manipulation of symbols in order to generate collective identity can prove counterproductive regarding the EU's strive for more democratic legitimacy.

Self-esteem booster function and European identity

This approach explains individuals' drive to develop attachment to groups and to construct communities against the background of the personal strategy of positive self-image enhancement via membership in a social group. We should expect that the European identity would not be an exception in this respect. As one's self-esteem is produced and upheld by a favourable social comparison to the out-group, in most of the cases an in-group projects certain characteristics both into the behaviour of the in-group and the out-group. The degree of permeability of the in-group is a factor in dealing with the positive self-image, since in groups with rigid boundaries or extensive territories (and therefore greater in-group mobility options, as is the case with the EU), the exit option and hence joining a more attractive group is less likely, as compared to other groups.[67] In this perspective, a manipulation of in-group image appears to be more probable. This manipulation can, of course, assume different forms. For instance, as pointed out by the 'collective codes approach' to collective identity, social groups can define themselves as an expression of natural order and demonize the non-members of the group. Alternatively, communities can utilize projections of the in-group supremacy, which may lead either to missionary zeal of converting the outsiders or to a hegemonic endeavour of subordinating them. Consequently, the so-called 'Othering' is more than a mere categorization of citizens vs. non-citizens, since it becomes filled with political 'substance'.[68] In this sense, the difference plays a central role in identity formation, as the social identity approach assumes a behavioural relationship between self and Others. However, the differentiation between self and Others is merely a preliminary step of Othering, while the next step includes 'enrichment' of the self with positive images of the group. Thus, the self becomes parasite-like regarding the group, whereas the group attempts to remain (or to become) attractive in terms of positive image in order to attract members and to secure their allegiance.[69]

In the case of the EU, some authors argue that precisely because of its diversity, the EU is forced to define its identity with substantiated images of the Others. However, Othering does not occur in relation to every out-group. Rumelili proposes three constitutive dimensions along which self–other relationships vary in producing Othering. They include the nature of difference between the self and Other, social distance as well as the response of the Other. He observes that the EU's interactions with Morocco, Turkey, and Central and Eastern Europe (CEE) vary with regard to the construction of the Othering, as they are situated differently on the proposed dimensions.[70] Even though the relation with CEE (prior to their EU accession) exemplified a type of self/Other interaction, it was not characterized by a relationship of Othering. The EU's relationship with Morocco is also characterized by an interaction that is not characterized by a relationship of Othering, whereas the processes of Othering occur visibly in the case of Turkey.[71]

While the dichotomy of citizen/non-citizen or of citizen/immigrant allows for a purely negative categorization (frequently entailing an exclusion from the host society), Othering uses commonalities activated in a social-historical context and thus stresses the specific historical legacy and socio-economic reality of a given country.[72] The codes of European collective identity therefore utilize particular European narratives and apply them with regard to Others.[73] As noted previously, codes of collective identity are socially constructed boundaries that segregate group similarity against group strangeness. In contrast to many other communities, the EU primarily uses transcendental codes of collective identity.[74] We can identify three basic images of the EU that are used to fulfil the function of a self-esteem booster. They include the image of the EU as an embodiment of cosmopolitanism, the EU image as normative power and the image of the EU as a civilizing force. European identity has to rely on positive images of its collective identity for two reasons. On one hand, it seeks to be attractive to its own members, and it uses the narrative of expansion in order to include new members on the other. In the latter case, the EU reflects the concept of missionary pedagogy of universalistic and transcendental codes of collective identity.[75]

Positive self-images of the EU

The first type of positive imaginary tools used by some scholars to describe the EU substantive identity is cosmopolitan Europe.[76] One of the most well-known and fervent proponents of cosmopolitan Europe is Jürgen Habermas and his supporters, who believe that the European Union can be based on a 'thin' collective identity stemming from a set of abstract universalistic principles such as human rights, but evolves and thickens from this Kantian cosmopolitan conception into the European constitutional patriotism, which is expected to replace the ethnic bonds of European nations.[77] Since the EU represents a 'post-national constellation', European citizens, induced by the process of European constitution-making, are expected to develop a sense of loyalty and solidarity 'among strangers' with regard to each other by abstracting from their particular identities.[78] This cosmopolitan Europe is also associated with a constitution rather than a state, and is anchored in a shared culture of universal and liberal values.[79] In this case, we deal with a relatively open and inclusive citizenship, since neither ethnic belonging nor particular cultures are expected to be an obstacle for constitutional patriotism. Nevertheless, the cosmopolitan image of Europe shows normative boundaries, which distinguish Europe for instance from the USA. Jürgen Habermas and Jacques Derrida regard the historical and institutional peculiarities of Europe (such as secularization, the priority of the state over the market, the primacy of social solidarity over achievement, scepticism concerning technology, awareness of the paradoxes of progress, rejection of the law of the stronger, and the commitment to peace as a consequence of the historical experience of loss)[80] as an appropriate boundary-mechanism, which as a consequence allows for Othering.[81]

Nonetheless, other scholars also base collective identity in Europe on its constitutional distinctiveness where the USA remains the major object of Othering, while Europe maintains both cosmopolitan (fundamental role of reason in the public life, individual liberty, tolerance, and democracy) and particularistic features.[82] In accordance with Habermas, Wojciech Sadurski offers a set of constitutional identity distinctions between the EU and the USA, which politically perpetuated could construct and strengthen European identity. The main feature of European constitutional identity that distinguishes it from the USA points to a much more favourable conception to the state, which is treated not only as the source of threat but also as an ethical institution for creation of justice and protection of citizens against misfortunes stemming from inequalities and irrationalities of the market.[83] A further fundamental difference would pertain to minority rights, since European constitutional identity exhibits less faith in the positive effects of individualistic liberal principles, particularly when the societal diversity is associated with anti-minority prejudices and discrimination. In contrast, American constitutionalism is regarded as hostile to minority rights, since it is based on the liberal approach to the American immigrant society, where the main concern of new minorities is to enjoy the same rights as the older population, whereas European minorities' main concern is to enjoy special group rights as structurally disadvantaged minorities. Moreover, there is a crucial difference between American and European constitutionalism with regard to the secularity of the state. Since in the USA the constitutional doctrine protects a far-reaching separation of state and religion, many practices of European states (such as tax collecting by the German state for the Church or favouring certain churches as in the case of the Church of England) would be deemed unconstitutional. Nevertheless, the political culture in Europe is less tolerant of frequent references to God and religion in the public discourse, which is apparently a feature of the American political culture.[84] These differences are expected to function as a 'difference engine', thus fostering European common identity and simultaneously being ingrained in universalistic principles.[85]

Beyond the differences to the USA, the cosmopolitan image of the EU is expected to rest on the EU's transformed concept of power politics, according to which the EU exports the rule of law, democracy and human rights worldwide. Erik Oddvar Eriksen argues that the criteria for the EU's missionary activities can be derived from cosmopolitanism, suggesting that the EU subordinates its external policies to the constraints of a higher ranking law. In this perspective, the EU is regarded as different from the interest maximizing actors in the international politics, as it is able to act out of a sense of justice or duty pertaining mainly to the human rights. Consequently, infringements of human rights become sanctioned, whereby the EU increasingly fulfils the role of the forerunner of the new international order.

However, this self-image of the EU is not entirely mirrored in the reality. Eriksen points out that while inconsistent human rights policies within the EU and moral double standards are not exceptions, the EU can be deemed the most promising role model for other actors in its cosmopolitan zeal to anchor human rights in international politics.[86] Not only does the EU project its cosmopolitan image outside, but also attempts to enhance the positive image consistently between the externally projected and the internally applied standards. The EU Charter of Fundamental Rights is believed to be the indicator for these attempts.[87] Both approaches to construct a positive image (either via Othering towards the USA or its missionary cosmopolitanism) reflect universalistic codes of collective identity, which are based on a transcendental interpretation of its community values and an ethical supremacy vis-à-vis others.

However, the citizenship problem of the EU depicting itself as a cosmopolitan incarnation of human rights is as follows. It apparently reduces citizenship to a pursuit of moral principles, thus causing the political in the citizenship to fade away. Since the cosmopolitan image of Europe is based on morality and claimed legal superiority, there is not much space for political and moral plurality in the EU.[88] According to the cosmopolitan image, the European citizen is a bearer of rights and moral commitments rather than as a participant in the democratic decision-making. The cosmopolitan image of Europe, particularly in Habermas's approach, attempts to redirect the identification of citizens with their community towards more abstract moral norms.[89] Thus, this 'lean citizenship' attempts to substitute the 'thick' identity of communities based on participation and plurality with the legality and morality of transnational civil associations. Consequently, the 'lean citizenship' ignores the necessity of a distinct world as a basis for collective identity appealing to universalistic norms of conduct, but at the same time constructs an image of others who are deemed not complying with the norms.[90] This leads to an image of Europe as giving voice to 'better cosmopolitans' and being a 'community of fate' rather than a democratic community of self-governing citizens. It is a community of fate, rather than a community of self-determination, since the cosmopolitan European cannot explain how the cosmopolitan values of Europe came into existence and why they are supposed to be superior to other cosmopolitanisms.[91] Nonetheless, lean citizenship of the EU might not be sufficient for a development of a collective identity. It is argued that in order to spawn a more stable and sustainable collective identity the EU would need a 'thicker' political culture, which can provide the social capital necessary for enhanced cohesion of a multicultural and transnational order of the EU.[92]

A further positive image of the EU discussed in the debate pertains to the notion of the EU as a civilian power.[93] This issue has aroused considerable interest in recent years, since it seemingly gives the EU an additional feature to distinguish it from other global powers such as the USA. The notion of civilian power refers to the methods of international politics rather than the substance.[94] The EU is believed to pursue post-national or ethical interests by using methods of normative change rather than use of force. The civilian power Europe would act primarily in accordance with ideas and values, and not military or economic strength. In this sense, the EU's actions are believed to be more humanitarian and civilizing, which echoes the debate on the EU as a post-Westphalian political system.[95] In this perspective, the EU's external policies result from the 'post-modern', 'post-sovereign' and 'post-national' nature of the political system of the European Union.[96] One of the tenets of civilian power Europe is believed to be multiculturalism, which is a form of self-binding by law. Seen from this angle, the EU's objective is not to maximize its selfish interests, but to promote the development of an international society according to rule-based international order of multilateral institutionalism. The EU therefore fosters the power of international institutions and regional organizations that allow for an extensive coordination and cooperation of actors in international politics.[97] The goal is the creation of institutionalized and global governance capable of solving global and regional collective problems. Consequently, the principles of conduct are of major interest for the civilian power Europe, rather than particular interests.[98] The civilian nature of the EU is likely to be demonstrated particularly in the context of the EU foreign policy cooperation, which is believed to maintain a non-colonial civilizing identity towards its neighbours.[99] As opposed to the US, which defines its civilizing mission more internally, EU member states revert to deliberative and institutionalized cooperation mechanisms among themselves.[100] Consequently, even in an uncertain political environment, member states are expected to remain attached to deliberation and cooperation, which is an indicator of a basic trust between the member states.[101] In this sense, trust among nations is expected to play an important role in the European identity, as opposed to the anarchy of brute power outside the EU.[102]

Nevertheless, the issue remains how the elite-driven project of the civilian power Europe is associated with European citizenry. Foreign policy due to its strategic nature, civilian or not, is even in democracies considered insulated from public opinion to a higher degree than other policy fields.[103] The democratic control of foreign policy by the citizens occurs largely via national parliaments. The role of citizenship in the framework of the civilian image of Europe would not only mean mainly civil (non-military) conduct of foreign policy, but also the civil control over military that has increasingly gained significance in the EU with the new reform treaty.[104] However, as Wolfgang Wagner convincingly argues, the Europeanization of security and defence policy increases the democratic deficit of the EU, since it augments executive dominance, which cannot be compensated for by the European Parliament.[105] The creation of a military apparatus around the foreign policy in the EU enhances the danger of authority leakage to transnational military actors who cannot be effectively controlled by the European Parliament.[106] Consequently, the weakening of parliamentary control at the national level and the simultaneous growing significance of the military issues in the EU would paint a rather bleak picture of the civilian power of Europe. This in turn might not be very effective as a basis for positive identification, particularly in connection with citizenship.

The third image of European identity is the EU as a normative power, which is directly linked to the cosmopolitan and civilizing image. Here, the EU stresses its progressive stance in promoting and implementing human rights and environmental policies, and by so doing it asserts its leading role and depicts the US as a laggard. In other words, the EU promotes its positive image as the forerunner in advocating human rights worldwide and in the fight against climate change, thus claiming its moral supremacy.[107] Simultaneously, the EU represents the policies and concerns of the USA as illegitimate, as they are constrained by national boundaries, over-attached to the state sovereignty as well as to the economic and/or security interests.[108] Consequently, the EU uses the vanguard–laggard dichotomy in order to describe its own identity in contrast to the US. In this case, the EU uses Othering techniques associated with the construction of inferiority of the other with the aim of establishing and perpetuating its own positive image.[109] The image of the EU as a normative power is applied among other things to its ability to transform border conflicts and to promote selfless environmental politics. Since borders are socially constructed institutions, they rely on discursive processes of constructing a shared understanding among participants. Normative power Europe is expected to be capable of bringing about conflict transformation through the desecuritization of conflicts.[110] The EU apparently draws its 'security identity' from this source. The practice of its security identity is therefore possible because of Others who become objects of peaceful change.[111] There is considerable evidence that the European Union applies its institutional and discursive structures in order to project notions of peaceful coexistence into previously conflict-ridden territories within and beyond the EU borders. In this sense, the EU appears as capable not only of constructing its own identity as a 'peacemaker' with peaceful means, but also of intervening into the identity dynamics of others by transferring constitutive beliefs and practices through social learning.[112]

A further aspect of the European normative power image refers to its area of environmental diplomacy and bio-safety regulations, which are regarded as a reflection of distinctive societal values of European societies. Here again, the 'green' normative power defines itself through the difference to the USA, which becomes a constitutive factor pertaining to shared European identity.[113] However, this image of green normative power is empirically inconsistent. Robert Falkner argues that the EU's distinctive stance in environmental politics was not simply the outgrowth of a deep-rooted normative orientation but frequently the result of domestic conflicts over the future of biotechnology. In the debate on genetically modified (GM) food, the EU offered international leadership only after strong anti-GM sentiments appeared among the public. Prior to this, the EU attached little importance to the bio-safety talks. However, even after the EU claimed international leadership in that field, it sought to export its own domestic regulatory model, which would ensure that international rules would not damage the EU's economic interests in medical biotechnology.[114] This begs the question of who determines the European interests regarding the normative power and whether they reflect the diffuse character of European citizenry. Post-nationalism or post-materialism are rather diffuse values, whereas the European regulation and distribution activity frequently reflects constellations of concrete interests groups. Empirical studies demonstrate that there is a lobbying imbalance in the EU in favour of big business to the detriment of associations, whereby it is doubtful that the recent efforts at institutionalizing the political participation of civil society (for example, in the Lisbon Treaty) will compensate for this structural asymmetry.[115] However, we tend to speak of European citizenship primarily with regard to generalized European interests (or at least not narrowly in terms of special interest groups), which then creates the juxtaposition between special interests and European civil society (representing broader interests or interests difficult to organize usefully).[116] However, if the EU tends to represent rather narrow economic concerns of special interest groups in its regulations, rather than general interests of European citizenry, and at the same time disguises them as a normative position of the entire EU for the sake of constructing collective identity as normative power, we are dealing with manipulation as an identity technology. This brings us to the issue of whose identity is meant, when we speak of European identity. The positive self-images are represented and conveyed by the EU's political elites in order to boost the attractiveness of the EU to its population. Simultaneously, the same positive images of the EU are generated and perpetuated by scholars who present them as postulates and wishful thinking, rather than necessarily reflections of social reality. By so doing, academic elites also become agents of collective identity generation in the EU.

Collective memory in Europe

Collective memory is a social construction that is expected to generate the feeling of continuity and therefore identity in political communities. First, it is based on a narrative interpretation of the past, whose task is to provide a coherent framework for the collective memory.[117] For this purpose, historiography uses a number of identity techniques such as narrative 'smoothing' to construct collective memory as a sensible and seemingly logical series of events. There is therefore a difference between the actual historic events and their interpretation, which is functionally necessary for the instrumentalization of the past in order to construct collective memory. Second, collective memory is constructed among other things through the 'invention of traditions', which are remembered collectively in a repetitive and commemorative manner.

However, it is controversial whether the production of collective memory via invented traditions and rituals is efficient regarding the construction of European identity. Equally controversial remains the question of its normative validity.[118] Collective memory frequently becomes a part of a state ideology, which exhibits totalizing ambitions with regard to the collective identity of citizens.[119] By providing an integrated interpretative framework for citizens, collective memory has homogenizing effects. It impels citizens to define themselves intersubjectively, since it is shaped by shared historical events. In this sense, collective memory is a double common discriminating experience (right vs. wrong historical decisions as well as enemy vs. foe narratives) and a 'factual' commemoration with a veridical claim of the group's 'real' past.[120] However, if it becomes a part of an ideology it suppresses other explanations of the past and develops totalizing impacts on citizens' identity.

We can identify two main arguments in favour of substantial European identity, which can be experienced in repetitive rituals of commemoration.[121] They include the collective memory of war (recent past) and Christianity (distant past). The shared interpretation of recent history referring to the Second World War is expected to have a cohesive effect on Europeans, as the collective trauma resulting from the war marks a turn from the memory of heroes to the memory of victims.[122] Thus, anchoring the European collective identity in the context of the Second World War means a shift from a triumphant variant to the traumatic variant of collective memory.[123] In a larger perspective, collective memory of Europe would respond to the atrocities committed in the twentieth century.[124] Beyond the persecution and extermination of European Jews it would also include the genocide of the Armenians and more recent cases of ethnic cleansing in the Balkans, which are significantly more controversial issues.

Nevertheless, the plurality of possible narrations and the ongoing construction and deconstruction of myths of collective memory set limitations to the process of stable identity construction.[125] If they are to be freed from the attempt to establish the final truth on the European historic interpretation (which would equal a sort of European historic ideology), collective memory might prove to be unreliable as a source of collective identity. While the post-war tendency in Germany was to experience national identity as a source of shame or guilt, many other nations were more inclined to highlight their heroic past. In other words, Germany tends to narrate European collective memory as an overcoming of its 'dark legacy past', whereas other nations might not intend to discriminate against their national pasts, and they consequently do not regard the EU as a carrier for that. Even if the memory of collective trauma with the culture of ritual apologies regarding victims of the past may not be confined to Germany (as a number of European nations have officially acknowledged their country's role in collaborating with Nazi Germany), there exist diverse interpretations regarding who were the victims and what is to be done about it today. The best example is the recurrent conflictive disagreement between Poland and Germany on the destruction of Polish cultural heritage during the Second World War and the German claims of retrieval of German art items from Polish government. In the perception of Polish governments, the increasingly historically revisionist claims of Germany (be it government or private claim organizations) is distant from the Polish interpretation of history. Consequently, the hope that the horror of the past and the traumatic memory of perpetrators will become a unifying force in Europe might be over-optimistic. Shared tragic and traumatic memories do not resolve the issue of their interpretation, since collective memory is by definition a dialectical process of remembering and forgetting. Consequently, there is no rule for who decides what is remembered and what should be forgotten, which leads us to the idea that Europe, even (or especially) in historic terms, remains a contested concept and therefore a controversial basis for a shared collective memory.[126] The pluralism of interpretation may lead to an 'agonistic pluralism', which may be welcome as a democratic instrument against hegemonic interpretations of consensus.[127] However, it can also imply multifarious struggles for recognition, rather than commemoration of common roots and experiences.[128]

A further method of constructing collective memory in Europe by referring to the recent history would be to focus it on the process of European integration by selecting positive events that could be ritually commemorated. For instance, since 1985 the European Union has celebrated Europe Day every year on 9 May to commemorate the so-called 'Schuman Declaration' of 1950, in which the French foreign minister Robert Schuman proclaimed his plan for founding the European Community for Coal and Steel. European authorities attempt to load Europe Day with a strong symbolic meaning, as many nation-states do with national holidays. However, Europe Day is neither highly identifiable by the European citizens nor is it popular.[129] In addition, some authors doubt the predominant historiography of the EU, describing it as the outcome of a historical process whereby national institutions are superseded and replaced by supranational ones. This narrative tends to 'smooth' the EU history according to the progressive conception and simultaneously undermines the complexity of the EU.[130] Therefore, the potential of recent common history to become a carrier for European identity appears to be very limited and probably applicable only regarding young Europeans subject to the EU's education and exchange programmes.

The second argument in favour of European collective memory insists on emphasizing the historically distant common roots of classical antiquity and the idealized medieval Christian Europe. In particular, the rather essentialist connotation of Christian Europe as reflecting Christian values finds many supporters, as was visible during the negotiations on the European Charter of Fundamental Rights. However, the issue of Christianity being imprinted in the collective memory of Europe is controversial. Even though Christianity is a significant religion that influenced European history in an incomparable way by strengthening European cohesion in terms of a legal, political and cultural entity, the focus of European history on Christian Europe would not only present a danger of ideology, but it would exclude many European and non-Christian citizens. Since the function of collective memory is to serve as a common reference point for European citizens, the idea of a Christian Europe might cause the opposite. The heterogeneity and diversity of European societies prevent an application of a shared narrative as a focal point of a common identity. In this sense, a Christian Europe would run counter to the idea of free and equal citizens and would therefore be incompatible with the European citizenship. As Bo Stråth argues, since the Middle Ages the image of a Europe has rested on the religious or ethnic demarcation from non-Christian others such as the Turks or the Chinese. This demarcation was strengthened by the monotheistic competition between Christianity and Islam beginning with the Crusades, which during the next centuries led to a development of stable xenostereotypes (stereoptypes of others).[131] However, by insisting on the old xenostereotypes of Christian Europe, the idea of Christian Europe tends to maintain cultural demarcation lines, instead of promoting more inclusiveness in light of the European multi-ethnic and multi-religious social reality. While some authors warn about the essentialist and religious definition of European identity, others criticize the ideology of secularity by finding 'Christian deficit' in the European constitution. For the critics, the ideology of secularity is not the same as the neutrality of the state, which means that a refusal to include Christian values in the European Constitution reflects a particular ideological position.[132]

Against this background, the potential of Christianity as a carrier for inclusive European identity, grounded in European citizenship, has to be doubted. The production of common European memory, recent or distant, is a highly controversial issue, which often finds itself in opposition with historiographic technologies of national identity generation. However, the integrative power of secularism is also highly controversial, which leaves us with the doubt of whether the religion/secularism dichotomy can still be applied regarding the citizenship–collective identity nexus.[133]

Political functions of European identity

In Chapter 2 we also discussed political functions of collective identity, referring to national community building, legitimacy of political authority, and the solution of cooperation dilemmas. These three themes are also mirrored in the debate on the European identity, albeit with varying degrees of interest. For instance, the notion of European nationalism is rather exotic in social sciences, whereas the issue of legitimacy belongs clearly to the mainstream of inquiry in this field. The question of whether the EU can solve cooperation dilemmas is frequently discussed through the prism of research in international relations.

European nationalism

Some authors would like to reproduce the strength and resilience of the national bond in the EU by establishing a sort of European nationalism. The concept of constitutional patriotism proposed by Jürgen Habermas can be interpreted as a form of civic nationalism for the EU, as being grounded on a devotion to liberal and democratic principles of a European political community.[134] Even if constitutional patriotism rests on cosmopolitan values, it requires a contextualization with regard to a specific territory and a concrete community, which make possible the superseding of pre-political identities grounded in ethnic or national collectivities. In this view, not only could European constitutional patriotism supersede collective identities of nation-states, but it could also induce a European identity based on rational moral and political bonds.[135] Nonetheless, constitutional patriotism does not have to be interpreted as circumventing nationalism, but rather as close to the notion of civic nationalism, since both concepts exhibit communitarian features.[136] It remains controversial whether Habermas' position reflects constitutional patriotism, or rather civic nationalism, as he speaks of supportive political culture that would stabilize the allegiance to legal principles of political community.[137] According to this reading, Habermas' constitutional patriotism would still be nationalism, which brings us to the notion of European nationalism.[138]

Irrespective of the correct answer, the debate on European nationalism follows the controversy on how 'thick' the European identity would be, in the event that it was associated with constitutional patriotism.[139] For instance, Craig Calhoun argues that constitutional patriotism should be supplemented by a stronger approach to social solidarity, which would include creation and reproduction of social institutions and reconfiguration of social relations, as it is too weak to generate sustainable collective identity.[140] Consequently, he proposes a European form of civic nationalism that embraces both constitutionalism and social solidarity. However, it implies that the more constitutional patriotism shifts away from civic nationalism, the less collective and cohesive identity it can create. Whenever the cosmopolitan element in constitutional patriotism becomes dominating, it will lead to more inclusiveness, but it will also entail weaker collective bonds.

In the same vein, Philippe Schmitter and Michael W. Bauer argue in favour of expanding social citizenship in the European Union, which would entail stronger and more numerous redistributive measures in the EU.[141] This would shift the EU again in the direction of a welfare state with national character. Schmitter and Bauer want to enhance the visibility of the EU by bringing it closer to European citizens and thus to make it a part of their everyday lives. However, they apply devices of welfare nationalism without the existence of the European nation. This may increase the political salience of the EU, but can also exacerbate the legitimacy problem of the EU due to its heterogeneous and majoritarian nature.

The issue of thickness of European identity leads us to a debate on whether the EU is able to reproduce nationalism at a higher level. Anthony D. Smith argues that the desire for European identity arises from flawed assumptions about the end of the nation-states, which are naïve as they are unsubstantiated, as they ignore both the perseverance of nation-states and the rootedness of national identities. Moreover, Europe lacks a common ethnic base with a reliable and visible set of common historical memories, myths, symbols and values, since abstract allegiances lead to strong and stable identities. According to Smith, European historic traditions and memories of medieval

Christendom and the Holy Roman Empire are increasingly irrelevant due to the growing secularism of European societies, and hence their limited usability in everyday lives of European citizens.[142]

A further sceptic, David Miller, rejects the idea of European nationalism on the grounds of lacking trust between European citizens. According to Miller, the EU must justify material redistribution beyond self-interest, which leads to obligations between compatriots. These obligations are justifiable only against the background of reciprocity and trust, which can be provided only by a national community, since it embodies continuity between generations and holds up virtues of the ancestors by encouraging citizens to live up to them.[143] As the EU is unable to generate an equal level of trust and justify obligations, it suffers from a legitimacy deficit and enforces redistributive policies.[144]

Beyond the problem of the 'thickness' of European nationalism, there are some other methodological dilemmas voiced, for instance by Rogers Brubaker in his studies on nationalism. Brubaker questions the dichotomy between civic and ethnic nationalism on methodological and normative grounds. Regarding the criteria of 'thickness', civic nationalism does not have to be distinct from its ethnic variant, as civic communities are a culmination of a long past of common endeavours, sacrifice and devotion, which are stabilized by institutions, customs, historical memories and common values. In this sense, even civic nationalism or constitutional patriotism are not entirely chosen, but are also given, since they are incapable of generating collective identity without the backup of the common culture and collective memory.[145]

In addition, the normative assumption of civic nationalism as being inclusive, since it is based on citizenship and not on ascriptive features or descent, is questioned by Brubaker. He argues that civic nationalism is also exclusive, but differently exclusive from ethnic nationalism. Civic and ethnic nationalism manage the access to the nation differently, but they are both devices of social closure and exclusion.[146] The exclusionary aspects of the European Union are currently quite apparent, even without the internal bonds denoted as civic nationalism.[147] For instance, Anita Böcker and Tetty Havinga argue that statistics on asylum applications in the EU have been deliberately used in the debates on refugees and asylum policies in a highly selective manner to justify restrictive measures. Consequently, even with its dedication to cosmopolitanism and civility, the EU establishes and uses mechanisms of social closure and exclusion.[148]

The EU is perceived as endorsing multicultural values and attitudes. Even if this holds true, we could argue in accordance with Brubaker that civic and multicultural European identity (in the sense of European nationalism) could be associated with intolerance towards non-members. Laurent Licata and Olivier Klein suggest that even the mere creation of the status of 'Citizen of the Union' in Maastricht may promote intolerance towards resident foreigners, thus questioning the normative validity of European collective identity. In this case, a paradoxical situation could emerge, as citizens' degree of tolerance towards foreigners would contradict the values propagated by the EU. The results of a study conducted by Licata and Klein in Belgium show that although Europe is associated with humanistic values, strong European identifiers tend to exhibit more xenophobic attitudes than weak European identifiers.[149]

In sum, there are reasons to believe that European identity cannot or should not be based on the model of national identity. In the Habermasian view (if distilled correctly), it is neither possible nor desirable to melt national identities of the member states down into a European nation.[150] Therefore, a new form of (post-conventional and post-national) identity is supposed to rest on a community other than the nation-state (even if it may boil down to civic nationalism at the European level). For this purpose, a shared political and social space (for instance in the form of European civil society) should be promoted in order to generate new emotional attachments (or redirect emotional energy of national identities towards the EU) that would lie at the heart of European identity. Others argue that European identity cannot be easily produced as most Europeans are still strongly attached to their nations. For instance, Mathieu Deflem and Fred C. Pampel suggest that European citizens' concern with the interests of their own countries implies the persistence of national identity at the expense of post-national identity. They conclude that there exists a myth of post-national identity that does not reflect the reality of the European Union.[151] Other authors are even more sceptical concerning the chances of European nationalism. They argue that neither the EU nor other supranational forms of governance have been able to dethrone the nation-state as the dominant form of political organization in the contemporary world. Nationalism tends to adapt to the changing world of globalization, as violent secessionist movements, a growing backlash against immigration in Europe and North America and xenophobic attitudes continue to flourish.[152]

Notwithstanding the controversies on the possibility and necessity of European identity as European nationalism, the mainstream debate argues that the emergence of a collective European identity is central for the viability of the EU. It is expected to compensate for the lack of direct interactions among citizens, thus creating a symbolic illusion of unity in a space without social interaction. However, the functionality of European identity is not only to be viewed in terms of absent social interactions, but also regarding diverse, plural, heterogeneous language barriers, historical conflicts, and cultural cleavages. A strong sense of collective identity is needed to facilitate the formation of bonds between disparate and within diverse societies.[153]

Collective identity and legitimacy of the EU

The literature on the legitimacy and democracy deficit of the EU is as vast as proposals for alleviating the EU's legitimacy deficit are varied.[154] However, only a part of the debate links collective identity with legitimacy. For instance, J. Peter Burgess argues that the EU exhibits a tension between an understanding of Europe as a representative (and a supplier) of certain cultural identities and a technocratic project of European construction that is perpetuated in the name of the former. The central aspect of this tension is the relationship between identity and legitimacy, as the EU wants to produce legitimacy using the cultural system of values (thus referring to collective identity), but its main bulk of activities is anchored in a European system of regulations that are only loosely connected to the value system. In contrast to the fusion of collective identity and legitimacy within the nation-state, where the legitimating force of collective identity is integrated into the institutions of the state, the EU presents a cleavage between the contradictory aspects of its institutionalized legal system and the complex cultural value system of European identity.[155]

One school of thought in particular connects collective identity with legitimacy of political authority in the EU. It attempts to link collective identity with legitimacy in the EU through a notion of public sphere, rather than through a community of origin, heritage, collective memory, and ascriptive characteristics. It is argued that the post-national democracy in Europe relies on the emergence of a European communicative space that fulfils functions of a public sphere.[156] Public sphere connects civil society to the power structure of the political system both by enabling citizens' opinion formation and by giving the citizens the power to influence the decision-making. In this sense, the public sphere is essential for citizens to realize their claims to democracy as self-government. The corresponding collective identity, which develops in the process of citizens' participation in the public sphere, does not rest on origin-based or heritage-orientated identification, but rather on the practice of constructing commonality through communication processes that are expected to generate a collective self-understanding.[157] In differentiated and complex societies, the public sphere is not an institution with clear boundaries, but rather a network of numerous publics that are expected to be integrated at the communicative level. Simultaneously, this network should be constrained by the rules of discourse only and should allow for interaction among citizens without aiming for a particular result.[158]

In the context of the EU, the public sphere perspective regards European citizens not only as rights bearers but primarily as community members.[159] In this sense, public space promotes collective identity by anchoring citizens in a community as well as enhancing the legitimacy of the political system. However, the belonging to a community does not have to be underpinned by pre-political bonds, since the public sphere is capable of generating collective identity through equal participation, communicative opinion formation and autonomous law-making. Public spheres created as such rest on a reflexive identity, i.e. a shared understanding of commonality coupled with recognition of difference.[160]

Many authors argue that a new public space is emerging in the European Union. This new public space is associated with the institutions of the EU and their supranational development that transcend the boundaries of the nation-state. Philip Schlesinger argues that the multi-level political system of the EU also generates multi-level forms of political communication that include lobbying, and information campaigns as well as news reporting.[161] However, this complex communicative activity occurs not in an integrated European public arena network, which could induce a sort of collective identity, but rather in fragmented and even contradictory sub-arenas. As a consequence, Schlesinger suggests that we should rather assume a system of interrelated (but disintegrated) spheres of European publics. In addition, there is an asymmetry in the structure of the European publics. The growth of transnational media such as newspapers, magazines and television news perpetuates a rather restricted elite space rather than encouraging a generalized access to communication by European publics, which confirms the divide between citizens and the elite. Therefore, the notion of a transnational citizen with easy access to the European publics has to be assessed as unrealized.[162]

While Schlesinger observes an elite-citizenry divide in the European publics, Eriksen and Fosssum apply the differentiation between general and strong publics to examine European public space.[163] The concept of 'strong publics' refers to institutionalized deliberations that are also part of the publics (but in a condensed and more routinized form) and are close to the centre of the political system, as opposed to general publics. The proximity vis-à-vis the centre of the political system denotes the decision-making power of strong publics that reaches beyond the opinion or will-formation reserved for general or weak publics outside the formal political system. In general, strong publics relate to parliamentary assemblies and other deliberative institutions with formally organized structures that possess a codified stake in the decision-making process. For Eriksen and Fossum, in the context of the EU it is mainly the European Parliament

(EP) that fulfils the function of a strong public.[164] Since the EP is directly elected by the peoples of the member states, it can claim to be an expression of the will of the people, and thus the only direct democratic body to represent European interest.[165] Moreover, the EP has over the past half century been successively empowered by the member states.[166] In contrast to the Council, the EP is rather more strongly consensus-orientated and likely to be open for deliberation, as majorities can be more easily formed in the absence of the traditional division between government and opposition.

Moreover, Eriksen and Fossum regard European conventions (both the Charter Convention and the Constitutional Convention) as strong publics. Both conventions institutionalize communicative interaction, but beyond a mere aggregation of preferences, as is the case with the intergovernmental conferences. In the conventions, participants deliberated in an open debate, which was not only open to a variety of actors (such as parliamentarians, civil society actors etc.), but also had features of representatives assemblies. Therefore, the conventions assume a stronger normative force, as they were no longer entirely dominated by the executive and technocratic actors.[167] Even so, Eriksen comes to a similar conclusion as Schlesinger: although there are signs of an integrated public sphere with an easy and general access for citizens, segmented publics that show problems of fragmentation and communication distortions remain dominant and salient. Under these circumstances, collective will-formation is difficult, and a collective identity cannot be presumed. Even the strong publics specialized in collective will-formation cannot fulfil the integrative function and cannot generate a general collective will.[168]

In contrast, Hans-Jörg Trenz and Klaus Eder present a more optimistic view of European public space and its fruitful role in creating European democracy.[169] Trenz and Eder put the function of public sphere in the context of social learning of political actors. Through the interactions in the public sphere citizens experience each other as contingent Others and they develop individual coping strategies. In the case of the EU, we deal with a transnational public sphere, which has the potential of unfolding a transnational communicative resonance.[170] Since we can observe in the EU a growing communication network, the conclusion about a transnational resonance might be not unlikely.[171] In this sense, the more collective actors are contingent on the public, the more likely processes of collective learning contribute to the development of transnational democracy in the EU. Since constitutional reform of the EU is bound to the public performance of the EU, there are learning processes that create public resonance. In the process, networking actors present their activities before the general public and evoke its reactions either in the form of consent and loyalty or in the form of protest and voice. For Trenz and Eder, it was the European Convention that assumed the function of a carrier transforming the particularistic lobbying practices, specific for the EU governance into the specific mode of communication with the public.[172]

However, not all EU institutions are capable of establishing a communication mode of interaction with the public. Since information about political processes is a prerequisite for debates in the public sphere, it is crucial to identify how, for instance, the Commission communicates with the public. Patrick Bijsmans and Christina Altides suggest in their study that the Commission and the national media emphasize different aspects of the EU political process, which instead of integrating the communication structures in Europe, does the opposite.[173] It does not result even in a superficial integration of the European communication sphere, which would be a precondition for European citizens to act. In this perspective, European citizenship is given substance through the mass media by creating an informed and active public, which is a precondition for the democratic legitimacy of the EU.[174]

Other studies also indicate the absent transcendence of the European national spheres and the consequent fragmentation of the public sphere in the EU. John Downey and Thomas Koenig point out that even if there is an obvious European reference, such as in the Berlusconi–Schulz case, the framing of events occurs in a way that discourages deliberation among citizens, since the actors involved in the conflict are portrayed as representatives of national ethnicities rather than their respective political parties at the European level. Consequently, ethnicity shows more perseverance than expected, and makes deliberative change of opinion difficult.[175]

But even within an integrated public space, communication might not be sufficient to generate collective identity. Klaus Eder enriches the notion of communicative sphere with the idea of narrative boundary construction, which 'enhances' identity building processes with a different component. New boundaries reflect the old narratives (in a continuous or a discontinuous way), either as conservative continuation of a tradition or as a revolutionary break with it. This perspective breaks with the substantialist notion of Europe's borders, and leaves open whether the European integration carries on an old narrative or whether it discontinues it by embracing a new European narrative.[176] However, if communication and information are not sufficient, the EU's strategies to improve democratic legitimacy by strengthening its publicity will necessarily fail. This 'thin' understanding of public sphere and democracy may cause inappropriate institutional measures to be chosen in order to generate public attention. In this sense, the EU confounds public space with public relations and transparency with publicity. Therefore, improving democratic legitimacy would require more than just the publishing of its decisions and seeking attention.

Collective identity as a solution to cooperation dilemmas in the EU

Collective dilemmas can primarily be solved by using two methods. First, there is a third party with enough power to change the suboptimal outcome of the strategic constellation between actors. Second, there is a social structure allowing for and stimulating repeated interactions between the same actors, thus stabilizing expectations about each other, and even developing social resources such as trustworthiness and credibility.[177] These social resources pertain to the reciprocity that is expected to be promoted in the EU as a stable institution organizing actors' interactions.[178] Under the circumstances of reciprocity, conflict potential is likely to be reduced and the chances for cooperation increase.[179] In this perspective, the EU is an example of a complex international organization, which not only links different policy fields, but also generates social norms and knowledge, thus giving rise to a social order.[180] Even though interests of the political actors are still the major motivation for political action, they become modulated by norms of appropriate behaviour. Both social norms and reciprocity can 'thicken' into collective identity, increasing the chances of cooperation even further. The socialization (whose congealed form is collective identity) is expected to modify actors' preference formation from idiosyncratic to more collective-orientated.[181] This socialization to build bridges stresses the relevance of norms of appropriate behaviour within a collectivity.[182]

Some authors argue that certain types of norms are more central than others for the social and political order of the EU and consequently for the development of collective identity. Fundamental norms such as citizenship keep a community together, as they are linked with the polity level. The EU is an example not only of a complex organization, but also one that encompasses diverse European societies. Therefore, the socializing function of citizenship appears to be particularly crucial.[183] In other words, citizenship constitutes actors and their interests, as it provides individuals with an understanding as citizens, thus shaping interests and identities.[184] As for some authors citizenship pertains to the rule of law, fundamental freedoms and human rights, and democracy, the issue of European citizenship mirrors to a certain extent the debate on how cohesive a collective identity based on fundamental freedom and human rights can be. Human rights are promising to bridge differences and particular identities, but they equally lack a thicker communitarian component, as they are universalistic in their appeal. Therefore, one could argue that bridging differences is solely a precondition for collective identity, which would also require civic attachment and reciprocity.

In this context, Andreas Føllesdal regards European citizenship as a central measure for increasing reciprocity and trust among the citizens of Europe. In this sense, European citizenship is expected to act as an agent of collective identity. Citizenship as a special and fundamental institution is likely to habituate individuals into citizens by redirecting their interests and perceptions (at least to some extent) towards the collectivity, whereby the individual inclination to free-ride is reduced and their confidence in the behaviour of others increases. Therefore, institutions such as citizenship (with a built-in reference to collectivity) socialize individuals to abide by norms that generate cooperation.[185]

A more specific argument pertaining to collective identity regards the EU as a solution to war, which is a special case of non-cooperation. Eilstrup-Sangiovanni and Verdier argue that by developing binding properties the EU can solve credible commitment problems among member states, which applies even in the case of volatile preventive war dilemmas. The authors try to demonstrate that European integration since its beginnings was conceived as a mechanism of commitment for a weakened West Germany. The primary goal was to enhance the credibility of Germany as a non-aggressive state, which would via integration renounce pursuing military ends in Europe, which in turn was believed to preclude a preventive war against Germany. Eilstrup-Sangiovanni and Verdier show that even today's institutions of the EU still bear the mark of this commitment rationality.[186] Consequently, the aim of the EU was not to bind Germany in the sense of military and political power, but to establish and disseminate trust towards Germany.

In sum, the arguments with regard to the EU as a solution to collective action dilemmas are interested in the workings of collective identity – in other words, primarily in the production of trust, reciprocity and commitment towards collectivity. The nature of collective identity, its sources (essentialist vs. proceduralist) are irrelevant, as long as socialization processes lead to a modulation of mistrust and construct actors' interests in accordance with the collective identity. This perspective regards the EU as one among many international organizations with similar effects regarding solutions to collective problems. In addition, these approaches assume strong normative workings of the EU towards its own members and argue in favour of a structuralist bias, as they point to behaviour-modifying effects of international organizations. The problem of this approach is, however, its overemphasis on norms and an assumption of symmetry of effects. In other words, this approach can neither account for different behavioural modification nor can it explain cases of strategic circumvention of norms by the member states or the EU itself as a collective actor.

Recapitulation

In this chapter I discussed the debate on European identity in the functional perspective. The chapter shows not only that the notion of European identity is associated with many conceptual connotations and theoretical perspectives, but also implies that the exploration of the citizenship–collective identity nexus in the functional perspective, even if helpful in systematizing the research, is associated with deficiencies.

In the cognitive perspective on European identity I identified three main connotations pointing to the cognitive perspective: salience and perception, fluidity and hybridity as well as the manipulation of symbols. Whereas the cognitive perspective highlights mainly self-categorization processes in individuals, we can relate it also to the categorization technologies used by political authorities of the European Union. As the cognitive perspective also stresses fluidity of collective identity, European identity tends to be conceptualized as a layer of multiple identities or as a component of a hybrid identity. In this sense, European identity only becomes activated when there is a context relating directly to the EU and the individual becomes mobilized as an EU citizen. In this perspective, European identity is unlikely to replace other attachments, particularly the national ones. As the EU is characterized by cultural diversity, rather than unity, a cultural uniformization appears to be improbable. This refers to the issue of identity technologies, i.e. the policies of constructing collective identities in accordance with the images of European elites. This collectivistic stimulation of citizens' identity responding to cultural manipulation exhibits a predilection for authoritarian politics, since it enhances the inequality between the rulers and the ruled.

In contrast, the self-esteem booster approach to European identity explains individuals' drive to develop attachment to groups and to construct communities against the background of the personal strategy of positive self-image enhancement via membership in a social group. In this perspective, the EU fills the categorization of citizens vs. non-citizens with political 'substance' of positive self-images. In addition, I discussed the debate on European collective memory as a basis for collective identity. I identified three basic images of the EU that are used to fulfil the function of a self-esteem booster. They include the image of the EU as an embodiment of cosmopolitanism, the EU image as normative power and the image of the EU as a civilizing force. However, the EU exhibits cracks in consistency regarding the self-images, which may inhibit their socializing capacity. Furthermore, the positive self-images can be regarded as propaganda instruments with the goal of manipulating the EU population, as they are not entirely mirrored in the social reality and often espouse double standards. Moreover, the potential of recent or distant common history to become a carrier for European identity appears to be very limited. The production of common European memory remains a controversial issue, which often finds itself in opposition with historiographic technologies of national identity generation.

Political functions of collective identity relate to national community building, legitimacy of political authority, and the solution of cooperation dilemmas. While there are reasons to believe that European identity cannot or should not be based on the model of European nationalism, another school of thought attempts to connect collective identity with legitimacy of governance in the EU through a notion of an integrated public sphere allowing for a community-wide communication. However, studies suggest that the communicative activity in the EU occurs not in an integrated European public arena network, but rather in fragmented and even contradictory sub-arenas, which acts as an inhibitor on collective identity development. A further type of collective identity function relates to dilemmas of collective action. This perspective argues that both social norms and reciprocity can 'thicken' into collective identity, increasing the chances of cooperation. The socialization (whose congealed form is collective identity) is expected to modify actors' preference formation from idiosyncratic to more collective-orientated. The problem of this approach is, however, its overemphasis on norms and an assumption of symmetry of effects.

Since this chapter implied certain problems of the functional perspective, the next chapter will deal in more detail with the deficits of the functional approaches to collective identity in Europe.

4 Reconceptualizing the citizenship–collective identity nexus

The point of departure of this chapter is a discussion of deficits in the functional approaches to collective identity. Against the background of the weaknesses of the functional collective identity conceptualizations, an approach linking citizenship and collective identity will be proposed. I will begin by reconceptualizing the concept of collective identity, which will be explored with regard to both its semantic core and two semantic dimensions, which include its orientation and its internal dynamics. The semantic core of collective identity in political terms pertains to the notion of citizenship identity, which I have already touched upon in Chapter 1. After the exploration of the orientation and dynamics of collective identity I will discuss possibilities of linking citizenship with collective identity. Here, shared citizenship is regarded as a source of political collective identity. Even though many different political identities can exist, such as party identities or ideological identities, citizenship identity represents a 'master identity' that underpins citizens' behaviour in the public space. However, as citizenship can assume different forms, its variance finds its reflection in the thickness and strength of citizenship identity. This variance is mirrored in three generic models of citizenship (republican, liberal and caesarean citizenship) that correspond to different forms of collective identities. The chapter argues that precisely this differentiation between types of citizenship and their corresponding collective identities is crucial for the analysis of the citizenship–collective identity nexus. It can be applied to an analytical framework for the exploration of citizenship and collective identity in Europe.

Deficits of the functional approaches to collective identity

In the previous chapters I identified three major functions of collective identity and referred them to the debate on citizenship and to the debate on European identity. However, all three functions of collective identity (cognitive, self-esteem orientated, and political) exhibit methodological and theoretical deficits that shall be addressed in this chapter.

Disadvantages of the cognitive perspective

The cognitive perspective focuses on common perceptions and self-images of citizens highlighting the *salience* as a major factor in explaining self-categorization processes in citizens who define themselves as members of a collective. At the same time, the cognitive perspective concedes (implicitly) that political authorities can manipulate the criteria of salience by drawing attention to excluding categories, thus enhancing the perception of commonness.[1] Furthermore, political authorities can manipulate salience of certain categories by rendering institutional objects of identification such as the EU more identifiable. Espousing the concepts of multiple identities and hybridity of identity, the cognitive perspective stresses the activation possibility of different social identities in the same individuals. In this sense, European identity is regarded as one of several social identities that citizens can exhibit. As such it can be activated by stimulating European citizens with common symbols of the EU such as the common currency. Nevertheless, the cognitive perspective puts the notion of collective identity mainly into the context of perceptions and attitudes, without shedding much light on the durable behavioural implications. Besides discrimination effects that can ensue as a consequence of categorization policies, we do not learn much about the outcomes of the citizens' identification with the EU. As a consequence, the cognitive perspective is confronted with two limitations.

First, as some empirical studies demonstrate, European identity tends to be regarded by European citizens as a mere 'status identity'. Having citizenship of an EU member state can culminate in the conclusion that being European is logically unavoidable (like being German or French, as Germany and France are members of the EU). However, this derivative understanding of identity is neither based on a sense of belonging to a community nor is it particularly scrutinized with regard to one's own self-identity.[2] One categorizes oneself as European, but this category remains 'void' in terms of behavioural implications, without producing any expected behaviour differences between Europeans and non-Europeans. Even though the cognitive process of reducing social complexity by using the category of being European is assumed to have psychological benefits for individuals, it remains neutral with regard to their role as citizens. Instead, the cognitive perspective shows more interest in examining distributive constellations of multiple social identities, linking it to the argument of European identity being one layer among multiple identities. However, the insights on multiplicity and fluidity of identities are not necessarily conducive to a better understanding of the *kind* of European identity associated with European citizenship, since we need to learn more than merely general structural characteristics of fluidity, multiplicity and hybridity of European identity. The mere possibility of conceptualizing European identity as a layer of multiple identities or a component of a hybrid transnational syncretistic identity does not deliver much insight into the *meaning* of European identity to European citizens and its relevance for the citizens' behaviour. A conceptual link between collective identity and citizenship should promise to put more flesh on the bones of the behavioural implications of European identity.

By the same token, the position stating that all identities are in flux (which would certainly make European identity more likely to develop) seems to reduce the issue of European identity to an ephemeral phenomenon, since also here the implications of such identity remain uncertain. The issue of whether European identity is manageable as a multiple identity or instead appears as an exclusive identity replacing the national one might therefore be of secondary relevance, since this perspective does not supply much information on the possible 'chronic' European identity, with a minimal level of stability, necessary for identifying it.[3]

In the political context, fluid and hybrid identity in particular are associated with fragmented citizenship, which in turn could have a potential of destroying rather than bolstering shared citizenship identity at the European level.[4] Will Kymlicka's multicultural citizenship can have integrative effects in the national context, where indigenous groups have been discriminated against for a long time. However, in the EU exhibiting much higher overall diversity and heterogeneity, fragmented citizenship is likely to have counterproductive effects regarding a citizenship identity.[5] In this sense, the nature of potentially stable European identity should be explored, rather than the mere placement of European identity within the configuration of various identities. Also for this reason, we would need more insight into the nature of European identity, its thickness and its degree of collectivism.

Second, European identity is frequently conceptualized within the cognitive perspective as a support for EU policies and EU institutions.[6] However, some studies argue convincingly that support for the EU can be instrumental in nature and even be reversely associated with European identity. Support for the EU can depend on factors other than identification, such as expected costs and benefits of political actors or specific national economic and political environments.[7] In this context, Andrzej Marcin Suszycki suggests that actors exhibiting support for the 'deepening' of the European Union do not necessarily base it on a commitment to the European values. By the same token, discourses arguing against the national sovereignty loss to the EU may be located within the narratives of European identity. Examining the Swedish European discourse, Suszycki demonstrates that actors supporting a strictly limited transfer of the Swedish sovereignty to the EU proved to have a higher developed sense of Europeanness than the allegedly 'pro-European' majority.[8]

These findings show that the cognitive perspective highlighting citizens' attitudes does not necessarily help us to pin down the citizens' motives for their sense of Europeanness, nor does it deliver much insight into the intrinsic value of 'European identity' to individuals. An examination of identity rhetoric of political actors could allow us not only to shed light on the motives for identity politics and identity technology, but also to uncover political manipulation within the identity discourses of the EU, which could be difficult to discern from pro-European politics. If the pro-European arguments and support for the EU policies are used in favour of nationalism rather than European identity, then by measuring the support for the EU, we would in reality gauge politics of national identity and nationalism.

Limitations of the self-esteem booster approach

As opposed to the cognitive perspective, the self-esteem perspective on collective identity identifies European identity as a source of self-esteem for European citizens, which becomes generated and maintained mainly by a favourable social comparison to out-groups. Since the EU exhibits a great deal of diversity and heterogeneity, it is particularly likely to define its collective identity with substantiated images of the Others, thus attempting to become attractive to its members. Against this background, the EU is regarded through the prism of three basic collective self-images – the cosmopolitan image, the normative power image and the civilian power image. They all employ 'Othering' as an identity technology. In addition, the self-esteem of Europeans is thought to be produced through a sense of historic continuity, which uses narratives of the recent or distant past as frames for identity reference.

The challenge of the self-esteem orientated perspective is twofold. *First*, it is not certain who the carrier of the EU's collective identity is. While in social psychology individuals are 'receivers' of the identity, the positive images of the EU seem to be an expression of its own search for identity as a collective administrative and political actor, rather than a reflection of collective identity of European citizens. The identity technology of positive self-images implies that only after the EU can provide a consistent image of its own identity for itself can European citizens identify with it, rather than recognize each other as equal community members. In this sense, we deal with European identity of the EU's political elites or with normative postulates by scholars such as Jürgen Habermas, which do not necessarily reflect the collective identity of the EU population. Moreover, the positive self-images of the EU exhibit consistency cracks between the altruistic and moralist claims of the self-image and the interest-based reality of the EU. Against this background, the collective self-glorification by the EU as a collective actor may even be counterproductive regarding citizens' European identity, as it underestimates the reflexive character of citizens' identity.[9] The EU citizens may interpret the EU's self-identity politics as a crude construction for strategic purposes, thus leading to its rejection, particularly when similar self-images are provided by nation-states.[10]

Second, a further flaw of the positive images of the EU is that they intend to bolster identification with universalistic norms of conduct or moral values, rather than encourage collective identity as a mutual and shared relationship among citizens. As a consequence, the objects of identification of a citizenship identity and positive self-images of political authorities strongly differ. This applies in particular to the image of *constitutional patriotism*, which attempts to redirect attachment from the community level to the identification with abstract norms. By so doing, this redirection strategy attempts to shift collective identity from civic political space into the realm of ethics.[11]

Furthermore, constitutional patriotism and the civilian power image appear to be over-optimistic regarding the identity-inducing impact of norms and rights. Norms and rights are expected to frame citizens' perceptions of belonging. However, as norms and rights may be sufficient for bolstering identification with a certain value system and thus in boosting collective self-esteem, this perspective fails to explain how this abstract identity translates into thick identity entailing solidarity among citizens.[12] In particular, the cosmopolitan image is associated with 'lean' or 'thin' universalistic identity, which may on the one hand not generate sufficient resilience in the context of majority decisions and redistributive policies, thus not being sufficiently crisis-proof.[13] On the other hand, when surrendering the redistributive mechanism, the EU is likely to lose its attractiveness as a distinctive and wealth-furthering construction.

In addition, the search for a collective memory in Europe faces similar problems as manipulations of cultural symbols or mimicking national symbols. Whereas the manipulation of symbols is primarily aimed at the increase of visibility and identifiability of the EU, construction of collective memory is an identity technology focusing on stimulating feelings of collective continuity. The dilemma of this approach is the fact that, in contrast to relatively homogeneous historiographies of nation-states, the EU cannot draw on many similarities in the interpretation of the recent European past aside from the consensus on the horrors of the Second World War. However, even in this field the deeper-reaching questions of interpretations of guilt and the responsibility is far from frictionless and free of conflict. In contrast, there is an ongoing debate and reconstruction of the categorization of victims, aggressors and perpetrators, not only with regard to the Second World War, but also concerning political events prior to it.[14] Furthermore, especially after the Eastern enlargement of the EU, we can observe a shift of discourse of the past (for instance within the European Parliament) from a single focus on fascism and Nazism towards more attention on Stalinist and communist crimes.[15]

Against this background, the myth of a European value consensus appears to possess little convincing power. Consequently, recent European history may not be a reliable source of collective identity, even if the European historiography would refer collectively to the horrors of the Second World War as a collective trauma.[16] As Piotr Sztompka argues, cultural traumas can be coped with differently, as they can have varying impacts on different actors and the structure of European societies. Cultural traumas can entail strategies of obsessive cultivation of collective memory or attempts of cultural reconstruction involving strategies of forgetting.[17] These strategies are asymmetrically distributed across the EU member states, making a collective European interpretation almost impossible. The similar argument can be applied to the distant European past as a basis for collective identity. A narrow cultural or religious focus on a substantive European identity based in ancient Greek/Roman culture and Christianity would be likely to have a fragmenting impact, given the diversity and heterogeneity in Europe, rather than help unify. The history of Europe, particularly its long and bloody confessional conflicts appear to be an improper system of reference for the EU's ambitions to manage diversity. It was not only religious wars and confessional persecution in Europe that led to the counter-project of the USA as a tolerant society, but also the controversial role of the organized church with relation to the political power in the modernity.[18]

In sum, the collective self-esteem perspective of collective identity does not deliver convincing insights into why the EU should be regarded by the citizens as durably attractive in contrast to national attachments, which according to Liah Greenfeld provide individuals with personal dignity and empowerment through the principles of equality and popular sovereignty.[19] It does not mean that European identity should replace national identity, but it needs to be comparably attractive, either within the same criterion of comparison or by establishing new criteria for attractiveness. The EU's attempts to establish its normative and moral supremacy may thus be doomed to failure, since the positive self-images of the EU are contradiction-ridden and frequently exhibit empty claims that are likely to degenerate into politics of rhetoric. Additionally, even if Europeans agreed on the shared identification with certain norms, the 'thickness' of such identity in the context of redistributory measures and majority decisions would be questionable. Whereas the rejection of war as a method of conflict-solving or the rejection of the death sentence may be largely shared by the majority of Europeans, it is nowhere near enough to guarantee a stable consensus that would not be subject to daily fluctuations in public opinion, thus expressing a popular agreement above ideological and socio-economic cleavages.

Contradictions and weaknesses of the political functions

The political functions of collective identity include the idea of European nationalism, the focus on public space and the cooperation enhancement in the EU. Each of the political functions espouses contradictions and weaknesses regarding citizenship identity.

The idea of European nationalism is an attempt to apply nationalist technologies of collective identity with regard to the EU – a case of methodological nationalism. Methodological nationalism departs from the analytical and methodological template of the nation-state as a universal one and consequently seeks to remedy social and political problems by using the antidote of the nation-state or nationalism. However, concerning the EU this seems to be a fairly contradictory endeavour. On the one hand, most of the scholars negate the nation-state character of the EU by either using neologisms such as mixed polity, consortio, condominio, regulatory state and proto-federation[20] or by employing the rather vague term of *the sui generis system* for a lack of a precise description of the European polity.[21] On the other hand, the strategy of European nationalism expects to construct collective identity in the sense of national identity (be it civic or otherwise). Leaving aside the debate on the thickness of collective identity necessary to cement a diverse society confronted with majority decision-making and redistributive policies, European nationalism attempts to generate a national sense of belonging in a non-nation-state environment. However, negating the nation-state character of the EU and simultaneously requiring from the EU the fulfilment one of the main characteristics of the continental nation-states, modelled after national identity, is flawed. However, this methodological inconsistency could indicate more than just a methodological flaw; it could refer to the fact that the lack of a resilient collective identity may not necessarily be the deficit of the EU. On the contrary, it may be instead a problem of the application of the collective identity concept, which was originally tailored to refer to nation-states. Nation-states have developed a strong collective identity mainly due to the workings of nationalism, not necessarily present in other political regimes. Nationalism for different causes (for instance emancipation, integration, resentment) had had strong identity-forging influences on the nation-states. But as nation-states are not the only regime types that exist at present, there might be correspondingly different forms of collective identity. The other implication of methodological nationalism is its faulty assumption that most of the states in the international system are nation-states. In contrast, we can distinguish numerous forms of regimes coping differently with collective identity and societal diversity, whereby nation-state is one category among many. For instance, Michael Walzer discerns, among others, immigrant societies (USA), consociations (Switzerland, Belgium) and hybrid regimes like France, Canada and the European Union all evading the nation-state label.[22]

Furthermore, there are implications of European nationalism for the European citizenship identity. European nationalism, precisely because it has no certain roots, is associated with a danger or even a necessity of the EU elites engaging in propaganda actions and strategic socialization with the aim of attitude alteration of European citizens.[23] However, when we consider that state nationalism developed in Europe largely under non-democratic circumstances of elite-driven mobilization, it could imply that any European nationalism (as ideology of the EU and identity technology practised by the EU) would shift the focus within European citizenship more strongly from active citizen towards compliant subject.[24] In this sense, the strategy of European nationalism entails a tension in the relationship between citizenship and collective identity, as citizenship gives in to identity politics with elitist dominance. In this context, we have to address the problem of the worsening of the European democratic deficit.

In addition to the contradictions inherent in the strategy of European nationalism, the approach to public space in the EU also exhibits certain limitations. This approach to collective identity is based on the concept of shared communication and deliberation processes among citizens in an integrated public space, as communicating, deliberating and participating citizens are likely to develop bonds of reciprocity and commitment to mutual obligations, which generate commonality and social bonds. This approach bases its arguments on the perspective regarding communication and deliberation as inherently advantageous for the legitimacy and collective identity of polities. However, the role of deliberation in establishing agreement, consensus and commonality under the circumstances of diversity and heterogeneity is controversial and not to be taken for granted.[25] Deliberation can assume, for instance, a form of ideology and thus be significantly less conducive to a free exchange of arguments between citizens as expected by the supporters of the deliberative democracy theory.[26] Furthermore, a real life deliberation tends to deviate considerably from the noble ideals of deliberation theorists by exhibiting discrimination and other pathologies.[27] Even in the national context, deliberation does not always contribute to a democratic will-formation, as it is dependent on informational resources, rhetoric power and access, which are as a rule asymmetrically distributed. Therefore, it remains uncertain whether deliberation can indeed generate a feeling of belonging. This holds even for the ideal world deliberation, which is believed to establish consensus and mutual understanding.[28] However, it is questionable whether mutual understanding, which is issue-specific and thus needs to be re-established every time deliberation occurs, can be interpreted as an equivalent to collective identity. Particularly in divided or culturally diverse societies, deliberation may further political antagonism in the sense of 'conflict-riddenness', rather than collective understanding.[29] We could even reverse the argument by stating that for deliberative politics to be able to bolster mutual understanding there needs to be a common basis for a shared deliberative rationality, which we could interpret as a form of thin collective identity, since it represents a common value system.[30] However, even such deliberative rationality cannot guarantee mutual understanding and reciprocity as authentic, and serious public debates (also on constitutional questions) run the risk of rhetoric vehemence and of mutual castigation of opponents.[31] In the context of the EU, deliberation is discussed primarily as argument-based reasoning among experts or within the political elite, which is believed to be pivotal for efficient decision-making, rather than essential for citizenship identity.[32] Consequently, legitimacy of the EU is not drawn from a collective identity based on deliberative rationality and consensual problem solving via free exchange of arguments, but rather from the efficiency and effectiveness of elite-driven decision-making in the EU.

A further problem of deliberation in the European public sphere is its fragmented nature. Even if we are optimistic about strong publics in the EU, as seen for example in the European Parliament, the nature of the EU is rather multi-level, contextual, asymmetrical, complex and hybrid, all characteristics that are rather detrimental to a citizenship identity.[33] This has also implications for the deliberative settings in the EU, which are fragmented and functionally established. Therefore, we deal with a plethora of fragmented and frequently isolated deliberative settings that replace citizen participation with functionally defined rights and access for those affected by a given policy. As a consequence, citizen politics migrates from the institutions of representative democracy (with the claim of representing the interests of all citizens) to multiple networks and deliberative systems in the different areas of public policy. However, the fragmented and contextualized citizens' participation exhibits a functionally limited *intersubjectivity*, as a result of which the citizenship identity also becomes fragmented.[34] Against this background, one should be sceptical of whether strong publics in the EU are capable of the communicative integrating of the inherently fragmented citizenship.[35]

A further focus of the public sphere perspective on collective identity relates to the communicative structures in the EU. Some scholars argue in this context that the EU represents an integrated communication and action space, since the member states' mass media-conveyed publics share (despite cultural diversity) the same political topics with the same relevance and at the same time.[36] The EU should therefore be interpreted within a common communicative context, which in turn is indispensable for a mass democratic legitimacy via the public sphere. This communicative structure is expected to have an integrative impact even on diverse societies, as shared communicative horizons and experiences are likely to engender communities and therefore collective identity.[37]

However, this original perspective suffers from two weaknesses. First, the assumption of an emerging European community of communication, observable in the mass media, is based on measures of parallel national public spheres, rather than on a genuine transnational communicative space. In order to find out whether a European space for transnational processes of communicative community emerges, we should instead gauge the permeability of national public spheres to contributions by non-national actors. Preliminary studies suggest some embryonic transnational elements in the EU public space, but there is no common discourse observable in Europe. This does not support the thesis that a European public sphere as a genuine communicative community has already developed. Consequently, the EU remains largely dependent on the national political processes for its legitimacy.[38] Second, even if a communicative community had emerged in the EU, we would probably deal with a rudimentary collective identity, since communicative structures score even lower on the identity 'thickness' scale than a shared value system postulated by the supporters of the constitutional patriotism. It also implies that the thesis on the essential role of communication in the community-building process can be flawed in its causality, as it is based on reverse reasoning. It holds true that political communities exhibit more intense communication patterns, as compared to their environment. However, it cannot necessarily be concluded that every society displaying similar communicative features is a community.[39] This position clearly overlooks that more communication does not necessarily raise the consciousness for commonality, as it can equally foster the perception of cultural differences.[40] In other words, in making communication structures central categories of the analysis, we examine more a European society than a European community.[41] In other words, there is no certainty that similar semantic structures or shared discursive nods will generate a community or a perception of commonality in the political sense. This is particularly relevant in the context of the EU, where fragmentation of political contexts and segmentation of publics foster fragmented citizenship, rather than encourage an integrated citizenship identity.[42]

A further political function of collective identity relates to the assumption about its capacity to solve collective problems. In the case of the EU, the central question relates to who is expected to share collective identity. Since the EU is an elite-driven project, the cooperation dilemmas refer to the elites of (particularly) the member states, rather than European citizens. Therefore, even if the EU does generate social norms of reciprocity, as expected by approaches arguing in favour of common institutions solving collective action problems, they are likely to be found among the European officials, rather than European citizens.[43] In other words, citizens do not play cooperation games, as they are not primary actors in EU politics.[44] Certainly, cooperation, trust and reciprocity may also increase within the European citizenry as a result of the workings of European institutions.[45] However, as long as the citizens are 'receivers' of political decisions rather than the decision-makers, their collective identity would be of secondary significance for the solution of cooperation dilemmas within the EU.

A related question pertains to whether the social norms and patterns of reciprocity can 'thicken' into collective identity, increasing the chances of cooperation, or whether they result solely from stabilized expectations about the rational behaviour of other actors. It is therefore uncertain whether cooperation among the EU members is spawned by the socialization to 'build bridges' or rather by an interest calculation stemming from profitable long-term commitment secured by EU institutions. However, the latter would contradict the thesis on collective identity, even though we might observe similar cooperation effects, which we would assume to be resulting from collective identity.[46] Empirical studies are inconclusive regarding the cooperation willingness of the EU member states and, even more importantly, they cannot convincingly link the cooperation patterns in the EU with European citizenship.[47] An approach explaining the willingness of national publics to approve of and to support the decisions made by the EU in return for a more or less immediate and straightforward reward or benefit would be necessary as an indicator for collective identity linked to citizenship.[48]

In addition, scepticism should be expressed regarding the specific argument of the EU as a solution to war between otherwise belligerent states. Giving credit to the EU for its alleged peacemaking capability is a case of daring but uncertain causality. As many non-EU countries also experienced peace, we might find the causation running through other independent variables such as democracy, which would be consistent with the Kantian claim about perpetual peace.[49] An even more provocative thesis has been proposed by Hermann Lübbe, who argued that the peaceful nature of the EU member states vis-à-vis each other is a prerequisite for the successful functioning of the EU, rather than its result.[50] In this sense, there must be something common to the EU member states (for instance democracy, a shared value system, economic growth), which renders the EU a well-functioning organization. However, if this holds true, then the EU already possesses a sort of collective 'something' that makes the cooperation possible. In this case, the question would again be whether this kind of identity or collective characteristic is sufficient for legitimizing majority decisions and redistributory policies. These 'weak' or 'thin' commonalities might suffice to establish and maintain an international organization, but at the same time would be distant from a sufficient legitimizing strategy for a complex and redistributive polity such as the EU. Nonetheless, it is equally possible that the motivation for a peaceful coexistence and cooperation within a given international organization is based on self-interest, which can be maximized within an organization by providing lubricants for cooperation in forms of information and sanctions (reducing transaction costs).[51] Conversely, common cultural backgrounds might not be sufficient as a precondition for cooperation. Some empirical studies even suggest that violence is more likely among states with similar cultural ties.[52] Therefore, the causal relation between collective identity (at least in cultural terms) and cooperation between states might be too simplistic.

The deficits of all three functional approaches to European identity are presented in Table 4.1. This keyword-like recapitulation focuses, however, only on the main characteristics pertaining to the discussed deficits. In addition, Table 4.1 presents implications of the functional approaches for the citizenship identity.

Table 4.1 Deficits and implications of the functional approaches to European identity

Functional approach	Deficits	Implications for the citizenship–collective identity nexus
Cognitive approach	Status identity	Limited behavioural implications
Self-esteem booster perspective	Identity mainly through the out-group comparison	Uncertain integrative potential
Political functions	• European nationalism	• Methodological nationalism
	• Communicative space	• Over-optimistic assumptions about identity construction
	• Cooperation	• Problems of identity thickness

Conclusions

Each of the functional perspectives on collective identity exhibits limitations, and contradictions and offers ambivalent empirical accounts. In sum, all three perspectives (cognitive, self-esteem, and political functions) share *three* major methodological limitations, which could be remedied by employing an alternative approach.

First, the functional approaches to collective identity envisage only marginally the behavioural implications of collective identity. Whenever they do so, they remain mainly committed to a nomothetic idea of political function (European nationalism, communication space, cooperation fostering arrangements), and are thus incapable of addressing the potential variance between different political collective identities, particularly with regard to their varying strengths and their differing levels of collectivism. Consequently, an alternative approach linking citizenship with collective identity should on the one hand differentiate between social roles (or social identities) and political collective identity, the latter being of much more interest in the context of citizenship. On the other hand, the approach should account for the variance of collective identity, not necessarily referring to the different territorial multiple identities, but rather to various shades of a collective identity at the same level. In other words, European identity could assume different forms, develop varying strengths, and shift between strong individualism and strong collectivism. Furthermore, it implies that an alternative approach would be anchored within the boundaries of individualism, negating that collective identities are ontological entities existing independently from individuals. Therefore, collective identity should be regarded as a property of individuals, as it is connected with individual consciousness, but which connects the individual with a group. This connection entails behavioural implications, such as the fact that the individuals begin to consider the common good of group to be a relevant category for individual action.

Second, the functional approaches to collective identity are incapable of pinpointing *the* collective identity for Europe out of the maze of fluidity, multiplicity and hybridity, thus evading the issue of identity durability and its integrative workings. Instead, they frequently focus on the postulates or ideal self-images, even if frequently inconsistent with the actual activities of the EU. In the case of the fragmented, multiple and hybrid identities, we are confronted with the unidentifiable and disintegrated citizenship. In this context, citizenship ceases to be an integrative mechanism and becomes a strategic resource for identity politics competing with each other for the extraction of community resources. This ignores the very idea of citizenship, which is inextricably linked to a political collective identity espousing conception of an integrative mechanism, which cross-cuts other social identities. Against this background, citizenship identity represents political collective identity, as opposed to other social identities. The features of such political collective identity are a certain degree of durability, bridging capability and integrative performance. In this sense, citizenship represents political category pertaining to membership in a political community (from the perspective of the citizen) or a method of cultivating political community (from the perspective of the state/ polity), which makes it an integrative phenomenon. Therefore, the notion of citizenship identity potentially offers a more promising concept with which to link citizenship and collective identity.

Third, some other authors focus on identity technologies based on manipulation of cultural and political symbols, which in turn makes identity construction barely distinguishable from brainwashing. This mainly raises the question of tension in identity politics in the context of democratic politics, rather than delivering an overall picture of identity politics in the EU associated with citizenship. A possible method of remedying these problems would include a broad angle focus on the identity politics and identity technologies of the political authorities. The form of identity politics associated with types of citizenship could point to a certain direction in the maze of flux and multiplicity of identity. Therefore, out of many potential identities and their configurations, European politics of citizenship identity could help us explore the potentially emergent European identity or at least a collective identity envisaged by European political authorities beyond the focus on the manipulation of symbols.

Framing the argument

In this section I will frame my argument about the citizenship–collective identity nexus. This argument takes into account the deficits of the functional approaches to collective identity and attempts to avoid them. In particular, it is sensitive to the issue of integrative workings of citizenship by placing the notion of citizenship identity at the heart of the concept of collective identity. The argument is constituted of three aspects. The first aspect covers a reconceptualization of collective identity, which is explored with regard to both its semantic core and two semantic dimensions. The semantic core of collective identity pertains to the notion of citizenship identity. The semantic dimensions include the orientation of collective identity and its internal dynamics. The second aspect of the argument refers to generic models of citizenship, which include republican, liberal and caesarean citizenship. These models highlight each of the citizenship components (rights, obligations, compliance) discussed in Chapter 1. The third aspect of the argument links generic models of citizenship to different forms of collective identity/citizenship identity. Therefore, it accounts for identity variance and allows for an empirical analysis of collective identities in the context of citizenship. This alternative approach to collective identity attempts to come to terms with various objects of collective identity, different implications regarding its strength and durability and differing degrees of identity thickness. In this sense, the argument does not represent a theory in terms of causality, but should rather be viewed as an analytical framework. In the context of empirical analysis, the citizenship–collective identity nexus points inter alia to the expectations–outcome gap, which represents a potential mismatch between a specific form of citizenship identity and the identity technologies. If different types of citizenship are associated with diverse collective identities, ill-conceived identity politics would generate an expectations–outcome gap. By applying identity technologies that ignore the implications of the citizenship–collective identity nexus, political authorities will be unable to produce stable collective identity.

The concept of collective identity

The concept of collective identity can be explored with regard to both its *semantic core* and *two semantic dimensions*, which include its *orientation* and its *internal dynamics*. The semantic core of collective identity in political terms pertains to the notion of citizenship identity. It implies that despite many social roles, political preferences, self-government rights and specific territorial attachments, there is an overarching citizenship identity relating to the shared political community that individuals live in. Whereas the idea of differentiated citizenship divides individuals into separate communities, the concept of citizenship identity pertains to membership of an overlapping political community. From the perspective of the state, we deal here with a common citizenship strategy, which is expected to bridge cultural and political differences and thus becomes a source of unity and collective identity in a heterogeneous and diverse society. Such citizenship identity would be capable of integrating societies characterized by 'deep diversity', a notion Charles Taylor uses to describe the existence of cultural, national and ethnic structures of a society, entailing different collective goals.[53]

In this sense, political collective identity is referred to as a sense of political commonness between individuals that fosters a general commitment to the *public interest*. The sense of commonness means that individuals regard themselves as equal citizens belonging to the same political community, whereas the basis for this belonging is secondary. Therefore, this concept of collective identity has an explicitly political meaning in comparison to the other concepts of collective identity, which are anchored in various functions of collective identity. In this respect, collective identity is not solely based on the process of collective perception of difference and delimitation between 'us' and 'them', but also entails behavioural implications for citizens as members of political community.

Moreover, it is more than merely a function of self-esteem via group membership, in which collective identity reflects a self-perception of groups as unified entities attenuating their inner differences and exaggerating differences with other groups. While the functional perspectives highlight motivational, cognitive and legitimacy-orientated aspects of so-defined collective identity, this approach focuses on the behavioural aspect of it, arguing that collective identity is not only about self-definition, but also about the political consequences of it. It suggests that the political behaviour of citizens is likely to change under the impact of collective identity, as political collective identity is linked to citizenship. This distinguishes this explicitly political perspective from the functional perspective, in which collective identity had merely a *function* or a *by-product* of national community-building, legitimacy fostering and cooperation enabling. The commitment to public interest ties political collective identity to citizenship, as both categories refer to a political community. This implies that a general commitment to a public interest can be referred to as citizenship identity, which differs from other non-political and purely cognitive and perception orientated types of collective identity, for instance in forms of social roles or territorial self-concepts.

Orientation of collective identity

The *orientation* dimension of collective identity can be analyzed horizontally and vertically. *First*, there is a horizontal orientation of the We-feeling between individuals that denotes the sense of commonness irrespective of the sources of this feeling. This sense of belonging to a political community (regardless of its territoriality)[54] can assume for example a form of an emotional attachment.[55] The horizontal orientation of identity, i.e. the sense of belonging, ties individuals as members of the same group, thus relating to the internal relations within a community. Certainly, any form of belonging implies also a boundary-making, as it always excludes people not belonging to the group at hand. However, this is a methodological difference, whether we focus on the internal aspect of belonging as a main feature of horizontal orientation of collective identity or the excluding implications, which are concomitant of collective identity, but not necessarily the constituting characteristic of collective identity. Nevertheless, some forms of collective identity do rest on the concept of exclusion, from which they draw their bonding power. But in the case of citizenship identity, the intra-community relations among individuals/citizens are of greater significance, as these relations are based on the idea of a political equality between the community members. The horizontal orientation is a necessary condition for collective identity, but it is not a sufficient one. With only horizontal orientation covered, political identity assumes a significant, but preliminary, form, in which individuals perceive themselves as equal, similar or belonging to the same group or community.

Second, a fully fledged political collective identity should be additionally explored with regard to a vertical orientation, which pertains more strongly to the citizens' actions vis-à-vis the shared community. Within this vertical orientation, collective identity is defined by its effects upon individual action, thus covering behavioural implications. Whenever the sense of commonness does not result in a general commitment to the public interest, we cannot point to collective identity in the political sense. In this conception, specific collective feelings of belonging such as common pride in the winning of the football championship by the national team or subjective perception of cultural similarity or even an emotional attachment would cover the horizontal orientation of collective identity, but not necessarily with implications for citizens' actions. Hence, the vertical orientation of political collective identity describes citizens' behaviour in terms of moral resources such as loyalty or solidarity directed at the political community.[56] Loyalty towards the community generates refraining citizens' actions, whereas solidarity engenders committing actions. Depending on whether loyalty or solidarity dominates the vertical orientation, collective identity becomes stronger or weaker. We could even list moral resources as indicators of the 'thickness' of collective identity in a hierarchical order of loyalty, solidarity and sacrifice, where the latter represents the highest form of vertical commitment.[57] The term 'vertical orientation' suggests that citizens refer to an abstract idea of community, which transcends their perceptions of experienced similarity and their face-to face communication with other community members. The abstract idea of community appears at a higher level than the individual one, as the public good or the public interest becomes integrated into the citizens' behavioural preferences.

The vertical orientation relates to a commitment to the collectivity in terms of a disposition, rather than in terms of the revealed common will, as every citizen can freely interpret what collective good and public interest are. However, relating to public good or public interest we are frequently confronted with the problem of 'hijacking' of the collective will by political actors, who argue to be able to identify the revealed collective will. In contrast, the vertical orientation is a regulative principle stemming from an impersonal motivation vis-à-vis the community. As it pertains to civic resources of loyalty, solidarity and sacrifice, vertical orientation of collective identity frequently assumes a form of moral duty. Thus, collective identity assumes a generalized, unspecific and diffuse form.

Certainly, it depends on the type of citizenship, which civic resources (if any) are required from the citizens. Thus, solidarity appears to be a more demanding moral resource, since it is often associated with material redistribution, whereas the sacrifice of its own life reflects an absolute dominance of collective orientation to the detriment of individualism. This 'thick' collective identity is typical for instance for nationalist movements of irredentist character. In contrast, 'mere' loyalty can assume the form of giving up the exit option or refraining from damaging actions towards the community, without any additional active commitment. Conversely, if citizens exhibit low degrees of loyalty or solidarity, we cannot point to political collective identity in terms of citizenship identity. In this case, an individual might define himself/herself as belonging to a given community, and thus improve his/her own self-esteem or merely reduce the cognitive complexity, but s/he will not be prepared to adjust his/her preferences to the however defined public interest.

Dynamics of collective identity

Apart from the politically defined semantic core of collective identity and the orientation of collective identity, we can use the notion of identity dynamics to explore political collective identity even further. In this context, collective identity shall not be defined statically, but rather as a phenomenon that is perpetually constructed and reconstructed. The dynamic nature of collective identity stems from the relationship between the We-component and the I-component of individual identity. According to Norbert Elias, individuals maintain a We–I balance, where We-feelings relate to collective identity of individuals and the I-component describes the personal, idiosyncratic aspect of individual identity.[58] Hence, different constellations of individual identity can exist. The We–I balance might lean towards the I-component while containing a minimal amount of the We-feeling (weak collective identity). If there is a continuous long-term shifting process towards I-identity, we can label it *individualization*, during which the We–I balance turns to the I–We balance. Conversely, the We-component can dominate the We–I balance leading to a *collectivization* of identity (strong collective identity). In sum, collective identity can undergo long-term or medium-term changes in the process of identity construction, in addition to short-term identity politics.

The construction of collective identity in its political meaning, as a general commitment to the public interest, proceeds in association with different forms of citizenship. Since individuals are not born as citizens but instead undergo socialization qua the educational system, through the practice of citizenship such as the political participation in the polity and under the influence of identity politics, citizenship as it is relates strongly to political collective identity. Nonetheless, collective identity might face challenges when, for example, the model of citizenship hitherto present in the polity is under pressure due to societal changes or identity politics of the state. In this way, citizenship is closely associated with collective identity, which additionally supports the assumption that different models of citizenship may promote various collective identities.

For Norbert Elias, the major source of We-identity is the modern state, which advanced mass citizens' identity by integrating the hitherto excluded classes of the population. This development did not occur until the 20th century, as the loyalty and mobilization of the mass population gained significance for the mass warfare.[59] The resilient and strong collective identity generated by modern states resulted from the integration plane of the modern state via citizenship and its consequential role as a survival unit during the wars that engendered the emotional nature of the 'We-ness'.[60] The major issue is, however, whether nation-states can sustain this emotionally charged collective identity, even though the functional relevance of the nation-state, among other things as a result of growing transnational threats (security, ecology) is visibly diminishing. In this sense, it might become crucial for the supranational polity structure, be it the EU or others, to become new survival units by replacing or integrating nation-states. Otherwise, the likelihood for a resilient and vivid collective identity to develop outside the nation-states is bleak, and therefore we might be inclined to assume stronger individualization, in other words a shift in the We–I balance of collective identity.

The notion of We–I balance of identity cannot only be applied to the description of a relationship between individualization and collectivization, as in this case we describe macro-sociological processes. The concept of the We–I balance can be applied in three additional contexts, which are also related to the notion of citizenship identity. First, the We–I balance could enlighten the problem of identity fluidity by pinpointing the dynamic aspect of collective identity beyond the controversial claim that every identity is in flux and subject to individual choice.[61] In this context, fluidity and hybridization could be linked to the increasing individualization of modern societies, whereas collectivization could account for the simultaneous thrust of collectivization in the same societies. We could thus depict changes in the collective identity as non-synchronous events, allowing for integrating apparently contradictory phenomena.[62] Consequently, we could break down the macro-sociological perspective, preferred by Norbert Elias, to examine simultaneous realities of individualization and collectivization. Second, the notion of multiple identities (territorial or otherwise) could be enriched with the concept of the We–I balance, thus allowing for shifts between the levels or objects of identification. Here, we would analyze collective identity regarding its elasticity, rather than as a fixed attachment or stable preference structure. We would therefore move from an analysis of collective identity distribution across different levels or aspects towards a dynamic notion of multiple identities. Finally, we could address the issue of 'optimal' collective identity, particularly under the circumstances of hybridity of identity. The We–I balance of identity could account for identity formation in diverse societies, where the relational aspect of identity between minority and majority collective identity appears to be central. According to the optimal distinctiveness theory, individuals define themselves as much in terms of their group membership as in terms of their individual achievements.[63] As individuals can identify with different social groups, they do so in order to achieve and maintain a stable self-concept. Since an individual's self-concept is shaped by two opposing needs – the need for assimilation (collective identity) and the need for differentiation (individual identity) – people aspire to become part of larger social entities, while at the same time they want to feel unique and original. However, too much of either identity generates the opposite motivation, which provokes efforts to change the current level of social identification. This dialectics of individual and collectivist needs is likely to produce a momentary homeostatic balance between the opposing needs.

Consequently, we could face waves of collectivization and individualization running through different levels of collective identity: a wave of individualization would be followed for instance by a wave of nationalism, followed in turn either by another wave of individualization or Europeanization. Furthermore, the optimal distinctiveness theory would suggest that identity technologies might instigate an opposing effect on individuals when they are too pervasive and too intense, thus rendering efforts of identity construction counterproductive. When individuals become assigned to a majority group, they need to differentiate themselves in some way from this group, and thus tend to contrast away from their group. It would also imply that identification with a negatively valued group (for example with certain nations) could have a positive value, if such identification helped to restore homeostasis, thus achieving a greater balance between the opposing needs for assimilation and differentiation. This dynamic perspective negates that collective identity comes about as solely a self-esteem booster, as individuals prefer an optimal level of distinctiveness to increase their social identity, rather than boosting their esteem via membership in positively valued communities.

In sum, collective identity represents *an integrating category*, despite the fact that individuals can feel belonging to various groups or social units at the same time. Even though multiplicity, hybridity and variability are features of collective identities, collective identities integrate idiosyncrasies of individuals into group behaviour. However, this does not imply a uniformity of individual behaviour under the influence of collective identity. Collective identities operate under the circumstances of societal pluralism stemming from functional differentiation and the double process of individualization and globalization. This societal pluralism makes recombination of identities necessary. As every society is in a need of integration, this is provided by an overlapping collective identity sustained by various mechanisms.[64] The primary mechanism of *political integration* of societies is citizenship, which brings us back to the citizenship identity. The notion of citizenship identity addresses the systematic workings of political collective identity, particularly in terms of its double coding of collective identity, e.g. bonding and bounding. Citizenship is a double coded phenomenon, since it is associated with bonding among citizens and at the same time it gives rise to boundaries excluding the non-citizens. In addition, citizenship identity as an approach to political collective identity accounts for the variance of collective identity (its contextuality), which can be traced to different types of citizenship. This double-edged working of citizenship identity is essential for its effectiveness as an integrating mechanism, as it has to mediate between collectivization impulses inherent in any collective identity and fragmentation tendencies of the functionally differentiated modern societies.

Linking citizenship and collective identity

As an integrative device, shared citizenship identity does not annihilate differences, but is instead capable of superseding rival identities. In other words, shared citizenship can be a source of political collective identity. As citizenship can assume different forms, its variance finds its reflection in the thickness and strength of citizenship identity. Even though many different political identities can exist, such as party identities or ideological identities, citizenship identity represents a 'master identity' that underpins citizens' behaviour in the public space.

Potential critique

Two potential points of critique are used against the notion of citizenship identity in the debate on citizenship. First, a potential critique of this position could point to the quasi-monolithic conception of citizenship, which regards differentiated citizenship (particularly in its emphasis on special group rights) as an obstacle, rather than a lubricant for the integration of diverse society.[65] This critique would argue that the recognition and promotion of diversity and hybridity enhances the probability of minority identities to accept the dominant collective identity of a given society.[66] Nevertheless, this position sheds light on the problem of citizenship identity merely from the angle of minorities. Therefore, the primary interest of this perspective is to develop effective integration strategies towards minorities. In contrast, the concept of citizenship identity covers the entire society and its ability to develop overlapping and shared collective identity despite different ethnic, political and social identities and rivalries. In this sense, the idea that citizens' inequality could contribute to an overall integration of the society appears to be counter-intuitive, even if differentiated citizenship could have integrative effects regarding minorities.

Second, a further potential critique of the notion of citizenship identity could point to an allegedly semantic conservatism, whose origin could be located in the tradition of the nation-state. In this tradition, citizenship and collective identity (national identity) overlap and strengthen each other mutually via national identity politics. However, the notion of citizenship identity includes explicitly post-national configurations of citizenship and identity, thus allowing both for variance of citizenship and different degrees of collective identity. Moreover, the notion of citizenship identity does not contradict the reality of complex citizenship, which encompasses different levels of citizenship and identity, also including multi-level citizenship associated with multiple identities. Therefore, the issue at hand is rather whether this post-national (or in our case European) citizenship can generate a shared collective identity despite its complex and multi-layered form. Whereas the notion of citizenship identity highlights its integrating aspirations, it also questions the uniforming character of citizenship identity, according to which every citizen would exhibit similar degrees of identity thickness. This leads us to the difference between citizenship uniformity and citizenship identity.

Thin and thick identities

In contrast to citizenship uniformity, citizenship identity indicates a layer of commonness among citizens pertaining to a common denominator of shared identity. Nevertheless, there can potentially be a plethora of citizenship identities, as we can distinguish various types of citizenship. Thus, citizenship identity may vary in its degree of its resilience (thin versus thick identity), even though both forms of identity would employ the language of community.[67] However, thin citizenship identity would make use of the language of shared values and norms, derived from common institutions and procedures,[68] whereas thick identity citizenship would anchor the sense of 'We-ness' in more demanding civic resources such as loyalty, solidarity and sacrifice.[69] In addition, thick citizenship identity would most likely apply the language of *diffuse reciprocity*, bonding citizens stemming from an image of more highly amalgamated communities.

Against this background, there are also different expectations of performance regarding thin and thick citizenship identity. Thin identity relates to a shared normative environment and restrains from demanding claims of solidarity or sacrifice, since it operates under the circumstances of pluralism and individualism. Therefore, approaches expecting a transformation of a thin identity (anchored in a normative environment of society) into a thick identity, implying a change in citizens' behaviour, are likely to be over-optimistic.[70] While solidarity claims refer to solidarity with someone, i.e. with other citizens, a shared normative environment implies identification with norms and principles of appropriate conduct. Consequently, thin identity would require a stronger application of identity politics and identity technologies to stimulate citizens' behaviour modification towards more loyalty, solidarity and sacrifice. But even a thin identity cannot easily be generated in a short period of time, unless it involves pervasive and intense identity technology. In contrast, thick citizenship identity would merely require a catalyst to be activated, since citizens' moral resources are present. In the context of thick collective identity, we would rather expect modest identity politics. At this point, we can distinguish between the transformer and the catalyst identity politics where, in the case of the former, political authorities must use more invasive identity technologies to establish thick identity. In contrast, the latter identity politics would be less invasive, as they require merely a catalyst to encourage behavioural implications of citizenship politics.

Thick collective identity is expected to be 'sticky' and resistant, particularly in crises.[71] In addition, it alleviates the legitimacy problems of the majority rule, typical for modern mass democracies. Thanks to the existence of thick collective identity, political minorities accept decisions of the political majority, even if these are made to the detriment of the minority, since the political minority regards itself as part of a community. Under the circumstances of thick identity, redistribution of goods is expected not to cause legitimacy problems, as community members are bound by moral obligations vis-à-vis each other and the abstract idea of community. On the contrary, thin identity considers rights to be the foundation for collective identity. The difficulty of such collective identity is its derivation from natural and universalistic rights, rather than from specific entitlements within the community. Natural and universalistic rights exclude any distinctiveness between individuals (also in their capacity as citizens), as they are community-independent and therefore imply equally thick identity inside as outside the community. As a consequence, the bonds among citizens cannot be stronger than among the non-citizens. Paradoxically, in newly naturalized citizens, new rights could be expected to stimulate collective identity, unlike in in-born citizens, as their citizen status and dignity would be enhanced, thus strengthening their bonds with the new community. However, for the great majority of in-born citizens, their rights are an obvious attachment of citizenship, rather than a privilege. Additionally, as a result of the universalistic appeal of human and citizen rights, citizenship could be associated with diluted collective identity (as opposed to the diffuse identity), which would be slightly stronger than the identity among strangers, as solidarity and sacrifice among strangers turn out to be a notion as demanding as it is unrealistic. Therefore, thin identity is prone to 'tear' and to generate legitimacy problems, particularly with regard to diverse societies endowed with majority-orientated political systems maintaining extensive redistribution policies.

However, the greater the diversity, the weaker the strength of solidarity. Thin citizenship identity may breed enough trust for citizens to regard their compatriots not as enemies, but also not necessarily as friends. By the same token, thin citizenship identity is unlikely to induce a generalization of solidarity, which is a diffuse form of reciprocity. This case could apply to the EU, whose members might not wage wars against each others, but are different enough to regard the majority decisions of the EU as a legitimacy problem. In other words, the heterogeneity of the EU, which engenders legitimacy problems, might not be curable with a thin citizenship identity.

Furthermore, thin citizenship identity reflects attachments to ideas, norms and procedures, rather than attachments to other citizens. In this sense, this form of collective identity can modify citizens' actions according to norms of appropriate behaviour (derived from norms and rules), linking them to an abstract and desired image of community. However, this community image neither relates to fellow citizens, nor is it an expression of moral resources of citizens. Moreover, most identity approaches resting on rights, norms and procedures are at pains to explain how they become constructed (as they assume Kantian default rationality of individuals as an origin of citizens' understanding of norms and rights), which suggests that intense identity politics and identity technologies might be at work in the construction of norms of shared appropriate behaviour, for instance in the form of engagement in perpetual expansions or missionary activity (and internal bonding as a result of these activities). Nevertheless, thin citizenship identity remains prone to be 'torn' and strained by conflicts, rivalries and differences between the community members. In order to make a rights-based, 'legal' citizenship generate thick identity would require everyday investment of social resources among citizens in their social interactions. In the process, citizens would emotionally invest in their citizenship as well as habitually and consciously practise an active citizenship. However, this would mean a shift towards another type of citizenship. In the case of the EU, this particular version of active citizenship would stress European identity at the level of 'being specifically European' rather than a sense of being a 'cosmopolitan' or 'global' citizen.[72]

Citizenship as an independent variable

A further issue pertaining to citizenship identity is the choice of citizenship as an independent variable in explaining types of collective identity. The notion of citizenship identity does not suggest any fusion of these two concepts, but solely relates the collective identity of individuals to the political realm of citizenship, in which individuals become citizens. Citizenship can be regarded as the main framework for reference of political collective identity, since citizenship is the most fundamental and at the same time the most pervasive institution of any polity. It lays foundations for the cognitive, habitual and ethical components of citizens' activity.[73] Moreover, the experience of citizenship and the denial of citizenship are likely to result in behaviour modification due to the citizen's self-orientation regarding the category of collective identity. Since we would expect citizenship to become consequential, these consequences for collective identity would occur at two levels. On the one hand, the citizenship practice would become consequential for the collective identity of the EU, when specific entitlements and obligations (for instance, to live, work and pay taxes in Europe), would become relevant for those whose horizons and ambitions go beyond local and national labour markets. For the remaining citizens, this category might not be consequential regarding their collective identity.

On the other hand, whether citizenship becomes consequential for collective identity depends on the type of identity politics and identity technologies involved. As there are many simultaneous sources of collective identity, the EU finds itself in competition with the nation-states regarding identity construction. It does not mean that European and national identities are exclusive per se. Rather, it indicates that nation-states, despite their growing weaknesses, attempt to extract the consequentiality of citizenship primarily in the national framework, as citizenship due to the citizenship identity can draw on moral resources, which are invaluable as sources for mobilization and legitimacy for political actors. Since citizenship is legally still closely attached to nationality, and regardless of a liberalization of the access to citizenship, citizenship identity results from the primary socialization of individuals into citizens by the nation-state, rather than from the gratitude of the former immigrants who became new citizens. This is related to the subject of European citizenship being a mere derivative of national identity.[74] This, among other things, could be the reason why national identity is likely to remain the 'chronic identity' of European citizens. Even though member states of the EU allow a certain degree of European identity to grow, they will certainly claim the moral resources of their citizens to be embedded in the nation-state. Although multi-layered identities are possible and frequent, some communities will be more likely to be able to assert citizens' loyalty, solidarity and sacrifice during identity conflicts.

Certainly, the relationship between citizenship and collective identity is not a simple structure–agency causation, in which structure completely dominates the agency. A relevant part of collective identity construction runs through alternative mechanisms. Therefore, the notion of citizenship identity does not indicate a mono-causal relationship between citizenship and collective identity, as it would put excessive explanatory burden onto citizenship. Nevertheless, citizenship channels collective political identity as well as ordering and taming conflicts by labelling and classifying collective similarities and differences. In this sense, citizenship determines how and when differences may legitimately be represented, and who counts as 'equal' in the public space.[75] At the same time, citizenship defines the limits of state power by indicating where the private space of free individuals begins and ends, thus also delineating the boundaries of citizenship identity. Therefore, we can identify a tension between structure (citizenship as a complex institution) and agency (citizens as holders of collective identity) that both enables the individuals to be different and bridges differences into a citizenship identity. This tension can be productive, as long as the dialectics of citizenship and collective identity (forging shared identity versus acknowledging difference) shifts constantly between the identity politics as state activity (citizens as objects of citizenship) and opposing impulses of the citizens (citizens as subjects of citizenship). Whenever one of the extremities dominates, we are confronted with either collectivist identity politics aiming at annihilating differences, or with fragmentation of citizenship identity.

Indicating a tension between citizenship and collective identity is on the one hand a consequence of separation between these two concepts instead of their merger. On the other hand, the tension between citizenship and collective identity allows for an exploration of citizenship with regard to the state power. In this context, citizenship can be regarded as an aggregate or composite conception, which next to rights and obligations includes citizens' compliance vis-à-vis the statehood.

This composite concept integrates various semantic transformations of citizenship, exemplified by different political traditions of thought. The compliance to authority as one component of citizenship would thus reflect Jean Bodin's tradition of state sovereignty, whereas the rights component of citizenship would point to Locke's tradition and the obligations component would indicate the Aristotelian ethical concept of politics. In Bodin's tradition, citizenship is about subjecthood, rather than an active self-determination of citizens in terms of their actorness. Hence, subjecthood and compliance describe citizenship as belonging to the state in exchange for its effectiveness in producing security and welfare. This tradition of thought finds its reflection in some contemporary justifications of the welfare state, which is expected to produce an output legitimacy of the states, for instance via extensive social rights, rather than supporting active citizenship. This could imply a benevolent autocracy instead of democratic polity. In contrast, the natural rights tradition of John Locke put more emphasis on self-ownership of citizens (freedom, property and security) than their passive and receptive nature. In this tradition of thought, liberal citizens aim at their independence from the states and their maximization of liberty. A further component of citizenship stresses the active and community-orientated ideal of citizenship, which implies an active belonging without reservations.

Even though our conception of citizenship includes all three components (rights, obligations, compliance), we can identify generic models of citizenship based on the emphasis of each of the components. Our three generic models of citizenship therefore correspond to the components of citizenship of obligations, rights, and compliance, producing the republican, the liberal and the caesarean model of citizenship. Each model stresses a different component while maintaining the other components, even though these assume weak values.

Citizenship and its generic models

The three models of citizenship are ideal types in the Weberian sense. They do not exist in pure form, exactly as other typological categories. Their function is to order our thinking of social phenomena. The republican model of citizenship is based on the Aristotelian ideal of citizen as *zoon politikon*, the political man for whom politics is a means of leading a good life.[76] In contrast, the liberal tradition of citizenship draws strongly from the writings of John Locke and David Hume,[77] according to whom citizens are individuals whose primary concern is not realizing any human ideal of good but, on the contrary, lies in the realizing of their interests and passions.[78] In this conception of citizenship, politics is only an instrument for guaranteeing the realization of citizens' individual interests.[79] The third model is caesarean citizenship, the roots of which can be found in the writings of Thomas Hobbes and, in its modern version, in the works of Carl Schmitt.[80] Being a citizen means to think politics in categories of friend and enemy. The caesarean citizen delineates politics as a perpetual struggle against enemies, be it internal (Hobbes) or external enemies (Schmitt). Citizenship is thus about survival, security and the effectiveness of political decisions. Politics is therefore ubiquitous, although in a different manner from the republican model. The citizen does not realize any human good, nor does s/he pursue her/his purely private interests. Rather, the citizen authorizes the Caesar, a political leader with power who guarantees the survival of the individual and the nation in a hostile environment with foes. Therefore, the citizen must not only be aware of enemies but also be organized within a homogeneous nation aware of the danger, thus allowing for unanimous decisions.

These three ideal types of citizenship have their real-type correspondence, though not in the pure form. It has often to do with the place of their emergence. Republican model citizenship was practised in the Athenian polis, which served as a model for Aristotle's reflections on citizenship. Certain aspects, such as the active participation in the political process and civic self-defence of the country, were present in the citizenship model of the Polish Gentry Republic in the sixteenth through to the eighteenth centuries and are still visible in the contemporary Swiss concept of the citizen in the uniform as well as in its strongly participative democracy model. The property rights-based liberal model of citizenship was developed in Great Britain by Locke and spread into the Anglo-Saxon world, supporting the early development of capitalism.[81] In contrast, the concept of caesarean citizenship emerged in Hobbes' works, having resulted from his experience of civil war in Britain. It matured in Carl Schmitt's writings, which in turn followed his disappointment with the instability of the German Republic of Weimar. Moreover, citizenship developed not only in different historical contexts, but it also related to different political regimes. Athenian polis, Roman Empire, Italian city-state, the nation-states, and eventually the European Union have generated different and diverging models of citizenship.[82]

Republican citizenship

The republican approach to citizenship focuses on the obligations of the citizens in a democratic community. On the one hand, it follows the idea that political participation is the way of realization of human good, since only political participation allows for an active liberty – that is, freedom to make laws that one can live by.[83] On the other hand, there is a clear moral prescription for the citizen to politically participate in the affairs of the community. The citizen is primarily a 'holder of duties' vis-à-vis the polity, as the holding of political office is regarded as a necessary burden resulting from the republican aversion to a permanent political class. Therefore, republican citizenship stresses the obligation component of all citizenship components (rights, obligations, compliance) the most.[84] Hence, the republican citizenship is not only active and participatory, but it rests on patriotic virtue.[85] This model of citizenship does not clearly differentiate between the society and the democratic polity; rather these two categories are merged.[86] The political community, which Aristotle called *koinonia politike*, is viewed by proponents of the republican model as the only appropriate way of life for an individual, since people are citizens by nature and only in the political community do they find their human and moral fulfilment. The polity possesses an ontological and ethical priority with respect to the individual.[87] The public space of the polity is radically different from the structure of the *oikos*, the private space, where individuals live along economic and egoistic principles.[88] In the modern (and continental European) version of the republican model of citizenship, the welfare state replaces the society based on slavery, in which the citizen possessed the time and the resources to actively participate for the sake of public interest.[89] In ancient Greece, this was possible since the everyday production and distribution of goods was carried out by slaves. The welfare state is supposed to fulfil the same functions regarding this model of citizenship by guaranteeing social security (by regulating labour time, allocating resources to the old and poor, and providing education for the future citizens).[90] The welfare state is thus a modern basis for the republican citizenship model, since the citizen has to be materially and socially independent in order to make political decisions dedicated to the common good.[91]

At the same time, the republican tradition in its Aristotelian version is anti-bureaucratic and patriotic.[92] As Michael Ignatieff points out, the republican tradition is directed against a permanent political class as well as against a professional army.[93] It implies for instance a rotation of political offices, allowing as many citizens as possible to accept responsibility for the polity. Furthermore, the readiness to defend one's own country (in the modern state it is embodied by military service) is a significant aspect of the republican model of citizenship.[94] In this way, the patriotic virtue of the citizen comes to the fore, since citizenship might become a burdensome and dangerous duty requiring even the sacrifice of life. This particular service to the polity is still relevant in present republican writings. For example, one of the leading republican thinkers of the post-war period, Raymond Aron, regards the military service of citizens as requisite for citizenship. According to Aron, political rights can be conceived of as a corollary of the duty of military service.[95]

Republican citizens are equal to one another, and each of them possesses qualities necessary to participate in the ruling of the polity.[96] This feature of republican citizenship is particularly visible in Rousseau's ideal of citizenship.[97] He rejects political representation, since all citizens must participate equally and continuously in all actions of the Sovereign.[98] In modern versions of republicanism, citizens pursue the public interest not only because of their insight that this is the only way of leading a good life. They also defend their specific model of society, in which the welfare state can demand sacrifices from the citizens as a price for the high living standards. Political participation therefore means not only self-fulfilment, but also a duty.

The essence of republican citizenship became visible in the controversy on e-voting, which is rejected by proponents of republicanism. They do this on the basis that voting is not a private matter, to be executed from a personal computer (PC) at home. It is first and foremost a public affair, requiring turning up at a public voting booth.[99] Online voting or voting using the short message service (SMS) moves the citizens' activity from the public space into their individual privacy, where citizens follow their private interests. In this way, the essential difference between *oikos* and *koinonia politike* vanishes, thus destroying the republican model of citizenship.[100]

The deliberative theory of democracy offers a postmodern, although curtailed, version of republicanism, based on the obligation component of citizenship. The essential element of the deliberative democracy theory is the argumentative exchange between equal citizens who engage in consensus building.[101] Deliberation rests on the principle of a continuous debate between citizens in which only the power of argument is expected to count. The debate should be free, open and fair, and it ought to guarantee equal access for every interested citizen. Deliberative theory excludes voting procedures, since citizens should debate until they reach a consensus.[102] The only way to influence the political outcome is through the debate in which only better arguments succeed. Those arguments must not, however, be based on selfish preferences, since the goal of deliberation is not only to solve common problems but also, often primarily, to find what the public good is. Correspondingly, the arguments ought to relate to the common good and public interest.[103] In this deliberative perspective, the model of citizenship is active and participatory and citizens should be committed to the *res publica*.[104] In this sense, citizens are obliged to share discursive ethics, rather than sacrifice their lives.[105] In addition, the deliberative conception of citizenship hopes for integrative effects of deliberation, particularly in divided societies.[106] Although unmistakably republican, deliberative theory cuts down the role of the citizen to a communicative process, whilst putting aside issues of voting, the holding of political office and further duties to the polity.[107] Nevertheless, it is, as is the entire republican tradition of citizenship, driven by the logic of shared obligations, from which moral resources, societal integration and collective identity are drawn.[108]

Liberal citizenship

The liberal model of citizenship is rights-based, in contrast to the obligations-orientated republican citizenship.[109] This results from a paradigm in which individuals are guided in their actions by private interests and passions, with politics being just one area besides economy, religion, culture, science etc. Public space does not possess any moral supremacy since political power comes into being by the voluntary decision of rational creatures.[110] The government function is neither to fulfil a supreme human good nor are citizens' actions subordinated to the shared public interest. The elected government's main role is to deter citizens' transgressions of other citizens' rights. The gravest of these are offences against individual freedom and property.[111] Any number of individuals can exercise political power collectively by electing a government and replacing it any time they please. The political community entrusts political power to a government consisting of deputies for the people – trustees who can be discarded if they fail their electors.[112] The government can therefore be dissolved when the governors neglect their tasks or act contrary to the will of the citizens.[113] The political community comes into being by the consent of every individual by way of the social contract, which has to be constructed in a manner fair to everybody. Against this background, citizens enjoy by and large *passive liberty*, which is expressed in terms of the rule of law. In other words, citizens are not necessarily interested in participation but rather in an undisturbed well-being. To put it provocatively, a liberal citizen is likely to be more interested in accumulation of wealth than in democracy, as opposed to his republican counterparts.[114] A liberal citizen could even choose to live under a despotic regime but under the rule of law – one which allows him the freedom to advance his affairs in private and guarantees the security of his property – rather than to live in a democracy accompanied by insecurity and disorder.[115]

The role of the citizen is for an individual merely one among many.[116] S/he is an economic creature living in a market-based society, the logic of which is mainly competition.[117] However, liberal citizens are not equal in the market. On the one hand, some individuals lose due to competition, and therefore lean towards the social taming of the market by state. On the other hand, there are winners in the market competition who in turn view themselves primarily as taxpayers. These two major roles are decisive for the self-definition of individuals as citizens in the liberal model of citizenship. In the *libertarian version* of this model, individuals are interested in a small government that acts effectively with regard to the tasks entrusted to it. This is because an expanding government functions beyond the necessary minimum, potentially endangering the freedom of citizens. In his radical theory of justice, Robert Nozick points out that redistribution of resources by the state in a free society without the consent of everybody inevitably leads to enslavement, as taxpayers are forced against their will to contribute to the welfare of strangers.[118] There is, therefore, an imminent threat from government to citizens' freedom, meaning that it is in citizens' best interests to keep the government at bay. For this reason, the government is only allowed to execute actions necessary for the production of common goods, which cannot be produced individually. Since the expansion of government tasks means higher taxes, citizens tend towards reducing the costs of state activity, particularly since the government is not indispensable for the functioning of the society. As David Hume put it:

> though government be an invention very advantageous, and even in some circumstances absolutely necessary to mankind; it is not necessary in all circumstances, nor is it impossible for men to preserve society for some time, without having recourse to such an invention.[119]

In the *social version*, liberal citizenship, unlike its republican counterpart, also excludes political hyperactivity, since the primary concern of citizens is more with their material existence than with self-fulfilment in the polity and the quest for common good. In this perspective, political rights guarantee only a formal equality without addressing real inequalities induced by the market. Therefore, social rights in addition to civil and political rights are viewed as a necessary component of citizenship. Among other things, they encompass health care services, and social security, as well as state investment in citizens' education.[120] In this version, citizens are also private *holders of rights* (especially rights to welfare) and have at the same time minimal responsibilities if any (first and foremost taxpaying) vis-à-vis the government. Common good is thus not essential in this model of citizenship, since the individual, as a citizen, remains a private person, faithful mainly to himself. S/he balances her/his different roles in society to realize her/his utility. Certainly, it does not exclude civic virtues such as individualism and pluralism, which are tenets of liberal citizenship. However, these virtues differ visibly from republican civic virtues. As a liberal citizen is a member of a pluralist society, government represents the interests of the majority, since it cannot reconcile the preferences of all its citizens. However, this is acceptable for the liberal citizen of the political minority, since the minority can potentially become a political majority after the next election. In general, the model of liberal citizenship exhibits difficulties with the notion of public interests. As Kenneth Arrow argues, an accumulation of individual interests into one public interest may not be possible.[121]

Caesarean citizenship

Whereas republican citizenship aims for the common good, and the liberal citizenship highlights the individual's rights and interests, the caesarean model of citizenship is regarded by its protagonists as a remedy against the decline of political order. Caesarean citizenship is based on the idea of the self-preservation of individuals who construct the state or/and acknowledge its total authority for the sake of protection against enemies. Against this background, caesarean citizenship highlights the compliance component of citizenship.

In the writings of Thomas Hobbes, the peacekeeping state is the result of consent between individuals who decide to permanently surrender political authority over themselves to *Leviathan*, the omnipotent ruler.[122] Individuals are unfit to live peacefully by themselves, as they cannot trust each other.[123] A strong ruler is thus regarded as the only solution to political chaos that would otherwise tear society apart and claim the lives of its citizens.[124]

However, with the conclusion of the contract of rule, citizens willingly surrender their political rights and pledge their obedience to the *Leviathan*.[125] Consequently, the ruler, like the Roman emperor Caesar, is free to make laws according to his will, even if capricious and despotic, for he guarantees the survival and security of his citizens. Moreover, Leviathan, or Caesar, possesses the ultimate authority of interpretation, since society suffers potentially from the chaos of different meanings, which begin, for example, with diverging interpretations of religious doctrines. Thus, in the case of the caesarean citizenship, we deal with the political and interpretational *decisionism*. Although citizens of the caesarean model are fully allowed to pursue their economic interests, politics is reduced to the arbitrary decisions of the ruler. As a consequence, the caesarean model of citizenship is not about the rights and obligations of citizens but about the effectiveness of political decisions and the compliance of the citizens who submit to an authority in the face of potential danger.

This train of thought had been further developed by Carl Schmitt in the first half of the twentieth century. According to Schmitt, the very essence of politics is the ability of citizens to think of the other in terms of 'enemies', to let themselves become politically mobilized and to make unanimous decisions. In his view, the democratic claim of equality cannot be resolved on the basis of liberal democracy that offers only temporary and occasional solutions to the existing problem of inequality. Whereas shifting majorities are sufficient for liberal citizens to cooperate with each other by entrusting the governors with political tasks, Schmitt regards it as mere *legality* as opposed to real *legitimacy*. Simple majorities cannot lay the claim to a general will. If the content of laws is decided by a majority of the people's representatives, for instance by a mere 51 per cent, it is not necessarily binding the large minority of 49 per cent. Therefore the majority becomes 'the state' itself, which leads to the tyranny of majority, a concern also expressed on many occasions by other political thinkers, most prominently by Alexis de Tocqueville.[126] Pre-legal and pre-constitutional means thus exist in order to come closer to the general will. Therefore, Carl Schmitt searches for answers pertaining to the question why individuals obey the laws besides the rational fear of sanctions. In his answer, he focuses on the collective acclamation of norms in which a homogeneous and concrete will of the demos manifests itself. Consequently, caesarean citizenship stresses the compliance component of citizenship, the subjecthood of the citizens and their fear-induced homogenization under the tutelage of the leader. The increasing bureaucratization of society gives presidential decrees a more enduring quality than the decisions of the parliament that only represent legislative majorities and which cannot claim to reflect the general will. As a result, the caesarean model of citizenship advocates non-parliamentary forms of political rule. Here, the relationship between the ruling and the ruled is defined in a top-down manner. It consequently redraws the boundaries of the political realm and rewrites the function of the citizen.

Only a decisive leader, who constructs the state legitimacy along the friend–enemy distinction, can guarantee the real equality of citizens, since solely by means of this distinction and in the presence of death and conflict can citizens feel responsibility for their own lives.[127] For the sake of political effectiveness, only the leader should possess the decisional authority, while the role of citizens is reduced to the confirmation of his decisions and compliance. This is a procedure similar to what Hobbes uses for legitimizing actions of Leviathan.[128] The ability to decide effectively in order to secure the survival and physical integrity of citizens is the Hobbesian criterion for state legitimacy.[129] However, political effectiveness can only be safeguarded when citizens accept the authority of the caesarean leader and comply with his decisions.[130] Shifting and thus transitory parliamentary majorities are incapable of delivering reliable, long-term policies, since political measures of one government are reversible after an electoral change. However, the state needs a stable authority in order to guarantee decisional efficiency.[131] In Schmitt's model of citizenship, the parliament attains only a derivative status in a system of plebiscitary procedures. As he puts it in the conclusion to *Legality and Legitimacy*:

> [t]he people can only respond yes or no. They cannot advise, deliberate, or discuss. They cannot set norms, but can only sanction norms by consenting to draft sets of norms laid before them. Above all, they also cannot pose a question, but can only answer with yes or no to a question placed before them. [132]

While the inefficiency and perhaps even a tyranny of the parliamentary majority poses a danger for the rule of the demos, the caesarean president in the ancient Roman manner redeems and rescues the decayed and corrupted republic. The president can rule using decrees, since qua direct legitimacy of the president they acquire a normative superiority. Due to his more legitimate decree-issuing power, he restores the power of law destroyed by the parliament. The laws issued by the president reflect the will of the entire people, while the parties in the parliament only threaten the popular unity. However, if they acclaim the president and his policies, they can be represented and embodied as a whole.[133]

Furthermore, Schmitt represents the view of political totality, since every aspect of societal life is potentially political, meaning that the enemy could be found everywhere, thus establishing the primacy of the political over other aspects of life.[134] While Hobbes primarily seeks the enemy within society, Schmitt instead highlights the importance of the friend–enemy distinction between the states.[135] According to Schmitt, institutions of liberal democracy should be replaced by a myth of homogeneity and the conjuration of homogeneity by citizens. On the one hand, democracy is not possible without a collective perception of homogeneity and without the unconditional belief by citizens in the legitimacy of the leader who represents the state. On the other hand, the leader guarantees the decisional effectiveness of the state, since he possesses the ultimate decisional authority (the approach of Schmitt is therefore labelled decisionism). The political role of the citizen thus confines itself to a confirmation through acclamation of the leader's decisions, which shifts the focus onto the compliance component of citizenship.

In the post-9/11 version, caesarean citizenship stresses security politics as the major concern of the state. Security politics become the basis for the collective identity construction, as the state increasingly uses technologies of surveillance and shifts the focus from a rights-orientated citizenship to neurotic citizenship.[136] A neurotic citizen defines politics in terms of its permanent insecurity, which can only be guaranteed by the state. His preference for liberty and freedom becomes surpassed by his fears of survival in view of organized criminality and possible terrorist attacks; collective identity thus becomes securitized.[137] In addition, the activity of the citizen focuses more strongly on reporting potentially dangerous situations and spying on his compatriots, rather than on elections, public space and ensuring the accountability of the government.[138] Consequently, the state producing collective identity is inclined to perpetuate the feeling of insecurity, thus transforming security politics into politics of insecurity.[139] As a result, the state demonstrates its indispensability (and thus legitimacy), whereas the fear-inclined citizens support the state almost unconditionally. In this way, a shared perception of danger and threat generates the feeling of homogeneity. However, it is not only a diffuse feeling of insecurity that is instigated as result of identity technologies; governments are instead likely to give the enemy a face and a name. Beyond terrorists and criminals, migrants and minorities can be used as a negative point of reference for caesarean citizenship and its homogenization practices.[140]

Citizenship models and collective identity

In this section, I argue that besides the diverging perspectives on what constitutes citizenship, the three outlined models of citizenship indicate quite different notions of collective identity. Whereas liberal citizenship is associated with a weak collective identity based on a similar rationality of citizens, the caesarean citizenship indicates perceptual homogeneity rather than collective identity in the sense described above.

Only the *republican model of citizenship* is accompanied by a *strong and resilient collective identity*. More precisely, it cannot exist without it. Republican citizenship not only requires civic altruism, but also the civic commitment to public interest.[141] The We–I balance of a republican citizen evens out on the We-component, which leads to an ethical subordination of private interests to the public space, since politics equals general commitment to the *res publica*. The republican citizenship therefore highlights civic obligations and responsibilities and underplays rights and compliance components of citizenship. However, it does not indicate any totalitarian domination of the political over any other aspects of life, as there is a strict separation between *koinonia politike* and *oikos*. Nonetheless, there is a cult of commonness in the public space, from which private matters are excluded. However, this commonness is not necessarily based on the similarity of citizens.[142] Citizens are allowed to interpret the public good differently. We can therefore point to a strong civic collective identity in the case of republican citizenship. Despite the accentuation of commonness, the republican model of citizenship is relatively open to everybody who accepts the rules of the democratic game. At the same time, the citizen shares with others the same philosophy of striving towards the human good through politics. Civic collective identity develops qua participation in the political process in which citizens become socialized in their acceptance of political obligations according to the public interest. Additionally, republican citizenship means common rule of equal citizens, since there is a strong anti-elitist aspect in this model.[143] As a result, collective identity has a strong horizontal dimension, as citizens rule themselves and perceive themselves as compatriots. They are obliged not only to defend the territorial integrity of the polity, but also to defend their compatriots or to act in accordance with their interests.[144] Simultaneously, the strong collective identity emanating from civic spirit makes free-riding relatively irrelevant, since citizenship is not about acquiring wealth and privilege, but first and foremost about obligations towards polity and community. Citizens are prone to moral actions towards their compatriots including loyalty, solidarity and sacrifice. These moral actions can become enriched with emotional attachments, which transcend republican responsibilities as of purely moral nature without replacing them.[145]

In the deliberative version of republican citizenship, political responsibilities of citizens primarily cover common discourse ethics pertaining to the common good orientation.[146] There is no voting in deliberative settings, since the actors are expected to debate until they reach a consensus. Additionally, no participant has the power to veto or delay the agreement. The only way to influence the outcome is through the debate in which only better arguments succeed. Those arguments must, however, relate to public interest, since the goal of deliberation is both to find what the public good is and to solve common problems. The core of deliberation is argument comprising persuasion and the convincing of others, since every participant must be ready to hear all arguments and to change his or her position and view when convinced. Most of the contemporary republican authors integrate deliberative elements into their republican models. It therefore seems that the deliberative arguments become anchored in the recent models of republicanism or perhaps will even replace the more traditional elements of republicanism such as the sacrifice-orientated national republicanisms of the nineteenth and twentieth centuries.[147] In the deliberative republicanism, public justification becomes a burden and a responsibility equal to moral obligations in more traditional versions of republicanism.[148] But even without moral obligations, deliberation is supposed to change citizens' minds to more collectivistic ones, as individuals become socialized during public deliberation, even though it is far from certain what competences the deliberative citizen should possess.[149]

The republican model of citizenship provides for strong horizontal and vertical collective identity, as there are special bonds among the compatriots and moral responsibilities towards each other. Even though the model stresses citizen activity and rotation of political offices, a more permanent political class of decision-makers may be acceptable for republican citizens. Still, they are regarded as representatives of the community acting in its best interests. Hence, the greatest danger for the republic is corruption of the political class, which can alienate itself from the community and degenerate into an oligarchy.[150]

Although open in principle, the civic and assimilatory collective identity of republican citizenship shows ambivalence towards multicultural societies.[151] On the one hand, some republican authors consider cultural heterogeneity a threat to the public interest, especially if minority groups enjoy special privileges, for instance in forms of affirmative action.[152] They argue that only the state can socialize the individuals into citizens. Responsible citizenship therefore cannot arise in the context of ethnic and religious minorities. At best, ethnic minorities might want to escape their civic responsibility as in the case of the passively law-abiding Amish People, who refuse to actively participate in the public space. At worst, ethnic minorities could undermine civic commitment to public interest by promoting loyalty towards the minority.[153] The state should therefore either compensate these insufficiencies of collective identity by using the state educational system and/or intervene in the inner structure of minority groups in order to extinguish particularistic attitudes and undemocratic practices. Special minority rights lead, in this view, to 'politicization of ethnicity', which is counterproductive in respect of civic collective identity. Ethnic minorities, particularly those endowed with special privileges, could promote a spiral of inter-group competition, distrust and antagonism.[154] Since the existence of ethnic minorities promotes fragmented identities, most republican authors regard them as a challenge to the citizenship identity. Nevertheless, some scholars argue to the contrary, namely that voluntary organizations, and ethnic and religious groups, might be considered schools of citizenship.[155] Through social interaction, individuals learn norms of reciprocity and thus adapt the civic 'habits of heart'. Consequently, special minority rights could foster civic collective identity by preventing the particular identities of minority groups from 'freezing'. In this perspective, the domination of the majority culture, which is imposed on minorities as the general basis for collective identity, can promote the feeling of vulnerability in minority groups, thereby strengthening particularistic and fragmented identities.[156] This could in turn hinder the participation of minorities in the public space and consequently discourage their commitment to the public interest. Advocates of this view support minority rights and also the so-called 'mirrored representation', according to which political institutions should reflect the ethnic composition of societies.[157] Public recognition of minority groups, and support for their identities, is supposed to foster their confidence in civic interaction and thus woo them to participate as equal citizens.[158] Conversely, minorities with an unclear status are more anxious and more defensive of their particular culture. Consequently, it could lead to the alienation of those minorities from the *collective citizenship identity*. This argument also applies to the deliberative variants of republicanism, in which a sincere public deliberation under the circumstances of cultural heterogeneity is either doubted or techniques such as inverse deliberation (using common good arguments only from the cultural context of the interlocutor) are allowed.[159] Regardless of whether more assimilationist or pluralist arguments are applied, both perspectives remain sensitive to the republican considerations for integrative identity, which is linked to a participative and common good orientated image of citizenship.

In comparison to the strong collective identity of republican citizenship, the *liberal model of citizenship* is associated with a notion of *weak collective identity*.[160] Whereas republican citizens are responsible members of a political community, liberal citizens are envisaged in a society of individuals.[161] Participation in the political process is, in the liberal model, not constitutive for being citizens. Politics is merely one of a plethora of various areas in which citizens construct their broad spectrum of preferences, although there is a meta-preference for cost sensitivity that plays an important role in deciding on the hierarchy of preferences. The We–I balance of a liberal citizen evens out on the I-component, which leads to an I–We-identity with no supremacy of the political community vis-à-vis the individual, as citizenship is about pre-political natural rights and (dis)trust towards the government.[162] Every individual enjoys natural rights, which may be infringed by others.[163] The main function of the government is thus to hinder the infringement of natural rights and punish legal transgressions by individuals. Therefore, there is no indication for a strong horizontal collective identity in the liberal model of citizenship.[164] In most cases, individuals are sufficiently reasonable to understand that only through cooperation are they able to realize their preferences, hence the belief in the workings of the market as an embodiment of freedom. In this case, we can point *at the most* to a weak or thin collective identity, which is anchored in the same rationality (or reasonableness) of citizens, but this identity is not *politically collective* in the sense of commitment to public good. We would rather point to a similarity in endowment of rationality between the citizens than to a political collective identity.[165]

Notwithstanding this thick or weak collective identity of liberal citizenship, there are variants of liberal thought highlighting so-called liberal virtues, which are necessary to sustain a liberal society. However, these virtues question mostly the collectivist orientation of the republican collective identity by stressing individualism, pluralism and toleration. For William A. Galston, for instance, liberal citizenship is more than the mere pursuit of self-interest, since '... [it] has its own distinctive restraints-virtues that circumscribe and check, without wholly nullifying, the promptings of self-aggrandizement'. However, the liberal virtues exhibit on the one hand a counter-collectivist twist, which leads to a strong I-accentuation in the We–I balance, and on the other they are 'meta-virtues', as liberal citizenship supports value pluralism.[166]

Even with liberal virtues or similar rationality, liberal citizens face dilemmas of collective action that can be resolved, for instance, by government interventions.[167] Those interventions refer to collective goods that cannot by and large be produced by individuals, as they are confronted by, among other things, the free-rider dilemma.[168] On the one hand, taxation is needed to finance state activity, but on the other hand excessive taxation is unacceptable, precisely because of the weakness of collective identity between individual citizens. In addition, there is weak collective identity between individuals and government, since the government is merely an instrument with responsibility to 'good governance'. What connects the rulers with the ruled is a temporary trust, which can disappear quickly when the government fails the citizens. In this model, it is the government that has obligations to citizens rather than *vice versa*. Furthermore, government is not to be regarded as self-government, but rather a temporary delegation of power for the sake of rationally motivated cooperation. The temporary and specific trust to the government is accompanied by a general distrust among citizens of the rulers. For this reason, the separation of powers plays an important role within the liberal model of citizenship. Within this model, citizens generally distrust the delegated rulers to act in the general interest. There is therefore an in-built mechanism that should impair power abuse. Such a mechanism against power abuse would be, however, against the republican logic of citizenship in which citizens trust each other by default. In contrast, the rights-based citizenship, almost deprived of any substantial duties, focuses on the legal status of citizens. In this sense, it highlights the rights-component of citizenship and underplays obligations and compliance. Liberal citizenship indicates equal status for all citizens, which can be legally claimed. However, these rights do not result from any collective identity, nor do they stem from participation in the political process. According to John Locke, rights are God-given, while in the classical typology of T. H. Marshall (encompassing civil, political and social rights – undeniable to any citizen) rights in turn result from historical sequence, based on a linear evolution of modern society.[169] Other authors claim the necessary extension of the rights proposed by Marshall, arguing that it arises from reasonable decisions of individuals reacting to societal changes. For example, some use the term 'technological citizenship', which addresses the new technological issues of modern society, such as environment policy or hazardous and energy supply-related political decisions.[170] This issue is a reaction to the fact that political decisions in modern societies are barely reversible in respect of complex and relevant technologies (e.g. use of nuclear energy). Technological citizenship would therefore indicate rights of popular approval (in comparison to a decision by government) regarding technologies that are difficult to reverse as a result of their complexity and sunk-costs investments. Some other authors argue in a similar way, albeit with regard to the 'ecological citizenship'.[171] They focus on the right of citizens to water supply, supposedly endangered by its commercialization. In modern variants of liberal citizenship, rights result from the insight of citizens into the changing structure of society, and thus into the necessity of addressing new societal problems in a specific way. Against this background, collective identity is not what connects individuals in the form of emotional belonging or a mutual responsibility, but it is rather the same basic motivation to realize interests and passions (albeit different ones) as well as the ability for rational decision-making of citizens that allows for cooperation in the market-like society. Liberal virtues of toleration, individualism and pluralism additionally support the I-component of We–I balance, which stresses weak/thick collective identity.

Irrespective of the strength of the collective identity, republican and liberal citizenship differ with regard to the *object* of collective identity. For the republican collective identity, the point of reference is the community of citizens who engage in mutual obligations, responsibilities and duties. Consequently, republican citizenship emphasizes group identity, whereas liberal citizenship highlights identification with rights and the institutions that sustain them, rather than compatriots. The liberal relation towards other citizens is a neutral one, and towards the ruling elite a suspicious one. Therefore, in the context of the liberal citizenship we would point to *identification* with rights, rather than *identification* or *identity* with others. However, not every type of rights has the same power in generating identity. Chris Hilson distinguishes between fundamental, community and citizenship rights and their different identity-generating functions. He departs from a liberal understanding of collective identity, defining it as identification with a given polity through rights. However, he criticizes the idea that fundamental rights and citizenship rights would have the power to generate identification, since they are associated with passive citizenship. Fundamental rights and citizenship rights are linked to judiciability and their enforcement leaves little space for citizens' activity and practice. But only rights in practice, i.e. community rights, could shape civic collective identity, as they bolster the agency aspect of identity. However, with this active understanding of community rights, Hilson adopts the republican vision of citizenship, which stresses the activist, engaged and civic identity of citizens. In other words, he doubts the identity-generating capability of liberal citizenship and views the potential of civic identity in the community-accentuated citizenship.[172]

In contrast, the *caesarean model of citizenship* shows features of strong collective identity as it is discussed in the cognitive perspective, but it is hardly collective identity in the political sense, as referred to above.[173] In the case of caesarean citizenship, we should instead refer to homogeneity with regard to common perceptions of danger and insecurity.[174] We can point to a rise of collectivism as an 'identity-signifier', as it becomes a response to insecurity and provokes attempts of reaffirmation of self-identity by approaching any collectivity that is expected to decrease insecurity and existential anxiety. Hobbesian contract of rule occurs on the basis of a homogeneous perception of threat. The motivation of the individuals is based on self-interest of survival, in which public interest is not a relevant factor, and nor does the identical perception of threat result in the joining of common resources, which could in turn cause general commitment to public interest.[175] As a result of general distrust and fear of each other (thus inability to cooperate), reasonable individuals instead renounce their right to self-determination and transfer their power to a third party. Consequently, there is neither collective identity in the state of nature, nor is there one evolving after the establishment of the Leviathan. After the instalment of the state, there is only one behavioural option for the citizens, which is obedience to authority, stemming from the contractual obligations of citizens.[176] Therefore, caesarean citizenship highlights the compliance component of citizenship and underplays rights and obligations. By means of the transfer of rights and obligations, citizens withdraw from every controversial public activity (including public expression of religious beliefs) that might cause conflict between them. Therefore, the homogeneity of the caesarean society radically increases after the installation of the state. However, commitment to public interest is only relevant in decisions of the Leviathan/Caesar, not the citizens, since there is no public space, and citizens are not free to take political decisions. As the legitimacy of the Leviathan/Caesar rests on his ability to sustain the internal peacekeeping function of the state, his commitment to public interest is an instrumental one. Consequently, there is no vertical collective identity in the caesarean model of citizenship. In Hobbesian theory, Leviathan is a body foreign to the society (himself not subject to the social contract) to guarantee the problem-solving capacity of the state. Consequently, Leviathan is legitimized solely by the effectiveness of his performance. However, in the Schmittian version of caesarean citizenship, this alien position of the leader undergoes a change, since the leader is regarded as the chosen one of the people for the sake of the people. Nonetheless, the leader manipulates the masses in order to guarantee his decisiveness and the masses accept the leader, as long as he can guarantee their security. In Schmitt's concept of the political, there is an even more explicit requirement of societal homogeneity of fear, as the societal plurality is to be suppressed by different methods. On the one hand, the friend–enemy distinction serves this purpose, since facing a threat gives the citizens the necessary motivation to mobilize against the enemy, while homogeneity of the people is forged in the process. The mobilizing role of the leader is thereby of great importance. On the other hand, society must be able to remove alien elements from its own 'tissue'. Whereas the republican citizenship is open for assimilation, caesarean citizenship instead isolates and removes alien elements. The perception of the other as the enemy leads to the establishment of homogeneity between citizens. In the process, homogeneity of society and the decisiveness of the state influence each other. Since there seems to be an imminent threat to the existence of citizens, the state must be able to make decisions; that is, to show political effectiveness. However, this effectiveness can be only safeguarded when the citizens accept the authority of the caesarean leader. Therefore, citizenship indicates a top-down relationship between the leader and the masses, in which there is no intersubjectivity between the citizens, since they are indistinguishable and depersonalized members of the masses who are convinced of their equality only in the face of a common threat. In this sense, the commonness is constructed only vis-à-vis external subjects, thus lacking horizontal orientation. In the post-9/11 world, the confrontational dichotomy of the caesarean citizenship does not run along the lines of citizen/non-citizen difference, as is the case in the cognitive perspective on collective identity. Instead, it highlights the difference between the citizen and the suspect. Therefore, the caesarean identity technology does not exhaust itself in the process of categorization, but it uses the very identifying process to strengthen collective responses and compliance. As biometric technologies and new methods of surveillance are employed to advance the restrictive practices of the caesarean citizenship, the goal of citizens and government agencies had become to secure identity.[177] We can therefore refer neither to horizontal nor vertical collective identity in the political sense. Citizens become mobilized by the leaders whenever they need citizens' support for the predetermined decisions. Collective identity as a commitment to public interest is visible only in the actions of the leaders who are supposed to ensure the survival of the polity. However, with regard to the collective body of citizens, we should point more to homogeneity than to a collective identity. Citizens are regarded as members of a political church (demos becomes ecclesia) to which they declare their belief and loyalty, and – unlike republican citizens – are not engaged in public discourse.

However, as Table 4.2 shows, there is a difference between collective identity in the liberal and caesarean model, even if both models score low on collective identity. Liberal citizens exhibit no extreme distrust towards each other, even though there are no strong community bonds among them. The distrust of the liberal citizen is directed against the government, as a potential source of power abuse. However, there is enough trust among liberal citizens to envisage that other individuals do not pose a permanent threat to their survival. While in the republican model we are confronted with the notion of civic friendship, liberal co-citizens are neither friends nor foes. In contrast, caesarean citizens distrust each other to such a degree that a third party becomes entrusted with the task of securing peace among people fearing each other. The neurotic citizen therefore cooperates with the state as guarantor of his security, rather than with other citizens who are potential foes and suspects. Consequently, the ability of caesarean citizens to act collectively in expectation of decreasing their insecurity and existential anxiety is greater than in the liberal model. However, it does not imply that horizontal collective identity in the caesarean model is stronger than in the liberal model, as caesarean citizens tend towards stronger collectivization. Nonetheless, this horizontal identity is weak in terms of citizenship identity as it is based on fear, rather than on more strongly pervasive forms of attachments. The weakness of the vertical dimension in collective identity is even more apparent in the caesarean model. In the liberal model, common good orientations of individuals are not very probable, but not excluded, since the selfish interest realization of the liberal citizen is embedded in liberal virtues of toleration, individualism and liberty. In contrast, the caesarean citizenship feeds on the perception of insecurity and anxiety by the citizens; the bonds of the community are not derived from moral resources, nor are produced by them. Although the caesarean model exhibits a certain notion of collective preservation, even if for selfish reasons, after the pact with the state is closed, collectivism of the neurotic citizen can be only maintained through a politics of permanent insecurity.[178] Therefore, we should identify in both models a lack of common good orientation, which contrasts with the notion of vertical collective identity. Therefore, the caesarean model scores even lower than the liberal citizenship on the strength of collective identity.

In addition, the caesarean citizenship relates to a different object of identity. Whereas republican citizenship stresses in-group bonds and liberal citizenship emphasizes identification with rights, caesarean citizenship fosters a faith and trust in Leviathan or Caesar. The relationship between the citizens (or rather subjects) and the Caesar does not exactly point to an identity, since the Caesar is a father figure rather than a representative of the people. He is the saviour of the people and the head of the political ecclesia who possess the supremacy of interpretation and decision. The citizens subordinate willingly with regard to his decisions and support him with acclamation. Therefore, it is the acclamation that unifies the Leader with his neurotic citizens seeking to be saved, rescued and defended against the many dangers of their insecure existence. Consequently, the Caesar remains the sole point of reference for the collectivist impulses of the citizens, rather than the community or rights.

Recapitulation

In this chapter I proposed my argument about the citizenship–collective identity nexus. First, departing from various deficits of the functional approaches to collective identity,

Table 4.2 Scoring models on collective identity

Citizenship	Horizontal orientation of collective identity	Vertical orientation of collective identity
Republican	+	+
Liberal	–	–
Caesarean	–	–

it focused on the integrative workings of citizenship by placing the notion of citizenship identity at the heart of the concept of collective identity. Citizenship identity as political collective identity was conceived of as a layer of commonness among citizens (horizontal orientation), which entails general commitment to public interest (vertical orientation). In contrast to citizenship uniformity, citizenship identity can vary in its degree of resilience (thin versus thick identity). Second, the argument referred to generic models of citizenship, which include republican, liberal and caesarean citizenship. These models highlight each of the citizenship components (rights, obligations, compliance). Third, the argument linked generic models of citizenship to different forms of collective identity/citizenship identity.

The chapter argued that precisely this differentiation between types of citizenship and their corresponding collective identities is crucial for the analysis of citizenship–collective identity nexus. Whereas liberal citizenship is associated with a weak collective identity based on a similar rationality of citizens, the caesarean citizenship indicates perceptual homogeneity rather than political collective identity. Only the republican model of citizenship is accompanied by a strong and resilient collective identity.

The We–I balance of a republican citizen evens out on the We-component, which leads to an ethical subordination of private interests to the public space. The republican citizenship therefore highlights civic obligations and responsibilities and underplays rights and compliance components of citizenship. The We–I balance of a liberal citizen evens out on the I-component, which leads to an I–We identity with no supremacy of the political community vis-à-vis the individual, as citizenship is about pre-political natural rights and distrust towards the government. In the case of caesarean citizenship, we should instead refer to homogeneity with regard to common perceptions of danger and insecurity. We can point to a rise of collectivism as an 'identity-signifier', as it becomes a response to insecurity and provokes attempts of reaffirmation of self-identity. In this sense, caesarean citizenship scores negatively on both the horizontal and vertical orientation of political collective identity, even though it is associated with identity politics of fear and insecurity.

This analytical framework will be applied in Chapter 5 to explore citizenship and collective identity in Europe. In the context of collective identity variance, we can point particularly to the *expectations–outcome gap*, which is a mismatch between the expected identity and the identity technologies utilized by the authorities. If different types of citizenship are associated with specific collective identities, ill-conceived identity politics would generate an expectations–outcome gap, rather than produce stable collective identity in tune with its citizenship model.

5 European citizenship and European collective identity

In the following section I will sketch the development of European citizenship up to this point in time. This section is thought of as an illustration of the theoretical argument proposed in Chapter 4 and simultaneously as a form of opening for the ensuing three empirical sections dealing with the current trends in European citizenship and European identity politics.

The main empirical sections are organized in tune with the typology of citizenship models including republican, liberal and caesarean citizenship. First, I will discuss the EU's republican attempts to engage in discursive ethics within the Constitutional Convention. In the process, I will offer an examination of the republican citizenship and republican identity politics in the Convention. Second, I will discuss the liberal model of European citizenship mainly with regard to the Charter of Fundamental Rights of the European Union. At this point, I will focus on the possibilities of the generation of a European collective identity on the basis of rights. Third, I will examine current trends in the EU's caesarean citizenship and caesarean identity politics. Here, I will discuss the development of the European Leviathan and the EU's politics of insecurity.

The development of European citizenship

European citizenship developed in stages during the entire process of European integration. Only as a result of the Maastricht Treaty in 1993 was the Union citizenship established. It was reaffirmed in the Treaty of Nice in 2000. The Union citizenship denominates a derivative status, which is contingent on the member state citizenship. The Amsterdam Treaty of 1999 even insisted on the supplementary role of Union citizenship, whose goal is notto replace national citizenship but only to extend territorially a pool of certain rights. Union citizenship covers four main rights, including passive and active entitlements. Union citizens have the right to move freely among and stay in other member states. They enjoy protection in non-EU countries by the diplomatic representatives of any other member state, in case one's own country is not represented. Moreover, Union citizenship encompasses political rights, such as the right to vote and run in local and European Parliament elections in the country of residence. In addition, European citizens have the right to petition the European Parliament and the European Ombudsperson.

With regard to the models of citizenship discussed in Chapter 4, I suggest that European citizenship has been hitherto a mixture of the caesarean and the liberal model, which supersede each other leading to a hybrid model of citizenship. Originally, the European Community (EC) evolved according to the *caesarean model of citizenship*.

It was established as a peacekeeping mechanism to prevent war between Germany and France, exactly as Hobbes would have recommended it. The mutual and historically anchored distrust between France and Germany had led to a pooling of sovereignty and its partial delegation to a third party, which was the EC. This mechanism has evolved over the years into influential leadership of the Franco-German tandem, without which it is believed a stagnation of European integration and incapacity to solve problems in European affairs would have occurred. However, it was not the only cause for the success of the EC. Hobbesian effectiveness in the first decades of the European project had led to the *permissive consensus*, which had excluded citizens from the decision-making process in the EC, with the approval of the citizens themselves.[1] The permissive consensus had meant a general compliance with decisions made by the EU, although the EU regulated citizens' lives to an ever higher degree, since an increasing amount of legislative activity occurred at the European level. Therefore, compliance of Europeans enhanced the decisional capability of the EC by excluding citizens as important veto players.[2] Furthermore, the EU's caesarean effectiveness was additionally strengthened by the emergence of an enemy and competitor, which was in tune with Carl Schmitt's postulates. The Eastern Bloc not only posed a threat to the political and physical survival of Western Europe (which has been shown in numerous confrontations inside and outside Europe), but it was until the beginning of the 1970s also regarded as a viable economic alternative, with high economic growth rates.[3] Against this background, European integration rescued the Western nation-states by enhancing their economic effectiveness and making them capable of better responding to their citizens' welfare demands. As Alan S. Milward puts it, 'integration was not the supersession of the nation-state by another form of governance as the nation-state became incapable, but was the creation of the European nation-states themselves for their own purpose, an act of national will'.[4] However, it was an act of national will without the participation of citizens. As a result of the threat from the East, as well as effectiveness enhancement of the nation-states, the EC acquired its legitimacy.

The first steps towards a *liberal model of citizenship* in the EC took place at the Paris summit in 1972, at which the necessity of gap narrowing between the EC and its citizens was stated. The heads of states and governments established in Paris that the first stage of European citizenship had to include mobility for students, the exchange of teachers and the harmonization of diplomas. As a result of the Paris summit the Council began to launch new policy instruments including the 'passport policy', aimed at the introduction of an EC passport, and took steps towards the abolition of border controls within the EC.[5] With the adoption of the Single European Act in 1986, the EC undertook measures against discriminatory national regulations and expanded the scope of free movement of citizens.

Even though in the official statements there were references to the term 'citizen', citizens themselves were neither consulted to approve of the decisions of the political elites, nor were they granted political rights in the process. Despite the expansion of certain rights, the caesarean orientation of European citizenship remained strong. While the permissive consensus left the destiny of emerging European citizens in the hands of the state elites, the construction of the European citizen was applied instrumentally by the European state elites. The goal of the construction of the European citizen was to remedy the inability of European states to cope with economic crises and the surge of mass unemployment. The oil crisis in 1973 and the breakdown of the Bretton Woods system of global economic management revealed the institutional inefficacy of the EU and showed the limitations of the welfare state in Europe. Against this background, the European Commission saw the necessity for a European identity that would strengthen Europe's assertion vis-à-vis the rest of the world.[6] In addition, the citizens' programme of the EC (established at the Fontainebleau summit in 1984), was the consequence of the realization of the technocratic project of internal market liberalization, rather than a shift towards democratization of the EU and strengthening of the citizenship. Since the right to move freely within the EC was regarded as advantageous for the economic goals of the EU, the establishment of the rights of free movement and residence was treated by EU decision-makers as means to economic goals rather than for the sake of genuine rights. Furthermore, the EU has remained strongly executive-orientated even until today, which suggests caesarean workings of the EU. Sonja Puntscher Riekmann points in this context to the emergence of the EU's supranational executive as an agent who is free from his democratic principal and rules in an uncontrolled manner.[7] In this sense, the EU leans strongly towards the Hobbesian perspective of the Leviathan, as the claim of democratic legitimacy in the EU has been replaced by the rule of law, which is per se not necessarily legitimate. Nonetheless, the ruled comply with the decisions of an effective ruler to implement the law, who in turn attempts to legitimize itself qua legislative output.

Only in the beginning of the 1990s did the first difficulties of caesarean citizenship occur in the EU. The end of the cold war posed a serious challenge to the caesarean elements in European citizenship, as the EU not only lost its geopolitical *raison d'être*, but also faced demands of accession from its former enemies and competitors. Only against this background has the issue of democratic deficit been put on the EU agenda. The European summit in Maastricht in 1991 decided to extend the pool of citizens' rights to include political rights to vote and to stand as candidates in municipal elections and elections to the European Parliament. Nevertheless, the involvement of citizens in the process of granting them political rights occurred in the Schmittian form of an acclamation of decisions previously taken by the elites. Even though the Treaty of European Union was rejected in Denmark in 1992, it was ratified in another referendum one year later as a result of an intensely pro-European campaign conducted by the Danish government. The EU has used the acclamation procedure eagerly ever since. The failed ratification of the Nice Treaty in the Irish referendum in 2001 led to another referendum, in which the Irish population decided per acclamation to ratify the same treaty, also as a consequence of a pro-European campaign by the Irish government. The Irish referendum on the Lisbon Treaty that failed in 2007 will probably be held again in 2009. Failed referenda in France and the Netherlands on the Constitutional Treaty in 2005 were circumvented by a parliamentary ratification of the Lisbon Treaty.

However, since 1991 much more emphasis has also been put on the rights of the citizens, which led to a more *liberal accentuation* of European citizenship. This has culminated in the work of the European Convention, which delivered the Charter of Fundamental Rights in 2001. Although there is a stronger focus on citizens' rights in the Charter of Fundamental Rights, there are controversies surrounding liberal elements in the European citizenship. One of them relates to the judiciability of the Charter of Fundamental Rights. Even though the Charter of Fundamental Rights contains fifty-four articles devoted to defining rights and freedoms, the nature of those rights, and particularly their judiciability, is ambiguous. Even though the Charter already presents an interpretational framework for the courts, it is controversial whether it can function as a source of law in terms of judiciability of rights.

Regarding the *republican model of citizenship*, as opposed to a plethora of rights (judiciable or not), Union citizens have virtually no obligations in the traditional civic sense. On the one hand, the EU does not require any substantive public engagement from the European citizens. Despite the political rights, there is a very low turnout at the European elections, notwithstanding the fact that voting for the European Parliament is viewed as a reaction of citizens to national issues, rather than an expression of European contestation and participation. On the other hand, there is virtually no political discourse on European public interest among European citizens that violates the core postulates of the republican citizenship. This republican deficiency is illustrated best by the debate on the Constitutional Treaty in the EU in 2005. The debates in France and the Netherlands, where the Constitutional Treaty was rejected, did not relate to the Constitutional Treaty per se, but rather to national issues with limited references to the provisions of the European Constitution. Instead, the Constitutional Treaty became a projection surface for controversial societal problems in member states as well as an object of manifestation for latent and new conflicts in the EU (such as the limitation of the right of free movement or the issue of a single currency). The citizens in France therefore did not discuss the content of the European Constitution, but the French model of society instead, which they view as endangered in the face of globalization and economic liberalization. Nor did the debate on the Constitutional Treaty in the Netherlands relate much to the constitution document. Rather, the citizens in Holland preferred to discuss the limitations of tolerance following the assassinations of two political figures.

However, there are new republican expectations concerning the Convention method in the EU, which are directed at strengthening certain aspects of republican citizenship in the EU. This will be discussed in the following section, which considers the current trends of republican citizenship in the EU.

Republican citizenship and the pathologies of deliberation

The republican approach to citizenship focuses on the obligations of the citizens in a democratic community. It is associated not only with moral prescriptions for the citizen to actively participate in the affairs of the community, but also with his commitment to the good of the community. As the citizen is primarily a 'holder of duties' towards the polity, republican citizenship stresses the obligation component in the citizenship triangle of rights, obligations and compliance.

In this context, the deliberation theory of democracy offers a version of republicanism where citizens are expected to share discursive ethics, rather than to sacrifice their lives, as they exchange arguments in the public space according to the requirements of communicative rationality: their arguments ought to relate to the common good and public interest. Thus, in this deliberative perspective, the model of citizenship is active, participatory and republican. The link between republicanism and the deliberation theory of democracy is stressed by several contemporary political theorists. For instance, Cass Sunstein argues that the best thing about republican thought is its commitment to deliberative democracy.[8] In this sense, the promise of deliberative democracy to produce morally justifiable solutions to common problems is based on the republican notion of mutual respect, recognition among citizens as equals and their commitment to shared discourse ethics. Therefore, Sunstein describes deliberative democracy as a 'republic of reasons', in which arguing and reason-giving play crucial roles.[9]

In addition, the deliberative conception of citizenship is associated with civic virtues that are believed to have integrative effects. This entails a republican notion of collective identity that leads to an ethical subordination of private interests to the public space as a result of citizens' commitment to the *res publica*. Whereas republican citizenship highlights civic responsibilities, it plays down the rights and compliance components of citizenship. Therefore, the autonomy of deliberative citizens is political or civic, rather than individualistic, as is the case with liberal citizenship. Moreover, we can trace deliberation theory to the classical republicanism of Aristotle, where the ability for public reasoning makes humans political animals.[10]

With regard to the EU, deliberation theory has experienced a surge in attention and research in the last ten years. Jürgen Neyer, as a leading representative of the EU deliberation research, posits even a 'deliberative turn' in the EU studies, suggesting that deliberation theory has become a new research paradigm on the one hand and that deliberation practices are a new feature of EU governance on the other.[11] The researchers' interest in deliberation settings is that they are expected not only to produce legitimate political decisions, but also by virtue of their democratic quality generate a sort of civic collective identity. In this sense, we deal here with claims of republican citizenship. The most prominent case of deliberative politics in the EU is considered the so-called convention method. In contrast to other deliberative perspectives on the EU, the convention method relates strongest to republican citizenship, whereas other approaches focus on well-informed and consensus-seeking communication processes in expert committees or in the entire EU as a complex negotiation system.[12] These approaches, however, are interested in efficiency of European decision-making, rather than in democratic decision-making processes in the form of republican citizenship.[13]

Against this background, I will explore the tenets of the republican citizenship in its deliberative version regarding the convention method in the European Union. In the process, I will refer to recent experience with the convention method applied within the Convention on the Charter of Fundamental Rights (1999/2000) and the Convention on the Future of the European Union (2002/2003), with particular emphasis on the latter. In the debate on the European constitution, many contributors praise the convention method of decision-making as a breakthrough in the European quest for democratization.[14] Many argue that the institutional set-up and procedures of the Convention show a deliberative character, openness and inclusiveness of different types of political actors, features corresponding to the tenets of republican citizenship. As a consequence, the convention method could be regarded not only as a realization of the virtues of democratic deliberation in the EU to an unprecedented degree, but also as a strengthening of republican citizenship in its deliberative version.

In contrast, I argue that even though deliberation can have benevolent effects on decision-making in the EU, the convention method should not be viewed as embodiment of republican citizenship. This is due to the pathologies of deliberation that can only be corrected by applying procedures beyond deliberative settings. In this sense, I focus on demonstrating the *dark side* of deliberation and its possible consequences for EU citizenship by arguing that the expectations about integrative workings of deliberation and consequently its identity-generating features might not only be overestimated, but may even produce negative outcomes for the European collective identity.

My point of departure is the observation of growing heterogeneity and diversity of the EU posing a considerable problem for a republican vision of citizenship and in particular for its identity implications. After a brief review of the expected republican potential of deliberative settings, I will turn to different types of deliberation pathologies constituting the anti-republican character of the convention method. These deliberation pathologies not only question the validity of republican claims made by deliberative democracy theory itself, but also exacerbate the likelihood of deliberative republican citizenship to engender collective identity. In the final section I will further elaborate on the issue of republican citizenship in light of those pathologies, and will conclude with the thesis that the convention method is not sufficient to promote republican citizenship in the EU, as it produces additional challenges to its democratic legitimacy.

Heterogeneity and the republican citizenship in the EU

As a result of its expansion, the heterogeneity of the EU societal structure is increasing considerably, causing not only the decision-making structures to grow more complex, but also placing a burden on the possibilities of the republican citizenship in the EU in terms of 'social choice' – of the collectivity possessing a shared set of political preferences.[15] It implies that given the growing heterogeneity of societal groups, their interests and identities, the formation of public good from actors' preferences that ought to be the essence of decisions according to republican citizenship, is becoming increasingly difficult.[16] With more societal heterogeneity there is an increasing chance that fewer citizens will be able to rediscover their preferences in the decisions taken at a European level. Since the European political system does not allow for swift changes of government in order to punish unpopular decision-makers, growing societal heterogeneity runs counter to republican tenets of citizen participation, anti-bureaucratic politics and in particular to the commitment to the common good that might be impossible to crystallize.[17]

In addition, heterogeneity is not only increased as a result of pure territorial expansion of the EU, but is also a result of the inner structural diversity of the EU, which can be described as 'clustered Europeanization' characterized by non-convergence and uneven commonality/difference generation. As Klaus H. Goetz argues, clustering is promoted by variety in the territory and temporality of the EU. While territory influences uneven Europeanization through 'families of nations' and centre-periphery structures, temporality matters as a result of the 'relative time of accession' in relation to domestic political and economic development of accession countries and in relation to the stage of European integration.[18] Growing heterogeneity and clustered diversity are likely to enhance the conflict potential between citizens (represented by collective political actors such as governments, regions or parties), rather than their commitment to the common good.

Diversity and heterogeneity pose a problem for republican citizenship, and civic and assimilatory collective identity of republican citizenship exhibits ambivalence towards diverse societies. The greater the diversity and heterogeneity, the weaker the strength of solidarity and other obligations among citizens. The republican model of citizenship implies thick collective identity, associated with special bonds among the compatriots and moral responsibilities towards each other. Thick collective identity of republican citizenship is expected to be 'sticky' and resistant, particularly in crises. Since thick republican identity solves the legitimacy problems of the majority rule, political minorities accept majority decisions by regarding themselves as a part of the community. However, cultural and ethnic heterogeneity is considered in the republican perspective to be mainly a threat to the public interest, especially if minorities enjoy particular privileges, be it special political representation rights or others. In this sense, diversity and heterogeneity make citizens want either to escape their civic responsibility by refusing to actively participate in the public space by withdrawing into their private sphere, or to exploit the public support for minorities by extracting material and political resources. In the worst case scenario, diversity can undermine civic commitment to public interest by promoting commitment towards particularist identities.[19] The EU is certainly a special case of heterogeneity, not easily comparable to multiculturalism of the Kymlickian sort, where indigenous groups acquire special group rights with the purpose of reintegration.[20]

Nevertheless, the republican citizenship has a rather tenuous relationship with diversity. The support for minority cultures and regional identities is thus believed to encourage politicization of heterogeneity, which in the context of republican citizenship is counterproductive regarding shared civic collective identity. The politicization of heterogeneity is likely to promote a spiral of competition, conflict, distrust and antagonism among citizens. Since diversity promotes fragmented identities, republicanism tends to regard it as a challenge to the citizenship identity in general and in the EU in particular.[21] The main concern of republican thinkers regarding the EU is therefore 'how to disentangle the issue of participation in an emerging polity from cultural and emotional dimensions of citizenship as pre-existing affinity and a confirmation of belonging'.[22]

According to the advocates of deliberation, deliberative citizenship represents a solution to antagonism, conflict of interests and contradictory identities.[23] Deliberative citizenship occurs against a background of a certain ethical psychology, which includes inter alia openness to persuasion by critical arguments. As a result, deliberation practices mediate or transform conflict of identities, since deliberation changes the substance of citizens' preferences by exposing and revising selfish interests and by stimulating reflection on common interest.[24] In this sense, deliberative democracies are believed to handle deep identity differences without surrendering the notion of civic citizenship. This can be achieved by transforming public space according to reason and orientation to the general interest, which would keep conflicts of interest to a minimum.[25] As deliberation helps to generate civic competence by inducing citizens to exchange arguments, republican and deliberative citizenship becomes crystallized.[26] Some authors go even further with their belief in the workings of deliberation, suggesting that prejudices can be transformed and hatred or racism annihilated through rational criticism and dialogue, which places deliberation even closer to the Aristotelian notion of civic friendship.[27] Consensus-driven deliberation is therefore expected to change pre-political aspects of particularistic interests and identities into political or common-good-orientated preferences reflecting civic identity.[28]

Expected republican potential of deliberative settings

The convention method was applied in the EU context for the first time in the period from October 1999 to autumn 2001, when the Convention on the Charter of Fundamental Rights was in operation. It comprised sixty-two members representing the governments, the President of the European Commission, the European Parliament and the national parliaments. The Presidium of the Convention consisted of members from each group of representatives. The drafting of the Charter took place without a formal vote. In the process, the members of the Convention submitted 205 written contributions, with the Presidium playing the decisive role. It is believed that the Charter was adopted without a vote due to the ongoing consensus-seeking process. Since the method seemed to be successful, the Laeken European Summit in December 2001 decided to apply it in the constitution-making process. The 2002 Convention comprised representatives of fifteen governments of the EU and of thirteen of the accession candidate countries' governments, plus representatives of thirty national parliaments, twenty-six national parliaments of the candidate countries, sixteen members of the European Parliaments and two members of the European Commission. As in the first Convention, there was a Presidium with a President who played a dominant role in the proceedings.[29] It was he who declared the compromise without taking a vote. Both Conventions allowed access for observers from various European institutions and the 2002 Convention also organized meetings with the representatives of European civil society.

Against this background, the proponents of the deliberative approach to democracy argued that the convention method offers an alternative method of decision-making in the European Union, since it features participative and inclusive forms of open deliberation, it respects and integrates minority positions, and it is conditioned by the method of consensus-building.[30] Advocates of these arguments highlight the relative strength of the convention method in comparison to the intergovernmental conferences (IGC), which have been the major mechanism of institutional change in the EU in the course of the European integration process. Whereas the IGCs are subject to diplomatic negotiations behind closed doors, which result in 'horse-trading' between the member states, the convention method is viewed as bringing about the spirit of deliberation in which different actors exchange arguments in public, thus fostering shared understanding and compromise among equals.[31] Following the deliberation theory of democracy,[32] supporters of the convention method argue that this not only reduced the democratic deficit of the EU by expanding public space, but also diminished the propensity of political actors to act according to their selfish interests.[33] According to this position, the convention method put a premium on reason-giving and arguing, rather than on interest-orientated bargaining. By requiring that speakers have to refer to commonly accepted norms in order to prove their points and by introducing consensus as decision rule, the convention method exhibits republican features. As a consequence, it is supposed to possess more potential for integration of diversity by generating collective identity than other institutional arrangements.[34] The convention method would thus present a republican method of decision-making in the EU. Therefore, as a result of its higher democratic value, it ought to be applied in cases of major institutional change, thus fostering the democratic legitimacy of the EU.

As a theoretical perspective, deliberation theory became viewed in the context of the convention method in contrast to the rational choice approach, based on the gain-orientated actions of political actors. Whereas this EU model highlights bargaining, negotiations and power,[35] the essential element of the deliberative democracy theory is the argumentative exchange between political actors who engage in consensus-building. Deliberation therefore rests on the principle of a continuous debate between participants in which only the power of argument counts, instead of the power of threats and sanctions, or the power of material compensation. The debate should be free, open and fair, and it should guarantee equal access for every interested actor. Furthermore, the participants should be formally (and in more radical versions even substantively) equal.[36] In such deliberative settings, no voting is envisaged, since the actors debate until they reach a consensus. Additionally, no participant has the power to veto or delay the agreement. The only way to influence the outcome is through the debate in which only better arguments succeed. Those arguments must not, however, be based on selfish preferences, since the goal of deliberation is not only to solve common problems, but also, often primarily, to identify what the public good is. Correspondingly, the arguments ought to relate to public good and common welfare, revealing a republican nature.

The core of deliberation is argument comprising persuasion and convincing of others, since every participant must be ready to hear all arguments and to change his or her position and view when convinced. Whereas the rational choice theory of democracy assumes fixed preferences that actors try to assert in political settings, deliberation theory implies that actors are free to challenge the validity claims inherent in every participant's statement (be it causal or normative). At the same time, they are willing to question their own beliefs and to change their world views and interests in the light of a better argument.[37] The behaviour of deliberative actors shall not be coordinated through selfish calculation of utility, but through acts of understanding and collective reasoning. Communication between actors in a deliberative setting is thus motivated by the desire to discover the truth about facts and causality with regard to the issue in question and to identify the common good for all participants or to understand what is, normatively seen, the right thing to do.[38] Deliberative communication is therefore conducive to political collective identity as a commitment to a common good.

In accordance with the deliberative democracy theory, advocates of the convention method praise it for its higher republican value and its higher decision-making efficiency. In contrast, the rational choice theory of democracy highlights the issue of power competition and the selection process in which the more powerful actors assert themselves. Only the resourceful participants can succeed in realizing their interests. In the context of EU politics, this approach finds its embodiment in bargaining and negotiations during the Intergovernmental Conferences as well as in everyday European politics.[39] In contrast, the deliberation approach to democracy is believed to have an intrinsic value of its own by creating republican citizens through the search for the common good as the basis of their political judgment.

Furthermore, the advocates of deliberation theory maintain that deliberative settings such as both European conventions further group identity and as a result promote citizens' readiness to cooperate.[40] This avoids conflict between participants, as well as the deadlocks that are related to negotiations. Moreover, nobody can disrupt or stall the decision-making process, since vetoing and voting are not allowed. Therefore, a stronger push towards collective identity is generated. However, it is not just any collective identity, but a civic one, as public discourses are also expected to have 'civilizing' effects on political actors. Justifying selfish interests is not possible in deliberative settings, since the actors must outline the validity of their arguments on the basis of common good or shared values. In other words, they have to play by the deliberative rules even if they remain egoistic utility calculators rather than becoming citizens in the republican sense, thus producing *nolens volens* an overall republican effect.

Anti-republican potential of the convention method

The aim of this section is not to test how deliberative both European conventions were with regard to the criteria of deliberative democracy theory, since there have already been studies published that have dealt with that question in detail.[41] Instead, I suggest examining the potential pathologies of deliberation and their implications for republican citizenship in the EU and consequently collective identity.[42] I argue that deliberation may unfold its *dark side*, which is contrary to republican citizenship and thus may become counterproductive in terms of collective identity.

The ideal type of deliberation takes place in the ideal-speech situation, where there are no relationships of power, no social hierarchies, and no asymmetries of access.[43] These criteria can certainly never be fulfilled in real life. Pointing this out merely means that a gap exists between the ideal type and the social reality. However, this is not the major drawback of deliberation settings regarding republican expectations. Instead I argue that deliberation processes, and especially deliberation via the convention method, can result in pathologies of republican citizenship. I distinguish three pathologies: false will-formation, rational 'hijacking' of deliberation, and perversity of deliberation.

Deliberation as false will-formation

I call the first pathology *false will-formation*, as due to their set-up and one-track deliberation the European conventions were not able to develop a European will-formation corresponding to collective will in the republican sense. I start with the distinction between deliberation among citizens and deliberation among representatives.[44] Whereas the bulk of literature on deliberation theory examines deliberative procedures among citizens with procedures such as citizens' juries or deliberative polls,[45] the aggregation of deliberative judgments and deliberation among representatives can pose a major problem to the republican interpretation of deliberation.[46] Since representatives in forums such as parliaments and constitutional conventions have loyalties to their 'ordering parties', they are unable to easily change their positions. In the European conventions, conventioneers represented their nations or their institutions, which set serious limits to the deliberation process. Even though the representatives did not formally have any imperative mandates, they were responsible to their 'principals', and therefore they were not free to change their preferences and world views. Even if they were personally convinced and persuaded otherwise as a result of the communicative process of deliberation, their function consists of representing the interests and world views of those who delegated them. Delegated deliberation is therefore likely to deviate strongly from deliberation among citizens.

According to the concept of *responsiveness*, political representatives, as opposed to technocratic decision-makers using technical and scientific arguments, have obligations towards their electors or other 'principals'.[47] However, this responsive deliberation has a priority over the deliberation among representatives, which in turn shifts from the relationship between the citizen and his representative towards the strength of an argument and thus becomes depersonalized.[48] Responsiveness implies a two-way deliberation between the citizens and their representatives, whereby the citizens-cum-electors as well as the representatives can change their preferences in the process.[49] Even though the representatives have the obligation to represent the interests of their electors, these private interests can be weighted by a more general consideration of public good. In this sense, the representatives may persuade their electors into modification of their private interests whenever these are in conflict with the public good, or whenever the electors maintain false causal beliefs about their interests. In other words, the representatives can civilize (in the sense of civicness) and enlighten their electors/citizens. Conversely, the electors can demand an effective representation of their interests, and they can use the sanction of non-re-election in the event that the representatives fail to fulfil the task. Moreover, they may withstand the persuasion of their representatives by better arguing. Against this background, delegated deliberation in European conventions does not correspond to deliberation among citizens, as the representatives are 'bound' in their argumentative elasticity and their mandate. Therefore, we cannot simply conclude that in the European conventions republican citizenship came to the fore and collective identity was generated, since the European conventions did not represent epistemic communities of experts and scientists.[50]

Furthermore, it appears plausible to assume that not every type of decision-maker is able to act in a responsive manner. In general, parliamentarians are likely to embrace their responsibility vis-à-vis their electors, if one benevolently omits their loyalty with regard to their parties or the German-like 'faction discipline' within the parliament. On the contrary, we should rather assume fixed preferences and the lack of responsiveness among executive representatives. They are directly responsible to their institutions, and are immediately held accountable by them. In cases of insubordination, they can be removed instantly from their posts, as executive decision-makers such as those of the European Commission do not enjoy the mercy of the delayed time horizon of parliamentary elections and the forgetfulness of the public. As a result, we can expect the representatives of governments and the European Commission in the European conventions to be on average less likely to change their preferences during the communication process.[51] In sum, there are reasons to believe that a deliberation among representatives would yield different results than deliberation among citizens, thus not corresponding to the informed public will highlighted by republican citizenship. In this sense, delegated deliberation would embody the elite-orientated and bureaucratic character of the polity, which republican citizenship is exactly directed against.

In the spirit of republican citizenship one could imagine institutional mechanisms that could at least reduce, if not remedy, the pathology of false will-formation. They could include facilitators or double deliberation.[52] The deliberation by the Convention could be followed by deliberation *with the public*. The representatives ought especially to debate the controversial issues with their citizens, rather than just subjecting the decisional outcome of the Convention to a referendum. Furthermore, since some types of political actors are by nature non-responsive, it should have consequences for the composition of the Conventions. Although it is not necessary to entirely exclude representatives of the executive branch from the proceedings, the composition of the Convention could be biased in favour of the parliamentarians. This proposal is reflected in the theory of deliberation, although with a different justification. Jon Elster argues that executives should not be represented in the Convention, since they are both decision-makers and the objects of the decision-making process.[53] In this respect, the Convention on the Charter of Fundamental Rights had a clear advantage over the Constitutional Convention, where the number and strength of European Parliament delegations shrank considerably. The power of the executive was clearly visible within the Convention on the Future of Europe, especially when one examines the pattern of alliance-building. For instance, government representatives did not engage with their party political groups. They submitted most of their contributions on their own. Only a few of the government representatives coordinated their actions with parliamentarians of their own nationality, frequently with those who were part of the government coalition.[54]

The pathology of false will-formation is associated with the republican belief that deliberation in the Conventions could give impetus to a true European will, representing civic collective identity. In a more radical version, the Convention on the Future of

Europe was actually the embodiment of the collective will, as it enriched raw preferences of individuals transforming them into enlightened, deliberative republican preferences. Claus Offe describes this type of ideology as 'left-republican elitism'.[55] It is left since it transcends the individual as a normative unit and gains an elitist and moralizing twist by postulating an institutional and collectivist supremacy. It draws its republican character from claims of collective production of common good and collective will-formation. In the case of the convention method, these claims, however, are far from reality, since under executive dominance and without feedback to the public (for instance in the form of double deliberation), the convention method only feigns the European will-formation. Consequently, we deal here with an illusion of will-formation that exhibits oligarchic features, rather than republican ones.

Against this background, one could go even further and claim that the convention method, as applied in the EU, possesses an illiberal core, as it fails to explain how outcomes correspond to individual judgments. The convention method therefore not only poses a problem regarding its republican claims, but also highlights a tension between democratic and deliberative aspects. Since deliberation does not automatically mean democracy, we can easily imagine elitist and authoritarian deliberation.[56] This point is highlighted by John Dryzek, who argues that courts in particular decide according to deliberative rules of public reason, without being democratic bodies.[57] This is also, however, frequently overlooked in scholarly literature, which tends to wrongly assume that both concepts are identical.[58] In comparison, bargaining can mitigate the problem of double deliberation, even though it cannot solve it. It is, namely, possible to either introduce semi-imperative mandates, which would be a list of acceptable concessions or arguments with which the representatives would be endowed, or to strengthen the feedback between the representatives and the public during the negotiations.[59] The representatives would be allowed to move argumentatively only within the list of acceptable arguments. It sets, of course, limits to deliberation that should take place without consideration for time and resources.

Rational hijacking of deliberation

The second pathology I shall call *rational hijacking of deliberation*. The theory of deliberation is a normative theory that presupposes an ideal world situation as the basis of the deliberation. However, it omits the real world effects of the selfish rationality of political actors in deliberation, and it ignores the manipulative use of arguments in the course of deliberation. Since the actors have to argue in public and justify their arguments with reference to the public or the common good, deliberation is intended either to transform the identity of the actors from individuals into members of a collective (strong assumption), or to contribute to the public good despite the selfishness of the actors (weak assumption). In the latter case, the actors remain selfish but are forced, by the mere fact of being in the public arena, to restrain their purely selfish interests, and to defend only those interests that correspond to the common good.

However, the likelihood of argumentative manipulation is seldom addressed by the advocates of the deliberation theory. For instance, even though Jon Elster discusses the possibility of manipulation, he argues that strong norms against opportunism and the necessity of argumentative consistency make the disguising of private interest as public good, as well as the manipulation of arguments, difficult.[60] Nonetheless, this over-optimistic view ignores the negative effects of rational behaviour of political actors in the course of deliberation, as the convention method not only allows but also promotes *rhetorical action*.[61] An important prerequisite of deliberation is the readiness of the actors to change their preferences, their beliefs, and even their identities under the influence of a better argument. However, political actors engaging in rhetorical action are not eager to change their own beliefs or to be convinced or persuaded. They argue strategically in order to realize their selfish interests.[62] This leads to a political debate rather than public reasoning, in which the argumentative process consists of purely rhetorical exchange but does not evolve towards true arguing. In this sense, the basis for rhetorical action is the selfish calculation of success, in which a more sophisticated justification, rather than a better argument, wins. By using arguments that refer to collective identity, collective ideology or the values and norms of the political community, actors gain political legitimacy for their selfish interest, and at the same time are able to de-legitimize the position of their opponents. The actors therefore use the arguments as a resource and the mechanism of *soft power* over other actors.[63] Others can be shamed into compliance by exposing their 'illegitimate' or inappropriate behaviour in public. Some authors point to the limits of the actors' manipulative behaviour within a political debate, as the manipulators must argue in a consistent manner. In other words, the arguments must match at different times and in different contexts,[64] otherwise they can become entrapped by their arguments and behave as if they had taken their arguments seriously. However, where there is only one context and a relatively short period of time, such as in the European conventions, the probability of self-inflicted entrapment diminishes and the incentives for rhetorical action increase.

When we apply the concept of rhetorical action to the Convention on the Future of Europe, one issue in particular stands out. Shortly before the draft of the Treaty on European Constitution had been concluded, the Convention Presidency, with former French President Giscard d'Estaing, introduced the new regulations on the decision-making system, which was to replace the system agreed upon in Nice in 2000.[65] The double majority system was strongly supported by Germany and France, with the argument that it makes the decision-making process more efficient by reducing the number of states able to form a blocking minority.[66] A more efficient decision-making system, it was argued, would be essential in the EU of twenty-five and more member countries.[67] As a result, the double majority system has been interpreted as a public good that ensures the proper functioning of an enlarged EU.[68] Countries that rejected the new decision-making system were accused, especially by Germany and France, of being nationalist or not civilized enough to understand the values of the community. German elites attempted to ridicule the Polish and Spanish rejection, while France focused on a shaming strategy, pointing to the lack of experience among the new members of the European club.[69]

At the same time, most of the German and French public seemed to be disinterested in the fact that the new decision-making system would give large countries, such as their own, much more power than had been intended by the Nice Treaty.[70] According to an analysis by the Vienna Institute of Higher Studies, the new system would move the balance of power (on the scale between equality and fairness) from 40 points (slightly in favour of small countries) to 80 points (massively in favour of large countries).[71] The new system would take the population of the countries more strongly into account, favouring Germany in particular.[72] This suggests that Germany and France used rhetorical action while pursuing selfish interests. Shaming and ridiculing strategies were easy to apply since these focused on Poland, which was about to become an EU member. The behaviour of the Polish government could be de-legitimized, since the country did not have any credibility with regards to having a strong commitment to Europe compared to the founding members such as Italy or the integration motor countries of France and Germany.[73]

This highly controversial issue of double majority was discussed in only one Convention session, on 15 and 16 May 2003. The debates on the first day were devoted in particular to the change of voting procedures into double majority, whereas on the second day the application of the new procedure in the field of foreign policy was discussed.[74] On the first day there was resistance observable against double majority, for instance from the Spanish delegate Dastis, who was in favour of Nice Treaty decision-making.[75] The Convention President Giscard d'Estaing had been silent on the issue of double majority in his most relevant speeches prior to 15 May.[76] Afterwards he mentioned it only very briefly in plenary sessions. On 13 June, Polish conventioneer Hübner declared that new decision-making rules should become the core of the debate during the upcoming IGC, as her resistance to double majority was ignored by the presidency of the Convention, who proclaimed a consensus.[77]

The 'great silence' of Giscard d'Estaing was consistent with the preferences of the large member states of the EU, particularly France and Germany, to modify power relations in the EU in their favour.[78] The Nice Treaty, which extrapolated the old system of weighting votes to ten new member states, was viewed in France and Germany as a mistake that had to be remedied.[79] Even before the Nice Treaty, France and Germany had voiced quite aggressively their critique of the EU decision-making system in order to make it more population-adjusted. It was frequently argued that one vote of a Luxembourg citizen has the power of 80,000 German votes, which makes the system undemocratic.[80] While France and Germany wanted to modify the decision-making system of the EU after the Nice Treaty, the Convention offered a welcome opportunity[81] and delivered the appropriate legitimacy to the power accumulation by the large member states.

Since the European Convention on the Future of Europe was linked to the constitutionalization of the EU, it not only promised to change the power relations within the EU, but also to 'freeze' them.[82] Constitutions can congeal hegemonic positions of certain political actors, and also legitimize radical shifts of power relations, as they offer a one-time opportunity to political actors for achieving a dominant position. Since constitutions are resistant to change, this stability or robustness of constitutions is one of the most relevant aspects of constitutionalism, a legal doctrine assuming that constitutions view the configuration of political processes as being supreme to the 'usual' legislation.[83] There are many hurdles that need to be jumped in order to change the constitution. In most countries there is a need for a supermajority to amend constitutions. This implies that decisions on political aims, values and procedures remain frozen and largely beyond democratic control. By the same token, the European constitution-making offered a unique opportunity for change and the freezing of new power relations, and also to deliver legitimating strategies by claiming its democratic legitimacy through deliberation in the European Convention. Even though the Constitutional Treaty in its original form was not adopted as a result of French and Dutch referenda, the Reform Treaty retained its substance.[84] Giscard d'Estaing argued that 'in the Treaty of Lisbon, the tools are largely the same. Only the order in which they are arranged in the tool-box has been changed. Admittedly, the box itself is an old model, which you have to rummage through in order to find what you are looking for.' In addition, references to the constitution had been removed 'above all to head off any threat of referenda by avoiding any form of constitutional vocabulary'.[85]

However, the change of power relations under the veil of deliberation is contrary to republican citizenship. The rational hijacking of deliberation not only questions the notion of citizens' equal influence on political outcome, but legitimizes oligarchies' decision-making structures, which may enhance the overall decision-making capacity of the EU, but simultaneously question the spirit of republicanism. That the Council on the Future of Europe has been mainly concerned with power shift was confirmed by the EU summit in Brussels in June 2007, which decided on the mandate for the Lisbon Treaty signed in December 2007.[86] In Brussels, the double majority was pushed through by German Presidency agenda-shaping powers against the more egalitarian Penrose square root solution.[87] However, most of the mathematical analyses confirm that the Penrose solution would equalize the individual power of European citizens, rather than balance it in favour of large countries.[88] The degressive weighting of votes denoted by the Penrose rule can be defended more plausibly against the background of republican equality of citizens than the double majority solution.[89]

The issue of rhetorical action does not confine itself to the question of which actors disguise their selfish interests as public good and which do not. The major issue is that actors have an incentive to act rhetorically, which leads to the classical prisoner's dilemma within the deliberation process. If I am the only one to play by the rules of deliberation, while everyone else pursues his or her private preferences by using rhetorical action, I find myself in the worst possible position. Not only will the common good not be served, but also my private well-being will suffer due to the exploitation of myself by others. As in every prisoner's dilemma, no one has the incentive to play by the rules of cooperation.[90] Therefore, every actor will try to use rhetorical action, and act strategically by disguising his true interests and by being argumentatively manipulative.[91] We deal here with pseudo-deliberation, in which most rational actors attempt to trick their opponents instead of engaging in consensus-seeking and problem-solving.

The probability of rhetorical action increases more during constitution-making conventions than in settings of a more deliberative character. As mentioned above, constitutions are devices for the long-term binding of others by limiting their freedom of action. They have this function for at least two reasons. First, political actors fear the abuse of power by others. The constitutions, therefore, secure human rights and power as well as divide political authority among several authorities. As a result, actors cannot afford the luxury of truth-seeking, while others try to 'bind' them. Second, political actors want the constitution to reflect their interests and identities, since constitutions are one-shot opportunities either to defend the individual preferences/identities or to be exploited. Since it is difficult to change the constitution, the actors in the Constitutional Convention have the incentive to secure power by acting rationally, and not deliberatively.

In sum, the convention method, particularly in European conventions, induces the political actors to behave in a rhetorical way. However, rhetorical action may take an even more radical form of ideological domination. Some actors with appropriate argumentative resources at their disposal may alter others' preferences into false beliefs.[92] The aim of deliberation is to change some people's beliefs with the assistance of a better argument. Contrary to the assumption of the theory of deliberation about formal and substantive equality of participants, deliberation takes place among unequal actors.[93]

We could even argue that if all participants had the same access to information and the same reasoning capacity, the deliberation would be superfluous, since each participant is disposed of equally good arguments, and there would not be any necessity to convince others. Only unequal actors, the stronger of whom can produce better arguments and are willing to argumentatively back up their interests, can convince others to accept false causal beliefs, for instance as a means of achieving a desired goal.[94] For example, the French government may persuade other deliberating participants that legitimacy of the EU can be boosted by increasing expenditure on the Common Agriculture Policy, while the real motivation behind the argument is not concern for the legitimacy of the EU but the representation of private interests of French farmers. Therefore, deliberation may result in the spread of false beliefs in favour of special interests. In this case, we deal with ideological domination, whereby two factors increase its probability. First, there is the presence of executive actors supported by large bureaucracies. Bureaucracies have more human and financial resources at their disposal than parliamentarians or other actors.[95] This allows for a much higher output of arguments backed by self-conducted statistics and opinion polls. If we take a look at the composition of the Convention on the Future of Europe, the presence and activity of the German and French foreign ministers strikes us as exceptional. The German Foreign Ministry has, of course, much more argumentative power than, for instance, a Lithuanian parliamentarian.[96] Against this background, an incorporation of Foucault's power-centred discourse theory into the deliberation theory may prove fruitful, as it stresses that knowledge and thus also arguments can be tools of power.[97]

It is not to say that deliberation is impossible in general, but that not all so-called deliberative settings, including the convention method, are conducive to genuine deliberation. Several empirical studies from political psychology suggest that deliberation in experimental settings may enhance the legitimacy of individual decisions, but only under strict institutional circumstances.[98] However, the convention method not only renders the use of rhetorical action possible, but it also promotes it. Interestingly enough, no one was able to trace back the initiative on the double majority. This is a further general deficit of the convention method. The lack of accountability makes the convention method open to political manipulation, since it fosters a dilution of responsibility. Nobody is held responsible for decisions taken in this institution. Characteristically, we speak of a *Convention* draft or a *Convention* proposal. This promotes loopholes whereby national interests can be followed without political actors being revealed. However, accountability is indispensable regarding any republican citizenship, as it represents a tool against corruption in the sense of interest particularism at the expense of the community. Therefore, the convention method does not fulfil the criteria of republican citizenship despite the hopes of advocates of deliberation theory. As rhetorical action allows for realization of national interests in a covered form and without citizens' control, the convention method provides an opportunity to disguise political interest under the veil of republican arguments, drawing on the common wealth and common interest. While side payments during negotiations can leave all parties satisfied, rhetorical action may aggravate feelings of impotence and betrayal in actors rhetorically manipulated. In this case, the chances of collective identity generation become bleak.

Simultaneously, deliberative manipulation cannot be reconciled with other tenets of republican citizenship resting on a concept of civic liberty. This collective liberty is based on non-domination and represents a civic achievement. As domination indicates an intension and capacity to diminish other citizens' scope of choice, not least through manipulation and subtle argumentative influence, it contradicts the republican spirit of citizenship. To avoid it there must be either proper institutions to control powerful actors with manipulative potential or those with power should choose not to exercise it.[99] The latter solution is certainly not a realistic one, yet some institutional settings such as the European Convention additionally empower the most powerful actors instead of keeping them at bay. Nonetheless, some republican authors use the republican concept of non-domination as a performance benchmark for the European Convention.[100] The non-domination republicanism focuses among other things on the *ideological domination* that unfolds in particular when a majority of participants face a small minority of opponents. Minorities can suffer conformity effects identified in Solomon Asch's experiment, which proved that individuals under group pressure change their correct beliefs about reality.[101] Consequently, small minorities may be easily indoctrinated into submission.[102] For example, the analysis by the Vienna Institute of Higher Studies mentioned above argues that a large majority of the members of the Convention on the Future of Europe were unaware of the consequences of double majority for the radical shift in the balance of power in the EU. The convention method not only makes indoctrination probable, but it has an additional mechanism that allows for the ignoring of minorities. Since there is no voting and vetoing in the Convention, alternative positions lying outside the argumentative mainstream can simply be ignored. For instance, the alternative minority report on the Europe of Democracies has been completely ignored in the Convention on the Future of Europe.[103] As the official draft put forward by the Presidium of the Convention was not accepted by the sceptical members, the convention method reflected the majority preferences, declaring it a consensus.

Against this background, it seems necessary to compensate for the negative effects of rational deliberation. For instance, secret voting at the end of the deliberation can fulfil this function. Since the rational deliberation unfolds its drawbacks in the specific social context, this context has to be neutralized. If the actors had the opportunity for a secret ballot after the closure of the Convention, the problems of rational actions and ideological domination could be reduced. This means that decisions taken via the convention method need to undergo public scrutiny in the form of a referendum, as referenda reduce group pressure and exclude justification of personal decisions among others by giving citizens an opportunity to decide for themselves without being exposed to group pressure or indoctrination.[104]

Other proposals suggest balanced discussions, rather than focusing on the common good arguments and consensus-seeking, as it misses the point of citizenship by depersonalizing the deliberation. Balanced presentation of alternative viewpoints is expected to integrate minority opinions. Lynn M. Sanders argues that sober exchange and weighing of reasons has historically made deliberation a tool for conservative politics, excluding those who did not succumb to the accepted method of 'reasoned' debate. In this sense, deliberation can entail disenfranchisement hidden in the pursuit of commonality, as not every particularism is an illegitimate one and can be interpreted as a case of corruption of the common good. Sanders pointed out that more inclusive talk could grant more accessible ways of communicating, including what she labelled 'testimony', in which citizens would state their own perspective in their own words without the necessity of defending or justifying its relevance.[105]

Perversity of deliberation in establishing collective identity

The third pathology I call the *perversity of deliberation*, which denotes a situation in which deliberation produces the reverse effect of what it seemingly intends. This can be caused by a more general problem of deliberation theory, which is a normative theory formulating ideals of a rational political order, but at the same time remaining unclear how such ideals are to be achieved, or even whether they *can* be achieved under the circumstances of the existing social realities.

First, we have to consider the possibility that deliberation can bring differences to the surface, and widen rather than narrow divisions. The theory of deliberation over-optimistically assumes that all interests can be reconciled, and an exchange of arguments will always foster a consensus, and thus shared identity. However, there is no particular reason to think that deliberation will bring people together. By exchanging arguments with others, actors may primarily realize their selfish interests as well as their distinctive identity. Actors' arguments do not float freely, but are anchored in their identities and world views, and these may be resistant to change. Moreover, there might be a citizenship problem with pressuring the change of identity in citizens, as it deprives the individual of his or her right to authenticity.[106] Apart from this argument, it might be almost impossible to persuade citizens to change their identity or world views during even a long series of deliberations. Whereas deliberation can work with regard to causal relations and facts, thus reducing informational deficits, simple information does not have the power to transform identities. Since political actors are socialized beings and identities and world views are at stake, citizens do not react to better arguments by default. They filter the arguments through the maze of their self-understanding, their ethical principles, and emotions.[107] Reducing political actors to highly selective devices (argument-senders and argument-receivers), the proponents of deliberation assume away the social reality and represent a mechanistic model of social action. Moreover, the deliberation theory underestimates the power of emotions in motivating citizenship. As Kostas Lavdas argues:

> not only do nationalist motivations rely on emotions and sentiments …, but the entire exercise of citizenship in such contexts may acquire predominantly emotional characteristics: emotional citizenship as well as cultural citizenship as facets of a particular mode of being involved in a political order.[108]

In this sense, the active dimension of citizenship derives its motivation and its focus on commonality from an emotional capital, where the exercise of participatory citizenship frequently has not much to do with reflection and critical reasoning.

Furthermore, actors may become conscious about their individual identity in the very process of deliberation. This 'consciousness-raising' occurs against the background of uncrystallized identities. Marxists argued that it would lead the working class to discover their interests to be irreconcilably at odds with those of employers, inducing the metamorphosis of the proletariat from a class in itself to a revolutionary class for itself, thus giving rise to working class identity.[109] A similar transformation may unfold as a result of deliberation. However, in this case, we would be confronted with a formation of fragmented identities, rather than a shared civic identity with a bridging capacity, a result not compatible with republican citizenship.

Moreover, political actors may not intend to reach a consensus, even though deliberation procedures are consensus-orientated. The proponents of deliberation posit the normative supremacy of consensus over dissent, just as the proponents of cooperation dismiss every kind of conflict, claiming its ethical inferiority. In contrast, actors refusing to settle their disagreements may perceive consensus as oppressive, and may wish to differentiate themselves from one another, which would entail a different mode of identity formation. Still, consensus and dissent are not to be regarded in a binary manner. The teleology of consensus in the convention method does not necessarily overlap with the politics of compromise. Whereas the former is directed against the republican citizenship, the latter could be a better tool for dealing with diversity, as it is more sensitive to pluralism and heterogeneity. Critics have argued that Habermas's and Cohen's focus on consensus prevents an alternative outcome of deliberation concluding that the interests and identities of the participants fundamentally conflict.[110] As a consequence, the collective pressure to frame arguments in terms of the common good can deform participants' understanding of the issue at hand, making it far harder to find genuine common ground.[111]

This reflects to some extent the agonistic critique of deliberation, which is in principle suspicious of consensus, since it can camouflage power relations.[112] An agonistic (temporary) compromise would thus be able to reconcile identity differences of citizens, as it includes continued contestation of the agreement and transforms antagonism into agonism. In this sense, deliberation theory searches for an invariant consensus-driven outcome, while the agonistic approach assumes that the will of the citizens changes.[113] Empirical research has already compared the consensus-orientated procedure with more adversarial procedures in public hearings. It found that the consensus-orientated procedure failed to detect significant conflicting interests among the citizens and as a consequence failed to discuss and negotiate these interests. Consequently, deliberative consensus-orientated procedures need to provide for dynamic updating on the existing and changing interest and identity structure before and during deliberation, with particular regard to the relevant lines of conflict. In this context, the role of facilitators is expected to help participants not only in forging common interests, but also in clarifying their conflicting interests and finding compromise.[114] None of these occurred in the European conventions, where the President simply proclaimed a consensus regardless of opposition from a number of conventioneers.[115] In this sense, we could construe the Constitutional Convention as institutionalizing an oppressive consensus, which has undermined the republican legitimacy of the results as being acceptable by every participant.

A further category of the perverse effects of deliberation can be described by reference to the law of group polarization. Deliberation may cause the members of a deliberating group to shift towards a more extreme point than the average participant had held in the pre-deliberation position.[116] When like-minded people participate in deliberation, an extreme movement is likely to occur in this group. As Cass R. Sunstein argues, group polarization is among the most robust patterns found in deliberation arrangements. Sunstein draws upon experimental literature from psychology in which two main factors are viewed as conducive to group polarization.[117] The first factor points to people's desire to maintain their reputation and their self-conception. Once a person hears what others believe, s/he adjusts his or her position in the direction of the dominant position. Individuals move their judgments in order to preserve their image among others and their own image of themselves. The second factor underlines the limited 'argument pool'. Members of a deliberating group may engage in *enclave deliberation*, not only rejecting alternative views, but also reinforcing their initial position in a more extreme form. Members of deliberating groups can only use a certain number of arguments to underline their initial position. If they hear like-minded people, they also tend to selectively perceive only arguments in support of the initial position. As a consequence, the person will express views less cautiously and move towards a more extreme version of the initial position. It implies that under certain circumstances and due to deliberation, moderate positions shift to extreme ones. Therefore, deliberation may not lead to a true reasoning, but simply entrench and strengthen only a fixed point of view. In this sense, deliberation may have perverse effects and should be regarded as undesirable.[118]

Besides fragmented identity formation and group polarization, deliberation may have corrosive effects on the relations between the members of the group, rather than fostering collective identity. Whether these effects occur depends on the cognitive types of actors engaged in deliberation. Diego Gambetta distinguishes between the analytical and indexical knowledge of political actors, stressing that different types of knowledge are not necessarily easy to integrate.[119] Analytical types engage in tentative rather than definitive exploration of knowledge, they value empirical verification, and they do not consider local ignorance dishonourable. A lack of knowledge in one field is not thought to be an indicator of overall ignorance. In contrast, indexical types assume their knowledge to be holistic, since it is one and indivisible.[120] As a result, 'local' ignorance is viewed as a disqualification and excellence as antithetical to specialization. Deliberating actors who show indexical beliefs present strong and decisive opinions, since they have an opinion on every subject. Therefore, their goal of deliberation is not insight, but winning an argument. Indexical types consider this goal more important than truth-seeking or compromise. Since losing an argument means admitting a more general kind of inferiority, it has important implications for deliberation. Indexical actors are not interested in the accumulation of knowledge or in finding the public good, as the exchange of arguments is believed to reveal one's superiority. In this case, it is not a better argument that wins, but the *person* with the better argument. Deliberation thereby degenerates into a contest of eloquence, where rhetorical action and discursive competition prevail. Whenever deliberation, as envisaged by Joshua Cohen and Jürgen Habermas, occurs among indexical actors, it can entail perverse effects. On the one hand, indexical types are not prepared to accept the arguments of others, as accepting them would imply surrender and a declaration of inferiority. On the other hand, indexical types will try to bully the others into agreeing with their opinions, thus pressuring into acceptance their version of consensus. Moreover, indexical types tend to become aggressive during the exchange of arguments, resulting in opinions coming to the fore in outbursts of destructive emotions such as rage or indignation. Even though emotions as such are not necessarily counterproductive in respect of compromise, destructive ones decrease the likelihood of constructing civil identity. As the arguments reflect the world view and identity of deliberating indexical actors, persuasion is likely to be difficult. As a result, deliberative interaction can take the form of criticizing, assaulting, and ridiculing others.[121] In these cases, the convention method can turn the deliberative setting into a discursive competition, thus preventing compromise, or it can produce a compromise being perceived by a minority as oppressive.

Conclusions

Even though the convention method increased the overall level of deliberation in the EU, it could neither fulfil criteria for republican citizenship nor was it able to produce shared collective identity associated with republicanism. Furthermore, it can have corrosive effects with regard to the EU as a political community. Although deliberation is not a danger to the EU that has to be avoided at any costs, deliberation theory does not deliver sufficient mechanisms for generating republican citizenship, which leads to an expectation–outcome gap. Far from demonizing deliberation theory, I argue that the aim of republican collective identity in the EU cannot be realized with the instrument of the convention method. The advocates of deliberation in the European conventions tend to share an illusion about its workings that underestimates the complexity of collective identity generation. In this sense, one-sided institutional solutions such as the convention method may have the opposite effect to that expected.

Since the convention method can breed disappointment and feelings of powerlessness, it appears to have a disruptive impact on collective identity. Moreover, it seems to support domination rather than promote equality, which is to be regarded as counterproductive for the generation of a republican collective identity based on mutual respect and recognition. The Convention on the Future of Europe seems not only to legitimize the preferences of the majority, but it also allows for radical shifts of power favouring more powerful members. It promoted the disguising of illegitimate particularism, thus being conducive to corruption of the polity, which is viewed as one of the greatest dangers to the *res publica*.

Furthermore, deliberative consensus-seeking works as a pressure in favour of majority or political actors with more deliberative resources such as executives. In this sense, it has conservative workings, to the detriment of minorities and the excluded. Therefore, deliberative consensus-seeking seems to contradict the general commitment to collective good, as it focuses solely on argumentative commitment, rather than on the substantial one. Consequently, the dichotomy of juxtaposing deliberation in contrast to bargaining does promise many insights into the issue of civic collective identity. As deliberation can entail corrosive effects for the political community, other institutional mechanisms such as double deliberations, testimonies or balanced discussions could support the republican citizenship more effectively than the prescribed remedies of deliberation theory.

Liberal citizenship and European identity through rights

As argued in the first section of this chapter, the European citizenship has exhibited an increasingly liberal accentuation as a result of its focus on rights, without surrendering its caesarean features. This rights focus culminated in the work of the Convention, which delivered the Charter of Fundamental Rights in 2000. The idea of the Charter of Fundamental Rights for the EU was pushed in 1998–1999 by the upcoming German presidency of the European Union.[122] The creation of a 'European Bill of Rights' was previously envisaged by the coalition agreement between the German SPD party and the Green Party, as they formed the federal government in 1999. As a consequence, the idea found a prominent place in the programme of the German EU Presidency and in official speeches by Chancellor Schröder and Foreign Minister Fischer. The Cologne European Council ending the German presidency in June 1999 made a decision on the preparation of a Charter of Fundamental Rights for the EU. The Council conclusions referred to the Charter as being essential for the respect for human rights within the EU as well as for its founding principles and legitimacy.[123] As a next step, the European Council decided in Tampere in October 1999 on the composition of the drafting institution, labelled the 'Convention'.[124] The Convention started its sessions in December 1999 under the chairmanship of former German president Roman Herzog. The drafting process itself was considered pioneering, as it combined deliberative and inclusive elements with a privileged representation of institutional representatives at the national and European level. In particular, the Council's General Secretariat charged with servicing the Convention exerted significant influence on the work of the Convention and on the subsequent outcome of its decision-making. The final draft of the Charter was adopted in October 2000 by the Convention and proposed to and approved by the informal European Council in Biarritz prior to the European Council in Nice in December 2000.

In this section, I will examine in more detail the rights component of European citizenship with an emphasis on the Charter of Fundamental Rights. In addition, I will explore some aspects of the rights-based mode of citizenship present in the draft Constitutional Treaty.[125] Even though the draft Constitutional Treaty could not be ratified in the EU as a result of negative referenda in France and the Netherlands in 2005, the substance of the document was incorporated in the so-called Lisbon Treaty signed in December 2007 by the European governments.[126]

The initial purpose of the Charter Convention was to codify rights already protected within Community law and make them 'more visible to the EU's citizens', thus increasing the salience of the EU as a community of rights. This in turn was expected to induce identity building effects among European citizens.[127] It was believed that by confirming and visualizing consensus on specific European rights, European citizens would be likely to develop stronger identification with the European Union.[128] As a consequence, the gap between the rights of Union citizens as legally constituted subjects of law and the emerging European identity could be bridged.[129]

This shifts the expected European identity more strongly towards a legal identity of liberal citizenship. However, in comparison to the strong collective identity of the republican model of citizenship, the *liberal model of citizenship* is associated with a *weak collective identity*.[130] Whereas republican citizens are conscientious members of a political community (which sets aims for citizens and suppresses to a certain degree their individual inclinations), liberal citizens live in a society of individuals, which is held together by means of a rational and individually motivated contract. Such a social contract reflects a set of preferences and goals endorsed by every citizen and its main aim is to protect citizens' liberty against infringements by the state.[131] The individual influence on a form and a scope of the political community makes the We–I balance of a liberal citizenship even out on the I-component, which leads to an I–We identity without obvious supremacy of the political community vis-à-vis the individual. In this sense, every individual citizen enjoys pre-political, natural rights that can be infringed by other citizens and the state; even special rights that are brought about by the social contract are to be guarded against the political authority. In most cases, individuals are sufficiently reasonable to understand that only through cooperative arrangements are they able to realize their preferences and guard their liberties. By the same token, social and political contract is possible only against the background of individual rationality and a minimum of common preferences.[132]

Against this background, a Charter of Fundamental Rights could be expected to express common preferences and common values of the EU. Therefore, some scholars regard the Charter of Fundamental Rights of the EU precisely as a foundation of the 'European social contract'.[133] In accordance with this reading, the Charter of Fundamental Rights reflects essential features of liberal citizenship, as it represents a common European legal system (*ius commune europaeum*), based on human dignity and the respect for each member of European society and their specific identities.[134] In this sense, instead of stressing thick collective identity, the Charter highlights diversity of identities and thus heterogeneity. In this context, European citizenship as membership in a political community is expressed above all in the equal treatment of citizens before the law. As a result, a sort of common thin political identity drawn from equal rights and principles is expected to develop.[135] However, this contractarian and thin collective identity mirrors solely a common normative basis for a future European democracy; it implies neither sticky collective identity nor does it require an integrated public sphere as a precondition for citizenship identity.[136] Therefore, approaches expecting a transformation of a thin identity (anchored in a normative environment of society) into a thick identity, implying a change in citizens' behaviour towards each other, are likely to be unrealistic. While solidarity claims of republican citizenship refer to solidarity with *someone*, i.e. with other citizens, a shared normative environment implies identification with norms and principles of appropriate conduct. As a result, liberal citizenship would require a stronger application of identity politics and identity technologies to stimulate citizens' behaviour modification towards more loyalty, solidarity and sacrifice, which may be contradictory regarding the rights-orientation of liberal citizenship. Here, we can refer to the differentiation made in Chapter 4 between the transformer and the catalyst identity politics where, in the case of the former, political authorities must use more invasive identity technologies to establish thick identity. In contrast, the latter identity politics would be less invasive, as it requires merely a catalyst to encourage behavioural implications of citizenship politics.

The following three sections deal with chances of collective identity generation through rights in the context of the EU. First, I will discuss the problems pertaining to the generation of collective identity by means of constitutionalization of rights. This focuses on the role of the European constitution (or constitutional treaty) in the European identity politics. Second, I will explore the chances of the construction of collective identity through inflation of rights. Here, I will put an emphasis on the provisions of the European Charter of Fundamental Rights, in particular the multiplication of rights in the Charter. Third, I will explore collective identity generation through rights to solidarity. Rights to solidarity are specific legal institutions that could be expected to spawn sticky collective identity, precisely because it is frequently associated with solidarity.

Collective identity through constitutionalization of rights

The Charter of Fundamental Rights of the EU represents an apogee of the liberal, rights-orientated citizenship in Europe. Within this framework, we can identify two approaches to collective identity in the EU: a minimalist and an ambitious. The minimalist approach can be associated with an attempt to generate collective identity among European citizens by enhancing the legal certainty of individuals in the EU. In this sense, the Charter is expected to secure consistent rights enforcement in the EU, even if the

Charter is nothing more than a codification of existing laws. Nonetheless, it gives more room to the European Court of Justice and the national courts when dealing with the EU law, thus strengthening the judicial branch believed to show considerations for citizens' rights.[137] In other words, the advocates of stimulating collective identity through legal certainty in the EU intend to achieve republican goals through legal means, which leads to an expectations–outcome gap.[138] Legal certainty is perfectly in tune with the core tenets of liberal citizenship, which lacks aspirations to thick identities.

In contrast, according to the ambitious approach to collective identity, the Charter of Fundamental Rights attempts to identify the basic rights and values of the EU and in the process to stimulate citizens' identification with them. In this sense, we deal here with identification of and identification with rights and values expressed by these rights. The recognition of a common set of rights in a single document should provide the possibility of shared identification by citizens with this basic set of rights, thus highlighting shared values in a political community.[139]

This line of argument stresses in particular the identity-generating effects of constitutions (with an emphasis on the Charter of Fundamental Rights) even with an absent community or a lacking societal consensus.[140] It assumes that a constitution can have symbolic effects independently of the societal structure and even in the absence of collective identity. This results from a presumption that constitutions are more than merely organizational statutes, since they are evaluative, cultural and affective systems of reference, through which citizens interpret their political experiences and develop their expectations. A constitution can therefore become a symbolic medium, which serves to construct the socio-cultural identity of a given society.[141] This influence of a constitution stems from its normative supremacy over the common law. For this reason, constitutions can become a relevant system of reference and a source of collective identity, and thus integrate even highly heterogeneous societies. Regarding the symbolic effect of a constitution, a Constitutional Court (which interprets it) plays an essential role, thus constructing political and social order with regard to the normative 'absolute' of the constitution. It can thus be argued that a constitution is a form of transcendental order, which permeates and constructs political reality and therefore also collective identity.[142] Therefore, constitutions not only legitimize political processes, but also remain a reliable source of normative answers, which neither the society itself nor the political elites are capable of responding to. In this sense, they invoke a higher normative authority, which has the power to integrate heterogeneous societies via the ongoing construction of a shared value system.

The Federal Republic of Germany is regarded as the classical case of the symbolic and integrative effect of a constitution.[143] Rulings by the Federal Constitutional Court give meaning to the political order and are expected to cause its internalization in the collective identity of the people. It is argued that the constitution could become a foundation for the so-called constitutional patriotism in Germany, because alternative integration devices such as 'nation' no longer have integrative effects on the society.[144] However, constitutions only develop their identity-generating effects if they are accepted by the society, and can become a sort of 'fetish' and object of cult.[145] It is believed that through cult and fetishism constitutions can affect societies by means of constructing trust towards the political system.[146] By generating trust, constitutions counterbalance the systemic distrust of liberal citizenship towards the government. Therefore, the cult of constitution, which is visible above all in the US and Germany, is thought to engender a permanent process of political identity building of the society. However, some authors argue that constitutions can only fulfil this integrative function if they remain open to different interpretations, thus giving heterogeneous societies an opportunity to integrate.[147] This is a highly relevant issue regarding sticky collective identity. Excessive ambiguity can be counterproductive in respect of citizenship identity, as constitutional narrowness can be unable to integrate diverse societies. This poses a certain dilemma for identity politics of constitutionalization in diverse societies. A constitution reflecting a coherent and 'dense' value system is more likely to have stronger identity effects. However, at the same time, it can alienate parts of a diverse society, thus being unable to integrate it. In turn, a constitution espousing ambiguity and contradictions can integrate more value sets, better reflecting the societal structure, but it can also lose its identity-generating power, as it cannot offer reliable value orientation for the citizens.

In the EU context, this train of thought suggests that a European constitution could play an integrative role even in the EU, which is a highly heterogeneous construction. In particular, approaches inspired by Jürgen Habermas suggest that even the mere process of constitution-making could have integrative effects on the heterogeneous European society by engendering shared identity. Such common political identity will be capable of withstanding conflicts and producing 'solidarity among strangers'.[148]

However, there are several problems with the argument that constitutionalization generates collective identity. I differentiate five points of critique of the link between constitutionalization and collective identity: lacking resonance of the European constitution, asymmetrical participation in the constitutionalization process, unstable effects between uniformization and diversification, systemic failures of the Charter and the 'judicialization' of politics.

First, since there is no European public space, the codification of rights within a constitution has to resonate with national public spaces to reach citizens of the EU as a prerequisite for their European citizenship identity. However, due to the segmentation of the European publics the debate on constitutionalization has not permeated the national public spaces (with some exceptions, such as Spain).[149] Despite the relatively transparent proceedings of the European Convention, the effect of the constitutional debate on public opinion in the EU was rather faint. Few citizens have shown interest in the subject of a European constitution, which was visible, for example, in the debate prior to the elections for the European Parliament, which exhibited a strong coloration of national debates within the member states.[150] One could argue that it takes time for the constitution to develop its effects, since the establishment of constitutional patriotism took several decades in Germany. However, the rejection of the European Constitution in France and the Netherlands, in which the constitution treaty, and the Charter in particular, was debated in a lively and intense manner, showed that the Constitutional Treaty has had the reverse effects to those expected. The debate on the constitution appeared to polarize European societies, while in France it almost caused an ideological break in the Socialist Party.[151] In this context, it is fairly unconvincing to present the Charter of Fundamental Rights (which was a component of the Constitutional Treaty) as a core of European values that is accepted by every EU member state.

Second, there is the issue of participation within the Charter of Fundamental Rights. The inclusion of the candidate states from Central and Eastern Europe (CEE) in the process of drafting the Charter was rather symbolic, as the Charter Convention envisaged only an 'exchange of views' with the applicant states instead of a debate in which the candidate state would enjoy real influence. As Wojciech Sadurski argues, the audition of the candidate countries within the Charter Convention, which took place in June 2000 in Brussels, was full of platitudes and diplomatic praise for the Charter drafters on the part of the member states and boasting about equivalents of the Charter in the national constitutions on the part of the applicant countries, rather than a genuine communicative exchange of the substance.[152] This rather symbolic participation of CEE in the sessions of the Charter Convention was not conducive to lending an overall legitimacy to the Charter of Fundamental Rights.[153] By the same token, a constitution can be questioned if it is perceived as a result of a hegemonic constitutionalization without sufficient inclusion.[154] In contrast, the corollary of hegemonic constitutions is their legitimacy shortfalls resulting from an excessive exclusiveness, as hegemonic constitutions seek to limit inclusion. The constitution debate in France highlighted that the constitution was rejected exactly as a result of fears associated with the Eastern enlargement.[155] In this sense, the Constitutional Treaty did not only render the EU visible, but also stressed the potential of value conflicts and the vulnerability of the EU as a political community.

This brings us back to the dilemma of constitutionalization in diverse societies. A rejection of the Constitutional Treaty bears serious consequences for its envisaged function as a promoting device for collective identity. On the one hand, the constitutional symbolism is lost upon the rejection of a constitution. In this sense, a series of national referenda under the circumstances of weak collective identity can be regarded as reckless, in particular on the part of the advocates of constitutional patriotism in the EU believing in the community-building effects due to the mere process of constitution-making. On the other hand, a perhaps more effective but less democratic constitution-making (with a modest participation of citizens and an asymmetric participation of member states) leads to a hegemonic constitutionalization and as a result to a governments' constitution, as opposed to a citizens' constitution.[156] However, hegemonic constitutionalization is likely to have limited identity effects at best. At worst, it can breed resistance and fragmentation instead of citizenship identity.

Whereas the democratic aspect of inclusion in the constitution-making appears to be particularly relevant to the CEE, the effects of the Charter are uncertain. Although the chaotic structure of the Charter of Fundamental Rights by the standards of classical constitutionalism resembles the constitutions of Central and Eastern European countries rather than constitutions of the old EU member states, an effect of a heteronomous constitution provided by an asymmetrical and barely transparent method can inhibit the legitimacy of the Charter as a basis for a shared identity. In particular, in view of the experiences of the so-called 'Stalinist' constitutions in CEE countries, the identity effects of the Charter may be limited in the new EU member states. Many charters of fundamental rights are brought into being to end tyranny. However, this is not the case with the EU. The CEE countries enjoyed a full measure of freedom and security from arbitrary and oppressive government prior to their EU membership, but the period of constitutional freedom has been fairly short. In this sense, the perception of heteronomy of a hegemonic constitutionalization can produce counterproductive results. It depends inter alia on the perception by the CEE countries whether the EU embraces a paternalist approach of the EU towards new member states or rather puts emphasis on the Charter as including constitution-making experiences of CEE, thus representing a shared enterprise and general commitment. In other words, the Charter of Fundamental Rights has to be regarded as an expression of commonality in CEE and at the same time to produce some added value for the CEE.[157]

Third, regarding the effects of the constitutionalization, we can identify them as varying between uniformization and diversification. Here, collective identity would not be generated by the process of the constitution-making, inclusion and an equal access to it, but the Charter of Rights would have supported a shared identity through the legal practice of the courts. As a consequence, a shared and coherent vision of European rights would produce identification with the institutions of the EU as embodying this vision. As the Canadian experience with a Charter of Fundamental Rights and Freedoms of 1982 demonstrates, Charters tend to have uniformization effects on a political community. They tend to further legal uniformity by suppressing legal diversity, which can prove to be disastrous in heterogeneous communities with a tenuous relationship between the national and supranational legitimacy.[158] The Canadian Charter has undermined the policy autonomy of the provinces by giving a policy veto to the Supreme Court, an institution that is more receptive to the policy preferences of central elites, rather than local elites.[159] Against this background, attempts to engender legal uniformity can be interpreted as non-liberal, as constitutional tolerance belongs to the liberal virtues of European citizenship.[160] Therefore, the Charter of Fundamental Rights (against its liberal rights-orientated aims) would entail non-liberal effects of uniformization. In this sense, it could be counterproductive regarding a construction of political identity for European citizens, since it could generate resistance rather than identification.[161] At this point, we can refer to the difference between citizenship uniformity and citizenship identity, introduced in Chapter 4. In contrast to citizenship uniformity, citizenship identity indicates a layer of commonness among citizens pertaining to a common denominator of shared identity without suppressing other identity differences. In this sense, it is supposed to have bridging, rather uniforming effects.

Fourth, there can be impediments of the identity construction as a result of systemic failures of the Charter. Two cardinal problems with far-reaching systemic implications can be differentiated. On the one hand, it is a question of whether member states will continue to be bound by EU fundamental rights in the event that they deviate from European Union law. On the other hand, it is unclear whether and under what circumstances the supremacy of Community/Union law can supersede national fundamental rights.[162] These unresolved issues make the Charter prone to producing conflicts between the EU legal system and national fundamental rights, thus contributing to conflicts rather than generating a common value system conducive to shared identity. Even though these conflicts could lead in the long term to a delimitation of the scope of rights and their better understanding through debate and case law, the middle term effects are likely to be disruptive.

In addition, the rights-orientated approach to European identity reflects more systemic problems of liberal citizenship, particularly regarding collective identity. On the one hand, the rights-based process of constitutionalization is built on the concept of individual autonomy, which establishes individual equality in the access to rights.[163] In the process, the visibility and identifiability of rights is believed to generate a perception of commonality among European citizens. On the other hand, by enhancing visibility of rights within a political document it enhances and even institutionalizes distrust towards political authorities of the EU as a potential threat to the rights, thus rendering identification with the EU more difficult.[164] This is an implication of liberal citizenship, which operates with trust and distrust, rather than thick collective identity. This implication could worsen if the Charter did not become any real source of rights for European citizens, as its legal status has long been uncertain.[165]

Fifth, by giving more voice to the courts the Charter will support the 'judicialization of politics', which was a further implication of the Canadian Charter of Fundamental

Rights. Since Charters are frequently ambiguous they tend to produce conflicts between different levels of political authority (in the case of the EU it would be European and national law), and the role of the judges in the process of political decision-making would increase. Some authors stress the positive side of this process, as political conflicts will be transferred into legal conflicts, thus depoliticizing the EU.[166] However, the depoliticizing of conflicts can have negative consequences in the case of the EU. On the one hand, depoliticizing goes hand in hand with a decrease in visibility, an effect the Charter was supposed to reverse. On the other hand, in view of its democratic deficit and the already elitist approach to legitimacy, the judicialization of politics would reduce even further the transparency of the EU decision-making and widen the gap between elites and the population.[167] As a consequence, it would mean even less influence of the EU citizens on the decisions at the European level, which is detrimental to the process of community-building and citizenship identity.[168]

This point of critique is consistent with a more general thesis of the new constitutionalism, which argues that there is a general shift towards juristocracy in democratic regimes, since judicial review replaces the parliamentary decision-making process. In this sense, constitutionalization may lead to a crisis of democracy.[169] In accordance with this position, the Charter of Fundamental Rights could have negative side effects not only in light of the liberal model of citizenship, but more generally with regard to democracy theory. Against this background, representative institutions would need to be reinvigorated to assume their democratic role of gatekeeper of the legislative process and to counterbalance the judicialization effects of the Charter in the EU. This implies that political decisions should be approved by a representative assembly and be subject to scrutiny by representative assemblies.[170] Paradoxically, a European constitution would need to neutralize the effects of the Charter by strengthening democratic elements.

Collective identity through inflation of rights

If rights are to spawn collective identity, they have to fulfil certain criteria including the type of rights, the range of rights and a minimum of coherence of rights.

First, the type of rights is consequential for collective identity. Fundamental rights have less identity-generating power than particular community rights, as the former frequently relate to human beings rather than to citizens. Group identification and commitment to the general interests of a particular political community is in general difficult to engender by rights, as opposed to obligations. However, fundamental or human rights score even lower in the scale of identity stimulation. As rights-based citizenship can be expected to produce thin political identity, it draws its limited power of identity-making from the particular character of citizenship. In this sense, the constitutionalization of fundamental or human rights with universalistic character is consistent with the EU's self-image as a civilizing normative power, but it runs counter to the efficacy of identity politics.[171]

Second, the range of rights is also significant for the construction of collective identity, even if only a thin one. The narrower the range is or the less effective the rights are in practice, the less likely it is that citizens will identify with a given set of rights, and hence the identity effects will be weakened.[172] The criterion of the range applies both to the scope of rights (political, social, and civil rights) and their legal 'bite'. A legally binding set of comprehensible rights, as opposed to a list of postulates with a merely declaratory character, will certainly have more identity-making power. At this point, the double-edged character of the identity-generating effects of rights becomes apparent again. While a binding set of rights enhances the visibility of citizenship, it simultaneously strengthens the role of courts, which is problematized by the notion of 'judicialization' of politics and its potentially negative implications for collective identity.

Third, a set of rights has to exhibit a minimum of coherence. This criterion mirrors the dilemma of constitutionalization in diverse societies. Constitutions or sets of rights reflecting a coherent value system are more likely to have stronger identity effects, but can alienate relevant social groups. In contrast, ambivalent sets of rights can have fragmenting effects, as they are incapable of delivering a reliable value orientation. This limits the second criterion without contradicting it, since it implies that more rights are not necessarily better than fewer. An inflation of rights delivers an impression of lacking seriousness, particularly if it leads to contradictions. This is not to say that systems of rights can avoid systemic contradictions, such as between liberty and equality. However, a set of rights will have a limited identity-forming capacity if it is based on an excessive listing of rights without much consideration for their coherence. In this sense, a set of rights ought to be able to set out a common vision, a shared set of constitutional ideals, which would generate a citizenship identity to be shared across national communities. However, this does not have to mean that constitutions have to be definite and obvious in every respect, since some degree of ambiguity (as opposed to semantic confusion) might be useful with regard to integration of diversity.[173] In other words, the goal of rights-orientated collective identity cannot be to inflate rights in order to make each citizen recognize in a given set of rights at least a part of his identity, but rather to offer shared rights as a basis for a shared identity.

Against this background, the provisions of the Charter of Fundamental Rights should be expected to have a limited identity-stimulating capacity at best. First, the provisions are not addressed to Union citizens, but to the institutions of the Union and to the member states only when they are implementing Union law (Chapter VII, Article 51 of the Charter).[174] As a result of this, it is uncertain whether Union citizens can legally claim the rights provided for in the Charter. Furthermore, many of the Charter provisions are vague, redundant, and often contradictory. For example, Article 14 states the right to education with the possibility of receiving free compulsory education: it is highly unclear if this right can be claimed legally. Article 21 forbids any discrimination on any ground, such as sex, and the first sentence of Article 23 guarantees additional equality between men and women. However, the second provision in Article 23 allows for discrimination on the grounds of sex in the form of specific advantages for the under-represented sex, which is quite contradictory.

Particularly problematic is the insistence on a division between 'rights' and 'principles' that upholds division between universal rights and particular socio-economic rights. This is mirrored in the wording of the rights. While the civil rights are expressed in the form of a fundamental right ('everyone has the right' to life, to freedom of speech and religion, to respect for private and family life etc.), socio-economic rights are formulated as positive rights, generally only in accordance with 'national law and practice'. For instance, Article 28 specifies that 'workers have the right to collective bargaining and to strike', but only 'in accordance with Community law and national laws and practices', which significantly limits the particular appeal of the socio-economic rights. Article 30 states that workers also have the right not to be unjustifiably dismissed, but only in 'accordance with Community law, national laws and practices'.[175] This division between universal and particular rights would not have been problematic if the role of particular rights was strengthened independently from the practices of the member states.

Apart from this, the Charter states the right to environmental protection (Article 37) as well as the right to health care (Article 35) and social security (Article 34-2), which are vaguely formulated. The degree of vagueness is also increased by the provisions that, instead of formulating a right directly, require the EU to recognize and respect pre-existing rights. For instance, Articles 25 and 26 state that the 'Union recognizes and respects the rights of' the elderly and disabled people; and Article 34-1 states that the 'Union recognizes and respects the right to social security benefits and social services'. Other examples include Article 22 (the 'Union shall respect cultural, religious and linguistic diversity') and Articles 37 and 38 (a high level of environmental and consumer protection should be 'integrated into or ensured' by EU policies).[176] This wording suggests duties and obligations. However, these are not duties of citizens, but obligations on the part of the EU, which are impossible to execute due to their vague and declaratory formulation. In fact, these 'duties' are goals of the EU activity. In the same vein, the Lisbon Treaty (adopting the wording of the draft Constitutional Treaty (CT)) mentions the fight against social exclusion and dicrimination as a Union objective as well as full employment and social progress as its goals (Article 2 in General Provisions 4).

Nonetheless, the Convention on the Charter of Fundamental Rights exhibits an apparent tendency towards universal rights, as opposed to specific European values.[177] A discourse analysis conducted by Marika Lerch demonstrates that the globally orientated human rights discourse in the Charter, which stresses the EU's international commitments and responsibilities, gained prominence during the debate and significantly shaped the discursive space for defining the fundamental rights.[178] Furthermore, the preamble of the Charter refers to the common and indivisible universal values on which the Union is founded and to diversity of cultures, tradition and identities in Europe. On the one hand, this leads us again to the question of whether the application of universal rights can be effective in respect to distinctive collective identity in the EU.[179] On the other hand, the emphasis on the diversity of identities in the EU suggests constitutional multinationalism, rather than constitutional patriotism.[180]

The Union citizenship establishes a derivate citizen born out of the European Community strategy to establish a single market. However, market citizens (according to the libertarian reading of liberal citizenship) do not exhibit any clear allegiance towards one political centre. Hence, the specific rights of Union citizens are mobility rights, necessary for the establishment and a proper functioning of a common market.[181] However, even regarding the essential freedom of movement, the EU does not confer an equal status on all citizens. With regard to the Eastern Enlargement (and previously the Southern Enlargement) of the EU, transition periods for some types of community workers and their families, for instance in the construction industry, have been introduced. This considers the services as well, but there are also transition periods with regard to the acquisition of property. There is therefore an asymmetry in the status of those rights that poses a serious problem for the conceptualization of citizenship as an equal status. This contrasts visibly with the principle of non-discrimination (Article 1a in the General Provisions 3 of the Lisbon Treaty), which is stated as an objective of the

European Union on the equal footing with fundamental freedoms. Constitutionalizing serious contradictions might not be, however, the best means to construct a shared value system, as it leads to constitutional fiction, rather than citizenship identity.[182] In this sense, we can identify a lack of coherence within the rights-based European citizenship: while the European Court of Justice uses citizenship to fill gaps left by primary and secondary law mostly with regard to non-discrimination,[183] the accession treaties have allowed a 'renationalization' of European freedoms, against the promises of equality inherent in the citizenship concept.[184]

Concerning the normative binding force of charters of fundamental rights, it is mostly the preamble that reflects the value system of the community in a condensed, but powerful, form. Although the European Charter is expected to generate a shared value system (as the basis for collective identity) rather than express it, we witness a normative helplessness, which is visible both in the preamble of the Charter of Fundamental Rights and the preamble of the Constitutional Treaty (and the Lisbon Treaty). The preamble of the Charter highlights the common values of the European peoples, in particular in their common pursuit of peace. In the preamble of the CT common values are mentioned in the context of humanism, as the human dignity plays a central role in the normative appeal of the preamble of the Charter. Both preambles put the 'human person', rather than the citizen, into their centre. In contrast, the Union citizens are not mentioned in the preamble, a decision that does not strengthen the political intersubjectivity of the citizens. In addition to frequent references in the CT to 'persons', a term lacking political meaning, the French proposal of 'EU peoples' prevailed. However, this proposal highlights diversity rather than shared citizenship. Even though the draft Constitutional Treaty mentions liberal values such as pluralism and tolerance (Article I-2 of the CT, Article 1a in the General Provisions 3 of the Lisbon Treaty), it fails to make an explicit reference to liberty, which suggests that the relevance of the democratic revolutions of 1989 have been underplayed with regard to European integration. This weakens the constitutional ideal of liberty, in particular relevant for liberal citizenship. Equally, the dark side of the European history is not referred to, which makes the sources of the European spiritual and moral heritage appear fairly vague. An explicit reference to European experiences with totalitarian and authoritarian regimes could have rendered the value system historically better situated and thus comprehensible for the entire citizenry. Moreover, it could give more consistency to the inflationary listing of values, rights and principles. The statement of bitter experiences in the preamble of the CT is too vague to be perceived as an historical point of reference for most of the citizens.

Against this background, the most striking feature of the Charter is an overload of rights and vaguely formulated goals. Numerous rights in the field of environmental protection and social market economy are aims for state activity rather than judiciable rights of citizens. Nonetheless, these rights and goals highlight features of liberal citizenship, rather than republican obligations and duties of citizens. In contrast, duties and obligations of power-wielding bodies towards the citizens are the tenets of liberal citizenship, which institutionalizes civic distrust towards political power. In this sense, the Charter states not only the right to vote and to political accountability but also mentions the right to good administration, which includes for instance 'the obligation of the administration to give reasons for its decisions' (Article 41-2).[185]

Moreover, the Charter itself, in Article 51, questions the judiciability of the rights. This, however, occurs without any attempt to distinguish between judiciable 'rights' and non-judiciable 'principles'. While the EU is required to recognize and respect a right, there is nothing in the Charter to imply that this refers only to rights that have already been provided for by member states or at EU level.[186] As a consequence, we deal in this case with a dilution of rights, rather than their strengthening and visibility enhancement. This is particularly relevant with regard to expected functions of the Charter as a source of collective identity. The traditional function of a Charter as a weapon of a Court of Justice to temper legislation in accordance with fundamental rights, which is the case with the US Supreme Court, is in the EU less probable. The European Court of Justice has hitherto shown little ambition in striking down EU provisions for violations of human rights or rights of the EU.

The list of rights, values and solidarities in the Charter is lengthy. In addition, the CT in an obvious attempt to conjure the EU as a community of values, which would establish a direct link to shared identity, offers a particularly excessive list of values:

> The Union is founded on the values of respect for human dignity, freedom, democracy, equality, the rule of law and respect for human rights, including the rights of persons belonging to minorities. These values are common to the Member States in a society in which pluralism, non-discrimination, tolerance, justice, solidarity and equality between women and men prevail (Article I-2 of the CT, Article 1a of the Lisbon Treaty).

At this point, we should stress the difference between an interpretative openness of the Charter and an inflation of rights and values. As mentioned above, it is sometimes argued that constitutions can only fulfil the integrative function if it remains open to different interpretations, thus giving heterogeneous societies an opportunity to integrate. However, an interpretative openness does not imply an inflation of values and rights. Gary Schaal differentiates four modes of integration by means of constitution. They include integration by neutrality, integration by value consensus, integration by discourse, and integration by conflict.[187] In the case of the Charter, the frequent references to common values suggest a preference of the Convention for integration by value consensus (and identity resulting from it). Nonetheless, the superfluity and excess of rights and values in the Charter of Fundamental Rights increases the likelihood of value conflicts and, as a consequence value neutrality, as overabundant values and rights that can generate value indifference among citizens.

The mere articulation and listing of values and rights pulls the EU into the contradiction of legality and legitimacy. The constitutionalization of a plethora of rights and values follows an underlying logic of confounding rights and political demands. Wishful states of the world become political demands and they in turn become codified as rights and values, which not only increases the probability of conflict between values and rights, but also reduces the identity-stimulating effects of the constitution. If the constitution reflects almost every right, value and political demand there is, there cannot be any common ground for collective identity, since citizenship identity is a *shared* identity, which presupposed intersubjectivity. Against this background, an inflation of values points to an attempt to compensate for a lacking orientation and value consensus. The proliferation of rights mirrors the EU's absence of reflexive ability to find a shared solution to the problem of deep diversity. This unreflective codification of rights and values promotes more activity of the EU in its statehood characteristics and strengthens the interpretative power of European and national judiciary. For some authors, this overabundance results from the participations of the variety of civil society organizations in the consultations of the Convention, which in terms of democracy is a welcome development.[188] However, it had a negative side effect of inflation of rights, values and objectives in the Charter, which leads us back again to the dilemma of constitutionalization in diverse societies.

The Charter Convention decided to include as many rights as possible, thus creating a burgeoning and chaotic structure of the document. Inclusion of an uninhibited plurality of rights stems from an insufficient understanding of identity workings and its prerequisites, since articulation and conjuration of rights and values does not render them social reality. It can have counterproductive effects instead, as overburdened charters and constitutions degenerate into constitutional lyrics, which go hand in hand with a high probability of citizens' disappointment, rather than civic engagement and citizenship identity. An identity-stimulating constitution would not only state obvious rights, values and principles, but prioritize them and show how conflicts between rights and principles can be resolved. This is a precondition for a charter or constitution to develop a normative power, which would generate a mutual recognition between citizens as equal members of a political community. In this sense, the role of a charter or constitution is not a proliferation of rights and values in heterogeneous societies, but its ability to limit the identity claims of different groups in favour of a citizenship identity. The Charter of Fundamental Rights applied, however, a different approach, which put more emphasis on the recognition and articulating of differences, rather than the recognition and articulating of commonality.

In sum, the Charter exhibits a 'thin' normative status, which does not allow for the development of a meaningful collective identity as it inflates individual rights across the entire document. As the preamble reads, the European Union 'places the individual at the heart of its activities', which can be interpreted as an attempt to establish direct contact with the objects of identity construction. However, the Charter refers to universal values and avoids a formulation of particular European values and obligations. There is no explicit inspiration in shared cultural values, as the Union is merely 'conscious' of 'spiritual and moral heritage'. In addition, the Charter lacks a stronger collective orientation towards a community of destiny, even though there is a reference to 'destiny' present in the preamble of the draft Constitutional Treaty.[189] It remains unclear which kind of destiny it might be, besides the common pursuit of peace and unity in diversity. The construction of the Charter of Fundamental Rights as based on universal rights can have a 'thinning' effect with regard to citizenship rights of the member states. Substantive citizenship rights are pushed towards a universal category of human rights, which gives social, political and civil rights of national citizenship a universal twist, thus semantically equalizing all types of citizens of the EU (nationals, denizens, third country residents) with resident foreigners. However, this is also an observable development of the Union citizenship, as Gerard Delanty argues. He points to Europeanization of national citizenship regimes, which occurred under the impact of a cosmopolitan form of European citizenship. However, this development results in a deficit in the values of solidarity and social justice leading to a major crisis at the heart of the European project.[190] By the same token, the universal 'thinning' of citizenship due to the European project can hardly be regarded as a basis for a collective identity conjured by European political elites.

Collective identity through rights to solidarity

The traditional constitutionalism is based on the liberal constitutional ideal of freedom, which becomes realized in a political union of equal legal subjects whose freedom is protected through constitutionalized law. However, new constitutional ideals including solidarity are increasingly discussed in scholarly debates on constitutionalism.[191] As solidarity lies at the heart of the republican citizenship, the constitutionalizing of solidarity rights is expected to generate a form of republican civic identity with liberal means. In this sense, we deal here with a further case of an expectations–outcome gap. In addition, an increasingly popular argument finds identity-making mechanisms primarily in social rights, which would render the EU not only salient, but also attractive for the citizens.[192] As a consequence, a sort of utilitarian allegiance towards the EU is believed to develop, probably as a first step of a more resilient collective identity.

Against this background, I want to discuss the issue of solidarity rights both with regard to the Charter of Fundamental Rights and the solidarity provisions of the Constitutional Treaty in the field of foreign and defence policy.[193] The entire Chapter IV of the Charter of Fundamental Rights points to solidarity; however, it is highly unclear as to how far solidarity may be considered a right. Moreover, numerous references to solidarity rights can be found in the Charter of Fundamental Rights and the CT. Ambitious in its conception, the reference to solidarity represents an attempt to shift liberal EU citizenship from a market freedoms-based conception towards a Marshallian notion of citizenship, in which solidarity and social rights are expected to represent the final phase of citizenship development.[194] The wording of solidarity in the Charter relates to welfare and social rights, which can also be regarded as a part of the liberal citizenship, or more precisely its welfare-orientated versions. In the liberal tradition of Marshall, social rights and welfare rights had a function to support civil and political rights, whereas the issue of collective identity was of secondary relevance, as the notion of the rights triad was explored against the background of a pre-existing national community. Therefore, the reference to solidarity in the Charter could suggest either the existence of obligations to solidarity or point to the conjuration of non-existing solidarity in the EU by its political elites. However, the residence-derived European citizenship cannot draw on 'thick' identity resources of solidarity. As solidarity in the EU is a decentralized resource, it is difficult to institutionalize at the European level.[195]

These problems are visible in an uneasy relationship of the Charter towards the solidarity rights. As Augustín José Menéndez points out, only some rights to solidarity are defined as fundamental rights. These are mostly work-related rights, whereas universalistic rights to solidarity are formulated for instance as policy goals.[196] Nonetheless, even such an incorporation and reference to solidarity as a right might be used by the member states to constrain further freedoms of movement within the EU, which is considered a fundamental right. In this sense, an attempt to stimulate European identity by shifting its perceivable characteristics from rights relating to the Single Market towards more social dimensions of Europe can give some additional legal arguments for protective measures of the EU member states, thus strengthening national identities rather than encouraging collective European identity.[197]

The extensive, even if ambivalent usage of 'rights to solidarity' in the Charter of Fundamental Rights could not prevent the French rejection of the European Constitution, of which the Charter was a part. There was a strong perception among the French population that a dismantling of the French welfare state occurs through the European integration process. This perception related to the EU as a neoliberal deregulation machine based on liberal freedoms, rather than on social achievements of European history.[198] Nonetheless, the frequent reference to 'solidarity' is conspicuous throughout the entire CT, even though the meaning of these references varies strongly from case to case. There is a reference to solidarity between generations, social solidarity among member states and solidarity among peoples: 'As a part of social solidarity the EU shall combat social exclusion and discrimination, promote social justice and protection' (Article I-3 of the CT, Article 2 of the Lisbon Treaty).

Furthermore, there is reference to solidarity in the draft Constitutional Treaty, in particular in the articles on foreign and defence policy (Chapter V).[199] In this case, it is a solidarity between member states, but it relates to existential solidarity of survival, which would point to a stronger community element in the EU. Nonetheless, the idea of mutual security guarantees has been quite controversial in the Convention debates (Article I-43). The clause relates to states that are victims of terrorist attack or natural and man-made disasters. The implication of this provision is uncertain, particularly since Article III-214 of the draft CT (proposed by the European Convention prior to the changes at the Intergovernmental Conference in 2003), concerning closer cooperation on mutual defence and providing for a quite ambitious establishment of a collective defence system within the EU, has been entirely removed from the CT. In addition, Article I-40(7) of the draft CT stating, 'if one of the Member States ... is the victim of armed aggression on its territory, the other participating States shall give it aid and assistance by all the means in their power' has been deleted from the CT (Article I-41).[200]

The remaining articles on the solidarity clause are extremely vague, making it uncertain whether these provisions imply a real military defence guarantee or could be fulfilled by a mere condemnation of the aggression or even solely by a symbolic declaration of aid, especially by the non-NATO countries. Since the Article applies to every member of the EU, it posed a dilemma for the neutral member states – Austria, Finland, Ireland and Sweden – which realized during the IGC summit in December 2003 that a literal application of the solidarity clause would be inconsistent with their security policies. The Article was given a short-lived supplement in December 2003 with another vague statement saying that the solidarity clause '... shall not prejudice the specific character of the security and defence policy of certain Member States'. However, even this diluted version has been removed from the Constitutional Treaty.[201] Moreover, the declaration in Articles I-43 and III-329 of the CT states clearly that '... none of the provisions of Articles I-43 and III-329 of the Constitution is intended to affect the right of another Member State to choose the most appropriate means to comply with its own solidarity obligation towards that Member State'. Hence, an explicit defence clause is not provided by the supplemented Constitutional Treaty, which may lead to the conclusion that a solidarity obligation in the field of common security and defence policy has only a limited range.[202]

The issue of solidarity and solidarity rights stresses in particular the problems of identity generation through rights. An identity-stimulating constitution is an expression of a basic consensus in a given society. This consensus is not subject to daily fluctuations of the public opinion, as the constitution does not change frequently. It thus expresses a societal agreement pertaining to solidarity above ideological and socio-economic cleavages. As a result of the constitutional agreement, democratic societies are capable of productive processing of solidarity claims.[203] This position highlights that constitutions have identity-stimulating effects in democratic societies or embody a consensus relating to basic values and norms, rather than making visible the value divergences and deep diversity. Against this background, it is doubtful whether the Charter of Fundamental Rights and the European Constitution with its provisions integrated into the Lisbon Treaty will be capable of generating collective identity in the EU.[204] Regardless of the logic of liberal citizenship, which can only produce weak political identity, the particular construction of the Charter exhibits structural problems that are likely to reproduce contradictions, rather than contribute to a shared rights-based identity. Both the inflation of solidarities in the Charter and the ambiguity of solidarity provisions in the field of foreign and defence policy reflect an inability of the EU to react to the change in the traditional basis of solidarity and live up to its image as a postmodern polity.[205] Moreover, the inflation of solidarities can be perceived as a hidden agenda for the expansion of the state to the detriment of the political liberty, which is a major tenet of liberal citizenship.

Conclusions

The Charter of Fundamental Rights and the draft Constitutional Treaty show clear features of liberal citizenship. It is not just the overall focus on rights, including rights to solidarity, but a specific approach to rights in the EU. For instance, the rights to good administration are the cornerstone of liberal citizenship, as they codify the distrust of individual citizens towards their government of trustees.[206] Nevertheless, even liberal citizenship is anchored in certain values such as pluralism and tolerance, which can become constitutionalized and further a shared citizenship identity (even if only a weak one). However, inflation of rights, values and solidarities occurs to the detriment of coherence, which is necessary to promote political collective identity. A certain vagueness and openness of constitution might be necessary to stimulate a shared identity, but an incoherent listing of a plethora of rights, values and solidarities appear rather to weaken the identity-promoting ability of the liberal citizenship, rather than to increase it. The overload of rights and principles can cause a constitutional fiction, as a result of which rights degenerate into the declarations of wishful states of the world, and consequently lose their legal entitlement character. Against this background, this inflation of non-judiciable rights would have rather the opposite effect than the advocates of constitutional patriotism envisaged. It is therefore doubtful whether a redirection of citizens' affective attachments from national communities towards a post-national civic, rights-based community can be achieved with the Charter of Fundamental Rights.[207] Therefore, the draft Constitutional Treaty and the Charter of Fundamental Rights in particular cannot offer much identity guidance to European citizens, as the Charter Convention was mostly concerned with neutralizing controversies over fundamental rights, rather than with offering a coherent and stimulating framework for citizenship identity. As a consequence, the Charter contains solidarity-related references that distort the approach of liberal citizenship to collective identity. Nonetheless, the incoherent and superfluous usage of solidarities was introduced to escape the critique of neoliberalism in the EU. This non-substantive reference to solidarity as an 'excuse' has been additionally exacerbated by the merely declaratory application of the solidarity clause within the foreign and defence policy of the draft Constitutional Treaty (and consequently of the Lisbon Treaty).

In sum, identity politics of rights-based citizenship might not be the best way to forge a collective identity in the EU. There are two major implications highlighting scepticism in this respect. First, weak identity of liberal citizenship might require vigorous identity politics to establish collective identity. The differentiation between the transformer and the catalyst identity politics suggests that in the case of liberal citizenship a construction of collective identity cannot rely on catalyst impact of constitutionalization, but makes necessary more invasive identity technologies of the state in order to transform the thin identity character of liberal citizenship into a thicker and more sticky identity. However, liberal citizens are expected to be aware of the dangers of the expansive statehood associated with intense identity politics. In this respect, invasive identity politics might be counterproductive in the context of liberal values. More intense and invasive identity politics are a foreign body in the liberal citizenship, which institutionalizes citizens' distrust towards political authorities. Here, we can point to a mismatch between the efforts of the EU to establish more sticky collective identity and the identity logic of liberal citizenship. As long as the EU uses rights and rights-orientated mechanisms of constitutionalization as a basis for the generation of thick identity, we will be faced with an expectations–outcome gap.

Second, there is a further dilemma concerning a constitutionalization that attempts to facilitate a construction of post-national political identity using mainly references to rights. Constitutionalism reflects the principle of rule of law, rather than the political principle of democracy. In this sense, the idea of rule of law and the constitutionally bounded state is not inherently democratic. These concepts developed independently of the idea of democracy, as a constitutional state and its institutions of checks and balances, as well as the effective rule of law, were supposed to protect liberty by averting potential dangers following from the temptations of power.[208] Therefore, liberal principles of constitutionalism and rule of law serve the purpose of *limiting* the scope of democracy and avoiding the harmful consequences of democratic rule by majorities and elites. As modern democracies rest on two pillars – the constitutional one referring to the liberal precautions against an abuse of power, and the popular one referring to 'the expression of popular will and choice'[209] – an over-constitutionalized EU with an overabundance of rights, listings of values and numerous declaratory references to solidarities, would limit the scope of the still deficient democracy in the EU. This would be counterproductive in terms of a citizenship identity, as it would shift the focus of EU politics even further towards the elites and institutions and away from the citizenry. The existing imbalance between the constitutional principle and the popular principle could therefore be exacerbated even further.[210]

Caesarean citizenship and the European politics of insecurity

The current forms of caesarean citizenship in the EU can be assessed against the background of Urlich Becks' claim that we are now living in a global risk society.[211] Political governance of risks, above all in forms of restrictive migration control and the 'war on terror', have become major tenets of state activity and pervade citizenship practice of nation-states as well as the European Union. The citizenship practices of governing risk are neither exclusively nor predominantly military. The new citizenship practices include inter alia biometric categorization of citizens and non-citizens, an increase in surveillance, rendition of suspects, intelligence cooperation with authoritarian regimes, and exchange of DNA data files of citizens within the EU. The notion of a risk society in which there are uncontrollable and unpredictable threats and dangers promotes excessive activity by the state, which not only transforms citizenship practices but also makes it easier for political authorities such as the EU to perpetuate the *politics of insecurity* as an instrument of identity construction. The collective identity in the form of homogenization of threat perception is forged through securitization of the citizenship issues.[212] This does not necessarily mean that the only goal of political authorities is to generate collective identity via securitization and that all security concerns are illegitimate. Regardless of the motives of the political decision-makers, securitization practices entail identity effects that cannot be ignored.

This section deals with the current trends of caesarean citizenship in the EU by focusing on the European politics of insecurity. First, I will relate caesarean citizenship to the notion of the neurotic citizen and briefly sketch the politics of insecurity in the EU. Second, I will discuss in more detail the EU's immigration and asylum policies as identity management. As the immigrants and asylum seekers are depicted as a challenge to the protection of national and EU identity, migration becomes politically constructed as an issue pertaining to the security of European citizens. Furthermore, I will focus on the question of who is the European Leviathan in the field of migration policy. Third, I will discuss the fight against terrorism as an identity-generating device in the EU. Here, I will concentrate on the European approach to homeland security and will explore the issue of the European Leviathan in the 'war on terror'.

Caesarean citizenship, neurotic citizens and the European Union

Caesarean citizenship confronts citizens with threat scenarios highlighting their shared destiny and group belonging, as their security is in danger as a result of their membership of a specific community or group. For instance, the perception of being a collective target for terrorists increases feelings of belonging to the same (endangered) category. At the same time, political authorities redefine some citizenship aspects as a result of their security policies. If the citizenry responds positively to threat scenarios, political authorities frame their security policies to achieve the resonance of insecurity required to justify emergency measures.[213]

Against this background, politics of insecurity pertain to the caesarean citizenship, which produces collective identity in the sense of homogeneity of fear by establishing and reinforcing boundaries between friends and enemies and expands executive-centred government at the expense of popular influence.[214] However, as discussed in Chapter 4, this is not collective identity in the political sense as a general commitment to common interest, but rather a method of identity politics with a goal of establishing a shared perception of danger and threat, which would in turn generate the feeling of homogeneity and support for emergency measures. On the one hand, politics of insecurity aims at producing a diffuse feeling of insecurity. The feeling of insecurity makes the citizens call for additional state action, which causes a shift within citizenship from rights towards compliance or – put differently – from autonomous citizenship towards subjecthood. On the other hand, the identity technologies of political authorities attempt to give the enemy a face and a name by focusing on migration and minorities. In this sense, combating migration and terrorism as diffuse threats goes hand in hand with attempts to identify terrorists and migrants as a specific point of reference for caesarean citizenship and its homogenization practices.

In the caesarean model of citizenship, this dichotomy highlights the difference between the citizen and the suspect. As for instance biometric technologies and new methods of surveillance are employed to press forward with the restrictive practices of the caesarean citizenship, citizens tend to perceive themselves in terms of commonalities, rather than differences. The politics of insecurity is therefore associated with identity construction, as the political authorities promote and respond to the 'neurotic citizenship' of a risk society.[215] A neurotic citizen defines his citizenship through a prism of permanent insecurity, which can be addressed only by the state. The liberal citizen's preference for liberty and freedom is surpassed by her/ his fears of survival in a risk society. This has not only cognitive but also behavioural implications. On the one hand, the neurotic citizen calls upon the state to expand its activity as a response to security considerations. On the other hand, a neurotic citizen is not necessarily a passive one, as in the Hobbesian world. The focus of citizenship shifts from elections and participation in public life towards reporting potentially dangerous everyday situations and spying on compatriots. Under these circumstances, political authorities are inclined to perpetuate the feeling of insecurity, thus transforming security politics into politics of insecurity. By demonstrating its indispensability (and thus legitimacy), political authorities represent the new Leviathan, willingly supported by the fear-inclined citizens. However, the growing state activity in the realm of security, surveillance and discipline is not entirely a bottom-down issue of state control over its population: neurotic citizenship supplements the traditional mechanisms of state surveillance, since the panoptical subjects willingly watch over themselves. This corresponds to a *viewer society*, which relies decreasingly on trust and increasingly on mutual forms of horizontal supervision.[216]

In this context, Carl Schmitt's writings can be applied as a source for analyzing politics of insecurity. Both his friend–enemy antagonism and the politics as a state of exception are useful concepts for exploring current trends of identity construction through politics of insecurity.[217] Caesarean citizenship is reinforced when surveillance and biometrics as exceptions to normal politics become 'normalized'. This politics of exception becomes a part of contemporary identity construction and management, as it attempts to establish the state of exception as the norm. Both surveillance and biometric categorization question the validity of autonomous citizenship by regarding citizens as suspects.[218] As an essential element of the caesarean citizenship, politics of the state of exception reduces politics to bare survival, where the rights component of citizenship is shifted from citizens towards the Leviathan. The friend–enemy antagonism is buttressed by policies towards foreign citizens or non-citizens.

The ever-encroaching politics of exception highlights the relevance of the caesarean citizenship and its corresponding identity construction and management in the EU as well. However, the creation of a European Leviathan does not only aim to solve the security problems of the Union citizens outright, as is the case in the Hobbesian state. Instead, to construct collective feelings of insecurity, European authorities are likely to promote a 'culture of fear' that makes citizens overreact to risks, rather than resolve problems of security. For instance, propagation of fear induces citizens to invest in practices that constitute lower risks while higher risks are presented as minor and ordinary. The culture of fear therefore makes neurotic citizens react to risks disproportionately to actual dangers. As the politics of insecurity produces feelings of vulnerability, neurotic citizens of a risk society are prone to panic, which in turn promotes gated communities with a trend towards isolation and insularity.[219] In this sense, the feeling of commonality is not based on a general commitment to public interest, but on a much more basic drive to survive.

In the context of the EU, there are attempts to come to terms with the discrimination between friend and enemy as the major tenet of caesarean citizenship. For instance, the EU stresses politics of insecurity by exchanging passenger data with the US, harmonizing its biometric identification practices, regulating surveillance of telecommunications, etc. Furthermore, the EU has become more active by differentiating between citizens and suspects by improving the Schengen Information System, with 15 million records on persons and objects within the EU, as well as by establishing a database with fingerprints of asylum seekers (Eurodac).[220] In the European state of exception, individuals become increasingly bereft of their political subjectivity as criminal migrants and terrorists who lose their rights to asylum and due process.[221] Against this background, the politics of insecurity in the EU includes not only an increased exploitation of threat images, but also a shift from 'normal politics' to the Schmittian decisionist politics of the exception perpetuated by executive branches with 'operational powers'.[222]

In the case of the EU it is particularly striking that no policy field other than the EU justice and home affairs (JHA) became subject to such rapid and widespread Europeanization and made its way to the treaties and to the centre of the political agenda, even prior to the events of 9/11. There has been a significant increase in legislative output in the area of JHA since the early 1990s, while in 2000 the Council adopted a total of seventy-five JHA texts, with a higher share of legally binding acts than ever before.[223] As early as the 1970s, as a response to the wave of left-wing terrorism in Western Europe, some arrangements for policy coordination among the interior ministers of the European Community were introduced. The framework of the so-called TREVI group ('terrorisme, radicalisme, extrémisme et violence internationale') remained, however, outside the treaties and retained an informal character without much legislative activity. This changed in the early 1990s, as the Maastricht Treaty established 'justice and home affairs' as one of three pillars of the European Union, whereas the Amsterdam Treaty articulated a goal of creating an area of 'freedom, security and justice'.[224] After the events of 9/11 there was a new acceleration of legislative output and an increase in new institutional arrangements in the EU justice and home affairs.

In addition to the regulative output, the EU established specialized agencies in the field of JHA. Besides Europol, there is the cross-border agency Eurojust, which is primarily a coordinating body, but also serves as an information exchange in the prosecution of terrorism and human trafficking. The new European Agency for the Management of Operational Cooperation at the External Borders (Frontex), established in Warsaw in 2005, not only fulfils coordination functions, but it also participates in the management of the EU's external borders. There exist further EU institutions dealing with surveillance of citizenry. They provide analyses that are used for developing EU risk management strategies. In this sense, they contribute to the EU's caesarean identity construction and management. One of those is the European Monitoring Centre for Drugs and Drug Addiction (EMCDDA) in Lisbon. It supplies the EU with data and risk assessments for specific types of drugs and drug-related crimes as a part of the EU's fight against drug trafficking.[225] At the intergovernmental level, a special office of the EU's Counter-Terrorism Coordinator in the Council Secretariat-General has been established. The EU's Counter-Terrorism Coordinator manages all anti-terrorist activities within the Council and monitors the implementation of EU anti-terrorism measures by the member states. In addition, in order to facilitate the EU police cooperation, the 'Police Chiefs' Task Force' (PCTF) – consisting of member states' police chiefs – was set up in 2000. Its task is to institutionalize (together with

Europol) the exchange of evaluations and planning of common operations in the area of combating cross-border crime.[226]

All these institutions and arrangements follow the logic of identity construction through estrangement. Surveillance and data collection on citizens and non-citizens entail categorization, classification and exclusion, which are on the one hand methods of dealing with sectors of the population that are difficult to assimilate, difficult to control, and trouble-prone. The increasing usage and rationalization of e-security, biometry and the exchange of the passenger name records are directed against citizens as suspects, and attempt to legitimize a shift from the citizen as an empowered individual in the EU to the citizen as the object of control by supranational security agencies.[227]

On the other hand, estrangement defines external enemies who are to be kept away and expelled. As Zygmunt Bauman argues, this is a traditional method of identity construction:

> Slaves were confined to the slave quarters. So were the lepers, the madmen, the ethnic or religious aliens and outcasts. If allowed to wander beyond allotted quarters, they were obliged to wear the signs of their spatial assignment – so that every passer-by is aware that they belong to another space.[228]

With regard to the EU, we can identify two major areas of risk and identity management. First, the EU organizes its resources to fend off migration by establishing exclusion practices at its borders and on its territory. Second, the EU has engaged heavily in the fight against terrorism, particularly after the train bombings in Madrid in 2004 and underground bomb attacks in London in 2005 as well as after several foiled bomb attacks in Germany during recent years.

Migration control as identity management of the EU

Jef Huysmans argues that the EU's immigration policies are related to a wider politicization, as a result of which immigrants and asylum seekers are depicted as a challenge to the protection of national and EU identity.[229] Therefore, migration is politically constructed as an issue pertaining to the security of European citizens. Migration has been increasingly presented as a danger to public order, cultural identity, and labour market stability. In the process, technocratic and political actors of the EU debate and decide the criteria for membership in European societies.[230] The range of threat images is broad. However, these threat images are not necessarily driven by a rational assessment of the current situation, but instead serve identity politics. Presenting immigration as a security issue therefore becomes a part of a discourse of insecurity rather than of security. As a consequence, countering illegal immigration results in a feeling of insecurity, rather than establishing security.

The Europeanization of migration policies entails a trend towards a restrictive and control-oriented approach in this policy area.[231] Recent examples of this trend are coordination of visa policy within the EU and the readmission agreements with neighbouring countries that regulate the forced return of illegal immigrants from EU territory.[232] At the same time, the EU establishes a security discourse that defines migration in terms of identification of existential threats. Images of societal danger from a criminal and invading enemy are reified in the discourse. In the process, the security concerns are defined against the background of dangers to societal integration, threats to the community's conception of a good life and the welfare of the community. Migration is thus increasingly depicted as a threat to the community's survival in its current social and cultural form.

As a result, border control and asylum policies became the cornerstone of defensive collective identity construction perpetuated by the EU. Some authors even argue that the EU's migration policies are coloured by cultural and racist exclusion criteria, thus undermining the EU's self-image of civic community. Most of the asylum seekers in the EU are categorized and classified according to somatic criteria such as skin colour, height and facial characteristics, which is believed to institutionalize racial differentiation and create practices of Euro-racism. This differentiation is given a security connotation, since by introducing stricter border controls and restrictions the EU conveys a threatening image of the outsiders and strangers who attempt to 'invade' the EU.[233]

In addition, this trend in identity politics of migration becomes strengthened even further, as the EU uses biometric technologies in search of dangerous or illegitimate migrants and asylum seekers. Therefore, citizenship is to an increasing degree regarded in terms of its threat to society, as others – aliens, i.e. 'insecure bodies' – attempt to enter the territory of the state. In this context, Benjamin Muller applies Carl Schmitt's concept of 'politics as a state of exception' with regard to migration. As opposed to normal politics, citizens learn to live under the feeling of perpetual threat associated with migrants, since the danger comes from outside. The migrants give a new face to the enemy, which replaces the image of other states as major threats. The politics of citizenship as the state of exception includes the identity management, which distinguishes between qualified and unqualified persons and uses biometrics for authentication of legitimate and illegitimate migrants. A new identity-forging boundary therefore runs between legitimate residents on the territory and the entry-happy asylum seekers/migrants who are regarded as a potential menace to society.[234]

Immigration and asylum policies of the EU: threats to identity?

Sandra Lavenex highlights the duality of the migration discourse of the EU. She argues that the EU asylum and immigration policies are characterized by a tension due to two conflicting policy frames – the frame of internal security and the frame of humanitarianism. While the security frame stresses the necessity to restrict migration across EU borders, and to fend off illegal immigration, the humanitarian frame incorporates the human rights principles of freedom of movement and refugee protection. Lavenex argues that despite this duality the extension of asylum and immigration policies to the Central and Eastern European countries was dominated by the imperative to secure the new border against unwanted immigration.[235] However, securitization of migration is also found in recent initiatives on European borders such as the European Neighbouring Policy (ENP). The European Union recently launched an initiative towards its near abroad, officially in order to avoid a new division of the continent and to set up a circle of friendly countries around Europe. By enjoying peaceful and cooperative relations with these countries the EU can externalize some of its security concerns. Some authors argue, however, that, despite these goals, the ENP will reproduce and perhaps even reinforce the existing barriers between the EU and its neighbours and create new ones. Ruben Zaiotti suggests that the EU suffers from a 'gated community syndrome', which explains the tension between openness and closure, friendship and fences. It results from the 'Schengen culture of internal security', whose key tenet is the focus on security as the central feature of the political process. This focus entails the priority of security over other policy domains, fixation of the EU authorities and national states to protect Europe from internal and external threats, and suspicion towards third countries.[236]

The immigration policies of the EU (as in national communities) have thus become institutionally imagined and materially constructed, with the consequence of a collective perception of dangers. Therefore, the institutional imagination of the EU as a collectivity is generated partly through its immigration policies, as they construct collective boundaries. For the lack of European public space, this construction is conveyed by the national media that addresses the neurotic citizen. The dispersion of news on the EU immigration policies through national media allows for a subtle creation of insecurity and thus commonness of fear.[237] This functions similarly as 'banal nationalism', which in contrast to the irredentist nationalism is forged in the everyday language used by the mass media, particularly in news, rather than during national holidays and international crises. The boundary-making differentiation between 'us' and 'them' establishes a rather unconscious matrix for citizens who regard themselves as belonging to the same collective category.[238] In the case of the EU immigration policies, this collective category is based on a feeling of collective insecurity, as it lacks deeper forms of collective attachment. In particular, the dramatization of threats conveyed by the media is significantly more effective in the EU than positive forms of collective reference such as the anthem, a European holiday or historical European figures. Therefore, mediatized threats that elicit strong affective responses are likely to be central to the EU's efforts to legitimize its immigration policies. Even though the media focus on immigration (linking it with criminality and terrorism) is not entirely politically controllable due to the plurality of the media, political authorities can trigger 'affective epidemics' of insecurity that proliferate through news media and become vital to the legitimacy of regulatory practices of immigration policies. These 'affective epidemics' of insecurity develop a dynamic that resonates with the citizenry in the form of a climate of insecurity, cementing the society in perceived danger.[239]

However, the political discourse of capturing migration from outside the EU as a danger to the cultural identity of Europe appears contradictory. By highlighting the need to culturally integrate the migrants from outside the EU, political authorities of the EU convey a self-image of a culturally homogeneous European society, identifying migrants as a threat. This seems to be a paradox in light of the EU's heterogeneity and its goals of diversity. Nonetheless, the conjuration of homogeneity is a further feature of caesarean citizenship. By emphasizing the necessity to integrate outside migrants, the EU authorities indirectly present an EU image of a culturally homogeneous society prior to migration. The image that migrants are a threat to the EU's societal integration is associated with a further self-image of the EU as a different social model, for instance in comparison with the USA. As the EU member states are believed to share a common vision of a welfare state and a social market economy, the migrants are regarded as rivals in the labour markets and competitors in the distribution of social goods. In this sense, the migration policies are also directed at preserving welfare chauvinism. In the process, migrants are classified as criminals committing welfare fraud, since they want to profit from a community they do not belong to. As Thomas Faist argues, these policies of welfare chauvinism are supported by the application of threat scenarios using notions of an 'invasion' and 'flood' of asylum seekers.[240]

By using a defensive language, the EU conveys a self-image of a genuine community that should be protected. According to William Walters, this 'domopolitics' (protection of a community as home) relates to migrants and refugees as a threat to the European home. Since home is a place to be secured against intruders who threaten its values, its property, and its security through their strangeness, migrants can only remain in Europe as guests who should eventually return to their homes. Therefore, the EU as home can remain a safe and reassuring place of togetherness and unity only when European citizens stay among themselves; otherwise, the familiarity of the home is lost. This identity technology juxtaposes the community of trust and citizenship with the dangerous non-citizenship world of illegal refugees, traffickers and terrorists, whereby it configures social reality as threat scenarios of 'us' versus 'them'.[241]

This juxtaposition promotes attempts to pinpoint the collective identity of the EU under the circumstances of increasing individual mobility and ontological insecurity. Therefore, border controls and asylum restrictions at the European level point to a reterritorialization of the EU by means of a classical nation-state. Whereas border controls within the EU are lifted, external EU borders are increasingly guarded. As similar practices of reterritorialization are common in the Organisation for Economic Co-operation and Development (OECD) world (particularly in the USA, Canada and Australia), the experience of being an EU citizen becomes particularly vivid by crossing external borders, rather than staying home.[242] Therefore, this EU identity technology is linked with attempts to contain EU citizenship within well-guarded EU borders, thus upholding a statist conception of citizenship in the face of transnational mobility.[243]

However, apart from some serious practical human rights considerations, loopholes in democratic accountability are characteristic of caesarean citizenship. As the neurotic citizen surrenders an essential part of his autonomy in favour of his security, the transparency of decision-making and the protection of civil and political rights slip beyond the control of the citizens and become a prerogative of executive authorities.[244] As a result, the EU immigration policies become a part of caesarean citizenship, as not only the content but also the intent of the restrictive policies is strongly questioned by refugee rights activists who criticize the secretive manner of the decision-making and the lack of transparency and democratic scrutiny.[245]

In the case of the EU, there is not much evidence of a large-scale, uncontrolled migration. The ever more restrictive immigration policies of the EU are therefore based on the fears and insecurities of the citizenry.[246] By showing decisiveness and by externalizing migration problems, the EU highlights the seriousness of the problem and contributes to the dispersion of fear and affective epidemics of insecurity.[247] The issues of migration are dealt with mostly by executives using modes of European interstate cooperation, often in isolation from judicial and parliamentary scrutiny. As some authors argue, European executives exploit the absence of legal and administrative constraints at the European level to push through with restrictive migration policies that would not have been feasible at the national level due to more effective control mechanisms of the executives. The European integration of Justice and Home Affairs is therefore primarily driven by interior ministry officials taking advantage of the weakness of the democratic control at the European level. By stressing the link between asylum and internal security, these actors were able to place justice and home affairs at the heart of the European Union.[248]

However, the more restrictive approach to migration defined as a security threat can even exacerbate the problems linked to migration, as a reduction in asylum seekers' civil and social rights might contribute to further clandestinization and criminalization of migration as well as to increased social segregation and illegal employment. The growing focus on control and identification policies by the EU is aimed not only at inhibiting potential migrants from entering the EU, but also targets migrants settled within the EU borders. Policy goals are deterrence, segregation and, eventually, expulsion. As some studies demonstrate, the immigration database analyzes detention and expulsion policies as well as efficient modes of surveillance in anticipation of the counter strategies that migrants invent to escape detection and expulsion. This strategic game between the executives and irregular migrants limits considerably the migrants' capability to manoeuvre and further increases their dependence on criminal networks and institutions. As a result, the political authorities aggravate the problem they want to combat and at the same time strengthen the image of migration as a serious threat.[249] The criminalization of migration by the EU leads to an increase in criminality among migrants, thus representing in a certain sense a self-fulfilling prophecy.[250]

The reinforcement of security-related migration policies promotes the perception of the migrant, and especially the asylum seeker, as a category outside legality. As a consequence of the political link between immigration and criminality, the rights of foreigners in the EU member states have deteriorated. Restrictions were imposed on migrants' basic political and civil rights as well as on their access to economic and social rights, including the right to health care. This represents a contradiction to the human rights paradigm propagated by the EU itself, as the EU member states cooperate regarding interception and interdiction mechanisms, entailing securitization of migration and reinforcing deterrent measures of a preventive security state.[251] Some scholars argue that the increasingly restrictive EU policies plug permissive loopholes in the Geneva Convention, thus undermining global protection of human rights, especially the global asylum norm. The restriction of access to the EU territory, deterrence of applications and a shift of the burden of reviewing claims to third countries suggest that human rights are not the priority in this field.[252] Others propose closing these loopholes by treating migrants as minorities, thus allowing for the application of the normative framework of minority protection to migration and asylum law.[253]

Moreover, there is a further underlying tension between the civil rights of asylum seekers and securitization of migration in the EU. The international refugee law establishes obligations on the states not to return individuals to countries known for human rights abuses. This principle of *non-refoulment* was anchored in the Convention relating to the Status of Refugees signed in 1951. However, the Schengen Convention of 1985, later to be replaced by the Dublin Convention in 1990 as well as the general development of asylum practice in the EU, introduced a contradictory practice with regard to the *non-refoulment* by using the ideology of 'remote control' of migration.[254] The consequence was recourse to extraterritorial interventionism, whose goal was to prevent the refugees from reaching the territory of the EU, where they could claim civil rights.[255] Immigration control thus becomes externalized in order to lift the civil rights obligations of the EU member states towards the potential refugees. This has two implications. First, it causes a collectivization of migrants by treating forced migrants and illegal immigrants equally. This collectivization has homogenizing effects on the EU population by implying that migrants belong to the same homogeneous group. As a result, refugees' rights to asylum have been weakened, since individual claims for asylum have become subject to collective treatment.[256]

Second, it strips migrants of civil rights, thus criminalizing and dehumanizing them, as they are put into extraterritorial detention facilities, for instance in Northern Africa.[257] The goal of the detention facilities as well as the EU-coordinated actions such as Operation Hera 1 in the Canary Islands is mainly to identify who the refugees are.[258] This identity management consists of categorization of friends and enemies as well as inclusion and exclusion practices. This securitized and bureaucratized realm of identity management applies, among others, the biometric technologies for identifying and authenticating threats. This identification entails the allocation of civil rights to refugees considered legitimate and rejection of civil rights to illegitimate refugees. Collective identity of Europeans is therefore mirrored in identification of the collective enemy, in terms of his authentication: biometrics, databanks, and electronic surveillance are used to verify and to discriminate between the qualified others and the unqualified authentic others who are in turn subject to detention and deportation.[259]

These EU practices of identity management increased in the course of the Eastern enlargement.[260] They resulted not only in the geographical extension of Schengen and Dublin regulations to new member states as they had to implement the asylum *acquis,*[261] but also in an even more restrictive handling of asylum procedures in the applicant and later new member countries. As Byrne et al. argue for instance, the Czech Republic in its EU accession zeal had introduced as early as 1993 manifestly unfounded procedures into their asylum determination processes, even though there were on average only 800 applications submitted for refugee status per year. Poland emulated in the 1997 Aliens Act the comprehensive limitation of the rights to asylum that was introduced into the German Constitution in 1993.[262] It included the safe country principle, which allows for the circumventing of *non-refoulment* and thus the International Refugee Law. The adoption of the safe country principle of returning asylum seekers to safe third countries by all EU member states promised to establish a pool of host countries around the EU and to avoid responsibility for breaches of the 1951 Convention.[263] This new *cordon sanitaire* creates a 'sanitary' identity that is based on discrimination and the perception of a collective enemy as abnormal and criminal.[264] However, this enemy is no longer defined in military terms, but rather as a threat to social cohesion, its welfare and the culture. Thus, the identity management establishes and fosters the difference between the citizen and the illegal and illegitimate others. Certainly, it does not mean that fortress Europe is a reality. It depicts rather the attempts of European executives to redraw boundaries in the EU, which has implications for specific collective identity generation associated with the imagery of caesarean citizenship.[265] Particularly striking is the zeal of the European law and order officials to fix the identity using unfoundedly restrictive migration policies and creating the soft (cross-border criminal) and hard (global terrorist) images of dangerous others. In many cases, these images are manipulative in nature. In Hungary, the executive used the shadow of the EU accession to argue that a more restrictive migration policy would need to conform to the EU standards in this realm. Since there was no tangible and precise EU standard, the Hungarian government used its own policy preferences in a manipulative way against its own public.[266]

Who is the European Leviathan in the field of migration policy?

The European executives act in the field of justice and home affairs as a collective European Leviathan with the goal of deterring and deflecting asylum seekers, thus enhancing the image of fortress 'Europe' and at the same time promoting the image of an effective and secure Europe.[267] This image goes hand in hand with new executive strategies reshaping the bureaucratic structure through internal reorganization, outsourcing, and supra-state security alliances giving birth in the case of the EU to a *corporate security state*, which in turn changes the relationship between the citizen and the state.[268] Nonetheless, the identity implications of this development include a tension between the European images as a community of values and its desire to undermine the civil rights of migrants. This tension is likely to grow with the establishment of the EU Fundamental Rights Agency, which is believed to illustrate a growing prominence of human rights within the EU.[269] This strongly conflicts with the securitization discourses of migration and asylum policies.

Let us turn now to the mechanisms and institutions the EU applies within its politics of insecurity in the area of immigration control. In recent years the EU has created a number of agreements and regulations that treat immigration as a security problem, thus making it subject to identity politics consistent with caesarean citizenship. One of the first steps towards a more restrictive EU migration policy was the Council directive 2001/40/EC on mutual recognition of the expulsion of third country nationals. The directive, issued in 2001, stipulated that an expulsion decision made by any EU member state can be implemented in any other EU country. A more comprehensive framework for migration policy in the EU was established by the Hague Programme in 2004. Its main goal was to implement an area of freedom, security and justice in the EU by 2010 by realizing common migration and asylum policies agreed upon in Tampere in 1999. The Hague Programme focused mainly on the security aspects of the EU migration policy, even though it was accompanied by some human rights rhetoric by the EU decision-makers.[270]

Together with the establishment of a common immigration and border policy, the EU began to create specialized agencies to implement and monitor the policy. The first institutional step was the Europol Convention, which was based on the Maastricht Treaty. It regulated the setting up of a European police office (Europol), which began its work in 1999.[271] Europol focuses on combating cross-border crimes, believed to be situated in so-called illegal immigration networks. One of the many objectives of Europol is to prevent and combat illegal immigrant smuggling. Even though it was established in 1994 to a limited extent as an agency fighting the drug trade, its activities extended considerably. Currently, Europol assists the member states with intelligence analysis of transnational crime, facilitates the exchange of information and participates in multinational investigations. In this sense, Europol is a part of a surveillance and investigation system of the EU aimed at the irregular migrants defined as a threat to the EU. Even though Europol officers lack executive powers such as wire tapping or house searches, the EU member states have agreed to grant Europol 'operational powers'.[272] Europol now has considerable influence on multinational investigations, in particular due to its access to intelligence and personal data. Since Europol has access to around 150,000 personal data files, it raises serious concerns of parliamentary and judicial control of its activities.[273] One of the many concerns relating to the executive and uncontrolled nature of Europol is the immunity of Europol officers, even if their activities infringe individual rights such as the right to privacy.[274] Moreover, neither national courts nor the European Court of Justice have jurisdiction over Europol, as a result of the immunity granted to Europol staff and the inviolability of Europol's archives, which again leads us to imagery of a European Leviathan.

A further agency central to the EU migration and asylum policy is the European Agency for the Management of Operational Cooperation at the External Borders (Frontex). The issue of the so-called integrated border management (IBM) has been defined by the EU since 2001 as crucial. The agency was inaugurated in 2005 and was designed to assist the member states in their control of the EU borders. Even though border controls are the responsibility of the member states, Frontex's main tasks include coordination of external border cooperation between the member states, training of national border guards, risk analyses, and monitoring of the research on control and surveillance of external borders.[275] Moreover, Frontex supports the EU member states in organizing joint return operations of irregular immigrants. It works together with other EU bodies, most importantly Europol, but also with the Commission directorate-general Joint Research Centre. In this sense, Frontex is a part of a supranational asylum and migration regime of the EU. In addition to Frontex's activities, the Commission proposed in 2006 to establish rapid border interventions teams, which would assist in dispatching staff with technical and operational know-how regarding border control and surveillance in crisis situations.[276] Although Frontex is already more than just a coordinating body, it is likely to further expand its powers and scope of activity at the expense of the member states. For instance, it declares that member states 'shall refrain from any activity which could jeopardize the functioning of the Agency or the attainment of its objectives'.[277] As a part of the European *corporate security state*, the agency is criticized for assisting in joint return operations, which can be regarded as a manifestation of its repressive powers earning it the label of an 'expulsion agency'. Moreover, Frontex lacks proper democratic control, which causes concerns for the legitimization and accountability of its operations. This being generally problematic with regard to the overtly executive character of the EU migration policy, it holds particularly true for the Frontex activities. The European Parliament is significantly isolated from Frontex information regarding for example the follow-up of its activities. It applies especially with regards to risk assessments, which are not delivered to the European Parliament.[278] Against this background, the activities of Frontex reflect the executive and security-orientated character of caesarean citizenship.

Apart from institutions and funds, the EU deals with unwanted immigration and asylum on the basis of specialized data gathering and data processing systems that are crucial for the EU's surveillance operations. The main EU information system is the Schengen Information System (SIS), which maintains and distributes data related to border security and law enforcement. The SIS stores data on the physical characteristics of individuals, whereas in its follow-up version – SIS II – it will register biometric data.[279] The Thessaloniki European Council from June 2003 called for a coherent approach on biometric identifiers (iris scans, facial recognition and fingerprints) to find EU-wide solutions for documents for third country nationals, EU citizens' passports and information systems.[280] Therefore, in addition to deterrence and expulsion strategies, the EU is digitalizing its borders and expanding the control over identity of individuals. Even though the EU's surveillance devices are mostly employed against migrants from outside the EU (or Europe in the larger sense, since Norway and Iceland also use the SIS), EU citizens also become objects of observation and information gathering, which clearly poses problems for civil rights.[281]

Furthermore, the Commission has proposed a Visa Information System (VIS), which is supposed to allow member states to exchange data on visas issued or denied in any of the EU states and thus to supplement the SIS II.[282] The VIS is a further technological device for identifying irregular immigrants and thus it is believed to 'contribute to the prevention of threats to internal security'.[283] The VIS represents the latest effort by the EU to establish control over identity, since this information system registers all visa applications and the fingerprints of individuals required to have a visa for the EU. It also includes data of the person or company that issued an invitation and is hence responsible for the cost of living of the visa applicant during their stay in the EU. Whereas SIS and SIS II target specifically cross-border criminal activity, the VIS is an instrument of less differentiating surveillance and control of migrants, EU residents and EU citizens. The goal of the VIS is to identify those migrants who legally entered the EU, but then illegally extended their stay. Upon the completion of the VIS, the EU will be able to control the immigrant population on its territory, in addition to its territorial borders.[284]

With the VIS still under construction, the EU possesses yet another information system that has already been operational since 2003. The Eurodac was set up to support the Dublin Regulation, which is to determine which member state is responsible for a given asylum application.[285] The system stores and processes fingerprints from asylum seekers and captured irregular immigrants crossing the EU external border. In this sense, the Eurodac is an essential part of the supranational biometric control regime, functioning as an automated fingerprint identification system.[286] The Eurodac database was designed to curtail the possibilities for so-called 'asylum shopping' of individuals applying for asylum in more than one EU country. Therefore, the Eurodac allows a community-wide comparison of fingerprints of asylum applicants and hence the determination of which member state is responsible for the asylum procedure.[287] Since a variety of instruments for controlling the identity of immigrants exists, the EU attempts to enhance interoperability between the SIS II, VIS and Eurodac. The interoperability is also believed to be reached through linking the SIS II to the Europol information system. This should result in an EU surveillance network, with which the 'protective Union' hopes to fulfil its functions as a European Leviathan.[288]

Moreover, the policies of identity management and control in the EU are accompanied by homogenizing processes regarding the migrants. As mentioned earlier, the securitization of migration produces a collective image of migrants as a threat without differentiating between different types of migrants. This is additionally reinforced by practices of externalization of border control. For instance, the EU obliges carrier firms such as airlines to return any illegal immigrant to their country of origin.[289] These carrier firms are made accountable and punished with financial sanctions where immigrants are unable to present legal documents during EU border controls. Apart from undermining the basic principles of refugee protection, the EU shifts the traditional state practice of checking travel documents and returning irregular immigrants to private firms. However, this shift is likely to put legitimate refugees and irregular immigrants into one category of threatening migrants who are to be prevented from entering EU territory, as the carrier firms are likely to avoid migrants in general, as a strategy of reducing potential costs of sanctions and returning the immigrants.[290]

In sum, EU migration and asylum policy developed into the field of identity management associated with the European identity politics of caesarean citizenship. It uses images and scenarios of threat from 'bogus asylum seekers' who are presented as a danger to the social integration and cohesion of the European societies. By so doing, the EU shifts its focus on citizenship from political participation and democracy towards the field of internal security, which bases its legitimacy in the bureaucratic power of surveillance, control, separation and expulsion. Didier Bigo coined in this context the term 'banopticon', which unlike the panopticon discriminates between those with access, and those to be monitored for possible detention and removal.[291]

In this sense, the Union citizenship is given a positive image, confronted with the chaos and danger outside of the EU. However, the main objective of citizenship becomes its preservation against external threats. It goes hand in hand with a construction of collective identity based on fear and insecurity of the neurotic citizen, who in order to preserve his collectively threatened lifestyle agrees to live in an increasingly disciplinary society. The EU offers a set of institutions, funds and surveillance instruments that help to separate the neurotic citizen from the dangers of the outside world, and shape at the same time his collective identity based on the perception of a collective threat. Therefore, the insecure society relies increasingly on executive powers of the new European Leviathan resting on dividing politics of border and population controls as well as on the expansion of surveillance networks. The networks of surveillance turn the entire EU territory into an expanded border, where biometric technologies become decisive for identity management practices.[292] At the same time, the insecure society and neurotic citizens become an essential part of the modern caesarean citizenship.

The fight against terrorism as an identity-generating device in the EU

The threat of terrorism is a further image within the politics of insecurity used by the EU, although it is frequently brought together with the immigration policy.[293] In this field, the EU policies are even more executive-dominated, particularly by police and security agencies, which decreases even further the transparency of the decision-making process, making it caesarean in character.

The politics of the fight against terrorism draws as equally as migration policies on the feeling of worry and fear in the population and at the same time perpetuates the experience of being vulnerable to risks. The fight against terrorism therefore not only responds to real threats and dangers, but also delivers risk and threat information through mass media, especially with participation of the so-called security experts. However, information on risk and threat is never reliable per se, as the experts make different judgments and their 'knowledge' is seldom reliable due to the secrecy surrounding security policy. Nonetheless, pure visibility of security experts and the availability of risk and threat information in mass media enhance the salience of security matters in the population. This contributes to collective feelings of threat and danger and simultaneously to feelings of ambivalence about how to deal with them. This ambivalence is particularly easy to manipulate in Western insurance-orientated societies.[294] Therefore, the imagery of terrorism and war is better suited for constructing collective perception of fear and worry than for instance the image of organized crime. The rhetoric of being under threat from terrorist attacks pushes the public to think in terms of the pure logic of self-preservation, where an assumption of a risk is sufficient justification for participating in a war on an unknown enemy.[295] The proclamation of the threat of terrorism (the public never knows how substantiated the threat is) therefore leads to the Schmittian view of political totality, where every aspect of societal life is potentially political, meaning that the enemy could be found anywhere. The post-9/11 war on terror in particular integrates the Hobbesian search for enemies within society with the Schmittian external enemy. This political totality of survival in light of terrorist threats seems to justify depriving the opponents of their fundamental rights.[296]

The image of terrorism renders confirming suspicion obsolete or even dangerous, since it inhibits the effectiveness of the fight against terrorism. As criminals are still entitled to their procedural human rights prior to their conviction as well as their substantive human rights following the conviction, they cannot serve as a totalizing image for construction of fear.[297] In contrast, the fight against terrorism is a preventive one, which makes the deprivation of prisoners of their rights as well as the emergency legislation reducing civil rights plausible for the public.

Furthermore, the politics of the fight against terrorism propagate a certain moral collectivization (not to be confused with the ethics of republican citizenship), since terrorists become dehumanized during anti-terror methods of detention and interrogation, not acceptable even with criminals. In this case, individual dignity is sacrificed to the collective interest in security, as the liberty and physical integrity of the person are set against an uncertain increase in the safety of the collectivity. Nonetheless, this dehumanization of the enemy seems to be acceptable, particularly when these individuals are defined as enemy combatants or members of a multinational terrorist network of fanatics, rather than suspects or soldiers (as the frequently used term 'war' might suggest).[298] This dehumanized enemy is contrasted with the image of 'people like us' who have nothing to fear from security measures, since the *collectively* fearful people are equalized with *collectively* decent people.

A fearful population is likely to support their government in its anti-terror legislation and implementation of anti-terror measures. However, the government is not accountable for the successful outcome of its policies, since realized terror attacks seem to increase the support for the government's anti-terror measures even further, thus delivering a strong argument in favour of war on terror as a state of exception, which in turn justifies curtailing civil rights. This leads us to a paradox of fear, where it is not the effectiveness of the government in the fight against terrorism that produces collectivization of fear, but rather the felt presence of terrorism. In this sense, a durable successful prevention of terrorist attacks might prove counterproductive in generating fear, according to the reasoning of why should we fear terrorism when the government can prevent it. In other words, a society might need to sooner or later experience a real terrorist attack; otherwise it can become reluctant to reassess the balance between security and liberty. A fear of *further* attack weighs more heavily in favour of security and against the protection of civil liberties than media-delivered information on prevented attacks.[299]

The approach to homeland security in the EU

Even though there are differences between the US approach to homeland security and terrorism and the EU's strategy of combating terrorism, the EU is increasingly active in this field.[300] As mentioned earlier, the EU (then the EC) established in the 1970s new forms of ad hoc intergovernmental cooperation dealing with different types of subversive terrorism, which paved the way for more integrated justice and home affairs policies.

Shortly after the 9/11 attacks, EU governments dedicated considerable resources to the fight against terrorism. On 8 October 2001, the European Council confirmed the willingness of the EU and its member states to play an active role in the global coalition against terrorism. The EU reiterated its determination to attack the financial sources of terrorism, in close cooperation with the USA. The EU governments created an EU-wide arrest warrant, drafted a common definition of terrorism and a common list of terrorist groups, and agreed on rules for joint operations between police forces.[301] Significant institution-building occurred with the gradual strengthening of counterterrorism branches and expansion of competences within Europol and the Joint Situation Centre (SitCEN). In the aftermath of the Madrid attacks, with the approval of the member states, Javier Solana appointed Gijs de Vries as the EU's counterterrorism coordinator.[302] De Vries was successful at pushing the EU into developing new counterterrorism policies.[303] For instance, the EU has adopted new laws to curb terrorist funding.[304]

Furthermore, member states gave Europol additional resources and established a counterterrorism task force consisting of national police officers.[305] The governments also created Eurojust, the EU's law enforcement agency, to assist member states on cross-border investigations. In addition, the counterterrorism task force of Europol established relations with their US counterparts with the goal of the joint evaluation of terrorist threats and exchange of information on national counterterrorist measures. Europol cooperates with the US authorities on the identification of terrorist organizations and at the same time grants the US representatives access to meetings of the second pillar counterterrorism working group (COTER) and the JHA anti-terrorism working group. Apart from the participation of the US representatives in the meetings of the heads of EU counterterrorist units, the EU has negotiated a formal agreement with the United States on the exchange of liaison officers between Europol and the US and on the transmission of personal data.[306]

The transfer of personal data to the US authorities in particular has been criticized for its illegal character. Even though the European Commission adopted an adequacy decision for the transfer of passenger name record data (PNR) to the US, the European Parliament has reacted to the Commission initiatives by expressing its disagreement. The EP called upon the Commission to withdraw the adequacy decision, claiming that it did not guarantee protection of personal data. The PNR may contain data revealing racial or ethnic origin, religious beliefs, or other sensitive data, but Directive 95/46/EC prohibits any processing of these sensitive data without specific authorizations, such as explicit consent or an obvious public nature. The first PNR agreement between the EU and the US, signed in 2004, was eventually annulled by the European Court of Justice. A second interim agreement was negotiated in 2006, while a third agreement was approved in July 2007.[307] On 10 July 2007, the EP adopted with an overwhelming majority a resolution heavily criticizing the new PNR agreement between the European Commission and the US Department for Homeland Security, considering it 'substantively flawed', in particular by 'open and vague definitions and multiple possibilities for exception'.[308] The EP considers that the new agreement still fails to offer an adequate level of data protection and that it has been concluded without any involvement of parliaments from both sides, lacking democratic oversight.[309] Even though racial or ethnic profiling is banned in the EU, there are attempts to shift European law on data protection in the opposite direction. Among other things, there is a new proposal by the EU Commissioner Frattini to establish an EU PNR system.[310] In November 2007, the European Commission proposed a PNR plan similar to the EU–USA PNR agreement. The EU PNR plan is part of a new package of proposals aimed at improving the EU's capabilities in the fight against terrorism.[311] With this new package the EU wants to step up the fight against terrorism.[312] Simultaneously, the Commission attempts to put more emphasis on certain types of risks and threats in the EU. In July 2007 it published a Green Paper on Bio-Preparedness in the EU, highlighting the danger of the deliberate release of harmful agents and pathogens by terrorists and its devastating consequences.[313]

Increasingly, surveillance seems to have become one of the crucial strategies of the EU. Since potential terrorists blend into the European societies (as was the case of the London bombings in July 2005) and are 'unexceptional', proactive forms of surveillance of suspect population are deemed essential for the preventive risk management. This, however, leads to a surplus supply of data and an exaggeration of threat perception, which in turn can provoke an indiscriminate surveillance of the entire population.[314] This goes hand in hand with growing resources and expanding executive powers for security services, police and other law enforcing agencies, which corresponds to the tenets of caesarean citizenship.[315] As a result, the EU puts more emphasis on surveillance technology. The recent EU Green Paper on surveillance technology adopted by the Commission in 2006 propagates standardization and integration of detecting systems into one system.[316] For that purpose, the EU aims to enhance the collaboration between the private and public sector in the creation of new, more efficient surveillance technologies.[317] Furthermore, a proposal for the creation of a centralized database of fingerprints from all twenty-seven EU countries was included in a new European Commission document that sets out the goals for 2008.[318] The fingerprints database will include sensitive information that could be shared with third parties, such as with the US security authorities. The database was planned to be operational by the end of 2008. However, the EU is behind schedule, as the costs soar and the EU runs into technical and legal problems.[319]

The fingerprint database would supplement the data retention directive passed by the EU in 2006. This directive requires all internet and telecommunications service providers to store all traffic data in Europe for up to 24 months and make the data accessible to law enforcement agencies.[320] The directive was controversially pushed through the European Parliament in December 2005, following threats from interior ministers to enforce an even more stringent legislation, in case the EP was unable to approve the proposed draft.

In addition to the transfer of the PNR data and the data retention directive, the 'SWIFT' (Society for Worldwide Interbank Financial Telecommunication) controversy illustrates the growing problems of the caesarean citizenship in the EU. It relates to the agreement between the Belgian operator of the SWIFT banking transfer system with the Central Intelligence Agency (CIA), which acquires data of individuals transferring funds around Europe without their knowledge or consent. As a Belgian-based company, SWIFT is subject to the European data protection law implemented by the Data Protection Directive (Directive 95/46/EC). However, SWIFT stores data on all financial transfers for a period of 124 days at two operation centres, one in Europe and one in the United States. In order to limit the negative effects of one server crashing, the European and US servers store an exact copy of the data. The Council Presidency and the Commission have attempted to legalize the data mirroring and the US access to the SWIFT data within the framework of the 'Safe Harbour' agreement. The 'Safe Harbour' agreement covers relations between two different subjects, one of them being on US territory. However, the SWIFT branch in the US does not have a legal personality, and nor does the 'Safe Harbour' agreement relate to the use of data for security purposes. As a consequence, the 'Safe Harbour' agreement 'legalizing' the uncontrolled access by the US authorities remains unresolved, which has been pointed out by the European Parliament in its resolution on that subject. The European Parliament reaffirms that the solutions envisaged so far by the Council and the Commission as well as by private companies do not adequately protect the personal data of EU citizens.[321]

Apart from the expanding surveillance instruments and creating law enforcement institutions, the EU has also worked on a common strategic approach to terrorism. During its extraordinary meeting on 21 September 2001, the European Council declared that terrorism was a 'real challenge to the world and to Europe' and that the fight against this phenomenon would be a priority objective of the European Union.[322] A more comprehensive common definition of terrorism as a security threat was formally achieved with the adoption by the European Council of the European Security Strategy (ESS) on 12 December 2003. In the ESS, the perception of the threat shifts from the focus on the globally organized al-Qaeda network towards the terrorist potential within the EU member states. Furthermore, the strategy highlights the complexity of the threat.[323] In particular, the EU considers the current terrorist threats directed not only at individuals but also at the foundations of the EU.[324] The ESS defines terrorism as being a form of warfare that threatens the European economic system and its social structures, thus highlighting the collective goals of terrorism.[325] Therefore, it obliges each member state to ensure that acts of collective violence such as bombings, shootings and kidnappings will be punishable as terrorist offences.[326] In addition, the ESS states that Europe is both a target and a base for terrorism. While European countries are targets and have already been attacked, logistical bases for terrorist cells have been discovered in several EU member states. The ESS stresses in particular the danger of terrorists using biological, chemical or even nuclear bombs on European soil.

However, the ESS employs a vague and broad definition of terrorism, which invites abuses and manipulation by security authorities. Even though the so-called security experts tend to interpret terrorism differently, they have a professional tendency to highlight insecurity as an underlying principle of politics. Security professionals and security agencies derive their authority and legitimacy from the definition of insecurities, since security expertise is always about what and how the public should collectively fear. The European Security Strategy prepared a conceptual ground for the EU Counter-Terrorism Strategy (EUCTS) that was adopted during the Dutch EU Presidency by the European Council on 15/16 December 2005. The EUCTS set out the objectives to prevent new recruitment into terrorist organizations, introducing mechanisms for protection of potential targets and pursuit and investigation of terrorists.[327] One of the most important elements of the EUCTS is prevention of terrorist attacks, among other things through cutting off the sources of terrorist funding and effective application of the European Arrest Warrant.[328] Even though the EU does not carry out its own counterterrorist operations, the EU measures such as the European Arrest Warrant are designed to help the governments in their efforts to identify, extradite and prosecute terrorists. On 25 March 2004, the EU published a Declaration on Combating Terrorism, which proclaimed measures including sharing intelligence, preventing the financing of terrorism and cooperation with the US. It was followed by the EU–US Declaration on Combating Terrorism on 26 June 2004, which again stressed the necessity of close cooperation between the EU and the USA. In addition, the European Council in its meeting on 17 and 18 June announced, over seventy-six pages, a revised plan of action involving seven strategic objectives and around 150 initiatives. The Action Plan is reviewed and updated every six months.[329]

With all its strategies, declarations and action plans, the EU seems to create a totalizing vision of a multidimensional security, which would privilege the fight against terrorism as the underlying principle of the EU politics. Under the label of the 'war on terror', a securitization of the European integration is observable, which shifts the EU towards a vision of comprehensive security within the EU security regime building. In the process, the EU assumes an executive-centred character, which exhibits a visible tension with the principles of international law and human rights principles.[330] These trends reflect the main tenets of caesarean citizenship highlighting the friend–enemy difference and threat images, which espouse homogenizing practices of identity-making. Threat-image construction is a useful resource for governments that intend to influence public opinion and legitimize their own actions. In the caesarean citizenship, enemy construction embodies the essence of the political, as it generates the perception of homogeneity and as a consequence can break down popular resistance to collective sacrifices, for instance in the form of curtailing civil liberties. However, the politics of insecurity is unlikely to be about benevolent construction of collective identity as a general commitment to public interest, since threat images always favour certain interests at the expense of others and legitimize shifts in political priorities.[331]

This leads us to the issue of the European Leviathan in the 'war on terror', which reflects new bureaucratic structures and supra-state security alliances changing the relationship between the citizen and the state and strengthening citizenship practices of the EU as a corporate security state.

Who is the European Leviathan in the 'war on terror'?

Security considerations relating to terrorism are common to many EU legislative and institutional activities. In particular, the already mentioned Hague Programme, adopted in November 2004 at a special European Council meeting, proposed a comprehensive JHA package covering numerous aspects of their security and justice cooperation, believed to be useful in the fight against terrorism. Furthermore, the interior ministers of the EU decided that they 'should have the leading role' in the EU's fight against terrorism, although they intend to take 'into account' the views of EU foreign ministers.[332]

This again shows not only that the politics of insecurity in the EU become increasingly executive-orientated, but also that security is shifted from the external dimension of politics towards the field of internal security.[333] The key element of the Hague Programme was the facilitation of the exchange of information between national authorities on the basis of the 'principle of availability'. According to the Hague Programme, this means that:

> throughout the Union, a law enforcement officer in one Member State who needs information in order to perform his duties can obtain this from another Member State and that the law enforcement agency in the other Member State which holds this information will make it available for the stated purpose, taking into account the requirement for ongoing investigations in that State.

In this context, some authors observe a thickening of police networks in the EU, which takes place as a result of institutional developments within the third pillar. In addition, as Europol officers begin to play a pivotal role in the EU law enforcement, they forge the development of a 'European police mentality'.[334] One of the two Council working groups devoted to the fight against terrorism is the Terrorism Working Group (TWG), composed of representatives of the member states' ministries of the interior and of law enforcement agencies. The TWG meets several times a year and deals with threat assessments and practical cooperation. In addition, the EU supports groups of governments to cooperate closely on joint investigations and prosecutions, as is the case with France and Spain, which in 2004 set up a joint counterterrorism unit to carry out common operations. In May 2003, the so-called G5 group – encompassing interior ministers from Britain, France, Germany, Italy and Spain – was established and convenes regularly to coordinate their counterterrorism efforts. Meanwhile, G5 became G6 by including Poland and now encompasses the six largest EU member states.[335]

Furthermore, the 'Salzburg group' (Benelux countries, Austria, the Czech Republic, Poland, Slovakia and Slovenia, with Ukraine as an observer) and the Baltic Sea task force (Denmark, Estonia, Finland, Germany, Iceland, Latvia, Lithuania, Norway, Poland, Russia and Sweden) also exist for similar purposes.[336]

On 27 May 2005, seven member states signed the Prüm Treaty to intensify cross-border cooperation, in particular in combating terrorism.[337] The Treaty's main goal is to accelerate the exchange of information among signatories via the supply of non-personal and personal data. The Prüm Treaty provides for the mutual exchange of information from national police DNA profile databases, databases of friction ridges (finger and palm prints, etc.) and vehicle registration databases of the signatories, as well as for information sharing in international events posing security risks.[338] The data are supplied, 'if any final conviction or other circumstances give reason to believe that the data subject ... poses a threat to public order and security'. By stressing 'beliefs', the Convention considers pure suspicion a legitimate ground for transferring non-personal and personal data. At the same time, the term 'threat to public order' remains vague and open to manipulation. Furthermore, the exchange of information will target individuals with identifiable political behaviour. As Article 16 of the Convention states clearly, apart from personal data the file will include the description of the circumstances giving reason for the 'belief' that the person might present a threat to public order.[339]

All these EU measures and institutions relate to the legitimacy of increasingly executive-centred government. These elements of caesarean citizenship rely excessively on rule by administrative and governmental decrees. They replace democratically legitimized laws with regulations that have the *force* of law but not its legitimacy.[340] In addition, the EU establishes institutions in the field of internal security that are characterized by a lack of parliamentary and judicial scrutiny at the European level and by a high level of secrecy. Whereas the lack of accountability always raises questions of legitimacy and of citizenship rights, it is evident in the agreements, institutions and procedures in the fields of security services, home affairs and policing.[341]

Apart from police networks and cooperation arrangements between ministers of interior, intelligence agencies seem to play an increasingly significant role in the caesarean citizenship of the EU. As terrorist threats are defined as complex and multidimensional, the technologies and techniques of intelligence gathering become more extensive. Therefore, profiling and surveillance tend to encompass the entire population. As a consequence, the institutional scope of intelligence is being enlarged accordingly. The idea of creating a European intelligence agency (EIA) was proposed in February 2004 by the Austrian and Belgian governments, who argued that the EIA would be endowed with resources to gather and process information needed for the assessment of threats to EU security. Regardless of whether the EU will eventually establish a European CIA, it already possesses bodies with similar functions such as the Intelligence Division (INTDIV) within the European Union Military Staff and SitCen, which functions within the second pillar of the Common Security and Foreign Policy and the European Defence and Security Policy.[342] All member states are provided by

SitCen with strategic analyses of terrorist threats. While SitCen is located in the Council secretariat and reports to Javier Solana, it brings together national experts to analyse intelligence assessments from the member states. Initially, SitCen analysts assessed mainly threats from outside EU territory. However, since 2005 they additionally use threat assessments from internal security services as well as from Europol.[343]

Even though the intelligence and security services of the Member States have cooperated in the fight against terrorism for a considerable time within the informal framework of the so-called 'Club of Bern', after the 9/11 attacks the intelligence heads of the EU member states established the Counter-Terrorism Group (CTG) in 2001. The group consists of the EU member states' intelligence counterterrorist experts along with their counterparts in Norway and Switzerland. The CTG meets every three months under the chairmanship of the service of the country holding the European Union presidency. The EU's counterterrorism activities centre on the exchange and processing of information, which makes the role of security services crucial. However, particularly in this case, secrecy and lack of accountability promote abuses of citizenship rights and fundamental rights. This raises not only the question of surveillance of citizens, but also of unlawful behaviour by using and processing foreign torture information provided by member states' security services.[344]

In the EU, recent investigations, for instance by the EP Temporary Committee, have shed light on the illegal practice of extraordinary renditions and unlawful detentions by foreign security services on European territory with the involvement of some member states, which suggests that the line between cooperation and complicity could have been crossed.[345] Some EU member states took advantage of extraordinary renditions and unlawful detentions. A year-long European parliamentary investigation into CIA flights transporting terror suspects to secret prisons has yielded a report pointing out Britain, Germany and other EU member states as cooperating with the US authorities on a secret detention programme, in breach of human rights standards.[346]

This shows the consequences of shifting the emphasis from the obligations and rights component of citizenship towards its compliance component. As caesarean citizenship rests on compliance as a price for guaranteeing citizens' security, a collectivization of security interests can contradict individual rights. The homogenization effects of a threat can even make caesarean practices of European executive agencies (endowed with extending operational powers) acceptable to the public. However, this homogenization can be maintained only as long as the threat is conveyed in a believable manner. Therefore, the European Leviathan can evolve an interest in itself, which seduces him into continuous designing of threat scenarios and danger projections. This again stimulates the expansion of executive-centred government in the EU to the detriment of parliamentary control and democratic accountability.

Conclusions

A homogenization of perception among citizens can be forged through securitization of the citizenship. It occurs when political authorities redefine some citizenship aspects as a matter of security. Politics of insecurity thus pertain to the caesarean citizenship, which attempts to produce collective identity in the sense of homogeneity of threat by establishing and reinforcing boundaries between friends and enemies. Securitization of citizenship in the EU is strongly associated with identity politics, as discourses of security have implications for the elaboration of the political subject (the collective self). Nevertheless, the securitization of citizenship does not generate collective identity defined as a general commitment to a common good, but represents attempts of establishing perceived identity via identity politics.[347]

Biometric technologies, detention facilities and new methods of surveillance are employed to establish the exclusionary and restrictive practices of the caesarean citizenship. The respondent of these practices is the neurotic citizen who defines citizenship in terms of permanent insecurity. His preference for liberty and freedom becomes surpassed by his fears of survival in a risk society.

In the EU the use of politics of insecurity upholding the fear goes hand in hand with a growing state activity in the realm of surveillance, control and restrictions. By demonstrating their indispensability (and thus legitimacy), political authorities represent the new Leviathan, supported by the fear-inclined citizens. Migration has been increasingly presented as a danger to public order, cultural identity, and labour market stability. In this sense, migration is increasingly depicted as a threat to the community's survival in its current social and cultural form. At the same time, the EU immigration and asylum policies are increasingly associated with a tacit acceptance of human rights abuses upon readmission, which contradicts the self-image of the EU as a normative power protecting and exporting human rights. The politics of the fight against terrorism draws on the feeling of worry and fear in the population and at the same time perpetuates the experience of being vulnerable to risks. In this sense, the fight against terrorism not only responds to real threats and dangers, but also delivers risk and threat information, especially with the participation of so-called security experts. Here, politics of insecurity become a domain of policy, security services and other law enforcement agencies. However, the identity generation based on caesarean citizenship is never completed, as it relies on the permanent feeling of insecurity and emergency. As a return to normality undermines the perception of a collective threat, the politics of insecurity (embodied by the Schmittian state of exception) are likely to increasingly dominate the political discourse of the EU.

Recapitulation

This chapter dealt with the current trend in the EU's citizenship practices on the basis of the typology of the republican, liberal and caesarean citizenship. *First*, I discussed the EU's republican attempts to engage in discursive ethics within the Constitutional Convention. I argued that even though deliberation can have benevolent effects on decision-making in the EU, the convention method should not be viewed as the embodiment of republican citizenship. This results from the pathologies of deliberation, which have implications for the citizenship–collective identity nexus. I established that the expectations about integrative workings of deliberation and consequently its identity-generating features might not only be overestimated, but may even produce negative outcomes for the European collective identity. I discussed different types of deliberation pathologies including the pathology of false will-formation, the rational hijacking of deliberation and the perversity of deliberation. For instance, the rational hijacking relates to rhetorical action that disguises actors' selfish interests as public good. By using arguments that refer to collective identity, actors gain political legitimacy and use the arguments as a resource and the mechanism of *soft power* over other actors. I also argued that deliberation can bring differences to the surface, and widen rather than narrow divisions. In this sense, it can have corrosive effects with regard to the EU as a political community. Although deliberation is not a danger to the EU that has to be avoided at any costs, deliberation theory does not deliver sufficient mechanisms for generating republican citizenship, which leads to an expectations–outcome gap.

Second, I discussed the liberal citizenship practice in the EU by focusing on the Charter of Fundamental Rights in the EU. As the Charter is expected to express common preferences and common values of the EU, it reflects essential features of liberal citizenship. In this sense, instead of stressing thick collective identity, the Charter highlights diversity of identities and thus heterogeneity. In this context, European citizenship as membership in a political community is expressed above all in the equal treatment of citizens before the law. As a result, a sort of common thin political identity drawn from equal rights and principles is expected to develop. However, this thin collective identity mirrors solely a common normative basis for a future European democracy. Therefore, approaches expecting a transformation of a thin identity (anchored in a normative environment of society) into a thick identity, implying a change in citizens' behaviour towards each other, are likely to be unrealistic. I discussed in particular arguments stressing the identity-generating effects of constitutions even with an absent community or a lacking societal consensus. These arguments assume that a constitution can have identity-generating effects, since they are evaluative, cultural and affective systems of reference for citizens. I argued inter alia that constitutionalizing serious contradictions might not, however, be the best means to construct a shared value system, as it leads to constitutional fiction, rather than citizenship identity. The particular construction of the Charter exhibits structural problems that are likely to reproduce contradictions, rather than contribute to a shared rights-based identity. This mirrors the more general dilemma of constitutionalization in diverse societies. Constitutions or sets of rights reflecting a coherent value system are more likely to have stronger identity effects, but can alienate relevant social groups. In contrast, ambivalent sets of rights can integrate more social groups, but they are incapable of delivering a reliable value orientation for citizens, thus having negative identity effects. In this sense, a mere articulation and inflationary listing of values and rights reduces the identity-stimulating effects of the constitution. In addition, the inflation of rights in the Charter and the ambiguity of solidarity provisions reflect an inability of the EU to react to the change in the traditional basis of solidarity and live up to its image as a postmodern polity. The differentiation between the transformer and the catalyst identity politics suggests that in the case of liberal citizenship a construction of collective identity cannot rely on the catalyst impact of constitutionalization, but makes necessary more invasive identity technologies of the state in order to transform the thin identity character of liberal citizenship into a thicker and more sticky identity. However, liberal citizens are expected to be aware of the dangers of expansive statehood associated with intense identity politics. In this respect, invasive identity politics appear to be counterproductive in the context of liberal citizenship.

Third, I explored the EU's caesarean citizenship practices against the background of risk society. I argued that the EU as the new Leviathan uses images of uncontrollable and unpredictable threats and dangers promoting its excessive activity, which not only transforms citizenship practices but also makes it easier to perpetuate the *politics of insecurity* as an instrument of identity construction. The collective identity in the form of homogenization of threat perception is forged through securitization of the citizenship issues. The Europeanization of migration policies entails a trend towards a restrictive and control-oriented approach in this policy area. At the same time, the EU establishes a security discourse that defines migration in terms of identification of existential threats. Images of societal danger from a criminal and invading enemy are reified in the discourse. In the process, the security concerns are defined against the background of dangers to societal integration, threats to the community's conception of a good life and the welfare of the community. In addition, this trend in identity politics of migration becomes strengthened even further, as the EU uses biometric technologies in search of dangerous or illegitimate migrants and asylum seekers. Therefore, citizenship is to an increasing degree regarded in terms of threats to society, as citizens learn to live under the feeling of perpetual threat associated with migrants, since the danger comes from outside. Next to migration policies, the EU uses the 'fight against terrorism' as the further aspect of its caesarean citizenship practices. With all its strategies, declarations and action plans, the EU seems to create a totalizing vision of a multidimensional security, which would privilege the fight against terrorism as the underlying principle of EU politics. Under the label of the 'war on terror', a securitization of the European integration is observable, which shifts the EU towards a vision of comprehensive security within the EU security regime building. In the process, the EU assumes an executive-centred character, which exhibits a visible tension with principles of international law and human rights principles. These trends reflect the main tenets of caesarean citizenship, highlighting the friend–enemy difference and threat images that espouse homogenizing practices of identity-making. Threat-image construction is a useful resource for governments that intend to influence public opinion and legitimize their own actions. In the caesarean citizenship, enemy construction embodies the essence of the political, as it generates the perception of homogeneity and as a consequence can break down popular resistance to collective sacrifices, for instance in the form of curtailing civil liberties. Nevertheless, the securitization of citizenship does not generate collective identity defined as a general commitment to a common good, but represents attempts to establish perceived identity via identity politics. However, the identity generation based on caesarean citizenship is never completed, as it relies on the permanent feeling of insecurity and emergency.

Conclusions

Citizenship and collective identity in Europe

The gist of the book

This book represents an attempt to explore the relationship between citizenship and collective identity in the EU. Its point of departure is a discussion of the conceptual variety of citizenship. As an alternative I offer a relational approach to citizenship that disaggregates citizenship into the three components of rights, obligations and compliance. This allows for an exploration of the relationship between the components of citizenship as well as the construction of generic models of citizenship with their respective collective identity.

Before turning to that I discuss the research on collective identity focusing on the cognitive function, the self-esteem booster function and the political functions of collective identity. Next, I organize and depict the current debates on European identity according to these functions of collective identity. I frame the main argument of the book against the background of the limitations of the functional approaches to collective identity. Here, I argue that various ideal types of citizenship are associated with differing collective identities. The disaggregation of citizenship into rights, obligations and compliance serves as a framework of reference for the generic models of citizenship. I use each of these components of citizenship to construct generic models of citizenship, to which I ascribe types of collective identity. These three generic models of citizenship include the republican, the liberal and the caesarean citizenship. Based on the conceptual and theoretical considerations of the citizenship–collective identity nexus, the empirical part of the book explores the EU's politics of citizenship and identity politics. Here I illustrate the EU's attempts to engage in discursive ethics within the convention method as a case of republican citizenship, the liberal model of European citizenship with regard to the Charter of Fundamental Rights, and also current trends in the EU's caesarean citizenship regarding the development of the European Leviathan and the politics of insecurity.

My approach to linking citizenship and collective identity reverts from a conceptual critique of making identity a component of citizenship and opening it up to values and attitudes, thus amalgamating the two separate phenomena. Therefore, the amalgamation of citizenship and collective identity is unhelpful in analyzing the phenomenon of European citizenship, since it dilutes the difference between citizenship as an institution of equality, and collective identity, which can be associated with different social categories. In contrast, I argue that collective identity should be regarded as analytically distinctive from citizenship. Therefore, we shall regard both concepts in an associative, rather than in a mutually constitutive relationship. Against this background, I argue in favour of an approach differentiating generic models of citizenship, which are endowed with specific collective identities.

Disaggregated citizenship: rights, obligations and compliance

The relational approach to citizenship disaggregates it into categories and reconfigures them into relational clusters. In this sense, citizenship appears as a patterned matrix of institutional relationships among political practices based on formalized and codified categories. Even though formal categories of citizenship are certainly not sufficient to analyze citizenship, we need to differentiate between the judiciable dimension of citizenship and a subjective practice of citizenship (without claiming normative priority of either of them).

Reverting from a minimal definition of citizenship as a shared membership in a political community, citizenship remains a relational phenomenon that is determined through the relationship among the citizens as well as between the citizens and the political authority. Therefore, the components of citizenship include rights, obligations and compliance. Rights reflect the ontological priority of the individual, and link the individual to a political community. At the same time, rights exclude non-members from the community by not ascribing these rights to them. Therefore, rights integrate members of the community and 'close' the community socially. Next to rights we identify obligations as a further component of citizenship. The main thrust of the obligation-based component of citizenship is that civic virtues such as solidarity, loyalty or trust (moral resources) are necessary features of living in freedom. In this sense, citizens demonstrate altruistic features, since they are concerned for the welfare of their friends for *their* friends' sake, not merely for their own. The bonds of citizenship are a basis for a political community whose goal is to fulfil civic obligations towards each other. Beyond the matrix of rights and obligations we identify a third component of citizenship, which is compliance. In this perspective, citizens are defined as the objects of political authority. However, it does not necessarily imply an arbitrary power or domination. Citizens possess enough rationality to understand the necessity of compliance to political authority, without which there would be no civilized existence and therefore no citizenship. Therefore, the goal of political discipline is to assure governance of modern states characterized by social complexity and management of risk.

Against this backdrop, citizenship can be depicted as a form of an 'interaction order' of three citizenship components that finds its reflection in a patterned behaviour of citizens. Rights, obligations and compliance are closely coupled with each other, whereas a 'loose coupling' exists between the interaction order and other social realms. The autonomy of the interaction order neither implies that we can reduce citizenship to contextualism or situationalism (as some practice-orientated approaches tend to do) nor that the interaction order has homogeneous effects. Although open towards social practice, the interaction order has its sources in the institutionalized dimension of citizenship, which includes formal rights, obligations and compliance, as constructed, codified and perpetuated by political authority.

In this sense, collective identity cannot be regarded as a component of citizenship. However, citizenship facilitates the construction of collective identity as an abstract category by structuring the non-face-to-face interactions among citizens on the basis of citizenship. Citizens assume that significantly more individuals belong to the same political group as they do and act upon this assumption. In other words, citizenship without collective identity would have to rely on situational and contextual ad hoc provision of collective identity based on the face-to-face experience. While the situational context does not suffice to construct collective identity as a stable pattern of reciprocity and recognition, reciprocity and recognition among participants in an interaction order requires a specific set of institutionalized values that can be provided by the institutions of citizenship.

In addition, the very notion of citizenship as membership of a political community implies a claim of collective identity as pointed out in the notion of *citizenship identity*. In the case of citizenship identity, collective identity pertains to the core of citizenship as delineating a community of which individuals define themselves as members, in which they participate and towards which they feel a sense of obligation. Therefore, citizenship identity assumes special ties binding citizens in a political community. How strong, extensive and stable these ties are depends in turn on the model of citizenship. These ties can relate to a thin collective identity found in a shared rationality, a thick collective identity stemming from mutually demanding obligations and specific responsibilities, or a specific collectivism of a shared perception of threat and danger.

Functional perspective of collective identity

Before turning to the different models of citizenship and their collective identities, I will briefly summarize the chapters discussing the functional view of collective identity in order to reconstruct the train of thought applied in the book. Despite various uses of the concept of collective identity, several distinct meanings can be discerned according to the expected function of collective identity. I differentiate between the cognitive function, the self-esteem function and political functions of collective identity.

Cognitive function departs from the assumption that human social relations are arranged through the definition and elaboration of collective self-categories, through which individuals organize their social relations. Collective self-categorization indicates that individuals perceive themselves as members of groups. This perception reduces social complexity for individuals by rendering it comprehensible and decreases perceived social complexity and thus social uncertainty. However, group identities and self-categorizations are fluid and context-dependent, which generates a collective identity with an unstable and highly dynamic mental structure. This perspective corresponds to the postmodern difference-accentuating conceptions of citizenship, which renounces the equality claim of citizenship in favour of fragmentation and contextuality of citizenship. Furthermore, the cognitive function of collective identity gives political authorities a tool for drawing boundaries in the society by recognizing and classifying people as group members.

In this context, European identity becomes increasingly associated with shared categories, images and frames used by the citizens in their perception. In this sense, European identity is reduced to shared images and common views of the EU, without considering how stable these perceptions are and whether they can indeed be conceptualized as collective identity. This brings us to the issue of technology of identity, which refers to the policies of constructing collective identities in accordance with the images of European elites and political authorities. Whereas the cognitive perspective highlights mainly self-categorization processes in individuals, we can relate it also to the categorization technologies used by the political authorities of the European Union. Political authorities categorize and classify people by assigning them to categories that are associated with consequential identities. Thus, they enhance and freeze the salience of certain collective identities through political practices of categorization, for instance by means of restrictive visa policies stressing the dichotomy between citizens and non-citizens.

Furthermore, European identity tends to be conceptualized as a layer of multiple identities or as a component of a hybrid identity. In this perspective, European identity is unlikely to replace other attachments, particularly the national ones. As the EU is characterized by cultural diversity rather than unity, a cultural uniformization appears to be improbable. Furthermore, the cognitive perspective increasingly stresses the hybridity of collective identities in Europe. The notion of hybridity puts emphasis on the fusion of identities, which is a result of the increasingly interwoven and multicultural nature of modern societies. The expansion of European borders and the consequent transnationalization of European societies are expected to foster not only cultural diversity, but also cultural hybridity. Since identities in the EU are likely to become increasingly multiple and hybrid, a sense of belonging to a particular territory or a community can be upheld alongside a simultaneous attachment to supranational collectivities such as the EU. In this sense, the socio-cultural dimension of the EU matches the notion of transnational syncretism. Not only are the citizens capable of having multi-layered and fluid identities, but these tend also to be inclusive and nested, rather than mutually exclusive.

Against this background, it is believed that the EU practises manipulation of cultural symbols pertaining to collective identity. One example of the EU's manipulation of cultural symbols is the introduction of the common currency in the EU. The establishment of a tangible symbol of the euro and its iconography raises the salience of Europeanness without the necessity of homogenizing European cultural diversity, since the euro allows for different iconographic connotations. Nevertheless, the EU tries to enhance its salience via the symbolic diffusion into the everyday life of citizens, but without relinquishing the symbolic ambiguity.

In contrast to the cognitive perspective, the self-esteem boosting function equally seeks to explain inter-group relations by focusing on the perceived similarities between members of the in-group as opposed to the out-group. However, the function of collective identity here is to acquire a positive image from membership of a social group. Therefore, the underlying motivation for membership of groups is the enhancement of self-esteem, whereby psychological gains are achieved through group identification and differentiation of one's own group from other groups. Two aspects of collective identity are central in this respect: the construction of the 'Other' and the establishment of a collective memory of the group. Collective identity is associated with demarcation and a juxtaposition of the in-group in relation to the 'Other', whereas the 'Other' frequently acquires a more durable image. Collective memory additionally provides a sense of group continuity, which is expected to make collective identity even more resilient. Particularly in times of crises, the significant Other becomes activated in the collective identity of individuals, since the binary construction of 'us' versus 'them' helps in overcoming the crises by using blaming and scapegoating strategies.

Regarding political functions of collective identity, I refer to national community building, legitimacy of political authority, and the solution of cooperation dilemmas. These three themes are also mirrored in the debate on European identity, albeit with varying degrees of interest. For instance, the notion of European nationalism is rather exotic in social sciences, whereas the issue of legitimacy clearly belongs to the mainstream of research in this field. The question of whether the EU can solve cooperation dilemmas is frequently discussed through the prism of international relations.

After the discussion of the functional perspective of collective identity, I offered a critique of the respective approaches. As some empirical studies demonstrate, European identity tends to be regarded by European citizens as a mere 'status identity'. Having citizenship of an EU member state can culminate in the conclusion that being European is logically unavoidable. While one categorizes oneself as European, this category remains 'void' in terms of behavioural implications, without producing any expected behaviour differences between Europeans and non-Europeans. Even though the cognitive process of reducing social complexity by using the category of being European is assumed to have psychological benefits for individuals, it remains neutral with regard to their role as citizens. By the same token, the position stating that all identities are in flux reduces the issue of European identity to an ephemeral phenomenon, since this perspective does not supply much information on the possible 'chronic' European identity, with a minimal level of stability.

In contrast, the challenges for the self-esteem orientated perspective include its uncertain integrative potential and its vagueness about who the object of the EU's identity politics is. The EU focuses frequently on the postulates or ideal self-images, even if frequently inconsistent with its actual activities. In addition, the positive evaluative strategies of the EU seem to be an expression of the identity of the EU's political elites and its administrative political apparatus, rather than a reflection of identity of European citizens. Furthermore, the construction of collective memory as an identity technology focusing on stimulating feelings of collective continuity is facing several problems. For instance, in contrast to relatively homogeneous historiographies of nation-states, the EU cannot draw on many similarities in the interpretation of the recent European past besides the consensus on the horrors of the Second World War. In sum, the collective self-esteem perspective of collective identity does not deliver convincing insights into why the EU should be regarded by the citizens as durably attractive in contrast to national attachments.

The political functions also espouse contradictions and weaknesses regarding citizenship identity. The idea of European nationalism represents an attempt to apply nationalist technologies of collective identity with regard to the EU. This methodological nationalism departs from the analytical and methodological template of the nation-state as a universal one and consequently seeks to remedy social and political problems by using the antidote of the nation-state or nationalism. In addition, I discussed the issue of communication processing establishing collective identity as a response to the legitimacy function. I argue inter alia that the European public sphere is rather multi-level, contextual, asymmetrical, complex and hybrid, all characteristics that are rather detrimental to a citizenship identity. However, this supports doubts about the European public sphere as a genuine communicative community. The EU remains largely dependent on the national political processes for its legitimacy. Even if a communicative community had emerged in the EU, we would probably be dealing with a rudimentary collective identity, since communicative structures score low on the identity 'thickness' scale.

A further political function of collective identity relates to the assumption about its capacity to solve collective problems. In the case of the EU, the central question relates to who is expected to share collective identity. Since the EU is an elite-driven project, the cooperation dilemmas refer to the elites of the member states, rather than European citizens. Therefore, even if the EU does generate social norms of reciprocity, as expected by approaches arguing in favour of common institutions solving collective action problems, they are likely to be found among the European officials, rather than European citizens. A particular scepticism should be expressed regarding the specific argument of the EU as a solution to war between otherwise belligerent states. Giving credit to the EU for its alleged peacemaking capability is a case of daring but uncertain causality. As many non-EU countries also experience peace, we might find the causation running through other independent variables such as democracy, consistent with the Kantian claim about perpetual peace.

The argument of the book: linking citizenship to collective identity

In contrast to the functional understanding of collective identity, I define collective identity as a sense of political commonness between individuals that leads to a general commitment to the *public interest*. The sense of commonness means that individuals regard themselves as equal citizens belonging to the same political community, while the basis for this belonging is secondary. Therefore, this concept of collective identity has an explicitly political meaning in comparison to the other concepts of collective identity, which are anchored in various functions of collective identity. In this respect, collective identity is not solely based on the process of collective perception of difference and delimitation between 'us' and 'them', but also entails behavioural implications for citizens as members of a political community.

As an integrative device, shared citizenship identity does not eliminate differences, but should be expected instead to supersede rival identities. Therefore, shared citizenship can be a major source of political collective identity. As citizenship can assume different forms, its variance finds its reflection in the thickness and strength of citizenship identity. Even though many different political identities can exist, such as party identities or ideological identities, citizenship identity represents a 'master identity' that underpins citizens' behaviour in the public space. Citizenship can be regarded as a cornerstone of political collective identity, since citizenship is the most fundamental and at the same time the most pervasive institution of a polity. It lays foundations for the cognitive, habitual and ethical components of citizens' activity.

However, to what extent citizenship becomes consequential for collective identity depends in addition to the type of citizenship also on the type of identity politics and identity technologies involved. As there are many simultaneous sources of identity politics, the EU finds itself in competition with the nation-states regarding identity construction. Even though European and national identities are not exclusive per se, nation-states attempt to extract the consequentiality of identity primarily in the national framework, as the national citizenship identity can draw on moral resources, which are invaluable as sources of mobilization and legitimacy for political actors. But the relationship between citizenship and collective identity is not a simple structure–agency causation in which structure completely dominates the agency. A relevant part of collective identity construction runs through alternative mechanisms. Therefore, the notion of citizenship identity does not indicate a mono-causal relationship between citizenship and collective identity. Nevertheless, citizenship channels collective identity, for instance by ordering and taming conflicts through labelling collective similarities and differences and through institutionalizing rights, obligations and compliance. In this sense, citizenship determines how and when differences may legitimately be represented, and who counts as 'equal' in the public space. At the same time, citizenship defines the limits of state power by indicating where the private space of free individuals begins and ends, thus also delineating the boundaries of citizenship identity. Therefore, we can identify a tension between structure (citizenship as a complex institution) and agency (citizens as holders of collective identity) that both enables the individuals to be different and bridges differences into a citizenship identity.

I argue that the specific form of political collective identity is channelled by the relationship between the three components of citizenship that in turn generates three models of citizenship. The type of collective identity therefore results from the domination of one of the citizenship components over the others, thus suggesting whether we deal with rights-orientated, obligations-accentuated or compliance-focused citizenship. The right-orientated citizenship leads to the model of liberal citizenship; the obligation-accentuated citizenship spawns the republican model of citizenship; and the compliance-focused citizenship produces the caesarean model of citizenship. These models of citizenship are coupled with differently strong and resilient collective identities, thus being associated with specific collective identities.

The republican model of citizenship is associated with the notion of citizen as a political man for whom politics is a means of leading a good life. In contrast, the liberal tradition of citizenship conceives citizens as individuals whose primary concern lies in the realizing of their (not necessarily political) interests and passions. In this conception of citizenship, politics is an instrument for guaranteeing the realization of citizens' individual interests, even though it highlights specific liberal virtues of toleration and pluralism. The third model is caesarean citizenship, which depicts citizens as thinking about politics in categories of friend and enemy. As the caesarean citizen delineates politics as a perpetual struggle against enemies, citizenship becomes an issue of survival, security and the effectiveness of political decisions. Therefore, the citizen authorizes the Caesar, a political leader with sufficient power to guarantee the survival of the individual and the society in a hostile environment.

However, only the republican model of citizenship is endowed with a strong and thick collective identity. It not only requires civic altruism, but also the civic commitment to public interest. As republican citizenship propagates a cult of commonness in the public space, this commonness is not necessarily based on the similarity of citizens. Citizens are allowed to interpret the public good differently, preferably during public deliberation that brings about consensus and forges commonness. In the deliberative version of republican citizenship, political responsibilities of citizens primarily cover common discourse ethics pertaining to the common good orientation, as the only way to influence the outcome is through debate in which only better arguments succeed. The core of deliberation is argument comprising persuasion and the convincing of others, since every participant must be ready to hear all arguments and to change his or her position and view when convinced. The republican approach to citizenship focuses on the duties of the citizens in a democratic community. As the citizen is primarily a 'holder of duties' towards the polity, republican citizenship stresses the obligation component in the citizenship triangle of rights, obligations and compliance.

In comparison to the strong collective identity of republican citizenship, the liberal model of citizenship is associated with a notion of weak or thin collective identity. Whereas republican citizens are responsible members of a political community, liberal citizens live in a society of individuals. Participation in the political process is, in the liberal model, not constitutive for being a citizen. Politics is one of a plethora of various areas in which citizens construct their broad spectrum of preferences. This rights-based citizenship focuses primarily on the legal status of citizens. In this sense, it highlights the rights-component of citizenship and underplays obligations and compliance. Liberal citizenship indicates equal status for all citizens, which can be legally claimed. However, these rights do not result from any collective identity, nor do they stem from participation in the political process.

In contrast, the caesarean model of citizenship shows features of strong collective identity as discussed in the cognitive perspective, but it barely represents collective identity in the political sense. Here, we should instead refer to homogeneity with regard to common perceptions of danger and insecurity. Therefore, caesarean citizenship is associated with collectivism as an 'identity-signifier' that is a response to insecurity, and that provokes attempts at reaffirmation of self-identity, decreasing insecurity and existential anxiety. Citizens become mobilized by the leadership whenever he needs their support for his predetermined decisions. Therefore, with regard to the collective body of citizens, we should point to homogeneity, rather than collective identity in the political sense. Citizens are regarded as members of a political church (demos becomes ecclesia) to which they declare their belief and loyalty, and – unlike republican citizens – are not engaged in public discourse. In addition, the caesarean citizenship relates to a different object of identity. Whereas republican citizenship stresses in-group bonds and liberal citizenship emphasizes identification with rights, caesarean citizenship fosters a faith and trust in Leviathan or Caesar.

European identity: pathologies of deliberation, inflation of rights, and politics of insecurity

The empirical chapters of the book explore republican, liberal and caesarean citizenship in the EU. As a form of republican citizenship in the EU, I discussed the EU's attempts to engage in discursive ethics within the constitutional conventions. As an example of the liberal model of European citizenship, I analyzed the Charter of Fundamental Rights, which represents an apogee of the rights-centred approach to European citizenship and identity. Current trends in the EU's caesarean citizenship were discussed regarding the development of the European Leviathan and the politics of insecurity.

Inspired by the deliberation theory of democracy, the European republican citizenship relates strongly to the ideal type deliberation taking place in the ideal-speech situation, where there are no relationships of power, no social hierarchies, and no asymmetries of access. In accordance with the deliberative democracy theory, advocates of the convention method praise it for its higher republican value and its higher decision-making efficiency. I demonstrated that deliberation processes, and especially deliberation via the convention method, can result in pathologies of republican citizenship. I distinguished three pathologies: false will-formation, rational 'hijacking' of deliberation, and perversity of deliberation. The pathology of false will-formation is associated with the republican belief that deliberation in the conventions could give impetus to a true European will, representing civic collective identity. In a more radical version, the Convention on the Future of Europe was actually the embodiment of the collective will, as it enriched raw preferences of individuals transforming them into enlightened, deliberative republican preferences. In the case of the convention method, these claims, however, are far from reality, since under executive dominance and without much feedback to the public the convention method only feigns the European will-formation. Consequently, we deal here with an illusion of will-formation that exhibits oligarchic features, rather than republican ones. Furthermore, political actors engaging in rhetorical action are not eager to change their own beliefs or to be convinced or persuaded. They argue strategically in order to realize their selfish interests. This leads to a political debate rather than public reasoning, in which the argumentative process consists of purely rhetorical exchange but does not evolve towards true arguing. The actors therefore use the arguments as a resource and the mechanism of soft power over other actors. Others can be shamed into compliance by exposing their 'illegitimate' or inappropriate behaviour in public. However, the change of power relations in the EU decided upon in the Convention on the Future of Europe occurred merely under the veil of deliberation, rather than as a result of genuine deliberation. The rational hijacking of deliberation not only questions the notion of citizens' equal influence on political outcomes, but legitimizes oligarchies' decision-making structures, which may enhance the overall decision-making capacity of the EU, but simultaneously question the spirit of the republican citizenship. This is demonstrated with regard to the power shift that was introduced and legitimized by the Convention on the Future of Europe and afterwards by the EU summit in Brussels in June 2007. Moreover, I argue that the likelihood of rhetorical action increases more during constitution-making conventions than in settings of a more deliberative character, since constitutions are devices for the long-term binding of others by limiting their freedom of action. As a result, actors cannot afford the luxury of truth-seeking, while others try to 'bind' them.

Besides fragmented identity formation and group polarization, deliberation may have corrosive effects on the relations between the members of the group, rather than fostering collective identity. Even though the convention method increased the overall level of deliberation in the EU, it could neither fulfil criteria for republican citizenship nor was it able to produce shared collective identity associated with republicanism. Although deliberation is not a danger to the EU that has to be avoided at all costs, the deliberation theory and deliberation practice does not deliver sufficient mechanisms for generating republican citizenship. In this sense, we deal here with a case of an expectations–outcome gap regarding the citizenship–collective identity nexus. Far from demonizing deliberation theory, I argue that the aim of civic collective identity in the EU cannot be realized with the instrument of the convention method. Since the convention method can breed disappointment and feelings of powerlessness, it appears to have a disruptive impact on collective identity. Moreover, it seems to support domination rather than promote equality, which is to be regarded as counterproductive for the generation of a civic collective identity based on mutual respect and recognition.

Despite the temporary emphasis on the convention method as a republican project, European citizenship exhibits a strong liberal accentuation as a result of its focus on rights. This focus culminated in the work of the European Convention, which delivered the Charter of Fundamental Rights in 2001. This shifts European identity more strongly into a legal identity of liberal citizenship. However, in comparison to the strong collective identity of the republican model of citizenship, the liberal model of citizenship is associated with a weak or thin collective identity. Nonetheless, the Charter of Fundamental Rights was expected to express the common preferences and/or common values of the EU. Therefore, some scholars regarded the Charter of Fundamental Rights of the EU as a foundation of the 'European social contract'. In accordance with this interpretation, the Charter of Fundamental Rights reflects essential features of liberal citizenship, as it represents a common European legal system based on human dignity and the respect for each member of European society and their specific identities. In this sense, instead of stressing collective identity, the Charter highlights diversity of identities and thus heterogeneity. In addition, the rights-orientated approach to European identity reflects more problems of liberal citizenship regarding collective identity. On the one hand, the rights-based process of constitutionalization is built on the concept of individual autonomy, which establishes individual equality in the access to rights. In the process, the visibility and identifiability of rights is believed to generate a perception of commonality among European citizens. On the other hand, by enhancing the visibility of rights within a political document it enhances and even institutionalizes distrust towards the political authorities of the EU as a potential threat to the rights, thus rendering identification with the EU more difficult. In particular, the overload of rights and principles can cause a constitutional fiction, as a result of which rights degenerate into the declarations of wishful states of the world, and consequently lose their legal entitlement character. Against this background, this inflation of non-judiciable rights would have rather the opposite effect than the advocates of liberal citizenship envisaged. It is therefore doubtful whether a redirection of citizens' affective attachments from national communities towards a post-national civic, rights-based community can be achieved with the Charter of Fundamental Rights. The mere articulation and listing of values and rights pulls the EU into the contradiction of legality and legitimacy. The constitutionalization of a plethora of rights and values follows an underlying logic of confounding rights and political demands. Wishful states of the world become political demands and they in turn become codified as rights and values, which not only increases the probability of conflict between values and rights, but also reduces the identity-stimulating effects of the constitution. If the constitution reflects almost every right, value and political demand there is, there cannot be any common ground for collective identity, since citizenship identity relates to a specific shared identity. Therefore, identity politics of rights-based constitutionalism might not be the best way to forge a collective identity in the EU, especially since the advocates of liberal citizenship hope to achieve republican results of thick identity with liberal means. In this sense, hopes for thick identity through workings of the liberal citizenship lead to the expectations–outcome gap.

The caesarean citizenship in the EU refers to the political governance of risks, primarily in forms of restrictive migration control and the 'war on terror'. These fields have become major tenets of EU activity and pervade the European Union's citizenship practices. The new citizenship practices of governing risk include among other things dispersion of threat images, biometric categorization of citizens and non-citizens, an overall increase in surveillance and supranational security alliances within the EU, which give birth to the new European corporate security state. The notion of a risk society in which there are uncontrollable and unpredictable threats and dangers promotes excessive activity by the EU, which not only transforms citizenship practices but also makes it easier for the EU to perpetuate the politics of insecurity as an instrument of identity construction. The homogenization of threat perception is forged through securitization of the citizenship issues, as citizens are confronted with threat scenarios highlighting their shared destiny and group belonging. The feeling of insecurity makes the citizens call for additional state action, which causes a shift within citizenship from rights towards compliance. Furthermore, the identity technologies of political authorities attempt to give the enemy a face and a name by focusing on migration and minorities. In this sense, combating migration and terrorism as diffuse threats goes hand in hand with attempts to identify terrorists and migrants as a specific point of reference for caesarean citizenship and its homogenization practices. In the caesarean model of citizenship, this dichotomy highlights the difference between the citizen and the suspect. The politics of insecurity is therefore associated with identity construction, as the political authorities promote and respond to the 'neurotic citizens', whose preference for liberty and freedom is surpassed by fears of survival. Under these circumstances, political authorities are inclined to perpetuate the feeling of insecurity, thus transforming security politics into politics of insecurity.

As a result, border control and asylum policies became the cornerstone of collective identity construction perpetuated by the EU. They use images and scenarios of threat from 'bogus asylum seekers' who are presented as a danger to the social integration and cohesion of European societies. By so doing, the EU shifts its focus on citizenship from political participation and democracy towards the field of internal security, which bases its legitimacy on the bureaucratic power of surveillance, control, separation and expulsion. Simultaneously, the Union citizenship is given a positive image, confronted with the chaos and danger outside of the EU. The EU offers a set of institutions, funds and surveillance instruments that help to separate the neurotic citizen from the dangers of the outside world, and at the same time shape his collective identity based on the perception of a collective threat. The politics of the fight against terrorism draws as equally as migration policies on the feeling of worry and fear in the population and at the same time perpetuates the experience of being vulnerable to risks. The fight against terrorism therefore not only responds to real threats and dangers, but also delivers risk and threat information through mass media, especially with participation of the so-called security experts, whose pure visibility and the availability of risk and threat information in mass media enhance the salience of security matters in the population. Increasingly, surveillance seems to have become one of the crucial strategies of the EU. Since potential terrorists blend into European societies (the enemy transforms itself from an external to an internal one) and are 'unexceptional', proactive forms of surveillance of suspect populations are deemed essential for the preventive risk management. This, however, leads to a surplus supply of data and an exaggeration of threat perception, which in turn can provoke an indiscriminate surveillance of the entire population. With all its strategies, declarations and action plans, the EU seems to create a totalizing vision of a multidimensional security, which would privilege the fight against terrorism as the underlying principle of the EU politics. Under the label of the 'war on terror', a securitization of the European integration is observable, which shifts the EU towards a corporate security state. In the process, the EU assumes an executive-centred character, which exhibits a visible tension with principles of international law and human rights principles. Politics of insecurity thus pertain to the caesarean citizenship, which attempts to produce collective identity in the sense of homogeneity of the threat by establishing and reinforcing boundaries between friends and enemies. However, the identity generation based on caesarean citizenship is never completed, as it relies on the permanent feeling of insecurity and emergency. As a return to normality undermines the perception of a collective threat, the politics of insecurity are likely to increasingly dominate the political discourse of the EU, which in turn poses a serious problem for citizenship identity in the political sense.

Final remarks

The goal of the book was not only to systematize the relationship between collective identity and citizenship in Europe, but also to introduce ordering categories into the complexity of citizenship. The three models of citizenship are ideal types in the Weberian sense. Like other typological categories, they do not exist in a pure form. Their function is to order our thinking of social phenomena. By using ideal types of citizenship and their corresponding collective identities we can better come to terms with various aspects of collective identity, as collective identity can be related to both abstract norms and group members, such as fellow citizens as in the case of citizenship identity. In both cases, it is not only the nature of collective identity that differs, but also the implications regarding its strength and durability. Furthermore, the proposed approach attempted to account for the variance of collective identity, not necessarily referring to the different territorial multiple identities, but rather to various shades of a collective identity at the same level. As European identity can assume different forms, develop varying strengths, and shift between strong individualism and strong collectivism, a differentiation of various generic types of citizenship promises to account for the variety of collective identity at the level of citizenship identity.

As an empirical result, one major feature of European citizenship became particularly apparent, namely the *expectations–outcome gap*. The gap arises when there is a mismatch between the identity politics and the identity logic of the citizenship models. Thus, identity politics can produce contradictory outcomes when the political practice ignores the identity implications of the citizenship models by blurring the specific citizenship–collective identity nexus. For instance, liberal citizenship implying thin identity does not warrant republican expectations. Constitutional patriotism can be a useful political doctrine under the circumstances of democracy, but in undemocratic political regimes such as the EU, it can prove not only to be unable to promote a citizenship identity, but also to aggravate the problems of the democracy deficit. Liberal principles of constitutionalism and rule of law serve the purpose of limiting the scope of democracy and avoiding harmful consequences of democratic rule by majorities and elites. As modern democracies rest on two pillars – the constitutional one referring to the liberal precautions against an abuse of power, and the popular one referring to 'the expression of popular will and choice' – an over-constitutionalized EU with an overabundance of rights, listings of values and numerous declaratory references to solidarities, would limit the scope of the still-deficient democracy in the EU. This would be counterproductive in terms of a citizenship identity, as it would shift the focus of EU politics even further towards the elites and institutions and away from the citizenry, thus becoming an anti-republican project. However, an anti-republican project cannot be associated with republican effects concerning collective identity.

The *expectations–outcome gap* also applies to the republican citizenship in the EU. Republican citizenship in its deliberative version is associated with thick identity, anchored in discursive ethics. However, confronted with pathologies of deliberation, we face defunct republicanism. As deliberative consensus-seeking works as a pressure in favour of the majority or of political actors with more deliberative resources, such as executives, it has conservative workings, to the detriment of minorities and the excluded. Therefore, deliberative consensus-seeking seems to contradict the general commitment to the collective good, as it focuses solely on argumentative commitment, rather than on the substantial commitment. As deliberation can entail corrosive effects for the political community, other institutional mechanisms such as double deliberations, testimonies or balanced discussions could support the republican citizenship more effectively than the prescribed remedies of deliberation theory.

The caesarean citizenship of the EU shows not only an expectations–outcome gap, but also contradicts practices of the liberal and republican citizenship. The securitization of citizenship in the EU is strongly associated with identity, as discourses of security have implications for the elaboration of the political subject (the collective self). Nevertheless, the securitization of citizenship does not generate collective identity defined as a general commitment to a common good, but represents attempts at establishing perceived identity via identity politics. Moreover, homogenization associated with caesarean citizenship poses serious problems for the democratization of the EU, as the securitization of migration and terrorism as threat images entails the curtailing of civil rights and the extension of surveillance and control. Therefore, the EU practices of caesarean citizenship contradict the rights-orientation of the liberal citizenship as well as the democratic focus and the suspicion towards executive politics of the republican citizenship. Since caesarean citizenship is based on the institutionalizing of 'exception politics' and draws its legitimacy from 'decisionism' of the leadership, securitization and risk images have to assume a more permanent character in the EU, thus increasing the democratic deficit of the EU.

Regarding predictions for the citizenship–collective identity nexus, the empirical examination suggests two issues. First, the European citizenship will spawn diverse and often contradictory conceptions and practices of collective identity. Its *three-tiered* character with republican, liberal and caesarean elements is therefore likely to remain unstable and subject to internal dynamics in the future as well. As a result, we cannot expect a linear and uncontroversial development of collective identity in Europe.

Second, the citizenship–collective identity nexus will more strongly relate to the questions of the legitimacy deficit in the EU in the future, as the issue of legitimacy pervades all models of citizenship. Stronger and more invasive identity politics based on manipulation, propaganda or threat scenarios can worsen the legitimacy deficit of the EU in the eyes of the citizens and thus become counterproductive in terms of democratic legitimacy. Paradoxically, the very identity politics designed and applied to increase the acceptance of and support for the EU could turn out to be one of the EU's greatest challenges.

Notes

Introduction

1 Raymond Aron, 'Is multinational citizenship possible?', *Social Research* 41, no. 4 (1974), pp. 638–56; Elizabeth Meehan, *Citizenship and the European Community* (London: Sage, 1993); Elizabeth Meehan, 'Staatsbürgerschaft und die Europäische Gemeinschaft', in Heinz Kleger (ed.), *Transnationale Staatsbürgerschaft* (Frankfurt: Campus, 1997), pp. 42–63.

2 Carole Lyons, 'Citizenship in the constitution of the European Union: rhetoric or reality?' in Richard Bellamy (ed.), *Constitutionalism, Democracy and Sovereignty: American and European Perspectives* (Aldershot: Avebury, 1996), pp. 96–110; Joseph H. H. Weiler, *Legitimacy and democracy of Union governance: the 1996 intergovernmental agenda and beyond* (Oslo: ARENA, 1996), Working Paper 22.

3 Antje Wiener, *European Citizenship Practice: Building Institutions of a Non-state* (Boulder, CO: Westview, 1998); Jo Shaw, 'The interpretation of European Union citizenship', *Modern Law Review* 61, no. 3 (1998), pp. 293–317.

4 Richard Bellamy, 'The right to have rights: citizenship practice and the political constitution of the EU', in Richard Bellamy and Alex Warleigh (eds), *Citizenship and Governance in the European Union* (London: Continuum, 2001), pp. 41–70, esp. p. 50ff.

5 Thomas Faist, 'Social citizenship in the European Union: nested membership', *Journal of Common Market Studies* 39, no. 1 (2001), pp. 37–58; Philippe C. Schmitter and Michael W. Bauer, 'A (modest) proposal for expanding social citizenship in the European Union', *Journal of European Social Policy* 11, no. 1 (2001), pp. 55–65.

6 R. J. Barry Jones, 'The political economy of European citizenship', in Richard Bellamy and Alex Warleigh (eds), *Citizenship and Governance in the European Union* (London, Continuum, 2001), pp. 143–62; Dennis C. Mueller, *Rights and citizenship in the European Union* (Vienna: University of Vienna, 2003), CESIFO Working Paper 895.

7 Antje Wiener, *Assessing the constructive potential of Union citizenship – a socio-historical perspective*, European Integration online Paper 1 (17), 1997, http://eiop.or.at/eiop/texte/1997-017a.htm; Jo Shaw, 'The interpretation of European Union citizenship', *Modern Law Review* 61, no. 3 (1998), pp. 293–317; Cris Shore, 'Whither European citizenship? Eros and civilisation revisited', *European Journal of Social Theory* 7, no. 1 (2004), pp. 27–44; Seyla Benhabib, 'Twilight of sovereignty or the emergence of cosmopolitan norms? Rethinking citizenship in volatile Times', *Citizenship Studies* 11, no. 1 (2007), pp. 19–36.

8 Nick Stevenson, 'European cosmopolitan solidarity: questions of citizenship, difference and post-materialism', *European Journal of Social Theory* 9, no. 4 (2006), pp. 485–500; Gerard Delanty, 'European citizenship: a critical assessment', *Citizenship Studies* 11, no. 1 (2007), pp. 63–72.

9 Cf. Gerard Delanty and Chris Rumford (eds) *Rethinking Europe: Social Theory and the Implications of Europeanization* (London: Routledge, 2005); Bellamy, Richard et

al., *Making European Citizens: Civic Inclusion in a Transnational Context* (London: Palgrave, 2006).

10 Cf. Charles Tilly, 'Citizenship, identity and social history', *International Review of Social History* 40, Supplement 3 (1995), pp. 1–17.

11 Amy Gutman, *Identity in Democracy* (Princeton,NJ: Princeton University Press, 2003); Carolin Emcke, 'Between choice and coercion: identities, injuries, and different forms of recognition', *Constellations* 7, no. 4 (2000), pp. 483–95.

12 Arieh Gavious and Shlomo Mizrahi, 'Two-level collective action and group identity', *Journal of Theoretical Politics* 11, no. 4 (1999), pp. 497–517; Bert Klandermans, 'How group identification helps to overcome the dilemma of collective action', *American Behavioral Scientist* 45, no. 5 (2002), pp. 887–900.

13 Cf. Marcus Höreth, *Die Europäische Union im Legitimationstrilemma: Zur Rechtfertigung des Regierens jenseits der Staatlichkeit* (Baden-Baden: Nomos, 1998); Marcus Höreth, 'No way out for the beast? The unsolved legitimacy problem of European governance', *Journal of European Public Policy* 6, no. 2 (1999), pp. 249–68; Franz C. Mayer and Jan Palmowski, 'European identities and the EU – the ties that bind the peoples of Europe', *Journal of Common Market Studies* 42, no. 3 (2004), pp. 573–98.

14 Peter Graf Kielmannsegg, 'Integration und Demokratie', in Markus Jachtenfuchs and Beate Kohler-Koch (eds), *Europäische Integration* (Opladen: Leske+Budrich, 2003), 2nd edition, pp. 49–83, esp. p. 60.

15 David McCrone and Richard Kiely, 'Nationalism and citizenship', *Sociology* 34, no. 1 (2000), pp. 19–34; Richard Falk, 'The decline of citizenship in an era of globalization', *Citizenship Studies* 4, no. 1 (2000), pp. 5–17; Björn Hettne, 'The fate of citizenship in post-Westphalia', *Citizenship Studies* 4, no. 1 (2000), pp. 35–46.

16 Gerard Delanty, *Citizenship in a Global Age: Society, Culture, Politics* (New York: Open University Press, 2000); Richard Münch, *Nation and Citizenship in the Global Age* (Basingstoke: Palgrave, 2001); For the EU see Catherine Wihtol De Wenden, 'Post-Amsterdam migration policy and European citizenship', *European Journal of Migration and Law* 1 (1999), pp. 89–101; Michael Peter Smith, 'Transnationalism, the State, and the extraterritorial citizen', *Politics & Society* 31, no. 4 (2003), pp. 467–502.

17 Stephen Castles and Alastair Davidson, *Citizenship and Migration: Globalization and the Politics of Belonging* (Basingstoke: Palgrave, 2000).

18 Cf. Ernest Gellner, 'The importance of being modular', in John Hall (ed.), *Civil Society* (Cambridge: Cambridge University Press, 1995), pp. 32–55.

19 Of course, semantically we would also differentiate between collective identity and citizenship in the context of the modern nation-state, where these two categories overlap.

20 This position is more than merely a critique of the first method of linking citizenship and collective identity. It takes it to a higher level of negating the relevance of the first method.

21 Trevor Purvis and Alan Hunt, 'Identity versus citizenship: transformations in the discourses and practices of citizenship', *Social & Legal Studies* 8, no. 4 (1999), pp. 457–82.

22 Seyla Benhabib, 'Twilight of sovereignty or the emergence of cosmopolitan norms? Rethinking citizenship in volatile times', *Citizenship Studies* 11, no. 1 (2007), p.31; see also William Smith, 'Cosmopolitan citizenship', *European Journal of Social Theory* 10, no. 1 (2007), pp. 37–52.

23 Rainer Bauböck, 'Why European citizenship? Normative approaches to supranational union', *Theoretical Inquiries in Law* 8 (2007), pp. 439–74; see also Rainer Bauböck, *Transnational Citizenship: Membership Rights in International Migration* (Aldershot: Edward Elgar, 1994); Heinz Kleger (ed.), *Transnationale Staatsbürgerschaft* (Frankfurt: Campus, 1997); cf. also Heinz Kleger, 'Transnationale Staatsbürgerschaft oder: Lässt sich Staatsbürgerschaft entnationalisieren?', *Archiv für Rechts-und Sozialphilosophie* 62 (1995), pp. 85–99.

24 Justine Lacroix, 'For a European constitutional patriotism', *Political Studies* 50, no. 5 (2002), pp. 944–58; Omid Payrow Shabani, 'Constitutional patriotism as a model of postnational political association: The case of the EU', *Philosophy & Social Criticism* 32, no. 6 (2006), pp. 699–718.

25 Gerard Delanty, 'European citizenship: A critical assessment', *Citizenship Studies* 11, no. 1 (2007), pp. 63–72.

26 Cf. Will Kymlicka, *Finding our Way: Rethinking Ethnocultural Relations in Canada* (Toronto: Toronto University Press, 1998).

27 Cf. Ulrich Haltern, 'Das Janusgesicht der Unionsbürgerschaft', *Swiss Political Science Review* 11, no. 1 (2005), pp. 87–117.

28 Richard Bellamy, 'Introduction: the making of modern citizenship', in Richard Bellamy, Dario Castiglione, and Emilio Santoro (eds), *Lineages of European Citizenship: Rights, Belonging and Participation in Eleven Nation-States* (Basingstoke: Palgrave, 2004), pp. 1–21, esp. p. 9; Christian Joppke, 'Transformation of citizenship: status, rights, identity', *Citizenship Studies* 11, no. 1 (2007), pp. 37–48; Derek Heater, *Citizenship: The Civic Ideal in World History, Politics and Education* (London: Longman, 1990), p. 187; Antje Wiener, *European Citizenship Practice: Building Institutions of a Non-state* (Boulder, CO: Westview, 1998).

29 Christian Joppke, 'Transformation of citizenship: status, rights, identity', *Citizenship Studies* 11, no. 1 (2007), pp. 37–48, esp. p. 44.

30 Richard Bellamy, 'Introduction: the making of modern citizenship', in Richard Bellamy, Dario Castiglione, and Emilio Santoro (eds) *Lineages of European Citizenship: Rights, Belonging and Participation in Eleven Nation-States* (Basingstoke: Palgrave, 2004), pp. 1–21; Richard Bellamy, 'Evaluating union citizenship: belonging, rights and participation within the EU', *Citizenship Studies* 12, no. 6 (2008), pp. 597–611; Antje Wiener, *European Citizenship Practice: Building Institutions of a Non-state* (Boulder, CO: Westview, 1998), p. 23; Antje Wiener, 'Making sense of the new geography of citizenship: fragmented citizenship in the European Union', *Theory and Society* 26, no. 4 (1997), pp. 529–60. Antje Wiener maps citizenship along the criteria of rights, access to polity/welfare state and belonging/identity. Even though she concedes that national identity loses its appeal, particularly in the EU, other forms of collective identity become dominant (p. 530). They are related to class, gender, race, age, and other cleavages leading to fragmented citizenship. The problem with this argument is that it seems to be inconsistent. On one hand, identity is viewed as a component of citizenship, which is a political concept. On the other hand, alternative forms of identity become relegated into an extra-political or even pre-political status of belonging. Cf. also Antje Wiener, 'Zur Verfassungspolitik jenseits des Staates: Die Vermittlung von Bedeutung am Beispiel der Unionsbürgerschaft', *Zeitschrift für Internationale Beziehungen* 8, no. 1 (2001), pp. 73–104.

31 Jo Shaw, 'The interpretation of European Union citizenship', *Modern Law Review* 61, no. 3 (1998), pp. 293–317, esp. p. 294.

32 David McCrone and Richard Kiely, 'Nationalism and citizenship', *Sociology* 34, no. 1 (2000), pp. 19–34.

33 Cf. Antje Wiener, *European Citizenship Practice: Building Institutions of a Non-state* (Boulder, CO: Westview, 1998), p. 23.

34 Cf. David Taylor, 'Citizenship and social power', *Critical Social Policy* 9, no. 26 (1989), pp. 19–31.

35 Norbert Elias, *The Civilizing Process: Sociogenetic and Psychogenetic Investigations* (Oxford: Blackwell, 2000), p. 365.

36 Cf. Jean L. Cohen, 'Changing paradigms of citizenship and the exclusiveness of the demos', *International Sociology* 14, no. 3 (1999), pp. 245–68; Trevor Purvis and Alan Hunt, 'Identity versus citizenship: transformations in the discourses and practices of citizenship', *Social & Legal Studies* 8, no. 4 (1999), pp. 457–82.

37 Andreas Reckwitz, 'Toward a theory of social practices: a development of culturalist theorizing', *European Journal of Social Theory* 5, no. 2 (2002), pp. 243–63, esp. p. 249.

38 Max Weber, *Economy and Society: An Outline of Interpretative Sociology* (Berkeley, CA: University of California Press, 1978), ed. by G. Roth and C. Wittich, vol. 1, pp. 9, 21; Geneviève Zubrzycki, 'The classical opposition between civic and ethnic models of nationhood: ideology, empirical reality and social scientific analysis', *Polish Sociological Review* 3, no. 139 (2002), pp. 24–43.

39 Cf. Richard Bellamy, 'Introduction: the making of modern citizenship', in Richard Bellamy, Dario Castiglione, and Emilio Santoro (eds), *Lineages of European Citizenship: Rights, Belonging and Participation in Eleven Nation-States* (Basingstoke: Palgrave, 2004), pp. 1–21, esp. p. 9.

Chapter 1: The conceptual dimension of citizenship

1 J. G. A. Pocock, 'The ideal of citizenship since classical times', in Gershon Shafir (ed.), *The Citizenship Debates* (Minneapolis, MN: University of Minnesota Press, 1998), pp. 31–41; Nicholas Buttle, 'Republican constitutionalism: a Roman ideal', *Journal of Political Philosophy* 9, no. 3 (2001), pp. 331–49; Adrian Oldfield, 'Citizenship and community: civic republicanism and the modern world', in Gershon Shafir (ed.), *The Citizenship Debates* (Minneapolis, MN: University of Minnesota Press, 1998), pp. 75–89.

2 John Rawls, 'Justice as fairness in the liberal polity', in Gershon Shafir (ed.), *The Citizenship Debates* (Minneapolis, MN: University of Minnesota Press, 1998), pp. 53–72; John Rawls, 'Justice as fairness: political not metaphysical', *Philosophy and Public Affairs* 14, no. 3 (1985), pp. 223–51.

3 Max Weber, 'Citizenship in ancient and medieval cities', in Gershon Shafir (ed.), *The Citizenship Debates* (Minneapolis, MN: University of Minnesota Press, 1998), pp. 43–49.

4 T. H. Marshall, *Citizenship and Social Class* (London: Pluto Press, 1992 [1950]).

5 Cf. Seyla Benhabib, 'Twilight of sovereignty or the emergence of cosmopolitan norms? Rethinking citizenship in volatile times', *Citizenship Studies* 11, no. 1 (2007), pp. 19–36; Winfried Thaa, 'Lean citizenship: the fading away of the political in transnational democracy', *European Journal of International Relations* 7, no. 4 (2001), pp. 503–23; Philip J. Frankenfeld, 'Technological citizenship: a normative framework for risk studies', *Science, Technology & Human Values* 17, no. 4 (1992), pp. 459–84; R. Amy Elman, 'The limits of citizenship: migration, sex discrimination and same-sex partners in EU law', *Journal of Common Market Studies* 38, no. 5 (2000), pp. 729–49.

6 Cf. Angus Stewart, 'Two conceptions of citizenship', *British Journal of Sociology* 46, no. 1 (1995), pp. 63–78.

7 Nancy Fraser and Linda Gordon highlight the original meaning of 'citizen', relating it to the dwellers of medieval cities that were situated outside the grip of feudal relations of servitude. Nancy Fraser and Linda Gordon, 'Contract versus charity: why is there no social citizenship in the United States?', in Gershon Shafir (ed.), *The Citizenship Debates* (Minneapolis, MN: University of Minnesota Press, 1998), pp. 113–27.

8 Cf. Elaine R. Thomas, 'Who belongs? Competing conceptions of political membership', *European Journal of Social Theory* 5, no. 3 (2002), pp. 323–49.

9 For a similar differentiation see Rogers Brubaker and Frederick Cooper, 'Beyond identity', *Theory and Society* 29, no. 1 (2000), pp. 1–47.

10 Cf. Andreas Reckwitz, 'Toward a theory of social practices: a development in cultural theorizing', *European Journal of Social Theory* 5, no. 2 (2002), pp. 243–63; Andreas Reckwitz, 'The status of the "material" in theories of culture: from social structure to artefacts', *Journal for the Theory of Social Behaviour* 32, no. 2 (2002), pp. 195–217.

11 Ruth Lister, 'Inclusive citizenship: realizing the potential', *Citizenship Studies* 11, no. 1 (2007), pp. 49–61.

12 *Ibid.*, p. 55.

13 Cf. Peter Wagner, *A Sociology of Modernity: Liberty and Discipline* (London: Routledge, 1994).

14   Cf. Margaret R. Somers, 'Narrativity, narrative identity, and social action: rethinking English working-class formation', *Social Science History* 16, no. 4 (1992), pp. 591–630; Rogers Brubaker, *Ethnicity without Groups* (Cambridge, MA: Harvard University Press, 2004), pp. 7–27, esp. p. 11.

15   Cf. Heinz Kleger, 'Was heisst: "Die Idee der Demokratie ist reflexiv geworden"'? *Studia Philosophica* 58 (1999), pp. 167–96.

16   Charles Tilly, 'A primer on citizenship', *Theory and Society* 26, no. 4 (1997), p. 600.

17   There is a range of approaches attempting to move the concept of citizenship beyond the relationship between the individual and a political authority by rendering it more encompassing. By criticizing the private–public divide they plea for including social or private issues such as poverty or sexuality into an extended conception of citizenship. See for instance John Hoffman, *Citizenship Beyond the State* (London: Sage, 2004); Ruth Lister, 'Inclusive citizenship: realizing the potential', *Citizenship Studies* 11, no. 1 (2007), pp. 49–61.

18   Cf. Trevor Purvis and Alan Hunt, 'Identity versus citizenship: transformations and practices of citizenship', *Social & Legal Studies* 8, no. 4 (1999), pp. 457–82; Jean L. Cohen, 'Changing paradigms of citizenship and the exclusiveness of the demos', *International Sociology* 14, no. 3 (1999), pp. 245–68.

19   Cf. Etienne Balibar, 'Possessive individualism reversed: from Locke to Derrida', *Constellations* 9, no. 3 (2002), pp. 299–317.

20   Marshall presents an account of the citizenship development in Britain, in which civil rights were introduced in the eighteenth century, political rights followed in the nineteenth century and social rights in the twentieth century. Civil rights include personal liberties, the right to own property and other rights linked to individual freedom. Political rights pertain to those rights that enable individuals to participate in the exercise of political decision-making and social rights refer to the right to a certain level of economic well-being. T. H. Marshall, *Citizenship and Social Class* (London: Pluto Press, 1992 [1950]).

21   Cf. Charles Taylor, 'The politics of recognition', in Amy Gutmann (ed.), *Multiculturalism and the Politics of Recognition* (Princeton, NJ: Princeton University Press, 1992), pp. 25–73; Iris Marion Young, 'Polity and group difference: a critique of the ideal of universal citizenship', *Ethics* 9, no. 2 (1989), pp. 250–74; Will Kymlicka, *Multicultural Citizenship: A Liberal Theory of Minority Rights* (Oxford: Oxford University Press, 1995).

22   Cf. Brian Barry, *Culture and Equality* (Cambridge, MA: Harvard University Press, 2002), esp. pp. 91–103.

23   Cf. Claus Offe, 'Homogeneity and constitutional democracy: coping with identity conflicts through group rights', *Journal of Political Philosophy* 6, no. 2 (1998), pp. 113–41; Yasmeen Abu-Laban, 'Liberalism, multiculturalism and the problem of essentialism', *Citizenship Studies* 6, no. 2 (2002), pp. 459–82; Tariq Modood, 'Introduction', in Tariq Modood and Pnina Werbner (eds), *The Politics of Multiculturalism in the New Europe* (London: Zed Press, 1997), pp. 1–25.

24   Cf. Ulrich Haltern, 'Das Janusgesicht der Unionsbürgerschaft', *Swiss Political Science Review* 11, no. 1 (2005), pp. 87–117, esp. p. 90.

25   Will Kymlicka, *Multicultural Citizenship: A Liberal Theory of Minority Rights* (Oxford: Oxford University Press, 1995), esp. p. 101f.

26   Cf. Isaac Logs, 'The political philosophy of Aristotle', *Annals of the American Academy of Political and Social Science* 10 (1897), pp. 313–33.

27   Cf. Geoffrey Gershenson, 'The rise and fall of species-life: Rousseau's critique of liberalism', *European Journal of Political Theory* 5, no. 3 (2006), pp. 281–300; Kalu N. Kalu, 'Of citizenship, virtue, and the administrative imperative: deconstructing Aristotelian civic republicanism', *Public Administration Review* 64, no. 4 (2003), pp. 418–27.

28   Cf. Clive Bean, 'Testing the precepts of republican political theory against citizen attitudes, beliefs and practices', *Journal of Sociology* 37, no. 2 (2001), pp. 141–55.

29 D. E. Cooper, 'Collective responsibility', *Philosophy* 43, no. 165 (1968), pp. 258–68.

30 Cf. Philip Pettit, *Republicanism: A Theory of Freedom and Government* (Oxford: Oxford University Press, 1997); Quentin Skinner, 'Republican ideal of political liberty', in Gisela Bock, Quentin Skinner and Marizio Viroli (eds), *Machiavelli and Republicanism* (Cambridge: Cambridge University Press, 1990), pp. 293–309; Nicholas Buttle, 'Republican constitutionalism: a Roman ideal', *The Journal of Political Philosophy* 9, no. 3 (2001), pp. 331–49.

31 John Maynor, 'Another instrumental republican approach', *European Journal of Political Theory* 1, no. 1 (2002), pp. 71–89; Philip Pettit, 'Keeping republican freedom simple: on a difference with Quentin Skinner', *Political Theory* 30, no. 3 (2002), pp. 339–56.

32 Alexis de Tocqueville, *Democracy in America*, trans. George Lawrence, ed. J. P. Mayer (Garden City, NY: Doubleday, 1964).

33 Jane Mansbridge et al., 'Norms of deliberation: an inductive study', *Journal of Public Deliberation* 2, no. 1 (2006), pp. 1–47.

34 Robert E. Goodin, 'Democratic deliberation within', *Philosophy and Public Affairs* 29, no. 1 (2000), pp. 81–109.

35 Arne Johan Vetlesen, 'Hannah Arendt, Habermas and the republican tradition', *Philosophy & Social Criticism* 21, no. 1 (1995), pp. 1–16; Axel Honneth, 'The limits of liberalism: on the political–ethical discussion on communitarianism', *Thesis Eleven* 28, no. 1 (1991), pp. 18–34.

36 Lyn Carson, 'Improving public deliberative practice: a comparative analysis of two Italian citizens: jury projects in 2006', *Journal of Public Deliberation* 2, no. 1 (2006), pp. 1–18; Peter Levine et al., 'Future directions for public deliberation', *Journal of Public Deliberation* 1, no. 1 (2005), pp. 1–13.

37 Cf. Jürgen Habermas, *Faktizität und Geltung: Beträge zur Diskurstheorie des Rechts und des demokratischen Rechtsstaats* (Frankfurt: Suhrkamp, 1992); Jeffrey Flynn, 'Communicative power in Habermas's theory of democracy', *European Journal of Political Theory* 3, no. 4 (2004), pp. 433–54.

38 This shift from active citizenship towards compliance and obedience to political authority is attributed to Jean Bodin, who highlighted the problem of the state sovereignty to the detriment of civic freedom. Nonetheless, the compliance component of citizenship remained visible and influential in the modern versions of citizenship. Cf. Manfred Riedel, 'Bürger, Staatsbürger, Bürgertum', in Otto Brunner et al. (eds), *Geschichtliche Grundbegriffe: Historisches Lexikon zur politisch-sozialen Sprache in Deutschland* (Stuttgart: Klett-Cotta, 1972), pp. 673–725.

39 William Rasch, 'Conflict as a vocation: Carl Schmitt and the possibility of politics', *Theory, Culture & Society* 17, no. 6 (2000), pp. 1–32.

40 Cf. Robert J. Pranger, 'An explanation for why final political authority is necessary', *American Political Science Review* 60, no. 4 (1966), pp. 994–97.

41 Albert O. Hirschman, *Shifting Involvements: Private Interest and Public Action* (Princeton, NJ: Princeton University Press, 1982).

42 Andreas Hess, 'The economy of morals and its applications – an attempt to understand some central concepts in the work of Albert O. Hirschman', *Review of International Political Economy* 6 (1999), no. 3, pp. 338–59; James L. Perry and Lois Recascino Wise, 'The motivational bases of public service', *Public Administration Review* 50, no. 3 (1990), pp. 367–73.

43 Gabriel A. Almond and Sidney Verba, *The Civic Culture: Political Attitude and Democracy in Five Nations* (Princeton, NJ: Princeton University Press, 1963). For a newer reappraisal of the concept see John Street, 'Political culture – from civic culture to mass culture', *British Journal of Political Science* 24, no. 1 (1994), pp. 95–113.

44 Peter Wagner, *A Sociology of Modernity. Liberty and Discipline* (London: Routledge, 1994).

45 Peter Wagner, 'Liberty and discipline: making sense of postmodernity, or, once again, toward a sociohistorical understanding of modernity', *Theory and Society* 21, no. 4 (1992), pp. 467–92.

46 Barry Hindess, 'Divide and rule: the international character of modern citizenship', *European Journal of Social Theory* 1, no. 1 (1998), pp. 57–70.

47 Cf. Rogers Brubaker, *Citizenship and Nationhood in France and Germany* (Cambridge, MA: Harvard University Press, 1992), esp. p. 23; Christian Joppke, 'Exclusion in the liberal state: the case of immigration and citizenship policy', *European Journal of Social Theory* 8, no. 1 (2005), pp. 43–61.

48 Michel Foucault, *Discipline and Punish: The Birth of the Prison* (London: Allen Lane, 1977).

49 Cf. John T. Scholz and Neil Pinney, 'Duty, fear, and tax compliance: the heuristic basis of citizenship behaviour', *American Journal of Political Science* 39, no. 2 (1995), pp. 490–512.

50 Roy Coleman, 'Images from a neoliberal city: the state, surveillance and social control', *Critical Criminology* 12, no. 1 (2003), pp. 21–42.

51 Colleen Bell, 'Surveillance strategies and populations at risk: biopolitical governance in Canada's national security policy', *Security Dialogue* 37, no. 2 (2006), pp. 147–65; Paul Henman, 'Targeted!: population segmentation, electronic surveillance and governing the unemployed in Australia', *International Sociology* 19, no. 2 (2004), pp. 173–91.

52 Engin F. Isin, 'The neurotic citizen', *Citizenship Studies* 8, no. 3 (2004), pp. 217–35.

53 Jeremy Waldron, 'A right-based critique of constitutional rights', *Oxford Journal of Legal Studies* 13, no. 1 (1993), pp. 18–51; Blain Neufeld, 'Civic respect, political liberalism, and non-liberal societies', *Politics, Philosophy & Economics* 4, no. 3 (2005), pp. 275–99. For instance, Joseph Carens argues that citizen rights entail an extensive range of duties and responsibilities such as the obligation to vote, to fulfil the responsibilities of public office, and to defend one's country. Joseph Carens, 'Rights and duties in an egalitarian society', *Political Theory* 14, no. 1 (1986), pp. 31–49. Also Will Kymlicka and Wayne Norman argue that the importance of civic virtue has been acknowledged by liberals such as Amy Gutmann or William Galston, even though critics believe that rights-oriented commitment to liberty or individualism renders the concept of civic virtue unintelligible. Will Kymlicka and Wayne Norman, 'Return of the citizen: a survey of recent work on citizenship theory', *Ethics* 104, no. 2 (1994), pp. 352–81.

54 Cf. Raymond Aron, 'Is multinational citizenship possible?', *Social Research* 41, no. 4 (1974), pp. 638–56.

55 J. G. A. Pocock, 'The ideal of citizenship since classical times', in Gershon Shafir (ed.), *The Citizenship Debates* (Minneapolis, MN: University of Minnesota Press, 1998), pp. 31–34; Adrian Oldfield, 'Citizenship and community: civic republicanism and the modern world', in Gershon Shafir (ed.), *The Citizenship Debates* (Minneapolis, MN: University of Minnesota Press, 1998), pp. 75–89.

56 Cf. Ulrich Beck, 'The terrorist threat: world risk society revisited', *Theory, Culture & Society* 19, no. 4 (2002), pp. 39–55; Ulrich Beck, 'The silence of words: on terror and war', *Security Dialogue* 34, no. 3 (2003), pp. 255–67.

57 Cf. Jonathan Fox, 'The difficult transition from clientelism to citizenship: lessons from Mexico', *World Politics* 46, no. 2 (1994), pp. 151–84; Oskar Kurer, 'Clientelism, corruption, and the allocation of resources', *Public Choice* 77, no. 2 (1993), pp. 259–73; Leonard Wantchekon, 'Clientelism and voting behavior', *World Politics* 55, no. 3 (2003), pp. 399–422.

58 Cf. Yoram Barzel and Levis A. Kochin, 'Ronald Coase on the nature of social cost as a key to the problem of the firm', *The Scandinavian Journal of Economics* 94, no. 1 (1992), pp. 19–31; Donald H. Regan, 'The problem of social cost revisited', *Journal of Law and Economics* 15, no. 2 (1972), pp. 427–37.

59 Cf. Richard Ball, 'Individualism, collectivism, and economic development', *Annals of the American Academy of Political and Social Science* 573, no. 1 (2001), pp. 57–

584; Manley H. Thompson, 'Individualistic and collectivistic liberty', *The Journal of Philosophy* 37, no. 14 (1940), pp. 382–86; Günter Bierbauer, 'Toward an understanding of legal culture: variations in individualism and collectivism between Kurds, Lebanese, and Germans', *Law & Society Review* 28, no. 2 (1994), pp. 243–64.

60 Cf. Douglas N. Husak, 'Paternalism and autonomy', *Philosophy and Public Affairs* 10, no. 1 (1981), pp. 27–46; N. Fotion, 'Paternalism', *Ethics* 89, no. 2 (1979), pp. 191–98; Christopher Wolfe, 'Liberalism and paternalism: a critique of Ronald Dworkin', *Review of Politics* 56, no. 4 (1994), pp. 615–39.

61 Cf. Michel Foucault, 'The subject and power', *Critical Inquiry* 8, no. 4 (1982), pp. 777–95.

62 However, some scholars find a systemic antinomy between the individual and nationality without recurring to the globalization processes. See for instance Steven Grosby, 'Antinomies of individuality and nationality', *Qualitative Sociology* 18, no. 2 (1995), pp. 211–26.

63 Saskia Sassen, *Denationalization: Territory, Authority, and Rights in a Global Digital Age* (Princeton, NJ: Princeton University Press, 2004); Saskia Sassen, 'The participation of states and citizens in global governance', *Indiana Journal of Global Legal Studies* 10, no. 5 (2003), pp. 5–28.

64 For instance Gerard Delanty, *Citizenship in a Global Age* (Philadelphia, PA: Open University Press, 2000). A good review of the topic of citizenship and globalization is offered by Bryan S. Turner, 'Review essay: citizenship and political globalization', *Citizenship Studies* 4, no. 1 (2000), pp. 81–86.

65 Richard Falk, 'The decline of citizenship in an era of globalization', *Citizenship Studies* 4, no. 1 (2000), pp. 5–17; cf. also Björn Hettne, 'The fate of citizenship in post-Westphalia', *Citizenship Studies* 4, no. 1 (2000), pp. 35–46.

66 William Smith, 'Cosmopolitan citizenship: virtue, irony and worldlinesss', *European Journal of Social Theory* 10, no. 1 (2007), pp. 37–52.

67 Cf. Claus Offe, 'Homogeneity and constitutional democracy: coping with identity conflicts through group rights', *Journal of Political Philosophy* 6, no. 2 (1998), pp. 113–41; cf. also Seyla Benhabib, 'The democratic moment and the problem of difference', in Seyla Benhabib (ed.), *Democracy and Difference: Contesting the Boundaries of the Political* (Princeton, NJ: Princeton University Press, 1996), pp. 3–18.

68 Offe, *op. cit.*, p. 122.

69 *Ibid.*, p. 132. In contrast, Jürgen Habermas argues that a universally shared civic culture is possible, one which recognizes and accommodates cultural differences while at the same time providing a neutral public sphere in which various groups can communicate and compete under conditions of democracy. Jürgen Habermas, 'Multiculturalism and the liberal state', *Stanford Law Review* 47, no 5 (1995), pp. 849–53.

70 Considering citizen competences, Hubertus Buchstein distinguishes between cognitive competences, procedural competences and habitual competences. Cognitive competences pertain to the existence of informed, relevant and transitive preference of individual citizens, whereas procedural competences include strategic knowledge of the workings of the political system, in which these preferences should be realized. In contrast, habitual competences encompass civic virtues of obligations and responsibilities vis-à-vis other citizens such as the sense of citizenship, which evaluates selfish preferences against the background of the ethical commitment to the community. Hubertus Buchstein, 'Die Zumutungen der Demokratie. Von der normativen Theorie des Bürgers zur institutionell vermittelten Präferenzkompetenz', in Klaus von Beyme and Claus Offe (eds), *Politische Theorien in der Ära der Transformation* (Opladen: Westdeutscher Verlag, 1995), pp. 295–324. For the debate on citizen competences see for instance James H. Kuklinski, 'Citizen competence revisited', *Political Behavior* 23, no. 3 (2001), pp. 195–98; James H. Kuklinski and Paul J. Quirk, 'Conceptual foundations of citizen competence', *Political Behavior* 23, no. 3 (2001), pp. 285–311; Robert Weissberg, 'Democratic political competence: clearing the underbrush and a controversial proposal', *Political Behavior* 23, no. 3 (2001), pp. 257–84; Tali

Mendelberg, 'The deliberative citizen: theory and evidence', *Political Decision Making, Deliberation and Participation* 6 (2002), pp. 151–93. For its application in the context of the European Union see Dimitris N. Chryssochoou, 'Civic competence and the challenge to EU polity-building', *Journal of European Public Policy* 9, no. 5 (2002), pp. 756–73.

71 For the discussion of the requirements for the admission to citizenship see Hermann R. Van Gunsteren, 'Admission to citizenship', *Ethics* 98, no. 4 (1988), pp. 731–41.

72 Brian Barry, *Culture and Equality* (Cambridge, MA: Harvard University Press, 2002), p. 104.

73 Brian Barry distinguishes between acculturation and assimilation. While assimilation aims at rendering individuals more alike, acculturation preserves cultural distinctiveness of individuals, even if it endows them with an additional layer of cultural competences such as the language proficiency. Brian Barry, *Culture and Equality* (Cambridge, MA: Harvard University Press, 2002), p. 72ff. For the discussion of the thesis of exclusionary tendencies of citizenship see also Veit Bader, 'Citizenship and exclusion: radical democracy, community, and justice. Or, what is wrong with communitarianism?', *Political Theory* 23, no. 2 (1995), pp. 211–46.

74 Cf. Jeremy Waldron, 'Particular values and critical morality', *California Law Review* 77, no. 3 (1989), pp. 561–89; Jeremy Waldron, 'Special ties and natural duties', *Philosophy and Public Affairs* 22, no. 1 (1993), pp. 3–30.

75 Jeremy Waldron, 'Cultural identity and civic responsibility', in Will Kymlicka and Wayne Norman (eds), *Citizenship in Diverse Societies* (Oxford: Oxford University Press, 2000), pp. 155–74. For other approaches to diversity and equality see for instance Avigail Eisenberg, 'Diversity and equality: three approaches to cultural and sexual difference', *Journal of Political Philosophy* 11, no. 1 (2003), pp. 41–64; Rogers Brubaker, 'Citizenship in Soviet successor states', *International Migration Review* 26, no. 2 (1992), pp. 269–91.

76 Cf. Ruth Lister, 'Inclusive citizenship: realizing the potential', *Citizenship Studies* 11, no. 1 (2007), pp. 49–61.

77 Seyla Benhabib, 'Twilight of sovereignty or the emergence of cosmopolitan norms? Rethinking citizenship in volatile times', *Citizenship Studies* 11, no. 1 (2007), pp. 19–36; see also James Bohman, 'Republican cosmopolitanism', *Journal of Political Philosophy* 12, no. 3 (2004), pp. 336–52.

78 Christopher Osakwe, 'Recent Soviet citizenship legislation', *American Journal of Comparative Law* 28, no. 4 (1980), pp. 625–43; also Durward V. Sandifer, 'Soviet citizenship', *American Journal of International Law* 30, no. 4 (1936), pp. 614–31.

79 James Burk, 'The citizen soldier and democratic societies: a comparative analysis of America's revolutionary and civil wars', *Citizenship Studies* 4, no 2 (2000), pp. 149–65.

80 Margaret R. Somers, 'Citizenship and the place of the public sphere: law, community, and political culture in the transition to democracy', *American Sociological Review* 58, no. 5 (1993), pp. 587–620.

81 Erving Goffman, 'The interaction order', *American Sociological Review* 48 (1983), pp 1–17, esp. p. 3; Paul Colomy and J. David Brown, 'Goffman and interactional citizenship', *Sociological Perspectives* 39, no. 3 (1996), pp. 371–81; Anne Warfield Rawls, 'The interaction order sui generis: Goffman's contribution to social theory', *Sociological Theory* 5, no. 2 (1987), pp. 136–49.

82 Erving Goffman, 'The neglected situation', *American Anthropologist* 66, no. 6 (1964), pp. 133–36.

83 Cf. Maurice Roche, 'Citizenship, social theory, and social change', *Theory and Society* 16, no. 3 (1987), pp. 363–99; Dennis C. Mueller, 'Defining citizenship', *Theoretical Inquiries in Law* 3, no. 1 (2002), pp. 1–16; cf. also Robert Asen, 'A discourse theory of citizenship', *Quarterly Journal of Speech* 90, no. 2 (2004) pp. 189–211.

84 Erving Goffman, 'Embarrassment and social organization', *American Journal of Sociology* 62, no. 3 (1956), pp. 264–71.

85 Cf. John Kendon, 'Goffman's approach to face-to-face interaction', in Paul Drew and Anthony Wootton (eds), *Erving Goffman: Exploring the Interaction Order* (Boston, MA: Northeastern Press, 1988), pp. 14–40.

86 Erving Goffman, 'The interaction order', *American Sociological Review* 48, no. 1 (1983), p. 2; William A. Gamson, 'Goffman's legacy to political sociology', *Theory and Society* 14, no. 5 (1985), pp. 605–22; Erving Goffman, 'A reply to Denzin and Keller', *Contemporary Sociology* 10, no. 1 (1981), pp. 60–68.

87 Ian Hacking, 'Between Michel Foucault and Erving Goffman: between discourse in the abstract and face-to-face interaction', *Economy and Society* 33, no. 3 (2004), pp. 277–302; Velina Topalova, 'Individualism/collectivism and social identity', *Journal of Community & Applied Social Psychology* 7, no. 1 (1997), pp. 53–64.

88 Cf. Leonie Huddy, 'From social to political identity: a critical examination of social identity theory', *Political Psychology* 22, no. 1 (2001), pp. 127–56; Chantal Mouffe, 'Citizenship and political identity', *October* 61 (1992), pp. 28–32.

89 Cf. Bernd Simon and Bert Klandermans, 'Politicized collective identity: a social psychological analysis', *American Psychologist* 56, no. 4 (2001), pp. 319–31; cf. also Margarita Sanchez-Mazas and Olivier Klein, 'Social identity and citizenship', *Psychologica Belgica* 43, no. 1–2 (2003), pp. 1–8.

90 Cf. Charles Tilly, 'International communities, secure or otherwise', in Emanuel Adler and Michael Barnett (eds), *Security Communities* (Cambridge: Cambridge University Press, 1998), pp. 397–412; cf. also Katherine Fierlbeck, 'The ambivalent potential of cultural identity', *Canadian Journal of Political Science* 29, no. 1 (1996), pp. 3–22.

91 Cf. Liah Greenfeld, 'Is nation unavoidable? Is nation unavoidable today?' in Hanspeter Kriesi et al. (eds), *Nation and National Identity: The European Experience in Perspective* (Zürich: Verlag Rüegger, 1999), pp. 37–54; Will Kymlicka and Wayne Norman, 'Return of the citizen: a survey of recent work on citizenship theory', *Ethics* 104, no. 2 (1994), p. 377; José Medina, 'Identity trouble: disidentification and the problem of difference', *Philosophy & Social Criticism* 29, no. 6 (2003), pp. 655–80.

92 Cf. Anne Warfield Rawls, 'Language, self, and social order: a reformulation of Hoffman and Sacks', *Human Studies* 12, no. 1 (1989), pp. 147–72; Ulises Schmill, 'The dynamic order of norms, empowerment and related concepts', *Law and Philosophy* 19, no. 2 (2000), pp. 283–310; Veit Bader and Sawitri Saharso, 'Introduction: contextualized morality and ethno-religious diversity', *Ethical Theory and Moral Practice* 7 (2004), pp. 107–15.

93 Cf. Jean L. Cohen, 'Changing paradigms of citizenship and the exclusiveness of the demos', *International Sociology* 14, no. 3 (1999), p. 247.

94 Jeremy Waldron, 'Special ties and natural duties', *Philosophy and Public Affairs* 22, no. 1 (1993), pp. 3–30.

95 Cf. Rogers Brubaker, 'The return of assimilation?: Changing perspectives on immigration and its sequels in France, Germany, and the United States', *Ethnic and Racial Studies* 24, no. 4 (2001), pp. 531–48.

Chapter 2: Collective identity and its functions

1 Rogers Brubaker and Frederick Cooper, 'Beyond identity', *Theory and Society* 29, no. 1 (2000), pp. 1–47; Lynn Jamieson, 'Theorising identity, nationality and citizenship: implications for European citizenship identity', *Sociológia* (Slovak Sociological Review) 34, no. 6 (2002), pp. 507–32.

2 Cf. Dahlia Moore and Baruch Kimmerling, 'Individual strategies of adopting collective identities: the Israeli case', *International Sociology* 10, no. 4 (1995), pp. 387–407.

3 Cf. Zygmunt Bauman, 'Identity in the globalizing world', *Social Anthropology* 9, no. 2 (2001), pp. 121–29; Zygmunt Bauman, *Liquid Modernity* (Cambridge: Polity Press, 2000); cf. also Sanford F. Schram, 'Postmodern policy analysis: discourse and identity in welfare policy', *Policy Sciences* 26, no. 3 (1993), pp. 249–70; Peter Abrahamson, 'Liquid modernity: Bauman on contemporary welfare society', *Acta Sociologica* 47,

no. 2 (2004), pp. 171–79; Vince Marotta, 'Zygmunt Bauman: order, strangerhood and freedom', *Thesis Eleven* 70, no. 1 (2002), pp. 36–54.

4 Cf. Stephen Reicher, 'Psychology and the end of history: a critique and a proposal for the psychology of social categorization', *Political Psychology* 22, no. 1 (2001), pp. 383–407.

5 Michael A. Hogg, 'Subjective uncertainty reduction through self-categorization: a motivational theory of social identity processes', *European Review of Social Psychology* 11 (2000), pp. 223–55; Scott A. Reid and Michael A. Hogg, 'Uncertainty reduction, self-enhancement, and ingroup identification', *Personality and Social Psychology Bulletin* 31, no.6 (2005), pp. 804–17.

6 Emanuele Castano et al., 'Who may enter?: the impact of in-group identification on in-group/out-group categorization', *Journal of Experimental Social Psychology* 38, no. 3 (2002), pp. 315–22; S. Alexander Haslam et al., 'Social identity salience and the emergence of stereotype consensus', *Personality and Social Psychology Bulletin* 25, no. 7 (1999), pp. 809–18.

7 Steven J. Sherman, David L. Hamilton and Amy C. Lewis, 'Perceived entitativity and the social identity value of group memberships', in Dominic Abrams and Michael Hogg (eds), *Social Identity and Social Cognition* (Oxford: Blackwell, 1999), pp. 80–110; Bert Klandermans, 'How group identification helps to overcome the dilemma of collective action', *American Behavioral Scientist* 45, no. 5 (2002), pp. 887–900.

8 For a more interactive perspective on the influence between the group and its members see Tom Postmes et al., 'Social influence in small groups: an interactive model of social identity formation', *European Review of Social Psychology* 16, no. 1 (2005), pp. 1–42.

9 Mark Levine at al., 'Identity and emergency intervention: how social group membership and inclusiveness of group boundaries shape helping behavior', *Personality and Social Psychology Bulletin* 31, no. 4 (2005), pp. 443–53; Dominic Abrams, 'Social identity, social cognition, and the self', in Dominic Abrams and Michael Hogg (eds), *Social Identity and Social Cognition* (Oxford: Blackwell, 1999), pp. 197–229.

10 Marilynn B. Brewer, 'The many faces of social identity: implications for political psychology', *Political Psychology* 22, no. 1 (2001), pp. 115–25.

11 Matthew T. Crawford et al., 'Perceived entitativity, stereotype formation, and the interchangeability of group members', *Journal of Personality and Social Psychology* 83, no. 5 (2002), pp. 1076–94; Emanuele Castano et al., 'The perception of the other in international relations: evidence for the polarizing effect of entitativity', *Political Psychology* 24, no. 3 (2003), pp. 449–68; Susan Condor, 'Temporality and collectivity: diversity, history and the rhetorical construction of national entitativity', *British Journal of Social Psychology* 45, no. 4 (2006), pp. 657–82; Emanuele Castano et al., 'We are one and I like it: the impact of ingroup entitativity on ingroup identification', *European Journal of Social Psychology* 33, no. 6 (2003), pp. 735–54.

12 Rupert Brown, 'Social identity theory: past achievements, current problems and future challenges', *European Journal of Social Psychology* 30, no. 6 (2000), pp. 745–78; Bert Klandermans, 'How group identification helps to overcome the dilemma of collective action', *American Behavioral Scientist* 45, no. 5 (2002), p. 891; Kathleen M. McGraw, 'Contributions of the cognitive approach to political psychology', *Political Psychology* 21, no. 4 (2000), pp. 805–32.

13 Lowell Gaertner and John Schopler, 'Perceived ingroup entitativity and intergroup bias: an interconnection of self and others', *European Journal of Social Psychology* 28, no. 6 (1998), pp. 963–80; Castano et al., *op. cit.*

14 Cf. Joan W. Scott, 'Multiculturalism and the politics of identity', *October* 61 (1992), pp. 12–19; Trevor Purvis and Alan Hunt, 'Identity versus citizenship: transformations in the discourses and practices of citizenship', *Social & Legal Studies* 8, no. 4 (1999), p. 460.

15 Cf. Isis H. Settles, 'When multiple identities interfere: the role of identity centrality', *Personality and Social Psychology Bulletin* 30, no. 4. (2004), pp. 487–500; Richard J. Crisp and Miles Hewstone, 'Multiple identities in Northern Ireland: hierarchical ordering in the representation of group membership', *British Journal of Social Psychology* 40,

no. 4 (2001), pp. 501–14; Anna Melich, 'The nature of regional and national identity in Catalonia: problems of measuring multiple identities', *European Journal of Political Research* 14, no. 1–2 (1986), pp. 149–69. For the concept of fragmented citizenship in the EU see Antje Wiener, 'Making sense of the new geography of citizenship: fragmented citizenship in the European Union', *Theory and Society* 26, no. 4 (1997), pp. 529–60. For an argument against a homogeneous citizenship see Takashi Kibe, 'Differentiated citizenship and ethnocultural groups: a Japanese case' *Citizenship Studies* 10, no. 4 (2006), pp. 413–30.

16 Cf. Bronislaw Szerszynski and John Urry, 'Visuality, mobility and the cosmopolitan: inhabiting the world from afar', *British Journal of Sociology* 57, no. 1 (2006), pp. 113–31; Noel Cass et al., 'Social exclusion, mobility and access', *Sociological Review* 53, no. 3 (2005), pp. 539–55; Saskia Sassen, 'Territory and territoriality in the global economy', *International Sociology* 15, no. 2 (2000), pp. 372–93; Luke Desforges et al., 'New geographies of citizenship', *Citizenship Studies* 9, no. 5 (2005), pp. 439–51.

17 Linda Bosniak, 'Citizenship denationalized', *Indiana Journal of Global Legal Studies* 7, no. 2 (2000), pp. 447–509; Saskia Sassen, 'The repositioning of citizenship: emergent subjects and spaces for politics', *New Centennial Review* 3, no. 2 (2003), pp. 41–66; Saskia Sassen, 'Globalization or denationalization?', *Review of International Political Economy* 10, no. 1 (2003), pp. 1–22; Rainer Bauböck, 'Reinventing urban citizenship', *Citizenship Studies* 7, no. 2 (2003), pp. 139–60.

18 Eric Fong and Kumiko Shibuya, 'Multiethnic cities in North America', *Annual Review of Sociology* 31 (2005), pp. 285–304; Ayse S. Çaglar, 'Constraining metaphors and the transnationalisation of spaces in Berlin', *Journal of Ethnic and Migration Studies* 27, no. 4 (2001), pp. 601–13; Justus Uitermark et al., 'Reinventing multiculturalism: urban citizenship and the negotiation of ethnic diversity in Amsterdam', *International Journal of Urban and Regional Research* 29, no. 3 (2005), pp. 622–40; Mark Purcell, 'Citizenship and the right to the global city: reimagining the capitalist world order', *International Journal of Urban and Regional Research* 27, no. 3 (2003), pp. 564–90; Marisol García, 'Citizenship practices and urban governance in European cities', *Urban Studies* 43, no. 4 (2006), pp. 745–65. For a rather critical view of transnational citizenship see Monica W. Varsanyi, 'Interrogating urban citizenship vis-à-vis undocumented migration', *Citizenship Studies* 10, no. 2 (2006), pp. 229–49.

19 Cf. Anne McNevin, 'Political belonging in a neoliberal era: the struggle of the sans-papiers', *Citizenship Studies* 10, no. 2 (2006), pp. 135–51; Linda Bosniak, 'Universal citizenship and the problem of alienage', *Northwestern University Law Review* 94, no. 3 (2000), pp. 963–84.

20 Ruth Lister, 'Inclusive citizenship: realizing the potential', *Citizenship Studies* 11, no. 1 (2007), pp. 49–61.

21 Cf. Bart Cammaerts and Leo van Audenhove, 'Online political debate, unbounded citizenship and problematic nature of a transnational public sphere', *Political Communication* 22, no. 2 (2005), pp. 179–96; Agnes S. Ku, 'Beyond the paradoxical conception of civil society without citizenship', *International Sociology* 17, no. 4 (2002), pp. 529–48; Maurice Roche, 'The olympics and global citizenship', *Citizenship Studies* 6, no. 2 (2002), pp. 165–81.

22 Cf. Steven Seidman, 'The end of sociological theory: the postmodern hope', *Sociological Theory* 9, no. 2 (1991), pp. 131–46; John W. Murphy, 'Making sense of postmodern sociology', *British Journal of Sociology* 39, no. 4 (1988), pp. 600–614.

23 Cf. Steven Vertovec, 'Transantionalism and identity', *Journal of Ethnic and Migration Studies* 27, no. 4 (2001), pp. 573–82; Henry A. Giroux, 'Living dangerously: identity politics and the new cultural racism: towards a critical pedagogy of representation', *Cultural Studies* 7, no. 1 (1993), pp. 1–27; Pnina Werbner, 'Divided loyalties, empowered citizenship? Muslims in Britain', *Citizenship Studies* 4, no. 3 (2000), pp. 307–24; Feyzi Baban, 'From Gastarbeiter to Ausländische Mitbürger: postnational citizenship and in-between identities in Berlin', *Citizenship Studies* 10, no. 2 (2006),

pp. 185–201; Gershon Shafir and Yoav Peled, 'Citizenship and stratification in an ethnic democracy', *Ethnic and Racial Studies* 21, no. 3 (1998), pp. 408–27.

24 Cf. Damian Tambini, 'Post-national citizenship', *Ethnic and Racial Studies* 24, no. 2 (2001), pp. 195–217; Yoav Peled, 'Towards a post-citizenship society? A report from the front', *Citizenship Studies* 11, no. 1 (2007), pp. 95–104.

25 Catarina Kinnvall, 'Globalization and religious nationalism: self, identity, and the search for ontological security', *Political Psychology* 25, no. 5 (2004), pp. 741–67.

26 Cf. Steven J. Sherman, David L. Hamilton and Amy C. Lewis, 'Perceived entitativity and the social identity value of group memberships', in Dominic Abrams and Michael Hogg (eds), *Social Identity and Social Cognition* (Oxford: Blackwell, 1999), pp. 80–110.

27 Cf. Paul Hutchison et al., 'Protecting threatened identity: sticking with the group by emphasizing ingroup heterogeneity', *Personality and Social Psychology Bulletin* 32, no. 12 (2006), pp. 1620–32.

28 Julian A. Oldmeadow et al., 'Self-categorization, status, and social influence', *Social Psychology Quarterly* 66, no. 2 (2003), pp. 138–52.

29 Amélie Mummendey and Michael Wenzel, 'Social discrimination and tolerance in intergroup relations: reactions to intergroup difference', *Personality and Social Psychology Review* 3, no. 2 (1999), pp. 158–74; Michael Wenzel, 'A social categorization approach to distributive justice: social identity as the link between relevance of inputs and need for justice', *British Journal of Social Psychology* 40, no. 3 (2001), pp. 315–35.

30 Cf. Kristen Renwick et al., 'The psychological foundations of identity politics', *Annual Review of Political Science* 3, no. 1 (2000), pp. 419–47; Akhil Gupta and James Ferguson, 'Beyond culture: space, identity, and the politics of difference', *Cultural Anthropology* 7, no. 1 (1992), pp. 6–23; Richard Jenkins, 'Categorization: identity, social process and epistemology', *Current Sociology* 48, no. 3 (2000), pp. 7–25.

31 Henri Tajfel, 'Cognitive aspects of prejudice', *Journal of Biosocial Sciences* 1 (Supplement) (1969), pp. 173–91; Michael Billig, 'Henri Tajfel's cognitive aspects of prejudice and the psychology of bigotry', *British Journal of Social Psychology* 41, no. 2 (2002), pp. 171–88; Geoffrey J. Leonardelli and Marilynn B. Brewer, 'Minority and majority discrimination: when and why?', *Journal of Experimental Social Psychology* 37, no. 6 (2001), pp. 468–85; Emanuele Castano and Vincent Y. Yzerbyt, 'The highs and lows of group homogeneity', *Behavioral Processes* 42, no. 2–3 (1998), pp. 219–38.

32 Cf. Alberto Voci, 'Relevance of social categories, depersonalization and group processes: two field tests of self-categorization theory', *European Journal of Social Psychology* 36, no. 1 (2006), pp. 73–90.

33 Charles Tilly, 'A primer on citizenship', *Theory and Society* 26, no. 4 (1997), p. 601.

34 Rogers Brubaker et al., 'Ethnicity as cognition', *Theory and Society* 33, no. 1 (2004), pp. 31–64; Richard Jenkins, 'Categorization: identity, social process and epistemology', *Current Sociology* 48, no. 3 (2000), pp. 7–25.

35 Brubaker et al., *op. cit.*, p. 47.

36 Jan E. Stets and Peter J. Burke, 'Identity theory and social identity theory', *Social Psychology Quarterly* 63, no. 3 (2000), pp. 224–37; Henri Tajfel, 'social psychology of intergroup relations', *Annual Review of Psychology* 33, no. 1 (1982), pp. 1–39.

37 Brown, *op. cit.*

38 Cf. Riia Luhtanen and Jennifer Crocker, 'A collective self-esteem scale: self-evaluation of one's social identity', *Personality and Social Psychology Bulletin* 18, no. 3 (1992), pp. 302–18.

39 Joshua Correll and Bernadette Park, 'A model of the ingroup as a social resource', *Personality and Social Psychology Review* 9, no. 4 (2005), pp. 341–59.

40 Cf. Ernest Gellner, 'Nationalism', *Theory and Society* 10, no. 6 (1981), pp. 753–76.

41 Kristen Renwick Monroe et al., 'The psychological foundations of identity politics', *Annual Review of Political Science* 3 (2000), pp. 419–47; Michael Hogg et al., 'A tale of two theories: a critical comparison of identity theory with social identity theory', *Social Psychology Quarterly* 58, no. 4 (1995), pp. 255–69; Bert Klandermans, 'How

group identification helps to overcome the dilemma of collective action', *American Behavioral Scientist* 45, no. 5 (2002), p. 891f; Mathias Blanz et al., 'Responding to negative social identity: a taxonomy of identity management strategies', *European Journal of Social Psychology* 28 (1998), pp. 697–729.

42 Marilynn B. Brewer, 'The many faces of social identity: implications for political psychology', *Political Psychology* 22, no. 1 (2001), p. 119.

43 At the first glance, this might sound counterintuitive, since structural categories are expected to be more durable than strategic and actor-orientated ones. However, the cognitive perspective stresses the multitude of social roles and changing contexts, which render collective identity a situational phenomenon. In contrast, social identity theory anchors the more durable nature of collective identity in the motivational spectrum of human activity, as individuals are likely to seek long-lasting collective images.

44 Michael Billig, *Banal Nationalism* (London: Sage, 1995), p. 78.

45 Anna Triandafyllidou, 'National identity and the other', *Ethnic and Racial Studies* 21, no. 4 (1998), pp. 593–612.

46 Arash Abizadeh, 'Does collective identity presuppose an other? On the alleged incoherence of global solidarity', *American Political Science Review* 99, no. 1 (2005), pp. 45–60.

47 Billig, 1995, *op. cit.,* p. 80.

48 In this context, Pille Petersoo distinguishes between positive and negative, and external and internal 'Others' by illustrating the categories in the case of Estonia. According to Petersoo, Estonia has had a number of ethnic minorities, which can be described as positive internal 'Other'. The most influential have been the Baltic German community and the Swedish communities of the west coast of Estonia. In contrast, the Russian-speaking post-Second World War immigrants are constructed as a negative internal Other, since they are regarded as a threat to national integrity and identity. Pille Petersoo, 'Reconsidering otherness: constructing Estonian identity', *Nations and Nationalism* 13, no. 1 (2007), pp. 117–33.

49 S. N. Eisenstadt, 'The construction of collective identities: some analytical and comparative indications', *European Journal of Social Theory* 1, no. 2 (1998), pp. 229–54; Bernhard Giesen, 'Codes kollektiver Identität', in Werner Gephart and Hans Waldenfels (eds), *Religion und Identität* (Frankfurt: Suhrkamp, 1999), pp. 13–43; Gerard Delanty, 'Die Transformation nationaler Identität und kulturelle Ambivalenz europäischer Identität: Demokratische Identifikation in einem postnationalen Europa', in Reinhold Viehoff and Rien T Segers (eds), *Kultur, Identität, Europa* (Frankfurt: Suhrkamp, 1999), pp. 267–88.

50 Charles Tilly, 'Social boundary mechanisms', *Philosophy of the Social Sciences* 34, no. 2 (2004), pp. 211–36.

51 Cf. Klaus Eder et al., *Collective Identities in Action: A Sociological Approach to Ethnicity* (Aldershot: Ashgate, 2002).

52 S. N. Eisenstadt, 'The construction of collective identities: some analytical and comparative indications', *European Journal of Social Theory* 1, no. 2, p. 232.

53 There is a slight confusion in the debate on codes of collective identity due to differing nomenclature. Most of the authors base their conceptualization on the typology proposed by Edward Shils, who distinguishes between primordial, civil and sacred codes. Eisenstadt uses his already mentioned typology of primordial, civic and transcendent codes, whereas Giesen speaks of primordial, traditional and universalistic codes. However, there is a major overlapping of these categories despite their slightly differing labels. Furthermore, Gerard Delanty includes two additional types of codes, which are social and discursive codes. While social codes pertain to the everyday social practices of material goods and status, discursive codes incorporate identity itself as an object of communicative exchange in the society. Cf. Edward Shils, 'Primordial, personal, sacred and civil ties: some particular observations on the relationship of sociological research and theory', *British Journal of Sociology* 8, no. 2 (1957), pp. 130–45; Bernhard Giesen, 'Codes kollektiver Identität', in Werner Gephart and Hans Waldenfels (eds),

Religion und Identität (Frankfurt: Suhrkamp, 1999), pp. 13–43; Gerard Delanty, 'Die Transformation nationaler Identität und kulturelle Ambivalenz europäischer Identität: Demokratische Identifikation in einem postnationalen Europa', in Reinhold Viehoff and Rien T Segers (eds), *Kultur, Identität, Europa* (Frankfurt: Suhrkamp, 1999), pp. 267 – 288.

54   Cf. Emanuele Castano and Mark Dechesne, 'On defeating death: group reification and social identification as immortality strategies', *European Review of Social Psychology* 16, no. 7 (2005), pp. 221–55.

55   Marilynn B. Brewer, 'The many faces of social identity: implications for political psychology', *Political Psychology* 22, no. 1 (2001), p. 119.

56   Cf. Maurice Halbwachs, *The Collective Memory,* trans. F. J. Ditter and V. Y. Ditter, intro. by M. Douglas (London: Harper, 1950, orig. pub. 1926).

57   Barbara A. Misztal, 'Durkheim on collective memory', *Journal of Classical Sociology* 3, no. 2 (2003), pp. 123–43; Bo Rothstein, 'Trust, social dilemmas and collective memories', *Journal of Theoretical Politics* 12, no. 4 (2000), pp. 477–501.

58   Misztal, *op. cit.*, p. 126. Even though Misztal uses the commemorative rituals and emotion-loaded practices with regard to early societies, they are equally true for any mass society, in which they fulfil an integrative and mobilization function.

59   Cf. Margarita Sanchez-Mazas and Olivier Klein, 'Social identity and Citizenship', *Psychologica Belgica* 43, no. 1–2 (2003), pp. 1–8.

60   Cf. Jeff Spinner-Halev and Elizabeth Theiss-Morse, 'National Identity and self-esteem', *Perspectives on Politics* 1, no. 3 (2003), pp. 515–32.

61   Marilynn B. Brewer, 'The psychology of prejudice: ingroup love or outgroup hate?' *Journal of Social Issues* 55, no. 3 (1999), pp. 429–44.

62   Different variants of this argument can be found in writings inspired by Jürgen Habermas. Cf. Jürgen Habermas, 'Multiculturalism and the liberal state', *Stanford Law Review* 47, no. 5 (1995), pp. 849–53; Andrea T. Baumeister, 'Habermas: discourse and cultural diversity', *Political Studies* 51, no. 4 (2003), pp. 740–58; Shivdeep Singh Grewal, 'The paradox of integration: Habermas and the unfinished project of European Union', *Politics* 21, no. 2 (2001), pp. 114–23; Max Pensky, 'Cosmopolitanism and the solidarity problem: Habermas on national and cultural identities', *Constellations* 7, no. 1 (2000), pp. 64–79.

63   Cf. David Miller, *On Nationality* (Oxford: Oxford University Press, 1995).

64   John C. Turner, 'Some current issues in research on social identity and self-categorization theories', in Naomi Ellemers et al. (eds), *Social Identity: Context, Commitment, Content* (Oxford: Blackwell, 1999), pp. 6–34.

65   Mark Schafer, 'Cooperative and conflictual policy preferences: the effect of identity, security, and image of the other', *Political Psychology* 20, no. 4 (1999), pp. 829–44.

66   Tariq Modood, 'Anti-essentialism, multiculturalism and the recognition of religious groups', *The Journal of Political Philosophy* 6, no. 4 (1998), pp. 378–99; cf. also Floya Anthias, 'Where do I belong? Narrating collective identity and translocational positionality', *Ethnicities* 2, no. 4 (2002), pp. 491–514.

67   Joanna Goodey, 'Non-EU citizens' experiences of offending and victimisation: the case for comparative European research', *European Journal of Crime, Criminal Law and Criminal Justice* 8, no. 1 (2000), pp. 13–34.

68   See the seminal work on stigma by Erving Goffman. Erving Goffman, *Stigma: Notes on the Management of Spoiled Identity* (New York: Prentice Hall, 1963); cf. also Carol T. Miller and Cheryl R. Kaiser, 'A theoretical perspective on coping with stigma', *Journal of Social Issues* 57, no. 1 (2001), pp. 73–92; Brenda Major and Laurie T. O'Brien, 'The social psychology of stigma', *Annual Review of Psychology* 56 no. 1 (2005), pp. 393–421. With regard to stigma and citizenship see Martin Powell, 'The hidden history of social citizenship', *Citizenship Studies* 6, no. 3, pp. 229–44; Iris Marion Young, 'Polity and group difference: a critique of the ideal of universal citizenship', *Ethics* 99, no. 2 (1989), pp. 250–74.

69 Christian Joppke, 'Transformation of citizenship: status, rights, identity', *Citizenship Studies* 11, no. 1 (2007), pp. 37–48; Christian Joppke, 'How immigration is changing citizenship: a comparative view', *Ethnic and Racial Studies* 22, no. 4 (1999), pp. 629–52; Christian Joppke, 'Asylum and state sovereignty: a comparison of the United States, Germany, and Britain', *Comparative Political Studies* 30, no. 3 (1997), pp. 259–98.

70 Cf. Yasemin Nuholu Soysal, 'Citizenship and identity: living in diasporas in post-war Europe?', *Ethnic and Racial Studies 23*, no. 1 (2000), pp. 1–15; Suzanne Shanahan, 'Different standards and standard differences: contemporary citizenship and immigration debates', *Theory and Society* 26, no. 4 (1997), pp. 421–48.

71 Eleonore Kofman, 'Citizenship, migration and the reassertion of national identity', *Citizenship Studies* 9, no. 5 (2005), pp. 453–67.

72 Rogers Brubaker, 'The return of assimilation? Changing perspectives on immigration and its sequels in France, Germany, and the United States', *Ethnic and Racial Studies* 24, no. 4 (2001), pp. 531–48.

73 David Miller, *Citizenship and National Identity* (Cambridge: Polity Press, 2000), p. 29.

74 Laura Andronache, 'A national identity republicanism?', *European Journal of Political Theory* 5, no. 4 (2006), pp. 399–414.

75 Liah Greenfeld, 'Is nation unavoidable? Is nation unavoidable today?' in Hanspeter Kriesi et al. (eds), *Nation and National identity: The European Experience in Perspective* (Zürich: Verlag Rüegger, 1999), pp. 37–54; cf. also Paul Gilbert, 'Ethics or nationalism', *Journal of Applied Philosophy* 19, no. 2 (2002), pp. 185–87; Bernard Yack, 'Popular sovereignty and nationalism', *Political Theory* 29, no. 4 (2001), pp. 517–36.

76 Liah Greenfeld, *The Spirit of Capitalism: Nationalism and Economic Growth* (Cambridge, MA: Harvard University Press, 2001), p. 2; cf. Rogers Brubaker, 'In the name of the nation: reflections on nationalism and patriotism', *Citizenship Studies* 8, no. 2 (2004), pp. 115–27.

77 Yael Tamir, *Liberal Nationalism* (Princeton, NJ: Princeton University Press, 1993); Albert W. Dzur, 'Nationalism, liberalism, and democracy', *Political Research Quarterly* 55, no 1 (2002), pp. 191–211; cf. also Arash Abizadeh, 'Liberal nationalist versus postnational social integration: on the nation's ethno-cultural particularity and concreteness', *Nations and Nationalism* 10, no 3 (2004), pp. 231–50; Andrew Vincent, 'Liberal nationalism: an irresponsible compound?', *Political Studies* 45, no. 2 (1997), pp. 275–95; Sune Lægaard, 'Liberal nationalism and the nationalization of liberal values', *Nations and Nationalism* 13, no. 1 (2007), pp. 37–55; Pierre-Yves Bonin, 'Libéralism et nationalisme: où tracer la ligne?', *Revue Canadienne de Science Politique* 30, no. 2 (1997), pp. 235–56. David Miller, *On Nationality* (Oxford: Clarendon Press, 1995), p.26; Catherine M. Frost, 'Survey article: the worth of nations', *Journal of Political Philosophy* 9, no. 4 (2001), pp. 482–503; Bo Rothstein, 'Trust, social dilemmas and collective memories', *Journal of Theoretical Politics* 12, no. 4 (2000), pp. 477–501.

78 David Miller, *On Nationality* (Oxford: Clarendon Press, 1995), p.26; Catherine M. Frost, 'Survey article: the worth of nations', *Journal of Political Philosophy* 9, no. 4 (2001), pp. 482–503; Bo Rothstein, 'Trust, social dilemmas and collective memories', *Journal of Theoretical Politics* 12, no. 4 (2000), pp. 477–501.

79 For example Dieter Grimm, *Braucht Europa eine Verfassung?* Paper presented at the Siemens Foundation, 19 January 1994, München 1994; Joseph H. H. Weiler, 'Does Europe need a constitution? Demos, telos and the German Maastricht decision', *European Law Journal* 11, no 3 (1995), pp. 219–58; Amitai Etzioni, 'The community deficit', *Journal of Common Market Studies* 45, no. 1 (2007), pp. 23–42.

80 For a critique of this argument see Rogers Brubaker, 'Myths and misconceptions in the study of nationalism', in John Hall (ed.), *The State of the Nation: Ernest Gellner and the Theory of Nationalism* (Cambridge: Cambridge University Press, 1998), pp. 272–306.

81 Benedict Anderson, *Imagined Communities: Reflections on the Origin and Spread of Nationalism* (London: Verso, 1991); Tim Philips, 'Imagined communities and self-identity: an exploratory quantitative analysis', *Sociology* 36, no. 3 (2002), pp. 597–617.

82 Anderson, *op. cit.*, p. 44; cf. also Will Kymlicka, *Politics in the Vernacular: Nationalism, Multiculturalism, and Citizenship* (Oxford: Oxford University Press, 2001).

83 Cf. Margaret Canovan, 'Sleeping dogs, prowling cats and soaring doves: three paradoxes in the political theory of nationhood', *Political Studies* 49 (2001), pp. 203–15.

84 Ernest Gellner, *Nations and Nationalism* (Ithaca, NY: Cornell University Press, 1983), p. 40; Ernest Gellner, 'Nationalism', *Theory and Society* 10, no. 6 (1981), pp. 753–76; Ugo Pagano, 'Nationalism, development and integration: the political economy of Ernest Gellner', *Cambridge Journal of Economics* 27, no. 5 (2003), pp. 623–46.

85 Ernest Gellner, 'The importance of being modular', in John Hall (ed.), *Civil Society* (Cambridge: Cambridge University Press, 1995), pp. 32–55; D. L. Seiler, 'Peripheral nationalism between pluralism and monism', *International Political Science Review* 10, no. 3 (1989), pp. 191–207; Montserrat Guibernau, 'Anthony D. Smith on nations and national identity: a critical assessment', *Nations and Nationalism* 10, no. 1–2 (2004), pp. 125–41.

86 Cf. Bart Maddens and Kristine Vanden Berghe, 'The identity politics of multicultural nationalism: a comparison between the regular public addresses of the Belgian and the Spanish monarchs (1990–2000)', *European Journal of Political Research* 42, no. 5 (2003), pp. 601–27; Furio Cerutti, 'Can there be a supranational identity?', *Philosophy & Social Criticism* 18, no. 2 (1992), pp. 147–62.

87 Gellner 1995, *op. cit.*, p. 50.

88 Cf. Rudolf De Cillia et al., 'The discursive construction of national identities', *Discourse & Society* 10, no. 2 (1999), pp. 149–73.

89 Gellner 1981, *op. cit.*, p. 753.

90 David Miller, *Citizenship and National Identity* (Cambridge: Polity Press, 2000), p. 81; cf. Andrew Mason, 'Special obligations to compatriots', *Ethics* 107, no. 3 (1997), pp. 427–447; Hannah Arendt, *The Human Condition* (Chicago, IL: University of Chicago Press, 1998/1958), with an Introduction by Margaret Canovan, 2nd edition.

91 Cf. Margaret Canovan, 'Patriotism is not enough', *British Journal of Political Science* 30 (2000), pp. 413–32.

92 Cf. Robert M. Hayden, 'Imagined communities and real victims: self-determination and ethnic cleansing in Yugoslavia', *American Ethnologist* 23, no. 4 (1996), pp. 783–801; Taras Kuzio, 'The myth of the civic state: a critical survey of Hans Kohn's framework for understanding nationalism', *Ethnic and Racial Studies* 25, no. 1 (2002), pp. 20–39.

93 Ranjoo Seodu Herr, 'In defense of nonliberal nationalism', *Political Theory* 34, no. 3 (2006), pp. 304–27.

94 Yael Tamir, 'Is liberal nationalism an oxymoron? An essay for Judith Shklar', *Ethics* 105, no. 3 (1995), pp. 626–45.

95 Margaret Moore, 'Normative justifications for liberal nationalism: justice, democracy and national identity', *Nations and Nationalism* 7, no. 1 (2001), pp. 1–20.

96 Eric Kaufmann, 'Liberal ethnicity: beyond liberal nationalism and minority rights', *Ethnic and Racial Studies* 23, no. 6 (2000), pp. 1086–1119.

97 Vincent, *op. cit.*

98 Sune Lægaard, 'Liberal nationalism and the nationalization of liberal values', *Nations and Nationalism* 13, no. 1 (2007), pp. 37–55.

99 Joan Cocks, 'Collectivities and cruelty', *Political Theory* 32, no 3 (2004), pp. 419–26.

100 Peter A. Kraus, 'Cultural pluralism and European polity-building: neither Westphalia nor cosmopolis', *Journal of Common Market Studies* 41, no. 4 (2003), pp. 665–86.

101 Cf. David Easton, 'A re-assessment of the concept of political support', *British Journal of Political Science* 5, no. 4 (1975), pp. 435–57; David Easton, 'Theoretical approaches to political support', *Canadian Journal of Political Science* 9, no. 3 (1976), pp. 431–48.

102 Fritz W. Scharpf, *Governing Europe: Efficient and Democratic* (Oxford: Oxford University Press, 1998).

103 A good and comprehensive review of literature on identity politics is offered by Mary Bernstein. Mary Bernstein, 'Identity politics', *Annual Review of Sociology* 31, no. 1 (2005), pp. 47–74.

104 Cf. Joan W. Scott, 'Multiculturalism and the politics of identity', *October* 61 (1992), pp. 12–19; cf. also Jonah Goldstein and Jeremy Rayner, 'The politics of identity in late modern society', *Theory and Society* 23, no. 3 (1994), pp. 367–84.

105 Claus Offe, 'Homogeneity and constitutional democracy: coping with identity conflicts through group rights', *Journal of Political Philosophy* 6, no. 2 (1998), p. 133.

106 For a discussion of strategic essentialism see Dietmar Rost, 'Social science approaches to collective identity, essentialism, constructionism and strategic essentialism', in Dietmar Rost et al. (eds), *New Regional Identities and Strategic Essentialism: Case Studies from Poland, Italy and Germany* (Münster: LIT Verlag, 2007), pp. 451–503.

107 Cf. Erich Goode and Nachman Ben-Yehuda, 'Moral panics: culture, politics, and social construction', *Annual Review of Sociology* 20 (1994), pp. 149–71; Emanuele Castano et al., 'Protecting the ingroup stereotype: ingroup identification and the management of deviant ingroup members', *British Journal of Social Psychology* 41, no. 3 (2002), pp. 365–85.

108 Cf. Ian Hacking, 'Between Michel Foucault and Erving Goffman: between discourse in the abstract and face-to-face interaction', *Economy and Society* 33, no. 3 (2004), pp. 277–302.

109 Ernest Gellner, 'The importance of being modular', in John Hall (ed.), *Civil Society* (Cambridge: Cambridge University Press, 1995), 32–55; Caroline Howarth, 'Identity in whose eyes? The role of representations in identity construction', *Journal for the Theory of Social Behaviour* 32, no. 2 (2002), pp. 145–62.

110 This typology is a generalization of David Brown's differentiation between instrumental and ideological nationalism. David Brown, 'Why independence? The instrumental and ideological dimensions of nationalism', *International Journal of Comparative Sociology* 45, no. 3–4 (2004), pp. 277–96.

111 Anthony D. Smith, 'Culture, community and territory: the politics of ethnicity and nationalism', *International Affairs* 72, no. 3 (1996), pp. 445–58; Anthony D. Smith, 'The resurgence of nationalism? Myth and memory in the renewal of nations', *The British Journal of Sociology* 47, no.4 (1996), pp. 575–98.

112 George Herbert Mead, 'The genesis of the self and social control', *International Journal of Ethics* 35, no. 3 (1925), pp. 251–77; Nigel Edley, 'Unravelling social constructionism', *Theory & Psychology* 11, no. 3 (2001), pp. 433–41; Tom Postmes et al., 'Social influence in small groups: an interactive model of social identity formation', *European Review of Social Psychology* 16, no. 1 (2005), pp. 1–42; Andrew Thompson and Ralph Fevre, 'The national question: sociological reflections on nation and nationalism', *Nations and Nationalism* 7, no. 3 (2001), pp. 297–315; Richard T. Serpe, 'Stability and change in self: a structural symbolic interactionist explanation', *Social Psychology Quarterly* 50, no. 1 (1987), pp. 44–55; Gertrud Nunner-Winkler, 'Identität und Moral', in Jürgen Straub and Joachim Renn (eds), *Transitorische Identität: Der Prozesscharakter des modernen Selbst* (Frankfurt: Campus, 2002), pp. 56–84.

113 Peter L. Berger and Thomas Luckmann, *The Social Construction of Reality: A Treatise in the Sociology of Knowledge* (New York: Doubleday, 1966); Sheldon Stryker, 'The vitalization of symbolic interactionism', *Social Psychology Quarterly* 50, no. 1 (1987), pp. 83–94; Sergio Sismondo, 'Some social constructions', *Social Studies of Science* 23, no. 3 (1993), pp. 515–53.

114 The personification of the state fulfils a decisive role, for instance in Hegel's state theory. Cf. Georg W. F. Hegel, *Philosophy of Right*, translated by S. W. Dyde (New York: Prometheus Books, 1996), §§ 275–86; Charles Taylor, *Hegel* (Cambridge: Cambridge University Press, 1975), pp. 439ff.

115 Cf. Consuelo Cruz, 'Identity and persuasion: how nations remember their pasts and make their futures', *World Politics* 52, no. 3 (2000), pp. 275–312.

116 Cf. Marc W. Steinberg, 'Tilting the frame: considerations on collective action framing from a discursive turn', *Theory and Society* 27, no. 6 (1998), pp. 845–72.

117 Cf. Donald E. Polkinghorne, 'Explorations of narrative identity', *Psychological Inquiry* 7, no. 4 (1996), pp. 363–67; Donald E. Polkinghorne, 'Narrative Psychologie und Geschichtsbewusstsein. Beziehungen und Perspektiven', in Jürgen Straub (ed.), *Erzählung, Identität und historisches Bewusstsein: Die psychologische Konstruktion von Zeit und Geschichte* (Frankfurt: Suhrkamp, 1998), pp. 12 – 46.

118 Cf. Rudolf de Cilla et al., 'The discursive construction of national identity', *Discourse and Society* 10, no. 2 (1999), pp. 149–73; Jerome Bruner, 'The narrative construction of reality', *Critical Inquiry* 18, no. 1 (1991), pp. 1–21; J. R. Maze, 'Social constructionism, deconstructionism and some requirements of discourse', *Theory & Psychology* 11, no. 3 (2001), pp. 393–417.

119 Michael Billig, *Banal Nationalism* (London: Sage, 1995).

120 Oliver Zimmer, 'Boundary mechanisms and symbolic resources: towards a process-oriented approach to national identity', *Nations and Nationalism* 9, no. 2 (2003), pp. 171–93.

121 Cf. Stephen May, Tariq Modood, and Judith Squires (eds), *Ethnicity, Nationalism and Minority Rights* (Cambridge: Cambridge University Press, 2004); cf. Dietmar Rost, 'Social science approaches to collective identity, essentialism, constructionism and strategic essentialism', in Dietmar Rost et al. (eds), *New Regional Identities and Strategic Essentialism: Case Studies from Poland, Italy and Germany* (Münster: LIT Verlag, 2007), pp. 451–503.

122 Mancur Olson, *The Logic of Collective Action: Public Goods and the Theory of Groups* (Cambridge, MA: Harvard University Press, 1968); John Chamberlin, 'Provision of collective goods as a function of group size', *American Political Science Review* 68, no. 2 (1974), pp. 707–16; Mancur Olson, *The Rise and Decline of Nations: Economic Growth, Stagflation and Social Rigidities* (New Haven, CT: Yale University Press, 1982).

123 Cf. Elinor Ostrom, 'A behavioral approach to the rational choice theory of collective action', *American Political Science Review* 92, no. 1 (1998), pp. 1–22.

124 Cf. Robert Axelrod, 'Effective choice in the prisoner's dilemma', *Journal of Conflict Resolution* 24, no. 1 (1980), pp. 3–25; J. V. Howard, 'Cooperation in the prisoner's dilemma', *Theory and Decision* 24, no. 3 (1988), pp. 203–13; Kenneth Clark and Martin Sefton, 'The sequential prisoner's dilemma: evidence and reciprocation', *Economic Journal* 111, no. 468 (2001), pp. 51–68.

125 Cf. Robyn M. Dawes and Richard H. Thaler, 'Anomalies: cooperation', *Journal of Economic Perspectives* 2, no. 3 (1988), pp. 187–97.

126 Cf. Jianzhong Wu and Robert Axelrod, 'How to cope with noise in the iterated prisoner's dilemma', *Journal of Conflict Resolution* 39, no. 1 (1995), pp. 183–89; Robert Axelrod, *The Complexity of Cooperation* (Princeton, NJ: Princeton University Press, 1997).

127 Chien-Chung Yin, 'Equilibria of collective action in different distributions of protest thresholds', *Public Choice* 97, no. 4 (1998), pp. 535–67; Mark Granovetter, 'Threshold models of collective behavior', *American Journal of Sociology* 83, no. 6 (1978), pp. 1420–43; Gerald Marwell et al., 'Social networks and collective action: a theory of critical mass III', *American Journal of Sociology* 94, no. 3 (1988), pp. 502–34; cf. also Douglas D. Heckathorn, 'The dynamics and dilemmas of collective action', *American Sociological Review* 61, no. 2 (1996), pp. 250–77; Elinor Ostrom, 'Collective action and the evolution of social norms', *Journal of Economic Perspectives* 14, no. 3 (2000), pp. 137–58; Jon Elster, 'Rationality, morality, and collective action', *Ethics* 96, no. 1 (1985), pp. 136–55.

128 Cf. Amartya Sen, 'Goals, commitment, and identity', *Journal of Law, Economics, and Organization* 1, no. 22 (1985), pp. 341–55; Arieh Gavious and Shlomo Mizrahi, 'Two-level collective action and group identity', *Journal of Theoretical Politics* 11, no. 4 (1999), pp. 497–517.

129 Bert Klandermans, 'How group identification helps to overcome the dilemma of collective action', *American Behavioral Scientist* 45, no. 5 (2002), pp. 887–900.

130 Klandermans, *op. cit.,* p. 898; also Bert Klandermans et al., 'Identity processes in collective action participation: farmers' identity and farmers' protests in the Netherlands and Spain', *Political Psychology* 23, no. 2 (2002), pp. 235–51; Bert Klandermans and Dirk Oegema, 'Potentials, networks, motivations, and barriers: steps towards participation in social movements, *American Sociological Review* 52, no. 4 (1987), pp. 519–31.

131 Brent Simpson, 'Social identity and cooperation in social dilemmas', *Rationality and Society* 18, no. 4 (2006), pp. 443–70; Marilynn B. Brewer and Roderick M. Kramer, 'Choice behavior in social dilemmas: effects of social identity, group size, and decision framing', *Journal of Personality and Social Psychology* 50, no. 3 (1986), pp. 543–49; Brent Simpson and Michael W. Macy, 'Power, identity, and collective action in social exchange', *Social Forces* 82, no. 4 (2004), pp. 1373–1409.

132 Steven Pfaff, 'Collective identity and informal groups in revolutionary mobilization: East Germany in 1989', *Social Forces* 75, no. 1 (1996), pp. 91–117; cf. also Timur Kuran, 'Sparks and prairie fires: a theory of unanticipated political revolution', *Public Choice* 61, no. 1 (1989), pp. 41–74; Erich Weede and Edward N. Muller, 'Rebellion, violence and revolution: a rational choice perspective', *Journal of Peace Research* 35, no. 1 (1998), pp. 43–59; Edward N. Muller and Karl-Dieter Opp, 'Rational choice and rebellious collective action', *American Political Science Review* 80, no. 2 (1986), pp. 471–88.

133 Cf. Francesca Polletta and James M. Jasper, 'Collective identity and social movements', *Annual Review of Sociology* 27 (2001), pp. 283–305.

134 Rhys H. Wlliams, 'Constructing the public good: social movements and cultural resources', *Social Problems* 42, no. 1 (1995), pp. 124–44.; Jeffrey Berejikian, 'Revolutionary collective action and the agent-structure problem', *American Political Science Review* 86, no. 3 (1992), pp. 647–57.

135 Jon Elster, *Making Sense of Marx* (Cambridge: Cambridge University Press, 1985), p. 347ff.

136 Claus Offe and Helmut Wiesenthal, 'Two logics of collective action: theoretical notes on social class and organizational form', *Political Power and Social Theory* 1 (1980), pp. 67–115; William G. Roy and Rachel Parker-Gwin, 'How many logics of collective action?', *Theory and Society* 28, no. 2 (1999), pp. 203–37; cf. also Erik Olin Wright, 'The continuing relevance of class analysis – comments', *Theory and Society* 25, no. 5 (1996), pp. 693–716; Wendy Bottero, 'Class identities and the identity of class', *Sociology* 38, no. 5 (2004), pp. 985–1003.

137 Cf. Georg Lukacs, *History and Class Consciousness* (Cambridge, MA: MIT Press, 1971); cf. also Mark Warren, 'Ideology and the self', *Theory and Society* 19, no. 5 (1990), pp. 599–634; Adam Przeworski and Glaucio A.D. Soares, 'Theories in search of a curve: a contextual interpretation of left vote', *American Political Science Review* 65, no. 1 (1971), pp. 51–68.

Chapter 3: The debate on European identity in the functional perspective

1 Ireneusz P. Karolewski and Viktoria Kaina (eds), *European Identity: Theoretical Perspectives and Empirical Insights* (Muenster: Lit, 2006).

2 Hauke Brunkhorst, 'The legitimation crisis of the European Union', *Constellations* 13, no. 2 (2006), pp. 166–80; John Bohman, 'Constitution making and democratic innovation: the European Union and transnational governance', *European Journal of Political Theory* 3, no. 3 (2004), pp. 315–37; Jonathan Bowman, 'The European Union democratic deficit: federalists, skeptics, and revisionists', *European Journal of Political Theory* 5, no. 2 (2006), pp. 191–212.

3 Cf. Peter Graf Kielmannsegg, 'Integration und Demokratie', in Markus Jachtenfuchs and Beate Kohler-Koch (eds), *Europäische Integration* (Opladen: Leske+Budrich,

2003), 2nd edition, pp. 49–83; cf. also Winfried Thaa, 'Lean citizenship: the fading away of the political in transnational democracy', *European Journal of International Relations* 7, no. 4 (2001), pp. 503–23; Peter A. Kraus, 'Cultural pluralism and European polity-building: neither Westphalia nor cosmopolis', *Journal of Common Market Studies* 41, no. 4 (2003), pp. 665–86.

4   Bo Stråth, 'A European identity: to the historical limits of a concept', *European Journal of Social Theory* 5, no. 4 (2002), pp. 387–401.

5   Some scholars even speak of a 'cognitive turn' in EU studies. Cf. Susana Borrás, *The Cognitive Turn(s) in EU Studies*, Research Paper no. 6/99, Department of Social Sciences, Roskilde University, Denmark.

6   Cf. Brigid Laffan, 'The European Union polity: a union of regulative, normative and cognitive pillars', *Journal of European Public Policy* 8, no. 5 (2001), pp. 709–27, esp. p. 718; Yves Surel, 'The role of cognitive and normative frames in policy-making', *Journal of European Public Policy* 7, no, 4 (2000), pp. 495–512.

7   Juan Díez Medrano, *Framing Europe: Attitudes to European Integration in Germany, Spain, and the United Kingdom* (Princeton, NJ: Princeton University Press, 2003), p. 249f; cf. also Xenia Chryssochoou, 'Memberships in a superordinate level: re-thinking European Union as a multi-national society', *Journal of Community & Applied Social Psychology* 10, no. 5 (2000), pp. 403–20.

8   Cf. Emanuele Castano et al., 'We are one and I like it: the impact of ingroup entitativity on ingroup identification', *European Journal of Social Psychology* 33 (2003), pp. 735–54.

9   Thomas Risse, 'The Euro between national and European identity', *Journal of European Public Policy* 10, no. 4 (2003), pp. 487–505; Thomas Risse, 'Neofunctionalism, European identity, and the puzzles of European integration', *Journal of European Public Policy* 12, no. 2 (2005), pp. 291–309.

10 Cf. the notion of technology of collective identity. Nikos Prentoulis, 'On the technology of collective identity: normative reconstructions of the concept of EU citizenship', *European Law Journal* 7, no. 2 (2001), pp. 196–218; also Edward Moxon-Browne, 'The Europeanization of citizenship: a passport to the future', *Yearbook of European Studies* 14 (2000), pp. 179–96.

11 Elena Jileva, 'Visa and free movement of labour: the uneven imposition of the EU *acquis* on the accession states', *Journal of Ethnic and Migration Studies* 28, no. 4 (2002), pp. 683–700.

12 Cf. Emek M. Uçarer, 'Managing asylum and European integration: expanding spheres of exclusion', *International Studies Perspectives* 2, no. 3 (2001), pp. 288–304; Randall Hansen, 'Migration, citizenship and race in Europe: between incorporation and exclusion', *European Journal of Political Research* 35, no. 4 (1999), pp. 415–44; Virginie Guiraudon, 'The constitution of a European immigration policy domain: a political sociology approach', *Journal of European Public Policy* 10, no. 2 (2003), pp. 263–82; Sandra Lavinex and Emek M. Uçarer, 'The external dimension of Europeanization: the case of immigration policies', *Cooperation and Conflict* 39, no. 4 (2004), pp. 417–43.

13 Cf. Alexander Wendt, 'Collective identity formation and the international state', *American Political Science Review* 88, no. 2 (1994), pp. 384–96; Cris Shore, 'Inventing the people's Europe: critical approaches to European Community cultural policy', *Man, New Series* 28, no. 4 (1993), pp. 779–800.

14 Cf. William Walters, 'The power of inscription: beyond social construction and deconstruction in European integration studies', *Millennium: Journal of International Studies* 31, no. 1 (2002), pp. 83–108; Mark B. Salter, 'Governmentalities of an airport: heterotopia and confession', *International Political Sociology* 1, no. 1 (2007), pp. 49–66; cf. also the debate on the EU's 'community of exclusion' between Kostakopoulou and Howe. Theodora Kostakopoulou, 'Why a community of Europeans could be a community of exclusion: a reply to Howe', *Journal of Common Market Studies* 35, no. 2 (1997), pp. 301–8; Paul Howe, 'Insiders and outsiders in a community of Europeans:

a reply to Kostakopoulou', *Journal of Common Market Studies* 35, no. 2 (1997), pp. 309–14.

15 Cf. Eiki Berg and Piret Ehin, 'What kind of border regime is in the making?: towards a differentiated and uneven border strategy', *Cooperation and Conflict* 41, no. 1 (2006), pp. 53–71; Andrew Geddes, 'Europe's border relationships and international migration relations', *Journal of Common Market Studies* 43, no. 4 (2005), pp. 787–806; Virginie Mamadouh, 'The territoriality of European integration and the territorial features of the European Union: the first 50 years', *Tijdschrift voor Economische en Sociale Geografie* 92, no. 4 (2001), pp. 420–36.

16 Peo Hansen, 'European Citizenship, or where neoliberalism meets ethno-culturalism', *European Societies* 2, no. 2 (2000), pp. 139–65.

17 Else Kveinen, 'Citizenship in a post-Westphalian community: beyond external exclusion?', *Citizenship Studies* 6, no. 1 (2002), pp. 21–35. An opposite view is represented by Steffen Mau, who argues that despite some 'hardening' of exclusionary practices, the EU's border regime remains variable and diffuse since it relies on a multitude of non-rigid forms of cross-border cooperation and association. The EU itself is an open regime with expanding borders, which renders rigid external boundary-making virtually impossible. Steffen Mau, 'Die Politik der Grenze', *Berliner Journal für Soziologie* 1 (2006), pp. 115–32; cf. also Thomas Christiansen, *Towards Statehood? The EU's Move Towards Constitutionalization and Territorialization*, Arena Working Paper 21 (ARENA: University of Oslo, 2005).

18 Cf. Audrey Macklin, 'Who is the citizen's Other? Considering the heft of citizenship', *Theoretical Inquiries in Law* 8, no. 2 (2007), pp. 333–66.

19 Adam Luedtke, 'European integration, public opinion and immigration policy: testing the impact of national identity', *European Union Politics* 6, no. 1 (2005), pp. 83–112.

20 Clases H. de Vreese and Hajo G. Boomgaarden, 'Projecting EU referendums: fear of immigration and support for European integration', *European Union Politics* 6, no. 1 (2005), pp. 59–82.

21 Lauren M. McLaren, 'Immigration and the new politics of inclusion and exclusion in the European Union: the effect of elites and the EU on individual-level opinions regarding European and non-European immigrants', *European Journal of Political Research* 39, no. 1 (2001), pp. 81–108.

22 Matthias L. Maier and Thomas Risse (eds), *Europeanization, Collective Identities and Public Discourses, Final Report,* Robert Schuman Centre for Advanced Studies, European University Institute, Florence; cf. also Juan Díez Medrano and Paula Gutiérrez, 'Nested identities: national and European identity in Spain', *Ethnic and Racial Studies* 24, no. 5 (2001), pp. 753–78; Thomas Risse, 'The Euro between national and European identity', *Journal of European Public Policy* 10, no. 4 (2003), pp. 487–505.

23 See also the typology proposed by Bettina Westle, who distinguishes between a competition model, a concordance model and a sandwich model of collective identity in the EU. Bettina Westle, 'Europäische Identifikation im Spannungsfeld regionaler und nationaler Identitäten: Theoretische Überlegungen und empirische Befunde', *Politische Vierteljahresschrift* 44, no. 4 (2003), pp. 453–82; Bettina Westle, 'Europäische Identität und europäische Demokratie', *WeltTrends* 15, no. 54 (2007), pp. 69–83. Cf. also Jan W. van Deth (ed.), *Deutschland in Europa* (Wiesbaden: VS Verlag für Sozialwissenschaften, 2004).

24 Cf. Andrew Moravcsik, 'What can we learn from the collapse of the European constitutional project?', *Politische Vierteljahresschrift.* 47, no.2 (2006), pp. 219–41.

25 For an empirical estimate of European diversity see Dieter Fuchs and Hans-Dieter Klingemann, 'Eastward enlargement of the European Union and the identity of Europe', *West European Politics* 25, no. 2 (2002), pp. 19–54.

26 John Erik Fossum, *Still a Union of Deep Diversity? The Convention and the Constitution for Europe*, Arena Working Paper (21/03) (Arena: University of Oslo, 2003); John Erik Fossum, 'The European Union: in search of an identity', *European Journal of Political Theory* 2, no. 3 (2003), pp. 319–40; Charles Taylor, *Reconciling the Solitudes: Essays*

on Canadian Federalism (Montreal: McGill-Queen's University Press, 1993); Charles Taylor, *Sources of the Self: The Making of Modern Identity* (Cambridge: Harvard University Press, 1989), esp. p. 25; cf. also Ash Amin, 'Multi-ethnicity and the idea of Europe', *Theory, Culture & Society* 21, no. 2 (2004), pp. 1–24.

27 Markus Jachtenfuchs, 'Die Europäische Union – ein Gebilde sui generis?', in Klaus-Dieter Wolf (ed.), *Projekt Europa im Übergang? Probleme, Modelle und Strategien des Regierens in der Europäischen Union* (Baden-Baden: Nomos, 1997), pp. 15–35; Beate Kohler-Koch, *The European Union Facing Enlargement: Still a System Sui Generis?* MZES Working Paper III/No. 20, 1997.

28 Cf. Jan Zielonka and Peter Mair, 'Introduction: diversity and adaptation in the enlarged European Union', *West European Politics* 25, no. 2 (2002), pp. 1–18.

29 Antje Wiener, 'Making sense of the new geography of citizenship: fragmented citizenship in the European Union', *Theory and Society* 26, no. 4 (1997), pp. 529–60, esp. p. 532.

30 David McCrone and Richard Kiely, 'Nationalism and citizenship', *Sociology* 34, no. 1 (2000), pp. 19–34, esp. p. 22.

31 Cf. Antje Wiener and Vincent Della Sala, 'Constitution-making and citizenship practice – bridging the democracy gap in the EU?', *Journal of Common Market Studies* 35, no. 4 (1997), pp. 595–614, esp. p. 605; Antje Wiener, 'From special to specialized rights: the politics of citizenship and identity in the European Union', in Michael Hanagan and Charles Tilly (eds), *Extending Citizenship – Reconfiguring States* (Lanham, MD: Rowman & Littlefield, 1999), pp. 195–227; Elizabeth Meehan, 'Europeanization and citizenship of the European Union', *Yearbook of European Studies* 14 (2000), pp. 157–77.

32 Cf. Jane Jenson, 'The European Union's citizenship regime: creating norms and building practices', *Comparative European Politics* 5, no. 1 (2007), pp. 53–69.

33 Liza Schuster and John Solomos, 'Rights and wrongs across European borders: migrants, minorities and citizenship', *Citizenship Studies* 6, no. 1 (2002), pp. 37–54, esp. p. 40; Rainer Bauböck, 'Why European citizenship? Normative approaches to supranational union', *Theoretical Inquiries in Law* 8 (2007), pp. 439–74; Ece Ozlem Atican, *Citizenship or Denizenship: The Treatment of Third Country Nationals in the European Union*, SEI Working Paper 85, Sussex European Institute, 2006; Jo Shaw, 'The interpretation of European Union citizenship', *Modern Law Review* 61, no. 3 (1998), pp. 293–317.

34 Alex Warleigh, 'The hustle: citizenship practice, NGOs and policy coalitions in the European Union – the cases of Auto Oil, drinking water and unit pricing', *Journal of European Public Policy* 7, no. 2 (2000), pp. 229–43.

35 Cf. Christian Joppke, 'How immigration is changing citizenship: a comparative view', *Ethnic and Racial Studies* 22, no. 4 (1999), pp. 629–52; David Fitzgerald, 'Rethinking emigrant citizenship', *New York University Law Review* 81 (2006) pp. 90–116. For a thesis that increasing immigration is associated with a reassertion of national identity see Eleonore Kofman, 'Citizenship, migration and the reassertion of national identity', *Citizenship Studies* 9, no. 5 (2005), pp. 453–67. For a differentiated view of inclusion and exclusion mechanisms associated with immigration see Liza Schuster and John Solomos, 'Rights and wrongs across European borders: migrants, minorities and citizenship', *Citizenship Studies* 6, no. 1 (2002), pp. 37–54.

36 Steven Vertovec, 'Transnationalism and identity', *Journal of Ethnic and Migration Studies* 27, no. 4 (2001), pp. 573–82; Thomas Faist, 'Jenseits von Nation und Post-Nation: Transstaatliche Räume und Doppelte Staatsbürgerschaft', *Zeitschrift für Internationale Beziehungen* 7, no. 1 (2000), pp. 109–44; Anke Strüver, 'Spheres of transnationalism within the European Union. On open doors, thresholds and drawbridges along Dutch–German border', *Journal of Ethnic and Migration Studies* 31, no. 2 (2005), pp. 323–43; Jan Zielonka, 'How new enlarged borders will reshape the European Union', *Journal of Common Market Studies* 39, no. 3 (2001), pp. 507–36; Margit Kraus and Robert Schwager, 'EU enlargement and immigration', *Journal of Common Market Studies* 42,

no. 2 (2003), pp. 165–81. Cf. also Adrian Favell and Randall Hansen, 'Markets against politics: migrations, EU enlargement and the idea of Europe', *Journal of Ethnic and Migration Studies* 28, no. 4 (2002), pp. 581–601; José Itzigsohn, 'Immigration and the boundaries of citizenship: the institutions of immigrants' political transnationalism', *International Migration Review* 34, no. 4 (2000), pp. 1126–54.

37 Ayse S. Çaglar, 'Hyphenated identities and the limits of culture: some methodological queries', in Pnina Werbner and Tariq Modood (eds), *The Politics of Multiculturalism in the New Europe: Racism,Identity, Community* (London: Zed Books, 1997), pp. 169–85; Matthias Kaelberer, 'The euro and European identity: symbols, power and the politics of European Union', *Review of International Studies* 30 (2004), pp. 161–78, esp. p. 173; Martin Kohli, 'The battlegrounds of European identity', *European Societies* 2, no. 2 (2000), pp. 113–37, esp. p. 130ff.

38 Cf. Thomas Faist, 'Transnationalisation in international migration: implications for the study of citizenship and culture', *Ethnic and Racial Studies* 23, no. 2 (2000), pp. 189–222, esp. p. 214; Elizabeth Meehan, 'Europeanization and citizenship of the European Union', *Yearbook of European Studies* 14 (2000), pp. 157–77; Furio Cerutti, 'A political identity of the Europeans', *Thesis Eleven* 72, no. 1 (2003), pp. 26–45; Christian Joppke, 'Transformation of citizenship: status, rights, identity', *Citizenship Studies* 11, no. 1 (2007), pp. 37–48, esp. p. 38.

39 Cf. Heinz Kleger (ed.), *Transnationale Staatsbürgerschaft* (Frankfurt: Campus, 1997); Rainer Bauböck, *Transnational Citizenship: Membership Rights in International Migration* (Aldershot: Edward Elgar, 1994); Veit Bader, 'The cultural conditions of transnational citizenship: on the interpenetration of political and ethnic cultures', *Political Theory* 25, no. 6 (1997), pp. 771–813; Antje Wiener, 'From special to specialized rights: the politics of citizenship and identity in the European Union', in Michael Hanagan and Charles Tilly (eds), *Extending Citizenship – Reconfiguring States* (Lanham, MD: Rowman & Littlefield, 1999), pp. 195–227; Chris Hilson, 'Legitimacy and rights in the EU: questions of identity', *Journal of European Public Policy* 14, no. 4 (2007), pp. 527–43.

40 Gary Marks, 'Territorial identities in the European Union', in Jeffrey Anderson, *Regional Integration and Democracy* (New York: Rowman & Littlefield, 1999), pp. 69–91.

41 Thomas Faist, 'Social citizenship in the European Union: nested membership', *Journal of Common Market Studies* 39, no. 1 (2001), pp. 37–58; cf. Maurizio Ferrera, 'European integration and national social citizenship: changing boundaries, new structuring?', *Comparative Political Studies* 36, no. 6 (2003), pp. 611–52; Maarten P. Vink, 'The limited Europeanization of domestic citizenship policy: evidence from the Netherlands', *Journal of Common Market Studies* 39, no. 5 (2001), pp. 875–96; Luise Ackers, 'Citizenship, migration and the valuation of care in the European Union', *Journal of Ethnic and Migration Studies* 30, no. 2 (2004), pp. 373–96.

42 Cf. for instance Hans Joas, *Praktische Intersubjektivität* (Frankfurt: Suhrkamp, 1989).

43 Daniel Fuss and Marita A. Grosser, 'What makes young Europeans feel European? Results from a cross-cultural research project', in Ireneusz P. Karolewski and Viktoria Kaina (eds), *European Identity: Theoretical Perspectives and Empirical Insights* (Muenster: Lit, 2006), pp. 209–41; Daniel Fuss, 'In Vielfalt geeint oder Festung Europas: Europäische Identität und das Fremde', *WeltTrends* 54, no. 15 (2007), pp. 39–51.

44 Marilynn B. Brewer, 'The many faces of social identity: implications for political psychology', *Political Psychology* 22, no. 1 (2001), p.121.

45 Cf. Antje Wiener, 'Contested meanings of norms: a research framework', *Comparative European Politics* 5 (2007), pp. 1–17; cf. also Gerard Delanty, 'Citizenship as a learning process: disciplinary citizenship versus cultural citizenship', *International Journal of Lifelong Education* 22, no.6 (2003), pp. 597–605.

46 Tomáš Tatranský, 'European citizenship policy: trying to stimulate the citizens' sense of belonging to the European Union', *Polish Sociological Review* 4, no. 156 (2006), pp.

489–503; Jos de Beus, 'Quasi-national European identity and European democracy', *Law and Philosophy* 20, no. 3 (2001), pp. 283–311; Percy B. Lehning, 'European citizenship: between facts and norms', *Constellations* 4, no. 3 (1998), pp.346–67.

47 Ireneusz P. Karolewski, 'Citizenship and collective identity in Europe', in Ireneusz P. Karolewski and Viktoria Kaina (eds), *European Identity: Theoretical Perspectives and Empirical Insights* (Muenster: Lit, 2006), pp. 23–58; cf. also Erin Delaney and Luca Barani, 'The promotion of symmetrical European Citizenship: a federal perspective', *Journal of European Integration* 25, no. 2 (2003), pp. 95–114.

48 Sergio Carrera, 'What does free movement mean in theory and practice in the enlarged EU?', *European Law Journal* 11, no. 6 (2005), pp. 699–721.

49 Ulrich K. Preuß, 'Two challenges to European citizenship', in Richard Bellamy and Dario Castiglione (eds), *Constitutionalism in Transformation: European and Theoretical Perspectives* (Oxford: Blackwell, 1996), pp. 122–40, esp. p. 139.

50 Gerard Delanty, 'European citizenship: a critical assessment', *Citizenship Studies* 11, no. 1 (2007), pp. 63–72, esp. p. 72. This argument is a European variant of the globalization critique pointing to an erosion of democracy and citizenship. Cf. for instance Philip G. Cerny, 'Globalization and the erosion of democracy', *European Journal of Political Research* 36, no. 5 (1999), pp. 1–26.

51 Gerard Delanty, *Citizenship in a Global Age: Society, Culture, Politics* (Buckingham: Open University Press, 2000), p. 114ff; cf. also Gerard Delanty, *Inventing Europe: Idea, Identity, Reality* (London: Palgrave, 1995).

52 Cf. Eva Jonas et al., 'Currencies as cultural symbols: an existential psychological perspective on reactions of Germans towards the euro', *Journal of Economic Psychology* 26, no. 1 (2005), pp. 129–46.

53 Jacques E. C. Hymans, 'The changing color of money: European currency iconography and collective identity', *European Journal of International Relations* 10, no. 1 (2004), pp. 5–31; cf. also Thomas Risse et al., 'To euro or not to euro? The EMU and identity politics in the European Union', *European Journal of International Relations* 5, no. 2 (1999), pp. 147–87.

54 Karen A. Cerulo, *Identity Designs: The Sights and Sounds of a Nation* (New Brunswick, NJ: Rutgers University Press, 1995).

55 Thomas Risse, 'The Euro between national and European identity', *Journal of European Public Policy* 10, no. 4 (2003), pp. 487–505.

56 Monica Sassatelli, 'Imagined Europe: the shaping of a European cultural identity through EU cultural policy', *European Journal of Social Theory* 5, no. 4 (2002), pp. 435–51.

57 *Ibid.*, p. 446.

58 Michael Bruter, 'On what citizens mean by feeling European: perceptions of news, symbols and borderless-ness', *Journal of Ethnic and Migration Studies* 30, no. 1 (2004), pp. 21–39.

59 Caryl Clark, 'Forging identity: Beethoven's ode as European anthem', *Critical Inquiry* 23, no. 4 (1997), pp. 789–807.

60 Cf. Franz C. Mayer and Jan Palmowski, 'European identities and the EU – the ties that bind the peoples of Europe', *Journal of Common Market Studies* 42, no. 3 (2004), pp. 573–98.

61 Michael Bruter, 'Winning hearts and minds for Europe: the impact of news and symbols on civic and cultural European identity', *Comparative Political Studies* 36, no. 10 (2003), pp. 1148–79; Michael Bruter, *Citizens of Europe? The Emergence of a Mass European Identity* (Basingstoke: Palgrave, 2005).

62 Cf. Ireneusz P. Karolewski, 'Constitutionalization of the common foreign and security policy of the European Union: implications of the constitutional Treaty', *German Law Journal* 6, no. 11 (2005), pp. 1649–66; cf. also Spyros Blavoukos et al., 'A president for the European Union: a new actor in town?', *Journal of Common Market Studies* 45, no. 2 (2007), pp. 231–52.

63 Kathleen M. McGraw and Thomas M. Dolan, 'Personifying the state: consequences for attitude formation', *Political Psychology* 28, no. 3 (2007), pp. 299–327.

64 Cf. Liah Greenfeld, 'Is nation unavoidable? Is nation unavoidable today?' in Hanspeter Kriesi et al. (eds), *Nation and National Identity: The European Experience in Perspective* (Zürich: Verlag Rüegger, 1999), pp. 37–54, esp. p. 39.

65 Cf. Seyla Benhabib, 'Twilight of sovereignty or the emergence of cosmopolitan norms? Rethinking citizenship in volatile times', *Citizenship Studies* 11, no. 1 (2007), pp. 19–36, esp. p. 21; Antonio Franceschet, 'Popular sovereignty or cosmopolitan democracy? Liberalism, Kant and international reform', *European Journal of International Relations* 6, no. 2 (2000), pp. 277–302.

66 Cf. Nikos Prentoulis, 'On the technology of collective identity: normative reconstructions of the concept of EU citizenship', *European Law Journal* 7, no. 2 (2001), pp. 196–218; Neil MacCormick, 'Democracy, subsidiarity, and citizenship in the European commonwealth', *Law and Philosophy* 16 (1997), pp. 331–56.

67 For the role of territory in the European identity formation see Mathias Albert, 'Territorium und Identität: Kollektive Identität und moderner Nationalstaat', *Österreichische Zeitschrift für Politikwissenschaft* 28, no. 3 (1999), pp. 255–68.

68 Cf. Ian Manners and Richard Whitman, 'The difference engine: constructing and representing the international identity of the European Union', *Journal of European Public Policy* 10, no. 3 (2003), pp. 380–404.

69 Cf. Kees van Kersbergen, 'Political allegiance and European integration', *European Journal of Political Research* 37, no. 1 (2000), pp. 1–17.

70 Bahar Rumelili, 'Constructing identity and relating to difference: understanding the EU's mode of differentiation', *Review of International Studies* 30, no. 1 (2004), pp. 27–47.

71 *Ibid.*, p. 46; cf. also Mehmet Ugur, 'Freedom of movement vs. exclusion: a reinterpretation of the insider–outsider divide in the European Union', *International Migration Review* 29, no. 4 (1995), pp. 964–99.

72 Cf. Anna Triandafyllidou, 'The political discourse on immigration in Southern Europe: a critical analysis', *Journal of Community & Applied Social Psychology* 10, no. 5 (2000), pp. 373–89.

73 Cf. Ian Ward, 'Identifying the European Other', *International Journal of Refugee Law* 14, no. 2–3 (2002), pp. 219–37; Gerard Delanty, 'Models of European identity: reconciling universalism and particularism', *Perspectives on European Politics and Society* 3, no. 3 (2002), pp. 345–59.

74 Cf. Gerard Delanty, 'Die Transformation nationaler Identität und kulturelle Ambivalenz europäischer Identität: Demokratische Identifikation in einem postnationalen Europa', in Reinhold Viehoff and Rien T Segers (eds), *Kultur, Identität, Europa* (Frankfurt: Suhrkamp, 1999), p. 270.

75 S. N. Eisenstadt, 'The construction of collective identities: some analytical and comparative indications', *European Journal of Social Theory* 1, no. 2 (1998), pp. 229–54.

76 Cf. Ulrich Beck and Edgar Grande, 'Cosmopolitanism: Europe's way out of crisis', *European Journal of Social Theory* 10, no. 1 (2007), pp. 67–85.

77 Cf. Jürgen Habermas, 'Making sense of the EU: towards a cosmopolitan Europe', *Journal of Democracy* 14, no. 4 (2003), pp. 86–100; Nick Stevenson, 'European cosmopolitan solidarity: questions of citizenship, difference and post-materialism', *European Journal of Social Theory* 9, no. 4 (2006), pp. 485–500; Daniele Archibugi, 'Cosmopolitan democracy and its critics: a review', *European Journal of International Relations* 10, no. 3 (2004), pp. 437–73; cf also Heidrun Friese and Peter Wagner, 'The nascent political philosophy of European polity', *The Journal of Political Philosophy* 10, no. 3 (2002), pp. 341–64.

78 Cf. Robert Fine and Will Smith, 'Jürgen Habermas's theory of cosmopolitanism', *Constellations* 10, no. 4 (2003), pp. 469–87.

79 For the argument that human rights can have a symbolic and identity promoting function see Thorsten Bonacker and André Brodocz, 'Im Namen der Menschenrechte: Zur symbolischen Integration der internationalen Gemeinschaft durch Normen", *Zeitschrift für Internationale Beziehungen* 8, no. 2 (2001), pp. 179–208. Cf. Also Omid Payrow Shabani, 'Constitutional patriotism as a model of postnational political association: the case of the EU', *Philosophy and Social Criticism* 32, no. 6 (2006), pp. 699–718; Justine Lacroix, 'For a European constitutional patriotism', *Political Studies* 50, no. 5 (2002), pp. 944–58. For a more basic debate on the constitutional patriotism see for instance Ciaran Cronin, 'Democracy and collective identity: in defence of constitutional patriotism', *European Journal of Philosophy* 11, no. 1 (2003), pp. 1–28; Clarissa Rile Hayward, 'Democracy's identity problem: is constitutional patriotism the answer?', *Constellations* 14, no. 2 (2007), pp. 182–96; Jan-Werner Müller, 'Three objections to constitutional patriotism', *Constellations* 14, no. 2 (2007), pp. 197–209.

80 Jürgen Habermas and Jacques Derrida, 'February 15, or what binds Europeans together: a plea for a common foreign policy, beginning in the core of europe', *Constellations* 10, no. 3 (2003), pp. 291–97; Shabani, *op. cit.*, p. 705.

81 Cf. Mark Murphy, 'Between facts, norms and a post-national constellation: Habermas, law and European social policy', *Journal of European Public Policy* 12, no. 1 (2005), pp. 143–56.

82 Wojciech Sadurski, *European Constitutional Identity?* EUI Working Papers, Law No. 2006/33, p. 9ff; cf. also Sergio Fabbrini, 'American democracy from a European perspective', *Annual Review of Political Science* 2, no. 1 (1999), pp. 465–91; Mirjan R. Domaška, 'Reflections on American constitutionalism', *American Journal of Comparative Law* 38, no. 1 (1990), pp. 4221–443; Michel Rosenfeld, 'American constitutionalism confronts Denninger's new constitutional paradigm', *Constellations* 7, no. 4 (2002), pp. 529–48.

83 Sadurski, *op. cit.* p. 13ff. For a view on European constitutionalism as 'responsible and inclusive' see Jo Shaw, 'Process, responsibility and inclusion in the EU constitutionalism', *European Law Journal* 9, no. 1 (2003), pp. 45–68; Jo Shaw, 'Postnational constitutionalism in the European Union', *Journal of European Public Policy* 6, no. 4 (1999), pp. 579–97; On the features of the American constitutionalism see for instance Richard Bellamy and Dario Castiglione, 'Constitutionalism and democracy – political theory and American Constitution', *British Journal of Political Science* 27, no. 4 (1997), pp. 595–618.

84 Sadurski, *op. cit.* p. 19f.

85 Cf. Ulrich K. Preuß et al., 'Traditions of citizenship in the European Union', *Citizenship Studies* 7, no. 1 (2003), pp. 3–14; Judith Squires, 'Liberal constitutionalism, identity and difference', in Richard Bellamy and Dario Castiglione (eds), *Constitutionalism in Transformation: European and Theoretical Perspectives* (Oxford: Blackwell, 1996), pp. 208–22.

86 Cf. also Sandra Lavenex, 'The Europeanization of refugee policies: normative challenges and institutional legacies', *Journal of Common Market Studies* 39, no. 5 (2001), pp. 851–74.

87 Erik Oddvar Eriksen, 'The EU – a cosmopolitan polity?', *Journal of European Public Policy* 13, no. 2 (2006), pp. 252–69.

88 For the normative issues connected to the EU accession of Turkey see Thomas Diez, 'Turkey, the European Union and security complexes revisited', *Mediterranean Politics* 10, no. 2 (2005), pp. 167–80.

89 Patchen Markell, 'Making affect safe for democracy? On constitutional patriotism', *Political Theory* 28, no. 1 (2000), pp. 38–63.

90 Winfried Thaa, 'Lean citizenship: the fading away of the political in transnational democracy', *European Journal of International Relations* 7, no. 4 (2001), pp. 503–23.

91 *Ibid.*, p. 510.

92 Percy B. Lehning, 'European citizenship: towards a European identity?', *Law and Philosophy* 20, no. 3 (2001), pp. 239–82; cf. also Cécile Leconte, 'The fragility of the

EU as a community of values: lessons from the Haider affair', *West European Politics* 28, no. 3 (2005), pp. 620–49.

93 Cf. Björn Hettne and Fredrik Söderbaum, 'Civilian power of soft imperialism? The EU as a global actor and the role of interregionalism', *European Foreign Affairs Review* 10, no. 4 (2005), pp. 535–552.

94 For a review of the debate cf. Jan Orbie, 'Civilian power Europe: review of the original and current debates', *Cooperation and Conflict* 41, no. 1 (2006), pp. 123–28.

95 Cf. Helene Sjursen, 'What kind of power?', *Journal of European Public Policy* 13, no. 2 (2006), pp. 169–81; Gerard Delanty, 'The making of a post-Western Europe: a civilizational analysis', *Thesis Eleven* 72, no. 1 (2003), pp. 8–25.

96 Cf. Karen E. Smith, 'The European Union: a distinctive actor in international relations', *The Brown Journal of World Affairs* IX, no. 2 (2003), pp. 103–13; Christian Freres, 'The European Union as a global civilian power: development cooperation in EU–Latin American Relations', *Journal of Interamerican Studies and World Affairs* 42, no. 2 (2000), pp. 63–85.

97 Cf. Richard Youngs, 'Normative dynamics and strategic interests in the EU's external identity', *Journal of Common Market Studies* 42, no. 2 (2004), pp. 415–35.

98 Cf. Helen Sjursen, 'The EU as a normative power: how can this be?', *Journal of European Public Policy* 1, no. 2 (2006), pp. 235–51; Kalypso Nicolaïdis and Robert Howse, 'This is my EUtopia…: narrative as power', *Journal of Common Market Studies* 40, no. 4 (2002), pp. 767–92.

99 For the opposite argument of the post-colonial character of the EU see Enrica Rigo, 'Citizenship at Europe's borders: some reflections on the post-colonial condition of Europe in the context of EU enlargement', *Citizenship Studies* 9, no. 1 (2005), pp. 3–22. Cf. also Jan Ifversen and Christoffer Kølvraa, *European Neighbourhood Policy as Identity Politics*, Paper presented at the EUSA Tenth Biennial International Conference, Montreal, Canada, 17–19 May 2007.

100 However, some scholars argue that there is nothing altruistic about the EU's external policies. For instance, Sandra Lavenex demonstrates that the 'Europeanization' of some policy fields such as immigration control does not necessarily follow merely humanitarian considerations, since the shift 'outwards' can be regarded as a strategy to increase the autonomy of national ministers towards political, normative and institutional constraints on national policy-making. Sandra Lavenex, 'Shifting up and out: the foreign policy of immigration control', *West European Politics* 29, no. 2 (2006), pp. 329–50. In addition, the inclusiveness of European external policies can be interpreted as an attempt to counterbalance these policy fields, in which the EU is particularly vulnerable. The inclination to inclusive and multilateral politics is therefore merely a rational management of interdependencies, rather than politics resting on value and norms of appropriate conduct. Sandra Lavenex, 'EU external governance in wider Europe', *Journal of European Public Policy* 11, no. 4 (2004), pp. 680–700; Michael Smith, 'The framing of European foreign and security policy: towards a post-modern policy framework?', *Journal of European Public Policy* 10, no. 4 (2003), pp. 556–75; Michael Smith, 'The European Union and a changing Europe: establishing the boundaries of order', *Journal of Common Market Studies* 34, no. 1 (1996), pp. 5–28.

101 Jennifer Mitzen, 'Anchoring Europe's civilizing identity: habits, capabilities and ontological security', *Journal of European Public Policy* 13, no. 2 (2006), pp. 270–85; Federica Bicchi, 'Our size fits all: normative power Europe and the Mediterranean', *Journal of European Public Policy* 12, no. 2 (2006), pp. 286–303. Cf. also Jürgen Neyer, 'Discourse and order in the EU: a deliberative approach to multi-level governance', *Journal of Common Market Studies* 41, no. 4 (2003), pp. 687–706.

102 Cf. Andreas Føllesdal, 'Union citizenship: unpacking the beast of burden', *Law and Philosophy* 20, no. 3 (2001), pp. 313–43; Jonathan Mercer, 'Anarchy and identity', *International Organization* 49, no. 2 (1995), pp. 229–51.

103 However, there is disagreement about how isolated foreign policy is and therefore how irresponsive the governments of democratic states are vis-à-vis public opinion attitudes

in the field of foreign policy. See Robert Y. Shapiro and Benjamin I. Page, 'Foreign policy and the rational public', *Journal of Conflict Resolution* 32, no. 2 (1988), pp. 211–47; Thomas Risse-Kappen, 'Public opinion, domestic structure, and foreign policy in liberal democracies', *World Politics* 43, no. 4 (1991), pp. 479–512; Ole R. Holsti, 'Public opinion and foreign policy: challenges to the Almond–Lippmann consensus', *International Studies Quarterly* 36, no. 4 (1992), pp. 439–66.

104 Cf. Ireneusz P. Karolewski, 'Constitutionalization of the common foreign and security policy of the European Union: implications of the constitutional treaty', *German Law Journal* 6, no.11 (2005), pp. 1649–66.

105 Wolfgang Wagner, 'The democratic control of military power Europe', *Journal of European Public Policy* 13, no. 2 (2006), pp. 200–216.

106 Cf. Michael Smith, 'Comment: crossroads or cul-de-sac? Reassessing European foreign policy', *Journal of European Public Policy* 13, no. 2 (2006), pp. 322–27, esp. p. 325.

107 Cf. Adrian Hyde-Price, 'Normative power Europe: a realist critique', *Journal of European Public Policy* 13, no. 2 (2006) p. 217–34.

108 Sibylle Scheipers and Daniela Sicurelli, 'Normative power Europe: a credible utopia?', *Journal of Common Market Studies* 45, no. 2 (2007), pp. 435–57; Ian Manners, 'Normative power Europe reconsidered: beyond the crossroads', *Journal of European Public Policy* 13, no. 2 (2006), pp. 182–99.

109 Ian Manners and Richard Whitman, 'The difference engine: constructing and representing the international identity of the European Union', *Journal of European Public Policy* 10, no. 3 (2003), pp. 380–404; Thomas Diez, 'Constructing the self and changing others: reconsidering normative power Europe'; *Millennium: Journal of International Studies* 33, no. 3 (2005), pp. 613–636.

110 Ole Wæver, 'European security identities', *Journal of Common Market Studies* 34, no. 1 (1996), pp. 103–32; Tuomas Forsberg, 'Explaining territorial disputes: from power politics to normative reasons', *Journal of Peace Research* 33, no. 4 (1996), pp. 433–49.

111 Emilian R. Kavalski, 'Identity of peace: framing the European security identity of the EU', in Ireneusz P. Karolewski and Viktoria Kaina (eds), *European Identity: Theoretical Perspectives and Empirical Insights* (Muenster: Lit, 2006), pp. 91–112.

112 Thomas Diez et al., 'The European Union and border conflicts: the transformative power of integration', *International Organization* 60 (2006), pp. 563–93.

113 Robert Falkner, 'The political economy of normative power Europe: EU environmental leadership in international biotechnology regulation', *Journal of European Public Policy* 14, no. 4 (2007), pp. 507–26.

114 *Ibid.*, p. 521.

115 Cf. Rainer Eising, 'The access of business interests to EU institutions: towards elite pluralism?', *Journal of European Public Policy* 14, no. 3 (2007), pp. 384–403; Stijn Smismans, 'European civil society: shaped by discourses and institutional interests', *European Law Journal* 9, no. 4 (2003), pp. 473–95; Irina Michalowitz, 'What determines influence?: assessing conditions for decision-making influence of interest groups in the EU', *Journal of European Public Policy* 14, no. 1 (2007), pp. 132–51; Marcus Höreth, 'No way out for the beast? The unsolved legitimacy problem of European governance', *Journal of European Public Policy* 6, no. 2 (1999), pp. 249–68.

116 Cf. David Coen, 'Empirical and theoretical studies in EU lobbying', *Journal of European Public Policy* 14, no. 3 (2007), pp. 333–45; Andreas Broscheid and David Coen, 'Lobbying activity and fora creation in the EU: empirically exploring the nature of the policy good', *Journal of European Public Policy* 14, no. 3 (2007), pp. 346–65; Chris Rumford, 'European civil society or transnational social space? Conceptions of society in discourses of EU citizenship, governance and the democratic deficit: an emerging agenda', *European Journal of Social Theory* 6, no. 1 (2003), pp. 25–43; Paul Magnette, 'European governance and civic participation: beyond elitist citizenship?', *Political Studies* 51, no. 1 (2003), pp. 144–60.

117 Cf. Ron Eyerman, 'The past in the present: culture and the transmission of memory', *Acta Sociologica* 47, no. 2 (2004), pp.159–69; Bo Stråth, 'Methodological and

substantive remarks on myth, memory and history in the construction of a European community', *German Law Journal* 6, no. 2 (2005), pp. 255–71.

118 Cf. Thomas Mayer, *Die Identität Europas* (Frankfurt: Suhrkamp, 2004); Erika Harris, 'New forms of identity in contemporary Europe', *Perspectives on European Politics and Society* 4, no. 1 (2003), pp. 13–33.

119 Bo Stråth, 'Ideology and history', *Journal of Political Ideologies* 11, no. 1 (2006), pp. 23–42.

120 Cf. Consuelo Cruz, 'Identity and persuasion: how nations remember their pasts and make their futures', *World Politics* 52 (2000), pp. 275–312, esp. p. 276.

121 For the significance of experience and comprehensibility in the construction of identity see Hartmut Wagner, *Bezugspunkte europäischer Identität* (Münster: LIT, 2006).

122 On the notion of collective trauma see for instance Piotr Sztompka, 'Cultural trauma: the other face of social change', *European Journal of Social Theory* 3, no. 4 (2000), pp. 449–66.

123 Bernhard Giesen, *Triumph and Trauma* (Boulder, CO: Paradigm Publishers, 2004); Bernhard Giesen, 'National identity as trauma: the German case', in Bo Stråth (ed.), *Myth and Memory in the Construction of Community. Historical Patterns in Europe and Beyond* (Brussels: Peter Lang, 2000), pp. 227–47.

124 Cf. Christian Joerges, 'Introduction: constructing Europe in the shadow of its pasts', *German Law Journal* 6, no. 2 (2005), pp. 245–54.

125 Bo Stråth, 'Methodological and substantive remarks on myth, memory and history in the construction of a European community', *German Law Journal* 6, no. 2 (2005), p. 256.

126 Cf. Jan Ifversen, 'Europe and European culture – a conceptual analysis', *European Societies* 4, no. 1 (2002), pp. 1–26; Gerard Delanty, *Inventing Europe: Idea, Identity, Reality* (Basingstoke: Palgrave, 1995).

127 Cf. Lawrence J. Hatab, 'Prospects for a democratic agon: why we can still be Nietzscheans', *Journal of Nietzsche Studies* 24 (2002), pp. 132–47.

128 Cf. Mark Wenman, 'Agonistic pluralism and three archetypal forms of politics', *Contemporary Political Theory* 2, no. 2 (2003), pp. 165–86.

129 Cf. Fabrice Larat, 'Presenting the past: political narratives on European history and the justification of European integration', *German Law Journal* 6, no. 2 (2005), pp. 273–90, esp. p. 275.

130 Mark Gilbert, 'Narrating the process: questioning the progressive story of European integration', *Journal of Common Market Studies* 46, no. 3 (2008), pp. 641–62.

131 Bo Stråth, 'A European identity: to the historical limits of a concept', *European Journal of Social Theory* 5, no. 4 (2002), pp. 387–401, esp. p. 395.

132 Cf. Srdjan Cvijic and Lorenzo Zucca, 'Does the European constitution need Christian values?', *Oxford Journal of Legal Studies* 24, no. 4 (2004), pp. 739–48; Camil Ungureanu, 'A Christian or a laic Europe? Moving beyond a false dichotomy', *Romanian Journal of Political Science* 6, no. 2 (2006), pp. 5–34; Augustín José Menéndez, *A Pious Europe? Why Europe Should not Define itself as Christian*, Arena Working Paper (10/04) (2004), University of Oslo.

133 Cf. for instance Uri Ram, 'Why secularism fails? Secular nationalism and religious revivalism in Israel', *Journal of Politics, Culture and Society* 21, no. 1–4 (2008), pp. 57–73.

134 Cf. Patchen Markell, 'Contesting consensus: rereading Habermas on the public sphere', *Constellations* 3, no. 3 (1997), pp. 377–400.

135 Patchen Markell, 'Making affect safe for democracy? On constitutional patriotism', *Political Theory* 28, no. 1 (2000), pp. 38–63, esp. p. 39.

136 Cf. Justine Lacroix, 'For a European constitutional patriotism', *Political Studies* 50, no. 5 (2002), pp. 944–58, esp. p. 945ff; Richard Bellamy and Dario Castiglione, 'Lacroix's European constitutional patriotism: a response', *Political Studies* 52, no. 4 (2004), pp. 187–93.

137 Lacroix, *op. cit.,* p. 955.

138   See, however, Jan-Werner Müller for an opposite view. Jan-Werner Müller, 'A European constitutional patriotism? The case restated', *European Law Journal* 14, no. 5 (2008), pp. 542–57.

139   Cf. Lars-Erik Cederman, 'Nationalism and bounded integration: what it would take to construct a European demos', *European Journal of International Relations* 7, no. 2 (2001), pp. 139–74.

140   Craig Calhoun, 'Constitutional patriotism and the public sphere: interests, identity, and solidarity in the integration of Europe', *International Journal of Politics, Culture and Society* 18, no. 3–4 (2005), pp. 257–80.

141   Philippe C. Schmitter and Michael W. Bauer, 'A (modest) proposal for expanding social citizenship in the European Union', *Journal of European Social Policy* 11, no. 1 (2001), pp. 55–65.

142   Anthony D. Smith, 'A Europe of nations. Or the nation of Europe?', *Journal of Peace Research* 30, no. 2 (1993), pp. 129–35; Anthony D. Smith, *Nations and Nationalism in a Global Era* (Cambridge: Polity Press, 1995), esp. Chapters 5 and 6.

143   David Miller, *On Nationality* (Oxford: Oxford University Press, 1995), p. 36.

144   For a critique of Miller's argument with regard to the EU see Andreas Føllesdal, 'The future soul of Europe: nationalism or just patriotism? A critique of David Miller's defence of nationality', *Journal of Peace Research* 37, no. 4 (2000), pp. 503–18. For the role of trust in the EU cf. also Rainer Schmalz-Bruns, 'The normative desirability of participatory governance', in Hubert Heinelt et al. (eds), *Participatory Governance in Multi-level Context: Concepts and Experience* (Leske+Budrich: Opladen, 2002), pp. 59–74.

145   Rogers Brubaker, 'The Manichean myth: rethinking the distinction between civic and ethnic nationalism', in Hanspeter Kriesi et al. (eds), *Nation and National Identity: The European Experience in Perspective* (Zürich: Rüegger, 1999), pp. 55–71, esp. p. 62.

146   *Ibid.*, p. 65.

147   Theodora Kostakopoulou, 'The protective union: change and continuity in migration law and policy in post-Amsterdam Europe', *Journal of Common Market Studies* 38, no. 3 (2000), pp. 497–518.

148   Anita Böcker and Tetty Havinga, 'Asylum applications in the European Union: patterns and trends and the effects of policy measures', *Journal of Refugee Studies* 11, no. 3 (1998), pp. 245–66; cf. also Jörg Monar, 'The dynamics of justice and home affairs: laboratories, driving factors and costs', *Journal of Common Market Studies* 39, no. 4 (2001), pp. 747–64.

149   Laurent Licata and Olivier Klein, 'Does European citizenship breed xenophobia? European identification as a predictor of intolerance towards immigrants', *Journal of Community and Applied Social Psychology* 12, no. 5 (2002), pp. 323–37.

150   Cf. Dominique Schnapper, 'Citizenship and national identity in Europe', *Nations and Nationalism* 8, no. 1 (2002), pp. 1–14; Philippe C. Schmitter, 'Citizenship in an eventual Euro-democracy', *Swiss Political Science Review* 4, no. 4 (1998), pp. 141–68.

151   Mathieu Deflem and Fred C. Pampel, 'The myth of postnational identity: popular support for European unification', *Social Forces* 75, no. 1 (1996), pp. 119–43.

152   Jon E. Fox and Cynthia Miller-Idriss, 'Everyday nationhood', *Ethnicities* 8, no. 4 (2008), pp. 536–76.

153   Cf. Klaus Eder and Willfried Spohn (eds), *Collective Memory and European Identity: The Effects of Integration and Enlargement* (Aldershot: Ashgate, 2005).

154   For some more recent positions on the issue of EU legitimacy see Christophe Crombez, 'The democratic deficit in the European Union', *European Union Politics* 4, no. 1 (2003), pp. 101–20; Andreas Føllesdal and Simon Hix, 'Why there is a democratic deficit in the EU: a response to Majone and Moravcsik', *Journal of Common Market Studies* 44, no. 3 (2006), pp. 533–62; Hauke Brunkhorst, 'The legitimation crisis of the European Union', *Constellations* 13, no. 2 (2006), pp. 166–80; Andrew Moravcsik, 'What can we learn from the collapse of the European constitutional project? *Politische Vierteljahresschrift*.47, no. 2 (2006), pp. 219–41; Amitai Etzioni, 'The community

deficit', *Journal of Common Market Studies* 45, no. 1 (2007), pp. 23–42; Ronald Holzhacker, 'Democratic legitimacy and the European Union', *Journal of European Integration* 29, no, 3 (2007), pp. 257–69.

155 J. Peter Burgess, 'What's so European about the European Union? Legitimacy between institution and identity', *European Journal of Social Theory* 5, no. 4 (2002), pp. 467–81.

156 Jürgen Habermas, 'Reconciliation through the public use of reason: remarks on John Rawls's political liberalism', *Journal of Philosophy* 92, no. 3 (1995), pp. 109–31; Jürgen Habermas, 'The public sphere', *New German Critique* 3 (1974), pp. 49–55.

157 Cf. Andrea T. Baumeister, 'Habermas: discourse and cultural diversity', *Political Studies* 51 (2003), pp. 740–58; S.N. Eisenstadt, 'Collective identities, public spheres, civil society and citizenship in the contemporary era – with some observations on the Israeli scene', *Citizenship Studies* 12, no. 3 (2008), pp. 203–13.

158 Erik Oddvar Eriksen, 'An emerging European public sphere', *European Journal of Social Theory* 8, no. 3 (2005), pp. 341–63.

159 Bernard Enjolras, 'Two hypotheses about the emergence of a post-national European model of citizenship', *Citizenship Studies* 12, no. 5 (2008), pp. 495–505.

160 Cf. Rainer Schmalz-Bruns, 'Deliberativer Supranationalismus: Demokratisches Regieren jenseits des Nationalstaates', *Zeitschrift für Internationale Beziehungen* 6, no. 2 (1999), pp. 185–224.

161 Philip Schlesinger, 'Changing spaces of political communication: the case of the European Union', *Political Communication* 16, no. 3 (1999), pp. 263–79.

162 *Ibid.*, p. 276.

163 Erik Oddvar Eriksen and John Erik Fossum, 'Democracy through strong publics in the European Union?', *Journal of Common Market Studies* 40, no. 3 (2002), pp. 401–24.

164 *Ibid.*, p. 411.

165 Cf. Berthold Rittbeger, 'No integration without representation: European integration, parliamentary democracy, and two forgotten communities', *Journal of European Public Policy* 13, no. 8 (2006), pp. 1211–1229; Wolfgang Wessels and Udo Diedrichs, 'A new kind of legitimacy for a new kind of parliament – the evolution of the European Parliament', *European Integration online Papers* (EIoP) 1, no. 6 (1997). For the role of the EP in the treaty reform see Daniela Kietz and Andreas Maurer, 'The European Parliament in treaty reform: predefining IGCs through interinstitutional agreements', *European Law Journal* 13, no. 1 (2007), pp. 20–46.

166 Berthold Rittberger, 'The creation and empowerment of the European Parliament', *Journal of Common Market Studies* 41, no. 2 (2003), pp. 203–25; Berthold Rittberger, *Building Europe's Parliament: Democratic Representation Beyond the Nation-State* (Oxford: Oxford University Press, 2005); Andreas Maurer, 'The legislative powers and impact of the European Parliament', *Journal of Common Market Studies* 41, no. 2 (2003), pp. 227–47. For an opposite view on the role of the European Parliament for the democracy in the EU see John Coultrap, 'From parliamentarism to pluralism: models of democracy and the European Union's democratic deficit', *Journal of Theoretical Politics* 11, no. 1 (1999), pp. 107–35.

167 Erik Oddvar Eriksen, 'An emerging European public sphere', p. 354f; Erik Oddvar Eriksen and John Erik Fossum, 'Democracy through strong publics in the European Union?', p. 416.

168 Erik Oddvar Eriksen, 'An emerging European public sphere', p. 358. For non-public types of deliberation see Christian Joerges, 'Deliberative political processes revisited: what have we learnt about the legitimacy of supranational decision-making', *Journal of Common Market Studies* 44, no. 4 (2006), pp. 779–802; Jürgen Neyer, 'Discourse and order in the EU: a deliberative approach to multi-level Governance', *Journal of Common Market Studies* 41, no. 4 (2003), pp. 687–706; Christian Joerges and Jürgen Neyer, 'Transforming strategic interaction into deliberative problem-solving: European comitology in the foodstuffs sector', *Journal of European Public Policy* 4, no. 4 (1997), pp. 609–25.

169 Hans-Jörg Trenz and Klaus Eder, 'The democratizing dynamics of a European public sphere: towards a theory of democratic functionalism', *European Journal of Social Theory* 7, no. 1 (2004), pp. 5–25.

170 *Ibid.*, p. 9.

171 Klaus Eder, 'Europa als besonderer Kommunikationsraum: Zur Frage der sozialen Integration einer kulturell heterogenen Gemeinschaft', *Berliner Journal für Soziologie* 1 (2007), pp. 33–50.

172 Hans-Jörg Trenz and Klaus Eder, 'The democratizing dynamics of a European public sphere: towards a theory democratic functionalism', p. 18.

173 Patrick Bijsmans and Christina Altides, 'Bridging the gap between EU politics and citizens? The European Commission, national media and EU affairs in the public sphere', *Journal of European Integration* 29, no. 3 (2007), pp. 323–40; cf. also Marianne van de Steeg, 'Rethinking the conditions for a public sphere in the European Union', *European Journal of Social Theory* 5, no. 4 (2002), pp. 499–519.

174 Jackie Harrison and Lorna Woods, 'European citizenship: can audio-visual policy make a difference?', *Journal of Common Market Studies* 38, no. 3 (2000), pp. 471–95.

175 John Downey and Thomas Koenig, 'Is there a European public sphere? The Berlusconi–Schulz case', *European Journal of Communication* 21, no. 2 (2006), pp. 165–87.

176 Klaus Eder, 'Europe's borders: the narrative construction of the boundaries of Europe, *European Journal of Social Theory* 9, no. 2 (2006), pp. 255–71.

177 Cf. Robert Axelrod, *The Evolution of Cooperation* (New York: Basic Books, 1984); Robert Axelrod, *The Complexity of Cooperation* (Princeton, NJ: Princeton University Press, 1997).

178 In contrast to the norm-based arguments of benevolent functions of collective identity for cooperation, a reverse argument is offered by Sylvia Kritzinger, who examines collective identity as a dependent variable seeking to explain its development. She argues that citizens' utilitarian expectations towards the European level can explain variations in European identity. As a consequence, it is argued that a political system that is expected to be efficient can gain identity. Sylvia Kritzinger, 'European identity building from the perspective of efficiency', *Comparative European Politics* 3, no. 1 (2005), pp. 50–75.

179 David Rousseau and A. Maurits van der Veen, 'The emergence of a shared identity: an agent-based computer simulation of idea diffusion', *Journal of Conflict Resolution* 49, no. 5 (2005), pp. 686–712; cf. also Erin I. Kelly and Lionel K. McPherson, 'Prisoner's mistrust', *Ratio* XX, no. 1 (2007), pp. 57–70.

180 Suzanne Lohmann, 'Linkage politics', *Journal of Conflict Resolution* 41, no. 1 (1997), pp. 38–67; Thomas Gehring, *Die Europäische Union als komplexe internationale Organisation: Wie durch Kommunikation und Entscheidung soziale Ordnung entsteht* (Baden-Baden: Nomos, 2002).

181 Cf. Morten Egeberg, 'Transcending intergovernmentalism? Identity and role perceptions of national officials in EU decision-making', *Journal of European Public Policy* 6, no. 3 (1999), pp. 456–74.

182 Cf. Michael Zürn and Jeffrey T. Checkel, 'Getting socialized to build bridges: constructivism and rationalism, Europe and the nation-state', *International Organization* 59 (2005), pp. 1045–79.

183 Antje Wiener, 'Contested meanings of norms: a research framework', *Comparative European Politics* 5 (2007), pp. 1–7; Antje Wiener, 'Comment: fact or artefact? Analysing core constitutional norms in beyond-the-state contexts', *Journal of European Public Policy* 13, no. 8 (2006), pp. 1308–13.

184 Cf. the argument with regard to institutions in a larger sense, Jeffrey T. Checkel, 'Social construction and integration', *Journal of European Public Policy* 6, no. 4 (1999), pp. 545–60. See also Thomas Christiansen et al. (eds), *The Social Construction of Europe* (London: Sage, 2001).

185 Andreas Føllesdal, 'Union citizenship: unpacking the beast of burden', *Law and Philosophy* 20, no. 3 (2001), pp. 313–43, esp. p. 315.

186 Mete Eilstrup-Sangiovanni and Daniel Verdier, 'European integration as a solution to war', *European Journal of International Relations* 11, no. 1 (2005), pp. 99–135.

Chapter 4: Reconceptualizing the citizenship-collective identity nexus

1 I will deal with this issue in more detail in the chapter on the politics of insecurity in the EU.

2 Daniel Fuss and Marita A. Grosser, 'What makes young Europeans feel European? Results from a cross-cultural research project', in Ireneusz P. Karolewski and Viktoria Kaina (eds), *European Identity: Theoretical Perspectives and Empirical Insights* (Muenster: Lit, 2006), pp. 209–241, esp. p. 229.

3 Cf. Jai Kwan Jung, 'Growing supranational identities in a globalising world? A multilevel analysis of the World Value Surveys', *European Journal of Political Research* 47, no. 5 (2008), pp. 578–609.

4 Andreas Føllesdal, 'Union citizenship: unpacking the beast of burden', *Law and Philosophy* 20, no. 3 (2001), pp. 313–43, esp. p. 322; cf. also Maeve Cooke, 'Beyond dignity and difference: revisiting the politics of recognition', *European Journal of Political Theory* 8, no. 1 (2009), pp. 76–95.

5 Cf. Gwendolyn Sasse, 'Kymlicka's odyssey lured by norms into the rocks of politics', *Ethnicities* 8, no. 1 (2008), pp. 265–70; Christine Chwaszcza, 'The theory and practice of multicultural theorizing', *Ethnicities* 8, no. 1 (2008), pp. 261–65.

6 Cf. Ronald Inglehart, 'Cognitive mobilization and European identity', *Comparative Politics* 3, no. 1 (1970), pp. 45–70.

7 Nicola Bücker, 'Returning to where? Images of Europe and support for the process of EU integration in Poland', in Ireneusz P. Karolewski and Viktoria Kaina (eds), *European Identity: Theoretical Perspectives and Empirical Insights* (Muenster: Lit, 2006), pp. 265–93, esp. p. 268; Juan Díez Medrano and Paula Gutiérrez, 'Nested identities: national and European identity in Spain', *Ethnic and Racial Studies* 24, no. 5 (2001), pp. 753–78, esp. p. 755.

8 Andrzej Marcin Suszycki, 'European identity in Sweden', in Ireneusz P. Karolewski and Viktoria Kaina (eds), *European Identity: Theoretical Perspectives and Empirical Insights* (Muenster: Lit, 2006), pp. 179–207, esp. p. 200.

9 Cf. Krishan Kumar, 'The question of European identity: Europe in the American mirror', *European Journal of Social Theory* 11, no. 1 (2008), pp. 87–105.

10 Cf. Martin Kohli, 'The battlegrounds of European identity', *European Societies* 2, no. 2 (2000), pp. 113–37; cf. also Lea Ypi, 'Sovereignty, cosmopolitanism and ethics of European foreign policy', *European Journal of Political Theory* 7, no. 3 (2008), pp. 349–64.

11 Cf. Carlos Closa, 'Deliberative constitutional politics and the turn towards a norms-based legitimacy of the EU constitution', *European Law Journal* 11, no. 4 (2005), pp. 411–31.

12 Cf. Chris Hilson, 'Legitimacy and rights in the EU: questions of identity', *Journal of European Public Policy* 14, no. 4 (2007), pp. 527–43.

13 I will deal with this issue in more detail in the chapter on inflation of rights in the EU.

14 Cf. for instance Carla Hesse, 'Revolutionary historiography after the cold war', *Journal of Modern History* 73, no. 4 (2001), pp. 897–907; Jeremy Leaman, 'The decontamination of German history: Jürgen Habermas and the Historikerstreit in West Germany', *Economy and Society* 17, no. 4 (1988), pp. 518–29; Jürgen Habermas, 'A kind of settlement of damages', *Economy and Society* 17, no. 4 (1988), pp. 530–42; Stephen Brockmann, 'The politics of German history', *History and Theory* 29, no. 2 (1990), pp. 179–89; Waldemar Westergaard, 'Danish history and Danish historians', *Journal of Modern History* 24, no. 2 (1952), pp. 167–80; Jacques Adler, 'The jews and Vichy: reflections on French historiography', *Historical Journal* 44, no. 4 (2001), pp. 1065–82; Ulrich Schlie, 'Today's view of the Third Reich and the Second World War in German historiographical discourse', *Historical Journal* 43, no. 2 (2000), pp.

543–64; James J. Sheehan, 'What is German history? Reflections on the role of the nation in German history and historiography', *Journal of Modern History* 53, no. 1 (1981), pp. 1–23; Norman M. Naimark, 'The Nazis and the East: Jedwabne's circle of hell', *Slavic Review* 61, no. 3 (2002), pp. 476–82; Theodore S. Hamerow, 'Review. Guilt, redemption, and writing German history', *American Historical Review* 88, no. 1 (1983), pp. 53–72.

15 Cf. Maria Mälksoo, *The Discourse of Communist Crimes in the European Memory Politics of World War II*, Paper presented at the ideology and Discourse Analysis conference 'Rethinking Political Frontiers and Democracy in a New World Order', Roskilde University, Denmark, 8–10 September 2008.

16 For the role of trauma regarding construction of identity and community see for instance the following articles: Emma Hutchinson and Roland Bleiker, 'Emotional reconciliation: reconstituting identity and community after trauma', *European Journal of Social Theory* 11, no. 3 (2008), pp. 385–403; Jeffrey Prager, 'Healing from history: psychoanalytic considerations on traumatic pasts and social repair', *European Journal of Social Theory* 11, no. 3 (2008), pp. 405–20.

17 Piotr Sztompka, 'Cultural trauma: the other face of social change', *European Journal of Social Theory* 3, no. 4 (2000), pp. 449–66, esp. p. 464.

18 Cf. Krishan Kumar, 'The question of European identity: Europe in the American mirror', *European Journal of Social Theory* 11, no. 1 (2008), pp. 87–105; Bryan Turner, 'Outline of a theory of citizenship', *Sociology* 24, no. 2 (1990), pp. 189–217, esp. p. 197; John T. S. Madeley, 'European liberal democracy and the principle of state religious neutrality', *West European Politics* 26, no. 1 (2003), pp. 1–22.

19 Liah Greenfeld, 'Is nation unavoidable? Is nation unavoidable today?' in Hanspeter Kriesi et al. (eds), *Nation and National Identity: The European Experience in Perspective* (Zürich: Verlag Rüegger, 1999), pp. 37–54, esp. p. 40.

20 Phillipe C. Schmitter, 'Representations and the future Euro-polity', *Staatswissenschaften und Staatspraxis* 3, no. 3 (1992), pp. 379–405; Giandomenico Majone, *Regulating Europe* (London: Routledge, 1996). Markus Jachtenfuchs et al., 'Which Europe? Conflicting models of legitimate European political order', *European Journal of International Relations* 4, no. 4 (1998), pp. 409–45.

21 Cf. Simon Hix, 'The study of the European Union II: the new governance agenda and its rival', *Journal of European Public Policy* 5, no. 1 (1998), pp. 38–65.

22 Michael Walzer, *On Toleration* (New Haven, CT: Yale University Press, 1997), esp. pp. 14–51.

23 Cf. Jan Ifversen, 'Europe and European culture – a conceptual analysis', *European Societies* 4, no. 1 (2002), pp. 1–26.

24 Cf. Carlos Closa, 'Between EU constitutionalism and individuals' self: European citizenship', *Law and Philosophy* 20, no. 3 (2001), pp. 345–71.

25 Cf. John S. Brady, 'Incorrigible beliefs and democratic deliberation: a critique of Stanley Fish', *Constellations* 13, no. 3 (2006), pp. 374–93.

26 Cf. Cass R. Sunstein, 'Ideological amplification', *Constellations* 14, no. 2 (2007), pp. 273–79; Robert L. Ivie, 'Rhetorical deliberation and democratic politics in the here and now', *Rhetoric and Public Affairs* 5, no. 2 (2002), pp. 277–85.

27 Cf. Kristina Boréus, 'Discursive discrimination: a typology', *European Journal of Social Theory* 9, no. 3 (2006), pp. 405–24.

28 Mihaela Czabor-Lupp, 'Intercultural understanding: a critical discussion of Habermas', *European Journal of Political Theory* 7. No. 4 (2008), pp. 430–48.

29 I will deal with these issues in more detail in the chapter on the deliberation pathologies in the EU.

30 Cf. Pablo Gilbert, 'The substantive dimension of deliberative practical rationality', *Philosophy and Social Criticism* 31, no. 2 (2005), pp. 185–210.

31 Gary Shiffman, 'Construing disagreement: consensus and invective in constitutional debate', *Political Theory* 30, no. 2 (2002), pp. 175–203.

32 Christian Joerges, 'Deliberative political processes revisited: what have we learnt about the legitimacy of supranational decision-making', *Journal of Common Market Studies* 44, no. 4 (2006), pp. 779–802; Jürgen Neyer, 'Explaining the unexpected: efficiency and effectiveness in European decision-making', *Journal of European Public Policy* 11, no. 1 (2004), pp. 19–38.

33 Cf. Jan Zielonka, 'The quality of democracy after joining the European Union', *East European Politics and Societies* 21, no. 1 (2007), pp. 162–80; Paul Blokker, 'Post-communist modernization, transition studies, and diversity in Europe', *European Journal of Social Theory* 8, no. 4 (2005), pp. 503–25.

34 Cf. Winfried Thaa, 'Lean citizenship: the fading away of the political in transnational democracy', *European Journal of International Relations* 7, no. 4 (2001), pp. 503–23, esp. p. 514.

35 Erik O. Eriksen argues himself that public sphere segmentation is the dominant feature of the EU. Erik O. Eriksen, *Conceptualizing European Public Spheres: General, Segmented and Strong Publics* (Oslo: Arena, Centre for European Studies at the University of Oslo, 2004), Working Paper 3/04.

36 Cathleen Kantner, *Kein modernes Babel: Kommunikative Voraussetzungen europäischer Öffentlichkeit* (Wiesbaden: VS Verlag, 2004), p. 163; Ruud Koopmans and Barbara Pfetsch, 'Obstacles or motors of Europeanization? German media and the transnationalization of public debate', *Communications* 31, no. 2 (2006), pp. 115–38.

37 Kantner, *op. cit.*, p. 175; cf. Klaus Eder, 'Cognitive sociology and the theory of communicative action: the role of communication and language in the making of the social bond', *European Journal of Social Theory* 10, no. 3 (2007), pp. 389–408.

38 Stefanie Sifft et al., 'Segmented Europeanization: exploring the legitimacy of the European Union from a public discourse perspective', *Journal of Common Market Studies* 45, no. 1 (2007), pp. 127–55; Maximilian Conrad, *A European Public Sphere and the Issue of Permeability: The Debate on the Constitutional Treaty in Two Swedish Quality Newspapers* (Lund: Centre for European Studies at Lund University, 2006), CFE Working Paper 31.

39 A similar argument has been made by Karl W. Deutsch, who argued that intensification of communication flows would eventually spawn a feeling of belonging or commonality. Karl W. Deutsch, 'On communication models in the social sciences', *The Public Opinion Quarterly* 16, no. 3 (1952), pp. 356–80; Karl W. Deutsch, 'The growth of nations: some recurrent patterns of political and social integration', *World Politics* 5, no. 2 (1953), pp. 168–95.

40 For a similar argument cf. Michael Zürn, *Regieren jenseits des Nationalstaates* (Frankfurt: Suhrkamp, 1998), p. 272.

41 Cf. Hans-Peter Müller, 'Auf dem Weg in eine europäische Gesellschaft? Begriffsproblematik und theoretische Perspektiven', *Berliner Journal für Soziologie* 1 (2007), pp. 7–31; cf. also Zygmunt Baumann, 'Chasing elusive society', *International Journal of Politics, Culture and Society* 18, no. 3–4 (2005), pp. 123–41.

42 Cf. Philippe C. Schmitter, 'Citizenship in an eventual Euro-democracy', *Swiss Political Science Review* 4, no. 4 (1998), pp. 141–68.

43 Cf. Morten Egeberg, 'Transcending intergovernmentalism? Identity and role perceptions of national officials in EU decision-making', *Journal of European Public Policy* 6, no. 3 (1999), pp. 456–74; Paul Magnette, 'European governance and civic participation: beyond elitist citizenship?', *Political Studies* 51, no. 1 (2003), pp. 144–60.

44 Cf. Fritz W. Scharpf, 'Games real actors could play: positive and negative coordination in embedded negotiations', *Journal of Theoretical Politics* 6, no. 1 (1994), pp. 27–53.

45 Cf. Helen Wallace, 'Whose Europe is it anyway? The 1998 Stein Rokkan lecture', *European Journal of Political Research* 35, no. 3 (1999), pp. 287–306.

46 Cf. Sylvia Kritzinger, 'European identity building from the perspective of efficiency', *Comparative European Politics* 3, no. 1 (2005), pp. 50–75.

47   Cf. Gerald Schneider and Claudia Seybold, 'Twelve tongues, one voice: an evaluation of European political cooperation', *European Journal of Political Research* 31, no. 4 (1997), pp. 367–96.

48   Kees van Kersbergen, 'Political allegiance and European integration', *European Journal of Political Research* 37, no. 1 (2000), pp. 1–17.

49   Cf. Klaus Armingeon, 'From the Europe of nations to the European nation: introduction', in Hanspeter Kriesi et al. (eds), *Nation and National Identity: The European Experience in Perspective* (Zürich: Verlag Rüegger, 1999), pp. 235–42, esp. p. 238; Bruce Russett, *Grasping the Democratic Peace: Principles for a Post-Cold War World* (Princeton, NJ: Princeton University Press, 1993); Thomas Risse-Kappen, 'Democratic peace – warlike democracies? A social constructivist interpretation of the liberal argument', *European Journal of International Relations* 1, no. 4 (1995), pp. 491–517.

50   Hermann Lübbe, *Abschied vom Superstaat: Vereinigte Staaten von Europa wird es nicht geben* (München: Siedler, 1994).

51   Cf. Joel M. Guttman, 'Repeated interaction and the evolution of preferences for reciprocity', *Economic Journal* 113, no. 489 (2003), pp. 631–56; Robert O. Keohane, 'Reciprocity in international relations', *International Organization* 40, no. 1 (1986), pp. 1–27.

52   Erik Gartzke and Kristian Skrede Gleditsch, 'Identity and conflict: ties that bind and differences that divide', *European Journal of International Relations* 12, no. 1 (2006), pp. 53–87.

53   Charles Taylor, *Reconciling the Solitudes: Essays on Canadian Federalism* (Montreal: McGill-Queen's University Press, 1993).

54   For the opposite idea of territorial identity see Gary Marks, 'Territorial identities in the European Union', in Jeffrey Anderson (ed.), *Regional Integration and Democracy* (New York: Rowman & Littlefield, 1999), pp. 69–91. The problem of the concept of territorial attachment is that it fails to account for citizens' behaviour. The attachment to territory cannot be translated into an attachment to community. We therefore do not know whether the territorial attachments of individuals have any impact on their commitment to their communities (territorial or otherwise).

55   Cf. Cris Shore, 'Whither European citizenship? Eros and civilization revisited', *European Journal of Social Theory* 7, no. 1 (2004), pp. 27–44.

56   Claus Offe, 'Homogeneity and constitutional democracy: coping with identity conflicts through group rights', *Journal of Political Philosophy* 6, no. 2 (1998), p. 115.

57   Some authors would add empathy to the list, which would shift it more strongly towards Rousseau's political thought. Cf. Andreas Føllesdal, 'Union citizenship: unpacking the beast of burden', *Law and Philosophy* 20, no. 3 (2001), p. 337.

58   Norbert Elias, *The Society of Individuals* (New York: Continuum, 1991), esp. Chapter III.

59   *Ibid.*, p. 207.

60   *Ibid.*, p. 219.

61   Cf. Zygmunt Bauman, 'Identity in the globalizing world', *Social Anthropology* 9, no. 2 (2001), pp. 121–29.

62   Klaus Eder, 'The two faces of Europeanization: synchronizing a Europe moving at varying speeds', *Time & Society* 13, no. 1 (2004), pp. 89–107.

63   Cf. Steven J. Sherman, David L. Hamilton and Amy C. Lewis, 'Perceived entitativity and the social identity value of group memberships', in Dominic Abrams and Michael Hogg (eds), *Social Identity and Social Cognition* (Oxford: Blackwell, 1999), pp. 80–110.

64   Cf. Niklas Luhmann, 'Differentiation of society', *Canadian Journal of Sociology* 2, no. 1 (1977), pp. 29–53.

65   Cf. Jos de Beus, 'Quasi-national European identity and European democracy', *Law and Philosophy* 20, no. 3 (2001), pp. 283–311.

66   Tariq Modood, 'Anti-essentialism, multiculturalism and the recognition of religious groups', *Journal of Political Philosophy* 6, no. 4 (1998), pp. 378–99.

67 Cf. Rogers Brubaker, 'Ethnicity without groups', in Rogers Brubaker, *Ethnicity without Groups* (Cambridge, MA: Harvard University Press, 2004), pp. 7–27, esp. p. 11.

68 Cf. Omid Payrow Shabani, 'Constitutional patriotism as a model of postnational political association: the case of the EU', *Philosophy and Social Criticism* 32, no. 6 (2006), pp. 699–718.

69 In this context, sympathy would be regarded as an unreliable moral resource, unable to generate thick identity.

70 Cf. Bert Klandermans, 'How group identification helps to overcome the dilemma of collective action', *American Behavioral Scientist* 45, no. 5 (2002), pp. 887–900.

71 Cf. Lars-Erik Cederman, 'Nationalism and bounded integration: what it would take to construct a European demos', *European Journal of International Relations* 7, no. 2 (2001), pp. 139–74.

72 Cf. Mikko Kuisma, 'Rights or privileges? The challenge of globalization to the values of citizenship', *Citizenship Studies* 12, no. 6 (2008), pp. 613–27.

73 Cf. Hubertus Buchstein, 'Die Zumutungen der Demokratie. Von der normativen Theorie des Bürgers zur institutionell vermittelten Präferenzkompetenz', in Klaus von Beyme and Claus Offe (eds), *Politische Theorien in der Ära der Transformation* (Opladen: Westdeutscher Verlag, 1995), pp. 295–324.

74 Ulrich K. Preuß, 'Two challenges to European citizenship', in Richard Bellamy and Dario Castiglione (eds), *Constitutionalism in Transformation: European and Theoretical Perspectives* (Oxford: Blackwell, 1996), pp. 122–40; Richard Bellamy, 'Evaluating Union citizenship: belonging, rights and participation within the EU', *Citizenship Studies* 12, no. 6 (2008), pp. 597–611.

75 Cf. Lynn Jamieson, 'Theorising identity, nationality and citizenship: implications for European citizenship identity', *Sociológia* (Slovak Sociological Review) 34, no. 6 (2002), pp. 507–32.

76 Aristotle, *Politics* 1253 a I; Isaac Logs, 'The political philosophy of Aristotle', *Annals of the American Academy of Political and Social Science* 10, no. 3 (1897), pp. 313–33; Patrick Coby, 'Aristotle's four conceptions of politics', *Political Research Quarterly* 39, no. 3 (1986), pp. 480–503.

77 Some authors also regard Baruch Spinoza as a co-founder of liberalism, while others disagree. Julie Cooper, 'Freedom of speech and philosophical citizenship in Spinoza's theologico–political treatise', *Law, Culture and the Humanities* 2, no. 1 (2006), pp. 91–114. That the works of John Stuart Mill were essential for the development of the liberal doctrine appears, however, to be consensual. See Shannon C. Stimson and Murray Milgate, 'Mill, liberty and the facts of life', *Political Studies* 49, no. 2 (2001), pp. 231–48.

78 John Locke, *Two Treatises of Government* (Cambridge: Cambridge University Press, 1988[1690]); David Hume, *Treatise of Human Nature* (New York: Prometheus Books, 1992[1739]); Margaret Kohn, 'The passion of liberalism', *Political Theory* 34, no. 4 (2006), pp. 499–505. For a comparison between liberalism and republicanism see Geoffrey Brennan and Loren Lomasky, 'Against reviving republicanism', *Politics, Philosophy and Economics* 5, no. 2 (2006), pp. 221–52; Richard H. Fallon Jr., 'What is republicanism, and is it worth reviving?', *Harvard Law Review* 102, no. 7 (1989), pp. 1695–1735.

79 David Hume, *Treatise of Human Nature*, p. 534ff; Christopher J. Finlay, 'Hume's theory of civil society', *European Journal of Political Theory* 3, no. 4 (2004) pp. 369–91.

80 Thomas Hobbes, *Leviathan, or the Matter, Form and Power of a Commonwealth, Ecclesiastical and Civil*, edited with an introduction by J.C. A. Gashin (Oxford: Oxford University Press (1996 [1651])); Carl Schmitt, *The Concept of the Political*, translated and with an introduction by George Schwab (Chicago, IL: University of Chicago Press, 1996 [1932]).

81 Thomas H. Marshall, *Citizenship and Social Class* (London: Pluto Press, 1992 [1950]).

82 Derek Heater, *Citizenship: The Civic Ideal in World History, Politics and Education* (London: Longman, 1990).

83 Jean-Jacques Rousseau, *Du contrat social ou principes du droit politique* (Paris: GF Flammarion, 1999 [1762]); Michael J. Sandel, 'Liberalism and republicanism: friends or foes? A reply to Richard Dagger', *Review of Politics* 61, no. 2 (1999), pp. 209–14; Marcia L. Colish, 'The idea of liberty in Machiavelli', *Journal of the History of Ideas* 32, no. 3 (1971), pp. 323–50; Carl K.Y. Shaw, 'Quentin Skinner on the proper meaning of republican liberty', *Politics* 23, no. 1 (2003), pp. 46–56.

84 Richard K. Dagger, 'What is political obligation?', *American Political Science Review* 71, no. 1 (1977), pp. 86–94; cf. also Shlomi Segall, 'Political participation as an engine of social solidarity: a sceptical view', *Political Studies* 53, no. 2 (2005), pp. 362–78.

85 David Miller, 'Holding nations responsible', *Ethics* 114, no. 1 (2004), pp. 240–68; Andrew Mason, 'Special obligations to compatriots', *Ethics* 107, no. 3 (1997), pp. 427–47; Paul Brest, 'Further beyond the republican revival: toward radical republicanism', *Yale Law Journal* 97, no. 8 (1988), pp. 1623–31; David Miller, 'Caney's international distributive justice': a response', *Political Studies* 50, no. 5 (2002), pp. 974–77.

86 Jean-Jacques Rousseau, *Du contrat social ou principes du droit politique*, p. 143; Angus Stewart, 'Two conceptions of citizenship', *Birtish Journal of Sociology* 46, no. 1 (1995), pp. 63–78; W. Jay Reedy, 'The relevance of Rousseau to contemporary communitarianism: the example of Benjamin Barber', *Philosophy and Social Criticism* 21, no. 2 (1995), pp. 51–84; Melissa Schwartzberg, 'Rousseau on fundamental law', *Political Studies* 51, no. 2 (2003), pp. 387–403.

87 Cf. Greg Hill, 'Citizenship and ontology in the liberal state', *Review of Politics* 55, no. 1 (1993), pp. 67–84; Christopher Nadon, 'Aristotle and the republican paradigm: a reconsideration of Pocock's Machiavellian moment', *Review of Politics* 58, no. 4 (1996), pp. 677–98; Frederic C. Lane, 'At the roots of republicanism', *American Historical Review* 71, no. 2 (1966), pp. 403–20.

88 Cf. Arne Johan Vetlesen, 'Hannah Arendt, Habermas and the republican tradition', *Philosophy and Social Criticism* 21, no. 1 (1995), pp. 1–16.

89 Cf. Richard Dagger, 'Neo-republicanism and the civic economy', *Politics, Philosophy and Economics* 5, no. 2 (2006), pp. 151–73; Joel Isaac, 'Republicanism: a European inheritance?', *European Journal of Social Theory* 8, no. 1 (2005), pp. 73–86.

90 Jon D. Michaels, 'To promote the general welfare: the republican imperative to enhance citizenship welfare rights', *Yale Law Journal* 111, no. 6 (2002), pp. 1457–98; Keith Faulks, 'Rethinking citizenship education in England. Some lessons from contemporary social and political theory', *Education, Citizenship and Social Justice* 1, no. 2 (2006), pp. 123–40; Ruth Lister, 'Towards a citizens' welfare state: the 3 + 2 'R's of welfare reform', *Theory, Culture & Society* 18, no. 2–3 (2001), pp. 91–111.

91 Cf. Robert Goodin, *Reasons for Welfare: The Political Theory of the Welfare State* (Princeton, NJ: Princeton University Press, 1988); David Schmidz and Robert Goodin, *Social Welfare and Individual Responsibility* (Cambridge: Cambridge University Press, 1998). See, however, the Hannah Arendt's critique of the welfare state: Ferenc Feher, 'The pariah and the citizen (on Arendt's political theory), *Thesis Eleven* 15, no. 1 (1986), pp. 15–29.

92 Cf. Lionel A. McKenzie, 'Rousseau's debate with Machiavelli in the social contract', *Journal of the History of Ideas* 43, no. 2 (1982), pp. 209–28; Ethan Putterman, 'Realism and reform in Rousseau's constitutional projects for Poland and Corsica', *Political Studies* 49, no. 3 (2001), pp. 481–94.

93 Michael Ignatieff, 'The myth of citizenship', in Ronald Beiner (ed.), *Theorizing Citizenship* (Albany, NY: State University of New York Press, 1995), pp. 53–78, esp. p. 58.

94 April Carter, 'Liberalism and the obligation to military service', *Political Studies* XLVI, no. 1 (1998), pp. 68–81; cf. also Dario Castiglione, 'Republicanism and its legacy', *European Journal of Political Theory* 4, no. 4 (2005), pp. 453–65.

95 Raymond Aron, 'Is multinational citizenship possible?', *Social Research* 41, no. 4 (1974), pp. 638–56.

96 Aristotle, *Politics*, 1275b, 1279a.

97 Geoffrey Gershenson, 'The rise and fall of species-life: Rousseau's critique of liberalism', *European Journal of Political Theory* 5, no. 3 (2006) pp. 281–300.

98 Rousseau, *Du contrat social,* 2001[1762]: I, II.

99 Hubertus Buchstein, *Private Öffentlichkeit: Online Wahlen und Demokratietheorie,* Paper presented in the section 'Politische Theorien und Ideengeschichte' at the 22nd congress of the DVPW on 23 September 2003, Mainz, esp. p. 28.

100 Cf. Maeve Cooke, 'A space of one's own: autonomy, privacy, liberty', *Philosophy and Social Criticism* 26, no. 1 (1999), pp. 23–53; Gal Gerson, 'Deliberative households: republicans, liberals, and the public–private split', *Political Research Quarterly* 57, no. 4 (2004), pp. 653–63.

101 Joshua Cohen, 'Deliberation and democratic legitimacy', in Alan Hamlin and Philip Pettit (eds), *The Good Polity: Normative Analysis of the State* (Cambridge: Blackwell, 1989), pp. 17–34.

102 Cécile Fabre, 'To deliberate or to discourse: is that the question?', *European Journal of Political Theory* 2, no. 1 (2003), pp. 107–15; Sally J. Scholz, 'Dyadic deliberation versus discursive democracy', *Political Theory* 30, no. 5 (2002), pp. 746–50.

103 Cf. Bernard Manin, 'On legitimacy and political deliberation', *Political Theory* 15, no. 3 (1987), pp. 338–68.

104 Denise Vitale, 'Between deliberative and participatory democracy: a contribution on Habermas', *Philosophy and Social Criticism* 32, no. 6 (2006), pp. 739–66.

105 Cf. Jeffrey Flynn, 'Communicative power in Habermas's theory of democracy', *European Journal of Political Theory* 3, no. 4 (2004), pp. 433–54; Bernard Yack, 'Rhetoric and public reasoning: an Aristotelian understanding of political deliberation', *Political Theory* 34, no. 4 (2006), pp. 417–38; Kenneth Shockley, 'On participation and membership in discursive practices', *Philosophy of the Social Sciences* 36, no. 1 (2006), pp. 67–85.

106 John S. Dryzek, 'Deliberative democracy in divided societies: alternatives to agonism and analgesia', *Political Theory* 33, no. 2 (2005), pp. 218–42; James Bohman, 'Reflexive public deliberation: democracy and the limits of pluralism', *Philosophy and Social Criticism* 29, no. 1 (2003), pp. 85–105.

107 Cf. Richard A. Epstein, 'Modern republicanism: or the flight from substance', *Yale Law Journal* 97, no. 8 (1988), pp. 1633–50.

108 Cf. Jürgen Habermas, 'Reconciliation through the public use of reason: remarks on John Rawls's political liberalism', *Journal of Philosophy* 92, no. 3 (1995), pp. 109–31. However, some republican authors see limitations of public deliberation in respect of cultural conflicts. Cf. James Bohman, 'Reflexive public deliberation: democracy and the limits of pluralism', *Philosophy & Social Criticism* 29, no. 1 (2003), pp. 85–105. In this sense, public deliberation would require a substantive dimension apart from the purely procedural propagated by Jürgen Habermas. However, giving public deliberation more substance shifts it again from procedural universalism towards republicanism. Cf. Pablo Gilabert, 'The substantive dimension of deliberative practical rationality', *Philosophy & Social Criticism* 31, no. 2 (2005), pp. 185–210.

109 Cf. Morag Patrick, 'Liberalism, rights and recognition', *Philosophy and Social Criticism* 26, no. 5 (2000), pp. 28–46; Jason A. Scorza, 'Liberal citizenship and civic friendship', *Political Theory* 32, no. 1 (2004), pp. 85–108.

110 Cf. Patrick Riley, 'Locke on voluntary agreement and political power', *Political Research Quarterly* 29, no. 1 (1976), pp. 136–45; Bart van Leeuwen, 'Social attachments as conditions for the condition of the good life? A critique of Will Kymlicka's moral monism', *Philosophy and Social Criticism* 32, no.3 (2006), pp. 401–28.

111 John Locke, *Two Treatises of Government* (Cambridge: Cambridge University Press, 1988 [1690]), esp. Chapter V; Charles Larmore, 'Political liberalism', *Political Theory* 18, no. 3 (1990), pp. 339–60; Jeremy Waldron, 'Theoretical foundations of liberalism', *Philosophical Quarterly* 37, no. 147 (1987), pp. 127–50.

112 Cf. Cynthia J. McSwain, 'Administrators and citizenship: the liberalist legacy of the constitution', *Administration and Society* 17, no. 2 (1985), pp. 131–48.

113   John Locke, *Two Treatises of Government*, esp. Chapter XIX; Martin Seliger, 'Locke's theory of revolutionary action', *Political Research Quarterly* 16, no. 3 (1963), pp. 548–68; Thomas S. Langston and Michael E. Lind, 'John Locke and the limits of presidential prerogative', *Polity* 24, no. 1 (1991), pp. 49–68.

114   Michael Ignatieff, 'The myth of citizenship', p. 61; Brian Barry, 'Liberalism and want-satisfaction: a critique of John Rawls', *Political Theory* 1, no. 2 (1973), pp. 134–53.

115   This is not to say that in the liberal citizenship democracy is associated with chaos and insecurity.

116   J. Donald Moon, 'Liberalism, autonomy, and moral pluralism', *Political Theory* 31, no. 1 (2003), pp. 125–35.

117   Cf. Philip Pettit, 'Freedom in the market', *Politics, Philosophy and Economics* 5, no. 2 (2006), pp. 131–49.

118   Robert Nozick, *Anarchy, State, and Utopia* (Oxford: Oxford University Press, 1974); Robert Nozick, 'Distributive justice', *Philosophy and Public Affairs* 3, no. 1 (1973), pp. 45–126; cf. also Christopher John Nock, 'Equal freedom and unequal property: a critique of Nozick's libertarian case', *Canadian Journal of Political Science* 25, no. 4 (1992), pp. 677–95.

119   David Hume, *Treatise of Human Nature*, p. 539.

120   T. H. Marshall, *Citizenship and Social Class*, p. 16; Janine Brodie, 'Citizenship and solidarity: reflections on the Canadian way', *Citizenship Studies* 6, no. 4 (2002), pp. 377–94.

121   Kenneth J. Arrow, *Social Choice and Individual Values* (New Haven, CT: Yale University Press, 1951); William Riker, 'Comment on Radcliff's "Liberalism, populism, and collective choice"', *Political Research Quarterly* 46, no. 1 (1993), pp. 143–49; Amartya Sen, 'Goals, commitment, and identity', *Journal of Law, Economics, and Organization* 1, no. 2 (1985), pp. 341–55.

122   Thomas Hobbes, *Behemoth or the Long Parliament*, edited by Ferdinand Tönnies, with an introduction by Stephen Holmes (Chicago: University of Chicago Press, 1990 [1682]); Thomas Hobbes, *The Citizen (De Cive)*, edited by Bernard Gert (Indianapolis, IN: Hackett Publishing Company, 1991 [1642]); Thomas Hobbes, *Leviathan, or the Matter, Form and Power of a Commonwealth, Ecclesiastical and Civil*, edited with an introduction by J. C. A. Gashin (Oxford: Oxford University Press, 1996 [1651]).

123   Thomas Hobbes, *The Citizen*, 1991 [1642], p. 100ff. Some authors discover liberal elements in Hobbes' state theory. However, the mainstream liberalism rejects Hobbes as a liberal author and regards the Hobbes-orientated school of thought as not more than 'vulgar liberalism'. See Patrick Neal, 'Vulgar liberalism', *Political Theory* 21, no. 4 (1993), pp. 623–42.

124   Cf. Samantha Frost, 'Hobbes out of bounds', *Political Theory* 32, no. 2 (2004), pp. 257–73. As a further caesarean author we could identify Jean Bodin due to his focus on state sovereignty regarding internal conflicts. Jean Bodin, *Les six Livres de la République* (Paris: Aalen, 1961[1583]); Wm. A. Dunning, 'Jean Bodin on sovereignty', *Political Science Quarterly* 11, no. 1 (1896), pp. 82–104; Max Adams Shepard, 'Sovereignty at the crossroads: a study of Bodin', *Political Science Quarterly* 45, no. 4 (1930), pp. 580–603; Jacques Maritain, 'The concept of sovereignty', *American Political Science Review* 44, no. 2 (1950), pp. 343–57.

125   Patricia Springborg, 'Hobbes's biblical beasts: Leviathan and behemoth', *Political Theory* 23, no. 2 (1995), pp. 353–75; Philip Pettit, 'Liberty and Leviathan', *Politics, Philosophy and Economics* 4, no. 1 (2005), pp. 131–51; Richard Boyd, 'Thomas Hobbes and the perils of pluralism', *Journal of Politics* 63, no. 2 (2001), pp. 392–413.

126   Carl Schmitt, *Legality and Legitimacy*, translated and edited by Jeffrey Seitzer with an introduction by John P. McCormick (Durham: Duke University Press, 2004[1932]), p. 14; cf. also Carl Schmitt, *The Crisis of Parliamentary Democracy*, translated by Ellen Kennedy (Cambridge, MA: MIT Press, 1988[1923]); cf. Marc de Wilde, 'Safeguarding the constitution with and against Carl Schmitt', *Political Theory* 34, no. 4 (2006), pp.

510–15; Alexis de Tocqueville, *Democracy in America,* trans. George Lawrence, ed. J. P. Mayer (Garden City: Doubleday, 1964).

127 Carl Schmitt, *The Concept of the Political,* translated and with an introduction by George Schwab (Chicago, IL: University of Chicago Press, 1996[1932]), esp. pp. 27 and 77; William Rasch, 'Conflict as a vocation: Carl Schmitt and the possibility of politics', *Theory, Culture and Society* 17, no. 6 (2000), pp. 1–32; Giovanni Sartori, 'The essence of the political in Carl Schmitt', *Journal of Theoretical Politics* 1, no. 1 (1989), pp. 63–75.

128 Hobbes, *The Citizen,* p. 166; Bill Scheuerman, 'Modernist anti-modernism: Carl Schmitt's concept of the political', *Philosophy and Social Criticism* 19, no. 2 (1993), pp. 79–95.

129 John P. McCormick, 'Fear, technology, and the state: Carl Schmitt, Leo Strauss, and the revival of Hobbes in Weimar and national socialist Germany', *Political Theory* 22, no. 4 (1994), pp. 619–52.

130 Cf. Andreas Kalyvas; 'Hegemonic sovereignty: Carl Schmitt, Antonio Gramsci and the constituent prince', *Journal of Political Ideologies* 5, no. 3 (2000), pp. 343–76.

131 Schmitt, *Legality and Legitimacy,* p. 90.

132 *Ibid.,* p .89.

133 *Ibid.,* p. 77.

134 Carl Schmitt, *The Concept of the Political,* p. 37; cf. also Heinrich Meier, *Carl Schmitt, Leo Strauss und der Begriff des Politischen: Zu einem Dialog unter Abwesenden* (Stuttgart: J.B. Metzler, 1988).

135 For a study of the intellectual influence of Carl Schmitt by Thomas Hobbes see *inter alia* Helmut Rumpf, *Carl Schmitt und Thomas Hobbes: Ideelle Beziehungen und aktuelle Bedeutung* (Berlin: Duncker & Humblot, 1972).

136 Engin F. Isin, 'The neurotic citizen', *Citizenship Studies* 8, no. 3 (2004), pp. 217–35; David Lyon, 'The new surveillance: electronic technologies and the maximum security society', *Crime, Law and Social Change* 18, no. 1–2 (1992), pp. 159–75.

137 Cf. David Lyon, 'Technology vs. terrorism: circuits of city. Surveillance since September 11th', *International Journal of Urban and Regional Research* 27, no. 3 (2003), pp. 666–78; David Lyon, 'Globalizing surveillance: comparative and sociological Perspectives', *International Sociology* 19, no. 2 (2004), pp. 135–49.

138 William Walters, 'Secure border, safe haven, domopolitics', *Citizenship Studies* 8, no. 3 (2004), pp. 237–60.

139 Jef Huysmans, 'Minding exceptions: the politics of insecurity and liberal democracy', *Contemporary Political Theory* 3 (2004), pp. 321–41; Jef Huysmans, 'International politics of insecurity: normativity, inwardness and the exception', *Security Dialogue* 37, no. 1 (2006), pp. 11–29.

140 William Walters, 'Deportation, expulsion, and the international police of aliens', *Citizenship Studies* 6, no. 3 (2002), pp. 265–92; Paul Roes, 'Securitization and minority rights: conditions of desecuritization', *Security Dialogue* 35, no. 3 (2004), pp. 279–94.

141 Kalu N. Kalu, 'Of citizenship, virtue, and the administrative imperative: deconstructing Aristotelian civic republicanism', *Public Administration Review* 64, no. 4 (2003), pp. 418–27.

142 Cf. David Miller, 'Democracy and social justice', *British Journal of Political Science* 8, no. 1 (1978), pp. 1–19; Katherine Fierlbeck, 'Redefining responsibility: the politics of citizenship in the United Kingdom', *Canadian Journal of Political Science* 24, no. 3 (1991), pp. 575–93.

143 In a modern version of the republican citizenship, some authors even point to so-called republican rights, which protect the *res publica* against powerful citizens involved in rent-seeking to the detriment of the collectivity. Thus, the republican patrimony is defended against actions of individuals. Luiz Carlos Bresser-Pereira, 'Citizenship and res publica: the emergence of republican rights', *Citizenship Studies* 6, no. 2 (2002), pp. 145–64.

144 Thus, republicans exhibit a priority for compatriots against cosmopolitan global duties. Veit Bader, 'Reasonable impartiality and priority for compatriots: a criticism of liberal nationalism's main flaws', *Ethical Theory and Moral Practice* 8, no. 1–2 (2005), pp. 83–103. However, there are some approaches attempting to conceive of global republicanism stressing obligations to humanity, rather than to compatriots. These conceptions probably share more with liberal universalism than traditional republicanism. See James Bohman, 'Republican cosmopolitanism', *Journal of Political Philosophy* 12, no 3 (2004), pp. 336–52; James Bohman, 'Rights, cosmopolitanism and public reason: interactive universalism in the claims of culture', *Philosophy and Social Criticism* 31, no. 7 (2005), pp. 715–26; cf. also Simon Caney, 'Cosmopolitan justice and equalizing opportunities', *Metaphilosophy* 32, no. 1–2 (2001), pp. 113–34; Max Pensky, 'Two cheers for cosmopolitanism: cosmopolitan solidarity as second-order inclusion', *Journal of Social Philosophy* 38, no. 1 (2007), pp. 165–84.

145 Cf. Bart Pattyn, 'The emotional boundaries of our solidarity', *Ethical Perspectives* 3, no. 2 (1996), pp. 101–8; Lawrence Wilde, 'The concept of solidarity: emerging from the theoretical shadows', *British Journal of Politics and International Relations* 9, no. 1 (2007), pp. 171–81.

146 Cf. Shane Doheny, 'Responsibility and the deliberative citizen: theorizing the acceptance of individual and citizenship responsibilities', *Citizenship Studies* 11, no. 4 (2007), pp. 405–20.

147 Cf. David Miller, *On Nationality* (Oxford: Oxford University Press, 1995); Laura Andronache, 'A national identity republicanism?', *European Journal of Political Theory* 5, no. 4 (2006), pp. 399–414; cf. also James Burk, 'The citizen soldier and democratic societies: a comparative analysis of America's revolutionary and civil wars', *Citizenship Studies* 4, no 2 (2000), pp. 149–65.

148 Cf. Samuel Freeman, 'The burdens of public justification: constructivism, contractualism, and publicity', *Politics, Philosophy & Economics* 6, no. 1 (2007), pp. 5–43.

149 Gerry Mackie, 'Does democratic deliberation change minds?', *Politics, Philosophy & Economics* 5, no. 3 (2006) pp. 279–303; Dieter Misgeld, 'Discourse and conversation: the theory of communicative competence and hermeneutics in the light of the debate between Habermas and Gadamer', *Cultural Hermeneutics* 4, no. 4 (1977), pp. 321–44; Anne van Aaken, 'Deliberative institutional economics, or Does Homo oeconomicus argue? A proposal for combining new institutional economics with discourse theory', *Philosophy & Social Criticism* 28, no. 4 (2002), pp. 361–94.

150 S. M. Shumer, 'Machiavelli: republican politics and its corruption', *Political Theory* 7, no. 1 (1979), pp. 5–34. For the deliberative republicanism, corruption would equal paternalism and domination in public deliberation. Cf. Christian F. Rostbøll, 'Preferences and paternalism: on freedom and deliberative democracy', *Political Theory* 33, no. 3 (2005), pp. 370–96; Lasse Thomassen, 'The inclusion of the other? Habermas and the paradox of tolerance', *Political Theory* 34, no. 4 (2006), pp. 439–62.

151 Even though republicanism is open in principle, it shows ambivalence towards opening of borders and immigration, as the claim of solidarity loses its moral strength and validity with the enlarging scope of the community. Cf. Joseph H. Carens, 'Aliens and citizens: the case for open borders', *Review of Politics* 49, no. 2 (1987), pp. 251–73; Ratna Kapur, 'The citizen and the migrant: postcolonial anxieties, law, and the politics of exclusion/inclusion', *Theoretical Inquiries in Law* 8, no. 2 (2007), pp. 537–70; Randall Hansen, 'Migration, citizenship and race in Europe: between incorporation and exclusion', *European Journal of Political Research* 35, no. 4 (1999), pp. 415–44.

152 Cf. Susan M. Okin, 'Feminism and multiculturalism: some tensions', *Ethics* 108, no. 4 (1998), pp. 661–84; Eamonn Callan, *Creating Citizens: Political Education and Liberal Democracy* (Oxford: Oxford University Press, 1997); Seyla Benhabib, 'Beyond interventionism and indifference: culture, deliberation and pluralism', *Philosophy and Social Criticism* 31, no. 7 (2005), pp. 753–71; Christopher Jencks, 'Whom must we

treat equally for educational opportunity to be equal', *Ethics* 98, no. 3 (1988), pp. 518–33.

153 Cf. Claus Offe, 'Homogeneity and constitutional democracy: coping with identity conflicts through group rights', *Journal of Political Philosophy* 6, no 2 (1998), pp. 113–41; Yasmeen Abu-Laban, 'Liberalism, multiculturalism and the problem of essentialism', *Citizenship Studies* 6, no. 2 (2002), pp. 459–82.

154 Cynthia Ward, 'The limits of liberal republicanism: why group-based remedies and republican citizenship don't mix', *Columbia Law Review* 91, no. 3 (1991), pp. 581–607, esp. p. 598.

155 Michael Walzer, 'The civil society argument', in Roland S. Beiner (ed.), *Theorizing Citizenship* (Albany, NJ: State University of New York Press, 1995), pp. 153–74; Michael Walzer, 'Liberalism and the art of separation', *Political Theory* 12, no. 3 (1984), pp. 315–30.

156 Cf. Veit Bader, 'Taking religious pluralism seriously. Arguing for an institutional turn', *Ethical Theory and Moral Practice* 6, no. 1 (2003), pp. 3–22; Veit Bader and Sawitri Saharso, 'Contextualized morality and ethno-religious diversity', *Ethnical Theory and Moral Practice* 7, no. 2 (2004), pp. 107–15; Veit Bader, 'The cultural conditions of transnational citizenship: on the interpenetration of political and ethnic cultures', *Political Theory* 25, no. 6 (1997), pp. 771–813.

157 Jane Mansbridge, 'What does a representative do? Descriptive representation in communicative settings of distrust: uncrystallized interests, and historically denigrated status', in Will Kymlicka and Norman Wayne (eds), *Citizenship in Diverse Societies* (Oxford: Oxford University Press, 2000), pp. 99–123.

158 Cf. Adrian Favell, 'Applied political philosophy at the Rubicon: Will Kymlicka's multicultural citizenship', *Ethical Theory and Moral Practice* 1 (1998), pp. 255–78.

159 Cf. Elizabeth Markovits, 'The trouble with being earnest: deliberative democracy and the sincerity norm', *The Journal of Political Philosophy* 14, no. 2 (2006), pp. 249–69; Jeremy Waldron, 'Cultural identity and civic responsibility', in Will Kymlicka and Wayne Norman (eds), *Citizenship in Diverse Societies* (Oxford: Oxford University Press, 2000), pp. 155–74.

160 Numerous scholars openly criticize the inability of liberal citizenship to foster a sense of community. See for instance, H. N. Hirsch, 'The threnody of liberalism: constitutional liberty and the renewal of community', *Political Theory* 14, no. 3 (1986), pp. 423–49. In contrast, other authors attempt to enrich liberalism with republican or communitarian elements. Cf. Ralph D. Ellis, 'Toward a reconciliation of liberalism and communitarianism', *Journal of Value Inquiry* 25, no. 1 (1991), pp. 55–64; Patrick Neal and David Paris, 'Liberalism and the communitarian critique: a guide for the perplexed', *Canadian Journal of Political Science* 23, no. 3 (1990), pp. 419–39.

161 Cf. James Johnson, 'Liberalism and the politics of cultural authenticity', *Politics, Philosophy and Economics* 1, no. 2 (2002), pp. 213–36; Duncan Kelly, 'The political thought of Isaiah Berlin', *British Journal of Politics and International Relations* 4, no. 1 (2002), pp. 25–48; Daniel Jacobson, 'Mill on liberty, speech and the free society', *Philosophy and Public Affairs* 29, no. 3 (2000), pp. 276–309.

162 Cf. Ruth W. Grant, 'Locke's political anthropology and Lockean individualism', *Journal of Politics* 50, no. 1 (1988), pp. 42–63; Michael S. Rabieh, 'The reasonableness of Locke, or the questionableness of Christianity', *Journal of Politics* 53, no. 4 (1991), pp. 933–57.

163 Mark Tunick, 'John Stuart Mill and unassimilated subjects', *Political Studies* 53, no. 4 (2005), pp. 833–48.

164 This is why liberalism has been criticized on many occasions, mostly from the communitarian angle. Cf. Amy Gutmann, 'Communitarian critics of liberalism', *Philosophy and Public Affairs* 14, no. 3 (1985), pp. 308–22.

165 However, some scholars point to the paradox of rationality in liberalism. H. T. Wilson, 'The paradox of liberalism', *Philosophy of the Social Sciences* 10 (1980), pp. 215–26; cf. also Paul Franco, 'Oakeshott, Berlin, and liberalism', *Political Theory* 31, no. 4 (2003),

pp. 484–507. A similar point of critique is the self-subverting nature of liberalism, which is believed to be in need of a stronger collective identity than liberalism itself supposes, precisely for the proper functioning of the liberal citizenship. Cf. Michael Walzer, 'The communitarian critique of liberalism', *Political Theory* 18, no. 1 (1990), pp. 6–23.

166 William A. Galston, 'Liberal virtues', *American Political Science Review* 82, no. 4 (1988), pp. 1277–1290, esp. p. 1284; William A. Galston, 'Pluralism and social unity', *Ethics* 99, no. 4 (1989), pp. 711–26; William A. Galston, 'Value pluralism and liberal political theory', *The American Political Science Review* 93, no. 4 (1999), pp. 769–78; cf. also Charles Larmore, 'The moral basis of political liberalism', *Journal of Philosophy* 96, no. 12 (1999), pp. 599–625, esp. p. 601; John P. Anderson, 'Patriotic liberalism', *Law and Philosophy* 22, no. 6 (2003), pp. 577–95.

167 However, there is an increasingly popular school of thought that argues that spontaneous institutions fostering cooperation and correcting market failures are possible without government interventions, thus constituting governance without government. While some authors attribute this to the liberal rationality of self-interested individuals, others see republican and civic workings as a cause. Cf. Elinor Ostrom, 'Collective action and the evolution of social norms', *Journal of Economic Perspectives* 14, no. 3 (2000), pp. 137–58; Robert D. Putnam, *Bowling Alone: The Collapse and Revival of American Community* (New York: Simon and Schuster, 2000); Per Mouritsen, 'What's the civil in civil society? Robert Putnam, Italy and the republican tradition', *Political Studies* 51, no. 4 (2003), pp. 650–68.

168 Cf. J.V. Howard, 'Cooperation in the prisoner's dilemma', *Theory and Decision* 24, no. 3 (1988), pp. 203–13.

169 Cf. Steven Forde, 'Natural law, theology, and morality in Locke', *American Journal of Political Science* 45, no. 2 (2001), pp. 396–409; Thomas H. Marshall, *Citizenship and Social Class* (London: Pluto Press, 1992 [1950]).

170 Phillip, J. Frankenfeld, 'Technological citizenship: a normative framework for risk studies', *Science, Technology & Human Values* 17, no. 4 (1992), pp. 459–84; Thomas Saretzki, 'Technological governance – technological citizenship', in Hubert Heinelt et al. (eds), *Participatory Governance in Multi-Level Context: Concepts and Experience* (Opladen: Leske+Budrich, 2002), pp. 83–106.

171 Roland Roth, 'Participatory governance and urban citizenship', in Hubert Heinelt, et al. (eds), *Participatory Governance in Multi-Level Context: Concepts and Experience* (Opladen: Leske+Budrich, 2002), pp. 75–82, esp. p. 80. However, the rights-orientation of the liberal citizenships approaches sometimes fairly closely to the republican citizenship, particularly when it focuses on participatory rights. Here, the participatory rights can blend with the postulate of citizen activity and participation found in the republican model, even if this is differently justified.

172 Chris Hilson, 'Legitimacy and rights in the EU: questions of identity', *Journal of European Public Policy* 14, no. 4 (2007), pp. 527–43. Cf. also Michael Marinetto, 'Who wants to be an active citizen? The politics and practice of community involvement', *Sociology* 37, no. 1 (2003), pp. 103–20.

173 Cf. Steven J. Sherman, David L. Hamilton and Amy C. Lewis, 'Perceived entitativity and the social identity value of group memberships', in Dominic Abrams and Michael Hogg (eds), *Social Identity and Social Cognition* (Oxford: Blackwell, 1999), pp. 80–110; Julian A. Oldmeadow et al., 'Self-categorization, status, and social influence', *Social Psychology Quarterly* 66, no. 2 (2003), pp. 138–52.

174 Cf. Charles W. Nuckolls, 'Motivation and the will to power: ethnopsychology and the return of Thomas Hobbes', *Philosophy of the Social Sciences* 25, no. 3 (1995), pp. 345–59.

175 Patrick Neal, 'Hobbes and rational choice theory', *Political Research Quarterly* 41, no. 4 (1988), pp. 635–52.

176 Cf. Nick Ellison, 'Civic-subjects or civic-agents? The structure–agency debate in late modern perspective', *Theory, Culture & Society* 17, no. 2 (2000), pp. 148–56.

177 Cf. Benjamin J. Muller, '(Dis)qualified bodies: securitization, citizenship and identity management', *Citizenship Studies* 8, no. 3 (2004), pp. 279–94; William E. Scheuerman, 'Carl Schmitt and the road to Abu Ghraib', *Constellations* 13, no. 1 (2006), pp. 108–24; Mike Dee, 'The new citizenship of the risk and surveillance society: from a citizenship of hope to a citizenship of fear?' Centre for Social Change Research, School of Humanities and Human Services, Queensland University of Technology, 2002; Lucia Zedner, 'Securing liberty in the face of terror: reflections from criminal justice', *Journal of Law and Society* 32, no. 4 (2005), pp. 507–33.

178 There exist a number of approaches that reconceptualize the Schmittian friend–enemy dichotomy of conflict in more republican terms. One of them is particularly promising. Departing from different variations of 'agonistic politics', the theory of synagonism focuses on the interpretation and production of the common good in and through conflict. However, synagonism leans towards the republican common good orientation of citizenship and shifts away from the caesarean citizenship and its homogenization practices. Therefore, it should be discussed within the republican framework. See Nathalie Karagiannis and Peter Wagner, 'Varieties of agonism: conflict, the common good, and the need for synagonism', *Journal of Social Philosophy* 39, no. 3 (2008), pp. 323–39; Nathalie Karagiannis and PeterWagner, 'Towards a theory of synagonism', *Journal of Political Philosophy* 13, no. 3 (2005), pp. 235–62.

Chapter 5: European citizenship and European collective identity

1 Cf. Leon N. Lindberg and Stuart A. Scheingold, *Europe's Would-be Polity: Patterns of Change in the European Community* (Englewood Cliffs, NJ: Prentice-Hall, 1970).

2 Cf. George Tsebelis, *Veto Players. How Political Institutions Work* (Princeton, NJ: Princeton University Press, 2002). Regarding the concept and the application of the veto-player analysis to the EU cf. Alexander H. Trechsel, 'How to federalize the European Union … and why bother', *Journal of European Public Policy* 12, no. 3 (2005), pp. 401–18.

3 Paul Krugman, *Pop internationalism* (Cambridge, MA: The MIT Press, 1996), esp. p. 167.

4 Alan S. Milward, *The European Rescue of the Nation-State* (London: Routledge, 1992) p. 18.

5 Antje Wiener, 'Assessing the constructive potential of Union citizenship – a socio-historical perspective', European Integration online Paper 1, no. 17, http://eiop.or.at/eiop/texte/1997-017a.htm, esp. pp. 8–9.

6 Bo Stråth, 'A European identity: to the historical limits of a concept', *European Journal of Social Theory* 5, no. 4 (2002), pp. 387–401.

7 Sonja Puntscher Riekmann, *Die kommissarische Neuordnung Europas* (Wien: Springer, 1998), p. 195.

8 Cass Sunstein, 'Beyond the republican revival', *Yale Law Journal* 97, no. 8 (1988), pp. 1538–90, esp. p. 1539.

9 Cass Sunstein, *Partial Constitution* (Cambridge, MA: Harvard University Press, 1993), esp. Chapter 1.

10 Cf. Bernard Yack, 'Rhetoric and public reasoning: an Aristotelian understanding of political deliberation', *Political Theory* 34, no. 4 (2006), pp. 417–38.

11 Jürgen Neyer, 'The deliberative turn in integration theory', *Journal of European Public Policy* 13, no. 5 (2006), pp. 779–91.

12 Some authors argue that the deliberative decision-making process can be found in other institutional aspects of the EU such as the comitology or the European Parliament, or in the entire non-majoritarian EU governance. Christian Joerges, 'Deliberative political processes revisited: what have we learnt about the legitimacy of supranational decision-making', *Journal of Common Market Studies* 44, no. 4 (2006), pp. 779–802; Erik Oddvar Eriksen and John Erik Fossum, 'Democracy through strong publics in the European Union?' *Journal of Common Market Studies* 40, no. 3 (2002), pp. 401–24;

Jürgen Neyer, 'Discourse and order in the EU: a deliberative approach to multi-level governance', *Journal of Common Market Studies* 41, no. 4 (2003), pp. 687–706; Edwin Vink, 'Multi-level democracy: deliberative or agonistic? The search for appropriate normative standards', *Journal of European Integration* 29, no. 3 (2007), pp. 303–22; Mark A. Pollack, 'Control mechanism or deliberative democracy? Two images of comitology', *Comparative Political Studies* 36, no.1–2 (2003), pp. 125–55.

In the political theory, James Bowman postulates deliberative federalism for polycentric and diverse polity of the EU. James Bohman, 'Constitutional making and democratic innovation: the European Union and transnational governance', *European Journal of Political Theory* 3, no. 3 (2004), pp.315–37.

13   Cf. Jürgen Neyer, 'Explaining the unexpected: efficiency and effectiveness in European decision-making', *Journal of European Public Policy* 11, no. 1 (2004), pp. 19–38.

14   Cf. Christer Karlsson, 'Deliberation at the European Convention: the final verdict', *European Law Journal* 14, no. 5 (2008), pp. 604–19; Paul Magnette, 'La Convention Européenne: Argumenter et Négocier Dans Une Assemblée Constituante Multinationale', *Revue française de science politique* 54, no. 1 (2004), pp. 5–42; Carlos Closa, 'Deliberative constitutional politics and the turn towards a norms-based legitimacy of the EU Constitution', *European Law Journal* 11, no. 4 (2005), pp. 411–31; Thomas Risse and Mareike Kleine, 'Assessing the legitimacy of the EU's treaty revision methods', *Journal of Common Market Studies* 45, no. 1 (2007), pp. 69–80.

15   Joachim Ahrens, Martin Meurers, and Carsten Renner, 'Beyond the big-bang enlargement: citizens' preferences and the problem of EU decision-making', *Journal of European Integration* 29, no. 4 (2007), pp. 447–79. For the concept of social choice under circumstances of heterogeneity see the seminal work of Kenneth J. Arrow, *Social Choice and Individual Values* (New Haven, CT: Yale University Press, 1951).

16   Cf. Robert A. Dahl and Edward.R. Tufte, *Size and Democracy* (Stanford, CA: Stanford University Press, 1973).

17   Cf. Andrew Gamble, 'The European disunion', *British Journal of Politics and International Relations* 8, no. 1 (2006), pp. 34–49; Jan-Emmanuel de Neve, 'The European onion? How differentiated integration is reshaping the EU', *Journal of European Integration* 29, no. 4 (2007), pp. 503–21.

18   Klaus H. Goetz, 'Territory, temporality and clustered Europeanization' (Vienna: Institute for Advanced Studies, 2006), Political Science Series 109.

19   Cf. James Bohman, 'Reflexive public deliberation: democracy and the limits of pluralism', *Philosophy and Social Criticism* 29, no. 1 (2003), pp. 85–105.

20   Will Kymlicka, *Multicultural Citizenship: A Liberal Theory of Minority Rights* (Oxford: Oxford University Press, 1995), esp. Chapter 7.

21   Cf. David Miller, *Citizenship and National Identity* (Cambridge: Polity Press, 2000), pp. 62–80; Richard Bellamy and Alex Warleigh, 'From ethics of integration to an ethics of participation: citizenship and the future of the European Union', *Millennium: Journal of International Studies* 27, no. 3 (1998), pp. 447–70.

22   Kostas A. Lavdas, 'Republican Europe and multicultural citizenship', *Politics* 21, no. 1 (2001), pp. 1–10, esp. p. 4.

23   Cf. Seyla Benhabib, 'Beyond interventionism and indifference: culture, deliberation and pluralism', *Philosophy and Social Criticism* 31, no. 7 (2005), pp. 753–71; Andrea T. Baumeister, 'Habermas: discourse and cultural diversity', *Political Studies* 51, no. 4 (2003), pp. 740–58. Some deliberation theorists, however, point to the problems of large scope public deliberation beyond individual communities and therefore its limited practicability; cf. Will Friedman, 'Deliberative democracy and the problem of scope', *Journal of Public Deliberation* 2, no. 1 (2006), pp. 1–29.

24   Cf. Jack Knight and James Johnson, 'Aggregation and deliberation: on the possibility of democratic legitimacy', *Political Theory* 22, no. 2 (1994), pp. 277–98; David Miller, 'Deliberative democracy and social choice', in James Fishkin and Peter Laslett (eds), *Debating Deliberative Democracy* (London: Blackwell, 2003), pp. 182–99.

25 Jürgen Habermas, *The Structural Transformation of the Public Sphere: An Inquiry into a Category of Bourgeois Society* (Cambridge, MA: MIT Press, 1991[1962]), esp. pp. 130–31; Jeffrey Flynn, 'Communicative power in Habermas's theory of democracy', *European Journal of Political Theory* 3, no. 4 (2004), pp. 433–54; Denise Vitale, 'Between deliberative and participatory democracy: a contribution on Habermas', *Philosophy and Social Criticism* 32, no. 6 (2006), pp. 739–66.

26 Arthur Lupia, 'Deliberation disconnected: what it takes to improve civic competence', *Law and Contemporary Problems* 65, no. 3 (2002), pp. 133–50; Pablo Gilabert, 'The substantive dimension of deliberative practical rationality', *Philosophy and Social Criticism* 31, no. 2 (2005), pp. 185–210. For a more sceptical perspective on the 'changing minds power' of deliberation see Gerry Mackle, 'Does democratic deliberation change minds?', *Politics, Philosophy and Economics* 5, no. 3 (2006), pp. 279–303.

27 Bruce Ackerman, *Social Justice in the Liberal State* (New Haven, CT: Yale University Press, 1980), p. 353. For the modern interpretation of civic friendship see Sibyl A. Schwarzenbach, 'On civic friendship', *Ethics* 107 (1996), pp. 97–128; Andrew Mason, 'Special obligations to compatriots', *Ethics* 107 (1997), pp. 427–47.

28 Andrew Schaap argues at this point that in taking consensus as a regulative idea, deliberative democracy conflates moral and political community, thereby representing conflict as already communal. In this sense, individuals who enter deliberative settings are already citizens and do not need to become transformed into them. Andrew Schaap, 'Agonism in divided societies', *Philosophy and Social Criticism* 32, no. 2 (2006), pp. 255–77.

29 For a review of the institutional setting of the European Convention and its actors see Desmond Dinan, 'Governance and institutions: the convention and the intergovernmental conference', *Journal of Common Market Studies* 42, s. 1 (2004), pp. 27–42.

30 For a praise of the Charter Convention in the republican spirit see Richard Bellamy and Justus Schönlau, 'The normality of constitutional politics: an analysis of the drafting of the EU Charter of Fundamental Rights', *Constellations* 11, no. 3 (2004), pp. 412–33.

31 For an interesting opposing argument about the IGC having more deliberative settings than the conventions see Diana Panke, 'More arguing than bargaining? The institutional designs of the European Convention and intergovernmental conferences compared', *Journal of European Integration* 28, no. 4 (2006), pp. 357–79.

32 For instance Jürgen Habermas, *Faktizität und Geltung.Beiträge zur Diskurstheorie des Rechts und des demokratischen Rechtsstaates* (Frankfurt: Suhrkamp, 1992); Joshua Cohen, 'Deliberation and democratic legitimacy', in Alan Hamlin and Philip Pettit (eds), *The Good Polity: Normative Analysis of the State* (Oxford: Blackwell, 1989), pp. 17–34; Seyla Benhabib, 'Toward a deliberative model of democratic legitimacy', in Seyla Benhabib (ed.), *Democracy and Difference: Contesting the Boundaries of the Political* (Princeton, NJ: Princeton University Press, 1996), pp. 67–94; Jon Elster, 'Deliberation and constitution making', in Jon Elster (ed.), *Deliberative Democracy* (Cambridge: Cambridge University Press, 1998), pp. 97–122; John S. Dryzek, *Deliberative Democracy and Beyond: Liberals, Critics, Contestations* (Oxford: Oxford University Press, 2000).

33 Cf. Thomas Risse and Mareike Kleine, 'Assessing the legitimacy of the EU's treaty revision methods', *Journal of Common Market Studies* 45, no. 1 (2007), pp. 69–80.

34 There is a more general expectation among deliberation theorists that deliberative settings can integrate diversity and promote commonness. Cf. John S. Dryzek, 'Deliberative Democracy in divided societies: alternatives to agonism and analgesia', *Political Theory* 33, no. 2 (2005), pp. 218–42; Robert E. Goodin and John S. Dryzek, 'Deliberative impacts: the macro-political uptake of mini-publics', *Politics & Society* 34, no. 2 (2006), pp. 219–44.

35 The rational choice analysis focuses either on intergovernmental negotiations or on inter-institutional agenda-setting and decision-making powers of the EU actors. For the former see Andrew Moravcsik, *The Choice for Europe: Social Purpose and State*

Power from Messina to Maastricht (Ithaca, NY: Cornell University Press, 1998) for the latter George Tsebelis, *Veto Players: How Political Institutions Work* (Princeton, NJ: Princeton University Press, 2002).

36 Joshua Cohen, 'Deliberation and democratic legitimacy', in Alan Hamlin and Philip Pettit (eds), *The Good Polity: Normative Analysis of the State* (Oxford: Blackwell, 1989), pp. 17–34; Amy Gutmann and Dennis Thompson, 'Deliberative democracy beyond process', *Journal of Political Philosophy* 10, no. 2 (2002), pp. 153–74.

37 Thomas Risse, 'Let's argue!: communicative action in world politics', *International Organization* 54, no. 1 (2000), pp. 1–39, esp. p. 7.

38 In contrast to Jürgen Habermas, John Dryzek differentiates between deliberative democracy and discursive democracy. Whereas deliberative democracy requires that arguments and only arguments captured in the idea of public reason should be provided in support of collective decisions, discursive democracy acknowledges the centrality of arguments in translating preferences into collective decisions, but also introduces additional modes of communication such as rhetoric and storytelling. In this sense, discursive democracy regards collective decisions as a mixture of private and common interests. John S. Dryzek, *Deliberative Democracy and Beyond: Liberals, Critics, Contestations* (Oxford: Oxford University Press, 2000), p. 50. Cf. also Jürgen Habermas, *Theorie des kommunikativen Handelns* (Frankfurt: Suhrkamp, 1981), 2 vols.

39 Cf. Jonathan B. Slapin, 'Who is powerful? Examining preferences and testing sources of bargaining strength at European intergovernmental conferences', *European Union Politics* 7, no. 1 (2006), pp. 51–76.

40 Risse, *op. cit.*, p. 13.

41 For a deliberative-democratic analysis of the European Convention see for instance Augustín José Menéndez, 'Neither constitution, nor treaty: a deliberative-democratic analysis of the Constitutional Treaty of the European Union', Arena Working Paper 8, 2005, University of Oslo; John Erik Fossum and Augustín José Menéndez, 'The constitution's gift? A deliberative democratic analysis of constitution making in the European Union', *European Law Journal* 11, no. 4 (2005), pp. 380–410.

42 In the meantime, empirical studies suggest also that other allegedly deliberative settings in the EU do not fulfil the normative expectations of deliberation theory. Cf. for example Elissaveta Radulova, 'The OMC: an opaque method of consideration or deliberative governance in action?', *Journal of European Integration* 29, no. 3 (2007), pp. 363–80.

43 Jürgen Habermas, *Faktizität und Geltung.Beiträge zur Diskurstheorie des Rechts und des demokratischen Rechtsstaates* (Frankfurt: Suhrkamp, 1992), esp. p. 392; Seyla Benhabib, 'The utopian dimension in communicative ethics', *New German Critique* 35, Special Issue on Jürgen Habermas (1985), pp. 83–96; Damian Chalmers, 'The reconstitution of European public spheres', *European Law Journal* 9, no. 2 (2003), pp. 127–89; Anne van Aaken, 'Deliberative institutional economics, or Does Homo oeconomicus argue? A proposal for combining new institutional economics with discourse theory', *Philosophy and Social Criticism* 28, no. 4 (2002), pp. 361–94.

44 Deliberation among individuals is analysed by, for instance, Bruce Ackermann and James S. Fishkin in their contribution, in what they call 'Deliberation Day'. This new national holiday would be held one week before major national elections. Registered voters would be called to neighbourhood meeting places to discuss central issues raised by the campaign. In this way, deliberation should contribute to a democratic will-formation before elections. Bruce Ackermann and James Fishkin, 'Deliberation Day', in James Fishkin and Peter Laslett (eds), *Debating Deliberative Democracy* (London: Blackwell, 2003), pp. 7–30.

45 For instance Lyn Carson, 'Improving public deliberative practice: a comparative analysis of two Italian citizens' jury projects in 2006', *Journal of Public Deliberation* 2, no. 1 (2006), pp. 1–18; Janette Hartz-Karp, 'A case study in deliberative democracy: dialogue with the city', *Journal of Public Deliberation* 1, no. 1 (2005), pp. 1–15.

46 For instance Philip Pettit, 'Deliberative democracy, the discursive dilemma, and republican theory', in James Fishkin and Peter Laslett (eds), *Debating Deliberative Democracy* (London: Blackwell, 2003), pp. 138–62.

47 Cf. Hannah Pitkin, *The Concept of Representation* (Berkeley, CA: University of California Press). Jürgen Neyer makes a helpful distinction between different types of deliberation, one of which is the knowledge-based deliberation in epistemic communities among scientists and experts. Jürgen Neyer, 'Discourse and order in the EU: a deliberative approach to multi-level governance', *Journal of Common Market Studies* 41, no. 4 (2003), pp. 687–706; Claudio Radaelli, 'The public policy of the European Union: whither politics of expertise?', *Journal of European Public Policy* 6, no. 5 (1999), pp. 757–74.

48 The depersonalizing focus on reason in deliberation procedures leads to a liberal critique of rights of unreasonable citizens. Cf. Jonathan Quong, 'The rights of unreasonable citizens', *Journal of Political Philosophy* 12, no. 3 (2004), pp. 314–35.

49 In this sense, we do not deal here with a classical principal–agent model, in which there is only a one-sided relationship between the 'ordering party' and the agent. Cf. Jean-Jacques Laffont and David Martimort, *The Theory of Incentives: The Principal–Agent Model* (Princeton, NJ: Princeton University Press, 2002); Torbjörn Bergman, 'The European Union as the next step of delegation and accountability', *European Journal of Political research* 37 (2000), pp. 415–29.

50 Cf. Diana Panke, 'More arguing than bargaining? The institutional designs of the European Convention and intergovernmental conferences compared', *Journal of European Integration* 28, no. 4 (2006), pp. 357–79; Thomas Christiansen, 'The role of supranational actors in EU treaty reform', *Journal of European Public Policy* 9, no. 1 (2002), pp. 33–53.

51 Cf. Daniel Göler, 'Comment on "Time was of the essence: timing and framing Europe's constitutional convention" by Justus Schönlau', in Carlos Closa and John Erik Fossum (eds), *Deliberative Constitutional Politics in the EU* (Oslo: ARENA, 2004), pp. 273–84; Thomas König, 'Measuring and analysing positions on European constitution-building', *European Union Politics* 6, no. 3 (2005), pp. 259–67.

52 Christopher F. Karpowitz and Jane Mansbridge, 'Disagreement and consensus: the need for dynamic updating in public deliberation', *Journal of Public Deliberation* 1, no. 1 (2005), pp. 348–64; Matthias Kumm, 'The jurisprudence of constitutional conflict: constitutional supremacy in Europe before and after the Constitutional Treaty', *European Law Journal* 11. no. 3 (2005), pp. 262–307; John Gastil, 'Is face-to-face citizen deliberation a luxury or a necessity?', *Political Communication* 17, no. 4 (2001), pp. 357–61; Stephanie Burkhalter, John Gastil, and Todd Kelshaw, 'A conceptual definition and theoretical model of public deliberation in small face-to-face groups', *Communication Theory* 12, no. 4 (2002), pp. 398–422.

53 Elster, *op. cit.,* p. 117.

54 Cf. Ben Crum, 'Politics and power in the European Convention', *Politics* 24, no. 1 (2004), pp. 1–11.

55 Claus Offe, 'Micro-aspects of democratic theory: what makes for the deliberative competence of citizens?', in Claus Offe, *Herausforderungen der Demokratie: Zur Integrations-und Leistungsfähigkeit politischer Institutionen* (Frankfurt: Campus, 2003), pp. 297–320.

56 Cf. Ethan J. Leib, 'The Chinese Communist Party and deliberative democracy', *Journal of Public Deliberation* 1, no. 1 (2005), pp. 1–6.

57 John S. Dryzek, *Deliberative Democracy and Beyond: Liberals, Critics, Contestations* (Oxford: Oxford University Press, 2000), esp. p. 15.

58 Cf. Elster, *op. cit.,* p. 98f. An example of treating democracy and deliberation as identical can be found for instance in Gary S. Schaal, *Vertrauen, Verfassung und Demokratie: Über den Einfluss konstitutioneller Prozesse und Prozeduren auf die Genese von Vertrauensbeziehungen in modernen Demokratien* (Wiesbaden: VS Verlag, 2004), p. 12.

59 Cf. the concept of acceptability sets by Robert Putnam, although it was coined in a different context. Robert Putnam, 'Diplomacy and domestic politics: the logic of two-level games', *International Organization* 42, no. 3, (1988), pp. 427–60; cf. also Simon Hug and Thomas König, 'In view of ratification: governmental preferences and domestic constraints at the Amsterdam Intergovernmental Conference', *International Organization* 56, no. 2 (2002), pp. 447–76.

60 Elster, *op. cit.,* p. 103f.

61 Cf. Carolyn M. Hendriks, 'When the forum meets interest politics: strategic uses of public deliberation', *Politics and Society* 34, no. 4 (2006), pp. 571–602; Elizabeth Markovits, 'The trouble with being earnest: deliberative democracy and the sincerity norm', *Journal of Political Philosophy* 14, no. 3 (2006), pp. 249–69.

62 Frank Schimmelfennig, 'The community trap: liberal norms, rhetorical action, and Eastern enlargement of the European Union', *International Organization* 55, no. 1 (2000), pp. 47–80; cf. also Robert L. Ivie, 'Rhetorical deliberation and democratic politics in the here and now', *Rhetoric and Public Affairs* 5, no. 2 (2002), pp. 277–85.

63 Cf. Margaret Kohn, 'Language, power, and persuasion: towards a critique of deliberative democracy', *Constellations* 7, no. 3 (2000), pp. 408–29.

64 Schimmelfennig, *op. cit.,* p. 65.

65 Cf. George Tsebelis and Sven-Oliver Proksch, 'The art of political manipulation in the European Convention', *Journal of Common Market Studies* 45, no. 1 (2007), pp. 157–86. For an opposite view that Giscard d'Estaing had little influence on the outcome of the convention results see Mareike Kleine, 'Leadership in the European Convention', *Journal of European Public Policy* 14, no. 8 (2007), pp. 1227–48.

66 Ben Crum, 'Politics and power in the European Convention', *Politics* 24, no. 1 (2004), pp.1–11; Yener Kandogan, 'Power analysis of the Nice Treaty on the Future of European Integration', *Applied Economics* 37, no. 10 (2005), pp. 1147–56.

67 Cf. Dennis Leech, 'Designing the voting system for the Council of the European Union', *Public Choice* 113, no. 3–4 (2002), pp. 437–64.

68 Cf. David R. Cameron, 'The stalemate in the constitutional IGC over the definition of a qualified majority', *European Union Politics* 5, no. 3 (2004), pp. 373–91.

69 Cf. R. Daniel Kelemen, 'Comment: shaming the shameless? The constitutionalization of the European Union', *Journal of European Public Policy* 13, no. 8 (2006), pp. 1302–7; Paul Magnette and Kalypso Nicolaïdis, 'The European Convention: bargaining in the shadow of rhetoric', *West European Politics* 27, no.3 (2004), pp. 381–404; Paul Magnette, 'In the name of simplification: coping with constitutional conflicts in the convention on the Future of Europe', *European Law Journal* 11, no. 4 (2005), pp. 432–51.

70 Cf. Paul Magnette and Kalypso Nicolaïdis, 'Coping with the Lilliput syndrome: large vs. small member states in the European Convention', *European Public Law* 11, no. 1 (2005), pp. 83–102; Dan S. Felsenthal and Moshé Machover, 'The Treaty of Nice and qualified majority voting', *Social Choice and Welfare* 18, no. 3 (2001), pp. 431–64.

71 Bernhard Felderer, Iain Paterson, and Peter Silrászky, *Draft Constitution: The Double Majority Implies a Massive Transfer of Power to the Large Member States, Is this Intended?* (Vienna: Institute of Higher Studies, 2003); also Axel Moberg, 'The Nice Treaty and voting rules in the council', *Journal of Common Market Studies* 40, no. 2 (2002), pp. 259–82; Axel Moberg, 'Is the double majority really double? The second round in the debate of the voting rules in the EU Constitutional Treaty', Working Paper 30/5/2007, Real Instituto Elcano, Madrid.

72 Cf. Dan S. Felsenthal and Moshé Machover, 'Analysis of QM rules in the draft constitution for Europe proposed by the European Convention, 2003', *Social Choice and Welfare* 23, no. 1 (2004), pp. 1–20; Wojciech Slomczynski and Karol Zyczkowski, 'Penrose voting system and optimal quota', *Acta Physica Polonica* 37, no. 11 (2006), pp. 3133–43; Claus Beisbart, Luc Bovens, and Stephen Hartmann, 'A utilitarian assessment of alternative decision rules in the Council of Ministers', *European Union Politics* 6, no. 4 (2005), pp. 395–418.

73 Cf. Tobias Auberger and Krzysztof Iszkowski, 'Democratic theory and the European Union: focusing on interest or reason?', *Journal of European Integration* 29, no. 3 (2007), pp. 271–84; Thomas König, 'Measuring and analysing positions on European constitution-building', *European Union Politics* 6, no. 3 (2005), pp. 259–69.

74 European Convention, Summary Report of the Plenary Session, Brussels, 15 and 16 May 2003, CONV 748/03.

75 Cf. also Joaquín Roy, 'Between cherry-picking and salvaging the Titanic: Spain and the rescuing of the essence of the EU Constitution', Working Paper (41/2007), Real Instituto Elcano, Madrid.

76 Europäischer Konvent (Präsidium), Vorentwurf des Verfassungsvertrages, 28.10.2002, CONV 396/02; Europäischer Konvent (Präsidium), Entwurf von Artikeln für title IV des Teils I der Verfassung, 23.04.2003, CONV (691/03); Europäischer Konvent, Mündlicher Bericht des Konventspräsidenten an den Europäischen rat in Thessaloniki, 20.06.2003; European Convention, Report from the Presidency European Convention to the President of the European Council, 18 July 2003, CONV 851/03, European Convention, Note on the Plenary Session, 4 July 2003, CONV (849/03).

77 European Convention, Summary Report of the Plenary Session, Brussels, 11 and 13 June 2003, CONV 814/03.

78 Cf. Xenophon A. Yatangas, 'The Treaty of Nice: the sharing of power and the institutional balance in the European Union: a continental perspective', *European Law Journal* 7, no. 3 (2001), pp. 242–91.

79 Cf. Sebastian Kurpas and Henning Riecke, 'The 2007 German EU presidency: a midterm report', Swedish Institute for European Policy Studies, SIEPS 2007.

80 Cf. Andreas Maurer, *Parlamentarische Demokratie in der Europäischen Union. Der Beitrag des Europäischen Parlaments und der nationalen Parlamente* (Baden-Baden: Nomos, 2001), p. 51.

81 Cf. Fuad Aleskerov et al., 'European Union enlargement: power distribution implications of the new institutional arrangements', *European Journal of Political Research* 41, no. 3 (2002), pp. 379–94.

82 Ireneusz P. Karolewski, 'Constitutionalization of the European Union as a response to the Eastern enlargement: functions versus power', *Journal of Communist Studies and Transition Politics* 23, no. 4 (2007), pp. 501–24.

83 Cf. Astrid Lorenz, 'How to measure constitutional rigidity: four concepts and two alternatives', *Journal of Theoretical Politics* 17, no. 3 (2005), pp. 339–61.

84 Cf. Alexander Somek, 'Postconstitutional treaty', *German Law Journal* 8, no. 12 (2007), pp. 1121–32.

85 *The Independent*, 'EU Treaty is a constitution, says Giscard d'Estaing', 14 January 2008.

86 Conference of the representatives of the governments of the member states, Treaty of Lisbon amending the Treaty on European Union and the Treaty establishing the European Community, Brussels, 3 December 2007, CIG (14/07).

87 Council of the European Union, Brussels European Council 21–22 June 2007: Presidency Conclusions, 11177/1/07; cf. Ben Crum, 'Can the EU Presidency make its mark on interstate bargains? The Italian and Irish Presidencies of the 2003–4 IGC', *Journal of European Public Policy* 14, no. 8 (2007), pp. 1208–26; Jonas Tallberg, 'The agenda-shaping powers of the EU Council Presidency', *Journal of European Public Policy* 10, no. 1 (2003), pp. 1–19.

88 Cf. Encarnación Algaba, Jesús Mario Bilbao, and Julio Rodrigo Fernández, 'The distribution of power in the European Constitution', *European Journal of Operational Research* 176, no. 3 (2007), pp. 1752–66; Nicola Maaser and Stefan Napel, 'Equal representation in two-tier voting system', *Social Choice and Welfare* 28, no. 3 (2007), pp. 401–20.

89 Cf. Luc Bovens and Claus Beisbart, 'Factions in Rousseau's *Du Contrat Social* and federal representation', *Analysis* 67, no. 1 (2007), pp. 12–20; Pao-Li Chang, Vincet C.H. Chua, and Moshé Machover, 'L S Penrose's limit theorem: tests by simulation',

Mathematical Social Sciences 51, no. 1 (2006), pp. 90–106; Geoff Fielding and Hans Liebeck, 'Voting structures and the square root law', *British Journal of Political Science* 5, no. 2 (1975), pp. 249–56.

90 Claus Offe, 'Micro-aspects of democratic theory: what makes for the deliberative competence of citizens?', in Claus Offe, *Herausforderungen der Demokratie. Zur Integrations-und Leistungsfähigkeit politischer Institutionen* (Frankfurt: Campus, 2003), pp. 297–334.

91 Cf. Tali Mendelberg, 'The deliberative citizen: theory and evidence', *Political Decision-Making, Deliberation and Participation* 6, no. 1 (2002), pp. 151–93.

92 Adam Przeworski, 'Deliberation and ideological domination', in Jon Elster (ed.), *Deliberative Democracy* (Cambridge: Cambridge University Press, 1998), pp. 140–60.

93 Some deliberation theorists seem aware of this deficit, at least to a certain degree. Since deliberation is never fully free of power, Joshua Cohen points out that participants in deliberation settings should be 'substantively equal in that the existing distribution of power and resources does not shape their chances to contribute to the deliberation'. This caveat, however, enlarges even further the gap between 'norms and facts', rather than making the applicability of deliberation theory more realistic. Joshua Cohen, 'Deliberation and democratic legitimacy', in Alan Hamlin and Philip Pettit (eds), *The Good Polity: Normative Analysis of the State* (Oxford: Blackwell, 1989), pp. 17–34, esp. p. 23.

94 Cf. Michael Billig, 'Discourse, opinions and ideologies: a comment', *Current Issues in Language and Society* 2, no. 2 (1995), pp. 162–67.

95 In the context of the EU, studies show that officials play a key role in the treaty reform process, even though the final European Council is only the last phase, and not necessarily the most significant one, of a long negotiation process. Christine Reh, 'Pre-cooking the European Constitution? The role of government representatives in the EU reform', *Journal of European Public Policy* 14, no. 8 (2007), pp. 1188–1207.

96 Uwe Puetter argues that national finance ministers intervened effectively in the convention. Even though they remained largely hidden from public attention, they were able to block the increase of the Commissions' competences in the field of European economic governance. Uwe Puetter, 'Intervening from outside: the role of EU finance ministers in the constitutional politics', *Journal of European Public Policy* 14, no. 8 (2007), pp. 1293–1310.

97 For a thorough discussion of this issue see Tom Keenan, 'The paradox of knowledge and power: reading Foucault on a bias', *Political Theory* 15, no. 1 (1987), pp. 5–37; also Michel Foucault, 'The subject and power', *Critical Inquiry* 8, no. 4 (1982), pp. 777–95; Peter Digeser, 'The fourth face of power', *Journal of Politics* 54, no. 4 (1992), pp. 977–1007.

98 Cf. Tracy Sulkin and Adam F. Simon, 'Habermas in the lab: a study of deliberation in an experimental setting', *Political Psychology* 22, no. 4 (2001), pp. 809–26; Tore Ellingsen and Magnus Johannesson, 'Does impartial deliberation breed fair behavior? An experimental test', *Rationality and Society* 17, no. 1 (2005), pp. 116–36; Janusz Reykowski, 'Deliberative democracy and human nature: an empirical approach', *Political Psychology* 27, no. 3 (2006), pp. 323–46.

99 Cf. Philip Pettit, *Republicanism: A Theory of Freedom and Government* (Oxford: Clarendon Press, 1997); Philip Pettit, 'Keeping republican freedom simple: on a difference with Quentin Skinner', *Political Theory* 30, no. 3 (2002), pp. 339–56. For a discussion of Pettit's republican concept of non-domination see John Maynor, 'Another instrumental republican approach', *European Journal of Political Theory* 1, no.1 (2002), pp. 71–89. For the application of the concept to the EU see Richard Bellamy and Alex Warleigh, 'From ethics of integration to an ethics of participation: citizenship and the future of the European Union', *Millennium: Journal of International Studies* 27 (1998), pp. 447–70, esp. p. 463.

100 See in particular James Bohman, 'Constitution making and democratic innovation: the European Union and transnational governance', *European Journal of Political Theory* 3,

no. 3 (2004), pp. 315–37. In contrast to my interest in the convention method, Bohman searches for the republican moment in the legal order of the EU as the outcome of the European Convention, referring to the concept of deliberative federalism.

101 Solomon E. Asch, 'Studies of independence and conformity: a minority of one against a unanimous majority', *Psychological Monographs* 70, no. 9 (1956), entire volume. 416.

102 Cf. Christian F. Rostbøll, 'Preferences and paternalism: on freedom and deliberative democracy', *Political Theory* 33, no. 3 (2005), pp. 370–96; Lasse Thomassen, 'The inclusion of the other? Habermas and the paradox of tolerance', *Political Theory* 34, no. 4 (2006), pp. 439–62.

103 European Convention, Proposal for a Common Alternative, Minority Report: The Europe of Democracies, 30 May 2003, CONV(773/03).

104 Cf. Carlos Closa, 'Why convene referendums? Explaining choices in EU constitutional politics', *Journal of European Public Policy* 14, no. 8 (2007), pp. 1311–32.

105 Lynn M. Sanders, 'Against deliberation', *Political Theory* 25, no. 3 (1997), pp. 347–76. Cf. also John Gastil, 'How balanced discussion shapes knowledge, public perception, and attitudes: a case study of deliberation on the Los Alamos National Laboratory', *Journal of Public Deliberation* 2, no. 1 (2006), pp. 1–32.

106 Jeremy Waldron, 'Cultural identity and civic responsibility', in Will Kymlicka and Wayne Norman (eds), *Citizenship in Diverse Societies* (Oxford: Oxford University Press, 2000), pp. 155–74.

107 Sanders, *op.cit.*, pp. 347–76.

108 Kostas A. Lavdas, 'Republican Europe and multicultural citizenship', *Politics* 21, no. 1 (2001), pp. 1–10, esp. p. 4.

109 Ian Shapiro, 'Optimal deliberation?', in James Fishkin and Peter Laslett (eds), *Debating Deliberative Democracy* (London: Blackwell, 2003), pp. 121–37, esp. p. 123.

110 Cf. Jane Mansbridge, *Beyond Adversary Democracy* (New York: Basic Books, 1980); Jane Mansbridge, 'Using power/fighting power: the polity', in Seyla Benhabib (ed.), *Democracy and Difference: Contesting the Boundaries of the Political* (Princeton, NJ: Princeton University Press, 1996), pp. 46–66; Jack Knight and James Johnson, 'Aggregation and deliberation: on the possibility of democratic legitimacy', *Political Theory* 22, no. 2 (1994), pp. 277–96.

111 Cf. Gary Shiffman, 'Construing disagreement: consensus and invective in "constitutional" debate', *Political Theory* 30, no. 2 (2002), pp. 175–203.

112 Cf. for instance Chantal Mouffe, *The Democratic Paradox* (London: Verso, 2000); Chantal Mouffe, 'Democracy, power, and the political', in Seyla Benhabib (ed.), *Democracy and Difference: Contesting the Boundaries of the Political* (Princeton, NJ: Princeton University Press, 1996), pp. 247–56; Edwin Vink, 'Multi-level democracy: deliberative or agonistic? The search for appropriate normative standards', *Journal of European Integration* 29, no. 3 (2007), pp. 303–22.

113 Cf. Adolf G. Gundersen, *The Socratic Citizen: A Theory of Deliberative Democracy* (New York: Lexington Books, 2000).

114 Christopher F. Karpowitz and Jane Mansbridge, 'Disagreement and consensus: the need for dynamic updating in public deliberation', *Journal of Public Deliberation* 1, no. 1 (2005), pp. 348–64.

115 Heinz Kleger (ed.), *Der Konvent als Labor. Texte und Dokumente zum europäischen Verfassungsprozess* (Münster: Lit, 2004), p. 176.

116 Cass R. Sunstein, 'The law of group polarization', in James Fishkin and Peter Laslett (eds), *Debating Deliberative Democracy* (London: Blackwell, 2003), pp. 80–101; Cass R. Sunstein, 'Ideological amplification', *Constellations* 14, no. 2 (2007), pp. 273–79; Philip T. Neisser, 'Political polarization as disagreement failure', *Journal of Public Deliberation* 2, no. 1 (2006), pp. 1–33.

117 Sunstein, 2003, *op cit.*

118 However, experimental research shows that institutional solutions may exist for the problem of polarization. Patrick W. Hamlett and Michael D. Cobb argue that bias of group deliberation towards the original majority preferences can be reduced if two

key variables of deliberation are manipulated: task facilitation and the quality of the argument pool. As a result, it becomes possible to structure public deliberation to mitigate these known decision-making problems. Patrick W. Hamlett and Michael D. Cobb, 'Potential solutions to public deliberation problems: structured deliberations and polarization cascades', *Policy Studies Journal* 34, no. 4 (2006), pp. 629–48.

119 Diego Gambetta, 'Claro!: an essay on discursive machismo', in Jon Elster (ed.), *Deliberative Democracy* (Cambridge: Cambridge University Press, 1998), pp. 19–43.

120 *Ibid.*, p. 24.

121 Albert O. Hirschman distinguishes between three principal reactive-reactionary theses used with the strategic goal of arguing others into submission. He calls them the perversity thesis, the futility thesis, and the jeopardy thesis. According to the perversity thesis, proposals that aim at improving some feature of the political, social, or economic order only serve to deteriorate the condition one wishes to change. The futility thesis starts out from the assumption that the arguments of the opponents will not succeed in fulfilling their promise, that these will fail to achieve the desired outcome. Finally, the jeopardy thesis holds that the costs of an envisaged measure will be too high, thus endangering previous accomplishments or other significant goals. Albert O. Hirschman, *The Rhetoric of Reaction: Perversity, Futility, Jeopardy* (Cambridge, MA: Harvard University Press, 1991).

122 Gráinne De Búrca, 'The Drafting of the European Union Charter of Fundamental Rights', *European Law Review* 26, no. 2 (2001), pp. 118–34, esp. p. 129.

123 Cologne European Council, *Conclusions*, 3–4 June 1999, esp. Annex IV.

124 Tampere European Council, *Presidency Conclusions*, 15–16.10.1999, esp. Annex.

125 I distinguish between the draft Constitutional Treaty as the original document proposed by the European Convention and the Constitutional Treaty amended by the IGC; see European Convention, *Draft Treaty Establishing a Constitution for Europe* (Brussels, 2003).

126 In this chapter I will refer to the Constitutional Treaty (CT) as the original document. Even though the Lisbon Treaty is a more recent document adopting all the essential Articles of the CT, it has a less comprehensible and less quotation-friendly form. Cf. Treaty of Lisbon amending the Treaty on European Union and the Treaty establishing the European Community, signed at Lisbon, 13 December 2007, *Official Journal of the European Union*, Volume 50, 2007/C 306/01.

127 Cf. Sandra Fredman, 'Transformation or dilution: fundamental rights in the EU social space', *European Law Journal* 12, no. 1 (2006), pp. 41–60, esp. p. 55.

128 Cf. Marika Lerch, *European Identity in International Society. A Constructivist Analysis of the EU Charter of Fundamental Rights*, Constitutionalism Web-Papers, ConWEB no. (2/2003), http://ideas.repec.org/s/erp/conweb.html.

129 Jo Shaw, 'The interpretation of European Union citizenship', *Modern Law Review* 61, no. 3 (1998), pp. 293–317, esp. p. 316. However, some authors advocate constitutionalization of rights primarily in cases where they are already visible. Cf. Guido Schwellnus, 'Reasons for constitutionalization: non-discrimination, minority rights and social rights in the Convention on the EU Charter of Fundamental Rights', *Journal of European Public Policy* 13, no. 8 (2006), pp. 1265–83.

130 Some scholars even argue that not only are rights unable to produce collective identity, but collective identity (as a social bond) is a precondition for legal integration. Cf. Mette Jolly, 'A demos for the European Union?', *Politics* 25, no. 1 (2005), pp. 12–18.

131 William J. Brennan Jr., 'Why have a Bill of Rights?', *Oxford Journal of Legal Studies* 9, no. 4 (1989), pp. 425–40.

132 Cf. Robert Sugden, 'Rationality and impartiality: is the contractarian enterprise possible?' in David Gauthier and Robert Sugden (eds), *Rationality, Justice and the Social Contract* (Ann Arbor, MI: University of Michigan Press, 1993), pp. 157–76; Dario Castiglione, 'Contracts and constitutions', in Richard Bellamy, Vittorio Bufacchi and Dario Castiglione (eds), *Democracy and Constitutional Culture in the Union of Europe* (London: Lothian Foundation, 1995), pp. 75–102; Peter Häberle, 'The constitutional

state and its reform requirements', *Ratio Juris* 13, no. 1 (2000), pp. 77–94; Heidrun Abromeit and Tanja Hitzel-Cassagnes, 'Constitutional change and contractual revision: principles and procedures', *European Law Journal* 5, no. 1 (1999), pp. 23–44.

133 Ingolf Pernice and Ralf Kanitz, *Fundamental Rights and Multilevel Constitutionalism in Europe* (Walter Hallstein-Institut für Europäisches Verfassungsrecht: Humboldt-Universität zu Berlin, 2004) WHI – Paper 7/04.

134 *Ibid.*, p. 6.

135 *Ibid.*, p. 7.

136 Cf. Stephan Bredt, 'The European social contract and the European public sphere', *European Law Journal* 12, no. 1 (2006), pp. 61–77.

137 Cf. Erik Oddvar Eriksen, 'Why a Charter of Fundamental Human Rights in the EU?', *Ratio Juris* 16, no. 3 (2003), pp. 352–72.

138 Cf. Gianluigi Palombella, 'Whose Europe? After the constitution: a goal-based citizenship', *International Journal of Constitutional Law* 3, no. 2/3 (2005), pp. 357–82. For the difference between the legal and the sociological concept of citizenship see Norbert Reich, 'Union citizenship – metaphor or source of rights?', *European Law Journal* 7, no. 1 (2001), pp. 4–23, esp. pp. 6–7.

139 Christopher McCrudden, *The Future of the EU Charter of Fundamental Rights*, Jean Monnet Working Paper 10/0, NYU School of Law, 2001.

140 Cf. Franz C. Mayer and Jan Palmowski, 'European identities and the EU: the ties that bind the peoples of Europe', *Journal of Common Market Studies* 42, no. 3 (2004), pp. 573–98.

141 André Brodocz, *Die Symbolische Dimension der Verfassung. Ein Beitrag zur Institutionentheorie*, (Wiesbaden: Westdeutscher Verlag, 2003), p. 26.

142 *Ibid.*, p. 27.

143 Jutta Limbach argues with regard to Germany that the Federal Constitutional Court fulfils an educational function vis-à-vis the German society, socializing it to democracy. Jutta Limbach, 'Die Integrationskraft des Bundesverfassungsgerichts', in Hanns Vorländer (ed.), *Integration durch Verfassung* (Wiesbaden: Westdeutscher Verlag, 2002), p. 316; Jutta Limbach, 'The concept of the supremacy of the constitution', *Modern Law Review* 64, no. 1 (2001), pp. 1–10.

144 Cf. Dolf Sternberger, *Verfassungspatriotismus: Schriften* (Frankfurt/Main: Insel, 1990), vol. 10; cf. also Dieter Grimm, 'Integration by constitution', *International Journal of Constitutional Law* 3, no. 2–3 (2005), pp. 193–208.

145 Hanns Vorländer, 'Integration durch Verfassung? Die symbolische Bedeutung der Verfassung im politischen Integrationsprozess', in Hanns Vorländer (ed.), *Integration durch Verfassung* (Wiesbaden: Westdeutscher Verlag, 2002), p. 26; Dieter Grimm, 'Integration by constitution', *International Journal of Constitutional Law* 3, no. 2–3 (2005), pp. 193–208.

146 Cf. Gary Schaal, *Vertrauen, Verfassung und Demokratie. Über den Einfluss konstitutioneller Prozesse und Prozeduren auf die Genese von Vertrauensbeziehungen in modernen Demokratien* (Wiesbaden: VS Verlag, 2004), pp. 11–15.

147 André Brodocz, 'Chancen konstitutioneller Identitätsstiftung. Zur symbolischen Integration durch eine deutungsoffene Verfassung', in Hanns Vorländer (ed.), *Integration durch Verfassung* (Wiesbaden: Westdeutscher Verlag, 2002), p. 101–20.

148 Jürgen Habermas, 'Braucht Europa eine Verfassung? Eine Bemerkung zu Dieter Grimm', in Jürgen Habermas, *Die Einbeziehung des Anderen* (Frankfurt/M.: Suhrkamp, 1996), p. 189.

149 Some authors highlight the segmentation of the European publics as the main obstacle to a development of a European identity. In this respect, a pan-European integrated public would be a precondition for a shared collective identity. Cf. Erik Oddvar Eriksen, 'An emerging European public sphere', *European Journal of Social Theory* 8, no. 3 (2005), pp. 341–63.

150 Heinz Kleger (ed.), *Der Konvent als Labor. Texte und Dokumente zum europäischen Verfassungsprozess*, (Muenster: Lit, 2004).

151 Heinz Kleger, 'EU-Verfassung im Härtetest', *WeltTrends* 48, no. 13 (2005), pp. 93–107.

152 Wojciech Sadurski, 'Charter and enlargement', *European Law Journal* 8, no. 3 (2002), pp. 340–62, esp. p. 347; Jiři Přibáň, 'European Union constitution-making, political identity and Central European reflections', *European Law Journal* 11, no. 2 (2005), pp. 135–53.

153 Cf. Neil Walker, 'Constitutionalising enlargement, enlarging Constitutionalism', *European Law Journal* 9, no. 3 (2003), pp. 365–85.

154 Cf. Cindy Skach, 'We, the peoples? Constitutionalizing the European Union', *Journal of Common Market Studies* 43, no. 1 (2005), pp. 149–70.

155 Ireneusz P. Karolewski, 'Zwischen Machtstreben und Toleranz – Verfassungsdiskurs in Polen', *WeltTrends* 48, no. 13 (2005), pp. 115–20.

156 For the difference between governments' constitution and citizens' constitution see Alan C. Cairns, 'The Canadian experience of a Charter of Rights', in Erik Oddvar Eriksen, John Erik Fossum, and Augustín José Menéndez (eds), *The Chartering of Europe: The European Charter of Fundamental Rights and its Constitutional Implications* (Baden-Baden: Nomos, 2003), pp. 93–111. For hegemonic constitutionalization see Ran Hirschl, 'Preserving hegemony? Assessing the political origins of the EU Constitution', *International Journal of Constitutional Law* 3, no. 2 (2005), pp. 269–92.

157 One might be tempted to argue that the Charter of Fundamental Rights reflects rights already covered by national constitutions and the European Convention on Human Rights as well as by the Community Charter of Fundamental Social Rights of Workers. Cf. Bob Hepple, 'The implementation of the Community Charter of Fundamental Social Rights', *Modern Law Review* 53, no. 5 (1990), pp. 643–54; Paul Craig, 'Constitutions, constitutionalism and the European Union', *European Law Journal* 7, no. 2 (2001), pp. 125–50.

158 Cf. Matthias Kumm, 'The jurisprudence of constitutional conflict: constitutional supremacy in Europe before and after Constitutional Treaty', *European Law Journal* 11, no. 3 (2005), pp. 262–307; Christopher Lord, 'Contested meanings, democracy assessment and the European Union', *Comparative European Politics* 5, no. 1 (2007), pp. 70–86.

159 F.L Morton, 'The effect of the Charter of Rights on Canadian Federalism', *Publius: The Journal of Federalism* 25, no. 3 (1995), pp. 173–88.

160 Cf. Joseph Weiler, 'Federalism without constitutionalism: Europe's *Sonderweg*', in Kalypso Nicolaidis and Robert Howse (eds), *The Federal Vision, Legitimacy and Levels of Governance in the United States and the European Union* (Oxford: Oxford University Press, 2001), pp. 54–70, esp. pp. 57, 61–62.

161 Cf. Furio Cerutti, 'A political identity of the Europeans?', *Thesis Eleven* 72, no. 1 (2003), pp. 26–45; cf. also Antonio Estella, 'Constitutional legitimacy and credible commitments in the European Union', *European Law Journal* 11, no. 1 (2005), pp. 22–42.

162 Cf. Erich Vranes, 'The final clauses of the Charter of Fundamental Rights: stumbling blocks for the first and second convention', *European Integration Online Paper* 7, no. 7 (2003), http://eiop.or.at/eiop/texte/2003-007a.htm.

163 Günter Frankenberg, 'The return of the contract: problems and pitfalls of European constitutionalism', *European Law Journal* 6, no. 3 (2000), pp. 257–76.

164 For a broader discussion of constitutionalization in this context see Jeremy Waldron, 'A right-based critique of constitutional rights', *Oxford Journal of Legal Studies* 13 (1993), pp. 18–51. However, an alternative interpretation is also possible. Distrust and collective identity do not have to be construed as contradictory, but as short and long run perspectives of the same process, as distrust may build European collective identity by both strengthening the citizens against the institutions and in the long run make the institutions respect the basic rights. For this alternative interpretation I thank Atina Krajewska.

165 Numerous legal scholars have doubted for various reasons either the legal bite of the Charter or its added value. See for instance Norbert Reich, 'Union Citizenship –

metaphor or source of rights?', *European Law Journal* 7, no. 1 (2001), pp. 4–23, esp. p. 23. However, the Lisbon Treaty stipulates that the Charter of Fundamental Rights shall have the same legal status as treaties. See the General Provision 8 of the Lisbon Treaty, CIG 1/1/07 REV 1.

166 Christoph Engel, 'The European Charter of Fundamental Rights: a changed political opportunity structure and its normative consequences', *European Law Journal* 7, no. 2 (2001), pp. 151–70, esp. p. 159.

167 F.L. Morton, 'The political impact of the Canadian Charter of Rights and Freedoms', *Canadian Journal of Political Science* 20, no. 1 (1987), pp. 31–55; Charles R. Epp, 'Do bills of rights matter? The Canadian Charter of Rights and Freedoms', *American Political Science Review* 90, no. 4 (1996), pp. 765–79.

168 Cf. Kenneth A. Armstrong, 'Citizenship of the Union? Lessons from Carvel and the *Guardian*', *Modern Law Review* 59, no. 4 (1996), pp. 582–88.

169 Ran Hirschl, *Towards Juristocracy: The Origins and Consequences of the New Constitutionalism* (Cambridge, MA: Harvard University Press, 2004).

170 Ben Crum, 'Tailoring representative democracy to the European Union: does the European Constitution reduce the democratic deficit?', *European Law Journal* 11, no. 4 (2005), pp. 451–67, esp. p. 465.

171 Cf. Samantha Besson, 'The European Union and human rights: towards a post-national human rights institution', *Human Rights Law Review* 6, no. 2 (2006), pp. 323–60; Peter Wagner, 'The political form of Europe, Europe as a political form', *Thesis Eleven* 80, no. 1 (2005), pp. 47–73.

172 Christopher McCrudden, 'The future of the EU Charter of Fundamental Rights', Jean Monnet Working Paper (10/01), NYU School of Law, 2001, p. 19.

173 Cf. Jan Erk, 'Real constitution, formal constitution and democracy in the European Union', *Journal of Common Market Studies* 45, no. 3 (2007), pp. 633–52.

174 The numbering and the wording of the Articles correspond to the original version of the Charter of Fundamental Rights, since it did not become a part of the Lisbon Treaty; Charter of Fundamental Rights of the European Union, *Official Journal of the European Communities* (2000/C 364/01); cf. also R. Alonso García, 'The general provisions of the Charter of Fundamental Rights of the European Union', *European Law Journal* 8, no. 4 (2002), pp. 492–514.

175 Cf. Sandra Fredman, 'Transformation or dilution: fundamental rights in the EU social space', *European Law Journal* 12, no. 1 (2006), pp. 41–60, esp. p. 56.

176 *Ibid.*, p. 56.

177 An alternative position stresses that the so-called universal rights, as for instance envisaged by the UN Charter, reflect Western values and therefore are instruments of Westernization of the entire globe. In this sense, we could argue that universal values overlap with European values.

178 Marika Lerch, 'European identity in international society: a constructivist analysis of the EU Charter of Fundamental Rights', Constitutionalism Web-Papers, ConWEB no. (2/2003).

179 Cf. Michel Brand, 'Towards the definitive status of the Charter of Fundamental Rights of the European Union: political document or legally binding text?', *German Law Journal* 4, no. 4 (2003), pp. 395–409; cf. also Paul Brest, 'The fundamental rights controversy: the essential contradictions of normative constitutional scholarship', *Yale Law Journal* 90, no. 5 (1981), pp. 1063–1109.

180 Cf. Vito Breda, 'A European Constitution in a multinational Europe or a multinational constitution for Europe?', *European Law Journal* 12, no. 3 (2006), pp. 330–44; N. W. Barber, 'Legal pluralism and the European Union', *European Law Journal* 12, no. 3 (2006), pp. 306–29; John Erik Fossum, 'The European Union: in search of an identity', *European Journal of Political Theory* 2, no. 3 (2003), pp. 319–40.

181 Cf. Nikos Prentoulis, 'On the technology of collective identity: normative reconstructions of the concept of EU citizenship', *European Law Journal* 7, no. 2 (2001), pp. 196–218.

182 Cf. Armin von Bogdandy, 'The European Constitution and European identity: text and subtext of the treaty establishing a constitution for Europe', *International Journal of Constitutional Law* 3, no. 2/3 (2005), pp. 295–315, esp. p. 314; Joseph H.H. Weiler, 'On the power of the word: Europe's constitutional iconography', *International Journal of Constitutional Law* 3, no. (2–3) (2005), pp. 173–90; cf. also Terence Daintith, 'The constitutional protection of economic rights', *International Journal of Constitutional Law* 2, no. 1 (2004), pp. 56–90.

183 Cf. John Morijn, 'Balancing fundamental rights and common market freedoms in Union law: Schmidberger and Omega in the light of the European Constitution', *European Law Journal* 12, no. 1 (2006), pp. 15–40; Sergio Carrera, 'What does free movement mean in theory and practice in an enlarged EU?', *European Law Journal* 111, no. 6 (2005), pp. 699–721.

184 Cf. Norbert Reich, 'The constitutional relevance of citizenship and free movement in an enlarged Union', *European Law Journal* 11, no. 6 (2005), pp. 675–98; Erin Delaney and Luca Barani, 'The promotion of symmetrical European citizenship: a federal perspective', *Journal of European Integration* 25, no. 2 (2003), pp. 95–114.

185 Cf. Klara Kańska, 'Towards administrative human rights in the EU: impact of the Charter of Fundamental Rights', *European Law Journal* 10, no. 3 (2004), pp. 296–326.

186 *Ibid.*, p.57.

187 Gary S. Schaal, 'Vier normative Konzepte von Integration qua Verfassung', in Hanns Vorländer (ed.), *Integration durch Verfassung* (Wiesbaden: Westdeutscher Verlag, 2002), pp. 71–100.

188 Heinz Kleger (ed.), *Der Konvent als Labor. Texte und Dokumente zum europäischen Verfassungsprozess* (Münster: Lit, 2004), p. 215.

189 Cf. Massimo La Torre, 'The law beneath rights' feet. Preliminary investigation for a study of the Charter of Fundamental Rights of the European Union', *European Law Journal* 8, no. 4 (2002), pp. 515–35.

190 Gerard Delanty, 'European citizenship: a critical assessment', *Citizenship Studies* 11, no. 1 (2007), pp. 63–72.

191 Cf. Frank I. Michelman, 'The constitution, social rights, and liberal political justification', *International Journal of Constitutional Law* 1, no. 1 (2003), pp. 13–34; Winfried Brugger, 'Communitarianism as the social and legal theory behind the German Constitution', *International Journal of Constitutional Law* 2, no. 3 (2004), pp. 431–60; Erhard Denninger, '"Security, Diversity, Solidarity" instead of "Freedom, Equality, Fraternity"', *Constellations* 7, no. 4 (2000), pp. 507–21. See also responses to the proposed new constitutional ideals. Michel Rosenfeld, 'American constitutionalism confronts Denninger's new constitutional paradigm', *Constellations* 7, no. 4 (2000), pp. 529–48; Jürgen Habermas, 'Remarks on Erhard Denninger's triad of diversity, security, and solidarity', *Constellations* 7, no. 4 (2000), pp. 523–28.

192 Cf. Jo Shaw, *A Strong Europe is a Social Europe*, The Federal Trust, Online Paper 05/03; Philippe C. Schmitter and Michael W. Bauer, 'A (modest) proposal for expanding social citizenship in the European Union', *Journal of European Social Policy* 11, no. 1 (2001), pp. 55–65; Andrew Moravcsik, 'What can we learn from the collapse of the European constitutional project? *Politische Vierteljahresschrift* 47, no. 2 (2006), pp. 219–41.

193 The Lisbon Treaty refers to these Articles inter alia under the general provision 176.

194 Cf. Nathalie Karagiannis, 'Solidarity within Europe/solidarity without Europe', *European Societies* 9, no. 1 (2007), pp. 3–21.

195 For the partially opposing view cf. Deborah Mabbett, 'The development of rights-based social policy in the European Union: the example of disability rights', *Journal of Common Market Studies* 43, no. 1 (2005), pp. 97–120.

196 Augustín José Menéndez, 'The sinews of peace: rights to solidarity in the Charter of Fundamental Rights of the European Union', *Ratio Juris* 16, no. 3 (2003), pp. 374–98.

197 Cf. Miguel Poiares Maduro, 'Reforming the market or the state? Article 30 and the European Constitution: economic freedom and political rights', *European Law Journal* 3, no. 1 (1997), pp. 55–82.

198 Cf. Christian Joerges, 'On the disregard for history in the convention process', *European Law Journal* 12, no. 1 (2006), pp. 2–5.

199 The references to solidarity have been taken over from the Constitutional Treaty and are a part of the Lisbon Treaty, Title VII, General Provisions 176. Cf. also House of Commons (Foreign Affairs Committee), Foreign Policy Aspects of the Lisbon Treaty, Third report of Session 2007–8, January 2008.

200 Cf. Vanda Knowles and Silke Thomson-Pottebohm, 'The UK, Germany and ESDP: developments at the convention and the IGC', *German Politics* 13, no. 4 (2004), pp. 581–604.

201 Addendum to the Presidency Note, Conference of the Representatives of the Governments of the Member Sates, CIG (60/03) ADD 1, Brussels, 9 December 2003.

202 Ireneusz Pawel Karolewski, 'Constitutionalization of the Common Foreign and Security Policy of the European Union: implications of the Constitutional Treaty', *German Law Journal* 6, no. 11 (2005), pp. 1649–66.

203 Richard Bellamy and Justus Schönlau, *The Good, the Bad and the Ugly: The Need for Constitutional Compromise and the Drafting of the EU Constitution*, The Federal Trust for Education and Research, 2003, Online paper 33/03.

204 For a more optimistic evaluation see Augustín José Menéndez, 'Chartering Europe: legal status and policy implications of the Charter of Fundamental Rights of the European Union', *Journal of Common Market Studies* 40, no. 3 (2002), pp. 471–90. Menéndez argues that the symbolic value of the Charter arises through its impact on concrete EU policies such as social and economic goals or the enlargement process, thus rendering the EU more coherent. However, this argument shows little empirical validity, as it was formulated prior to the Eastern enlargement and the failed referenda on the Constitutional Treaty in France and the Netherlands. In both cases, the symbolic impact of the Charter was modest at best and divisive at worst. Cf. also Gráinne De Búrca, 'The European constitutional project after the referenda', *Constellations* 13, no. 2 (2006), pp. 205–17.

205 For the conceptual history and societal development of solidarity see Thomas Fiegle, *Von der Solidarité zur Solidarität* (Muenster et al.: LIT, 2003).

206 Cf. Cynthia J. McSwain, 'Administrators and citizenship: the liberalist legacy of the constitution', *Administration & Society* 17, no. 2 (1985), pp. 131–48.

207 Cf. Nathan Gibbs, 'Examining the aesthetic dimensions of the Constitutional Treaty', *European Law Journal* 11, no. 3 (2005), pp. 326–42.

208 Cf. Fareed Zacharia, 'The rise of illiberal democracy', *Foreign Affairs* 76, no. 6 (1997), pp. 22–43.

209 Yves Mény, 'De la démocratie en Europe: old concepts and new Challenges', *Journal of Common Market Studies* 41, no. 1 (2002), pp. 1–13, esp. p. 3.

210 Cf. Simone Chambers, 'Democracy, popular sovereignty, and constitutional legitimacy', *Constellations* 11, no. 2 (2004), pp. 153–173.

211 Ulrich Beck, 'The terrorist threat: world risk society revisited', *Theory, Culture & Society* 19, no. 4 (2002), pp. 39–55; Ulrich Beck, 'The silence of words: on terror and war', *Security Dialogue* 34, no. 3 (2003), pp. 255–67; Claudia Aradau and Rens Van Munster, 'Governing terrorism through risk: taking precautions, (un)knowing the future', *European Journal of International Relations* 13, no. 1 (2007), pp. 89–115.

212 Cf. Barry Buzan and Ole Wæver, 'Slippery? Contradictory? Sociologically untenable? The Copenhagen school replies', *Review of International Studies* 23, no. 2 (1997), pp. 241–50; Malcolm Anderson and Joanna Apap, *Changing Conceptions of Security and their Implications for EU Justice and Home Affairs Cooperation* (CEPS Policy Brief 26, 2002).

213 Cf. Paul Roes, 'Securitization and minority rights: conditions of desecuritization', *Security Dialogue* 35, no. 3 (2004), pp. 279–94, esp. p. 281; Thierry Balzacq, 'The three faces of securitization: political agency, audience and context', *European Journal of International Relations* 11, no. 2 (2005), pp. 171–201.

214 For an analysis of the executive-centred governance in the EU see Klaus H. Goetz, 'Europäisierung der öffentlichen Verwaltung – oder europäische Verwaltung?', in Jörg Bogumil, Werner Jann and Frank Nullmeier (eds), *Politik und Verwaltung* (Wiesbaden: VS Verlag für Sozialwissenschaften, 2006), pp. 472–90.

215 Engin F. Isin, 'The neurotic citizen', *Citizenship Studies* 8, no. 3 (2004), pp. 217–35.

216 Roy Boyne, 'Post-panopticism', *Economy and Society* 29, no. 2 (2000), pp. 285–307.

217 Cf. Jef Huysmans, 'Minding exceptions: the politics of insecurity and liberal democracy', *Contemporary Political Theory* 3, no. 3 (2004), pp. 321–41; Benjamin J. Muller, '(Dis)Qualified bodies: securitization, citizenship and identity management', *Citizenship Studies* 8, no. 3 (2004), pp. 279–94; William E. Scheuerman, 'Carl Schmitt and the road to Abu Ghraib', *Constellations* 13, no. 1 (2006), pp. 108–24.

218 Cf. Andrew W. Neal, 'Foucault in Guantánamo: towards an archaeology of the exception', *Security Dialogue* 37, no. 1 (2006), pp. 31–46.

219 Bülent Diken, 'From refugee camps to gated communities: biopolitics and the end of the city', *Citizenship Studies* 8, no. 1 (2004), pp. 83–106.

220 Cf. Mar Jimeno-Bulnes, 'After September 11th: the fight against terrorism in national and European Law: substantive and procedural rule, some examples', *European Law Journal* 10, no. 2 (2004), pp. 235–53; Elspeth Guild, 'Crime and the EU's constitutional future in an area of freedom, security and justice', *European Law Journal* 10, no. 2 (2004), pp. 218–34.

221 Juliet Lodge, 'EU homeland security: citizens or suspects?', *Journal of European Integration* 26, no. 3 (2004), pp. 253–79.

222 Cf. Muller, *op. cit.*, pp. 279–94.

223 Jörg Monar, 'The dynamics of justice and home affairs: laboratories, driving factors and costs', *Journal of Common Market Studies* 39, no. 4 (2001), pp. 747–64; Theodora Kostakopoulou, 'The protective Union: change and continuity in migration law and policy in Post-Amsterdam Europe', *Journal of Common Market Studies* 38, no. 3 (2000), pp. 497–518.

224 Cf. Joanne van Selm-Thorburn, 'Asylum in the Amsterdam Treaty: a harmonious future?', *Journal of Ethnic and Migration Studies* 24, no. 4 (1998), pp. 627–38.

225 Cf. Jörg Monar, 'Cooperation in the justice and home affairs domain: characteristics, constraints and progress', *Journal of European Integration* 28, no. 5 (2007), pp. 495–509.

226 *Ibid.*, p. 503.

227 Juliet Lodge, 'EU homeland security: citizens or suspects?', *Journal of European Integration* 26, no. 3 (2004), pp. 253–79.

228 Zygmunt Bauman, 'Social issues of law and order', *British Journal of Criminology* 40, no. 2 (2000), pp. 205–21, esp. p. 208.

229 Jef Huysmans, 'The European Union and the securitization of migration', *Journal of Common Market Studies* 38, no. 5 (2000), pp. 751–77.

230 Cf. Michael Collyer, 'Migrants, migration and the security paradigm: constraints and opportunities', *Mediterranean Politics* 11, no. 2 (2006), pp. 255–70.

231 Cf. Gabriele Orcalli, 'Constitutional choice and European immigration policy', *Constitutional Political Economy* 18, no. 1 (2007), pp. 1–20.

232 Cf. Sandra Lavenex, 'The Europeanization of refugee policies: normative challenges and institutional legacies', *Journal of Common Market Studies* 39, no. 5 (2001), pp. 851–74; Virginie Guiraudon, 'The constitution of a European immigration policy domain: a political sociology approach', *Journal of European Public Policy* 10, no, 2 (2003), pp. 263–82.

233 Michel Wieviorka, 'Racism in Europe: unity and diversity', in Ali Rattansi and Sallie Westwood (eds), *Racism, Modernity and Identity: On the Western Front* (Cambridge: Polity, 1994), pp. 185–88; cf. also Gallya Lahav, 'Public opinion toward immigration in the European Union: does it matter?', *Comparative Political Studies* 37, no. 10 (2004), pp. 1151–83.

234 Benjamin J. Muller, '(Dis)Qualified bodies: securitization, citizenship and identity management', *Citizenship Studies* 8, no. 3 (2004), pp. 279–94; William Walters, 'Secure border, safe haven, domopolitics', *Citizenship Studies* 8, no. 3 (2004), pp. 237–60; Bülent Diken, 'From refugee camps to gated communities: biopolitics and the end of the city', *Citizenship Studies* 8, no.1 (2004), pp. 83–106; Davina Bhandar, 'Renormalizing citizenship and life in fortress North America', *Citizenship Studies* 8, no. 3 (2004), pp. 261–78; Gwendolyn Sasse, 'Securitization or securing rights? Exploring the conceptual foundations of policies towards minorities and migrants in Europe', *Journal of Common Market Studies* 43, no. 4 (2005), pp. 673–93; Liza Schuster, 'A sledgehammer to crack a nut: deportation, detention and dispersal in Europe', *Social Policy & Administration* 39, no. 6 (2005), pp. 606–21.

235 Sandra Lavenex, 'Migration and the EU's new Eastern border: between realism and liberalism', *Journal of European Public Policy* 8, no. 1 (2001), pp. 24–42. For an opposite account cf. Alexander Caviedes, 'The open method of co-ordination in immigration policy: a tool for prying open fortress Europe? *Journal of European Public Policy* 11, no. 2 (2004), pp. 289–310.

236 Ruben Zaiotti, 'Of friends and fences: Europe's neighbourhood policy and the gated community syndrome', *Journal of European Integration* 29, no. 2 (2007), pp. 143–62; cf. also Dario Melossi, 'Security, social control, democracy and migration within the constitution of the EU', *European Law Journal* 11, no. 1 (2005), pp. 5–21.

237 Tamara Vukov, 'Imagining communities through immigration policies: governmental regulation, media spectacles and affective politics of national borders', *International Journal of Cultural Studies* 6, no. 3 (2003), pp. 335–53.

238 Cf. Michael Billig, *Banal Nationalism* (London: Sage, 1995).

239 Lawrence Grossberg, *We Gotta Get Out of This Place: Popular Conservatism and Postmodern Culture* (London: Routledge, 1992).

240 Cf. Thomas Faist, 'How to define a foreigner? The symbolic politics of immigration in German partisan discourse, 1978–92', in: Martin Baldwin-Edwards and Martin A. Schain (eds), *The Politics of Immigration in Western Europe* (Ilford: Frank Cass, 1994), pp. 50–71; cf. also Hein de Haas, 'The myth of invasion: irregular migration from West Africa to the Maghreb and the European Union', IMI research report (Oxford: International Migration Institute, University of Oxford, 2007).

241 Walters, *op. cit.,* p. 241.

242 Davina Bhandar, 'Renormalizing citizenship and life in fortress North America', *Citizenship Studies* 8, no. 3 (2004), pp. 261–78; Catherine Dauvergne, 'Security and migration law in the less brave new world', *Social & Legal Studies* 16, no. 4 (2007), pp. 533–49.

243 Cf. Dennis Broeders, 'The new digital borders of Europe: EU databases and the surveillance of irregular migrants', *International Sociology* 22, no. 1 (2007), pp. 71–92; Ian Leader, 'Policing, securitization and democratization In Europe', *Criminal Justice* 2, no. 2 (2002), pp. 125–53.

244 Joanna Apap and Sergio Carrera, *Maintaining Security within Borders: Towards a Permanent State of Emergency in the EU?* (CEPS Policy Brief 41, 2003).

245 Emek M. Uçarer, 'Managing asylum and European integration: expanding spheres of exclusion', *International Studies Perspectives* 2, no. 3 (2001), pp. 288–304, esp. p. 303.

246 Cf. Andrew Geddes, 'International migration and state sovereignty in an integrating Europe', *International Migration* 39, no. 6 (2001), pp. 21–42, esp. p. 36; Andrew Geddes, 'Europe's border relationships and international migration relations', *Journal of Common Market Studies* 43, no. 4 (2005), pp. 787–806.

247 Cf. Thomas Faist, 'Extension du domaine de la lutte: international migration and security before and after September 11, 2001', *International Migration Review* 36, no. 1 (2002), pp. 7–14.

248 Andreas Maurer and Roderick Parkes, *Asylum Policy and Democracy in the European Union from Amsterdam Towards the Hague Programme*, Working Paper FG 1, SWP Berlin, 2006, esp. pp. 3–4.

249 Dennis Broeders and Godfried Engbersen, 'The fight against illegal migration: identification policies and immigrants' counterstrategies', *American Behavioral Scientist* 50, no. 12 (2007), pp. 1592–1609.

250 Frances Webber uses the term 'crime of arrival' with regard to the policy of criminalization of migrants in the EU. Frances Webber, 'Crimes of arrival: immigrants and asylum-seekers in the new Europe', Statewatch, 2000.

251 François Crépeau et al., 'International migration: security concerns and human rights standards', *Transcultural Psychiatry* 44, no. 3 (2007), pp. 311–37.

252 Emek M. Uçarer, 'Managing asylum and European integration: expanding spheres of exclusion', *International Studies Perspectives* 2, no. 3 (2001), pp. 288–304.

253 Ryszard Cholewinski, 'Migrants as minorities: integration and inclusion in the enlarged European Union', *Journal of Common Market Studies* 43, no. 4 (2005), pp. 695–716. In a similar vein of exploring the security–rights nexus argues Gwendolyn Sasse. Gwendolyn Sasse, 'Securitization or securing rights? Exploring the conceptual foundations of policies towards minorities and migrants in Europe', *Journal of Common Market Studies* 43, no. 4 (2005), pp. 674–93; Gwendolyn Sasse, 'A research agenda for the study of migrants and minorities in Europe', *Journal of Common Market Studies* 43, no. 4 (2005), pp. 655–71.

254 Rosemary Byrne et al., 'Understanding refugee law in an enlarged European Union', *European Journal of International Law* 15, no. 2 (2004), pp. 355–79, esp. p. 360.

255 People seeking asylum in the EU are likely to encounter the EU before entering its territory. The points of encounter are extraterritorial EU visa consulates, the EU Immigration Liaison Officers at the airports of transit and origin countries of migration as well as in the Mediterranean patrolled by EU navy vessels. Cf. Thomas Gammeltoft-Hansen, 'The extraterritorialization of asylum and the advent of "protection lite"', DISS Working Paper 2, Danish Institute for International Studies, Copenhagen, 2007; Derek Lutterbeck, 'Policing migration in the Mediterranean', *Mediterranean Politics* 11, no. 1 (2006), pp. 59–82.

256 Andreas Maurer and Roderick Parkes, *Asylum Policy and Democracy in the European Union from Amsterdam Towards the Hague Programme*, Working Paper FG 1, SWP Berlin, 2006, esp. pp. 5–6.

257 Cf. Frontex, 'FRONTEX-led EU illegal immigration technical mission to Libya: 28.05–5.06.2007', Warsaw; Karin Fathimath Afeef, 'The politics of extraterritorial processing: offshore asylum policies in Europe and the Pacific', RSC Working Paper 36, Refugee Studies Centre, University of Oxford, 2006.

258 Roderick Parkes, 'Joint patrols at the EU's Southern border', SWP Comments 21, 2006; COM(2006) 733; cf. Niklas Bremberg Heijl, 'Between a rock and a hard place: Euro-Mediterranean security revisited', *Mediterranean Politics* 12, no. 1 (2007), pp. 1–16.

259 Muller, *op. cit.,* p. 287; William Walters, 'deportation, expulsion, and the international police of aliens', *Citizenship Studies* 6, no. 3 (2002), pp. 265–92.

260 Cf. Catherine Phuong, 'Enlarging fortress Europe: EU accession, asylum, and immigration in candidate countries', *International and Comparative Law Quarterly* 52, no. 3 (2003), pp. 641–64.

261 Cf. Lora Borissova, 'The adoption of the Schengen and the justice and home affairs *acquis*: the case of Bulgaria and Romania', *European Foreign Affairs Review* 8, no. 1 (2003), pp. 105–24.

262 Rosemary Byrne et al., 'Understanding refugee law in an enlarged European Union', *European Journal of International Law* 15, no. 2 (2004), pp. 355–79, esp. pp. 361 and 375.

263 Cf. Nazaré Albuquerque Abell, 'The compatibility of readmission agreements with the 1951 Convention relating to the status of refugees', *International Journal of Refugee Law* 11, no. 1 (1999), pp. 60–83; Sandra Lavenex, 'Migration and the EU's new Eastern border: between realism and liberalism', *Journal of European Public Policy* 8, no. 1 (2001), pp. 24–42; Sandra Lavenex, 'EU external governance in wider Europe', *Journal of European Public Policy* 11, no. 4 (2004), pp. 680–700.

264 Cf. Jorrit J. Rijpma and Marise Cremona, 'The extra-territoralisation of EU migration policies and the rule of law', EUI Working Paper 1, Department of Law, 2007.

265 Cf. Adrian Favell and Randall Hansen, 'Markets against politics: migration, EU enlargement and the idea of Europe', *Journal of Ethnic and Migration Studies* 28, no. 4 (2002), pp. 581–601.

266 Byrne et al., *op. cit.*, p. 364; cf. also Virginie Guiraudon, 'The constitution of a European immigration policy domain: a political sociology approach', *Journal of European Public Policy* 10, no. 2 (2003), pp. 263–82.

267 Cf. John P. McCormick, 'Fear, technology, and the state: Carl Schmitt, Leo Strauss, and the revival of Hobbes in Weimar and National Socialist Germany', *Political Theory* 22, no. 4 (1994), pp. 619–52.

268 Vida Bajc, 'Introduction: debating surveillance in the age of security', *American Behavioral Scientist* 50, no. 12 (2007), pp. 1567–91; Gallya Lahav, 'Immigration and the state: the devolution and privatisation of immigration control in the EU', *Journal of Ethnic and Migration Studies* 24, no. 4 (1998), pp. 675–94; Christina Boswell, 'The securitisation of migration: a risky strategy for European States', DIIS Brief, Danish Institute for International Studies, 2007; Rey Koslowski, 'European migration regimes: emerging, enlarging and deteriorating', *Journal of Ethnic and Migration Studies* 24, no. 4 (1998), pp. 735–49.

269 House of Lords (European Union Committee), Human Rights Protection in Europe: the Fundamental Rights Agency, 29th Report with Evidence 5–2006, London; Gabriel Nikolaij Toggenburg, 'Die EU-Grundrechteagentur: Satellit oder Letstern?', SWP-Aktuell 8, 2007.

270 Petra Bendel, 'Immigration policy in the European Union: still bringing up the walls for fortress Europe?', *Migration Letters* 2, no. 1 (2005), pp. 20–31; cf. Council (16054/04); JAI 559; Antonio Vitorino, 'The future of the European Union agenda on asylum, migration and borders', Speech/04/435; Franco Frattini, 'The Hague Programme: a partnership for the European renewal in the field of freedom, security and justice', Speech/05/441.

271 Council Decision establishing EUROPOL, SEC(2006) 1682; COM(2006) 817.

272 Cf. Wolfgang Wagner, 'Guarding the guards: the European Convention and the communization of police-co-operation', *Journal of European Public Policy* 13, no. 8 (2006), pp. 1230–46.

273 Cf. Europäisches Parlament (Ausschuss für bürgerliche Freiheiten, Justiz und innere Angelegenheiten), Arbeitsdokument zur Errichtung des Europäischen Polizeiamts (EUROPOL), 19.2.2007, DT\652813DE.doc.

274 Cf. Walter Peissl, 'Surveillance and security: a dodgy relationship', *Journal of Contingencies and Crisis Management* 11, no. 1 (2003), pp. 19–24.

275 Sergio Carrera, 'The EU Border Management Strategy: FRONTEX and the challenges of irregular immigration in the Canary Islands', CEPS Working Document No. 261, 2007.

276 COM(2006) 401; COM(2006) 67.

277 Council Regulation No 2007/2004 establishing Frontex, L 349/1.

278 Hélène Jorry, 'Construction of a European institutional model for managing operational cooperation at the EU's external borders: is the FRONTEX Agency a decisive step forward?', Challenge Project, Liberty and Security, Research Paper 6, 2007.

279 House of Lords (European Union Committee), Schengen Information System II, 9th Report of Session 2006–7, Report with Evidence (London: House of Lords, 2007); Marie McGinley and Roderick Parkes, 'Data protection in the EU's internal security cooperation: fundamental rights vs. effective cooperation?', SWP Research Paper 5, 2007.

280 Juliet Lodge, 'EU homeland security: citizens or suspects?', *Journal of European Integration* 26, no. 3 (2004), pp. 253–79, esp. p. 265; Council, Council Conclusions on the SIS II, the SUS 1+ and the enlargement of the Schengen area, 2768th Justice and Home Affairs Council meeting, Brussels, 4–5 December 2006, CONCL 3, (14292/04).

281 Juliet Lodge, 'eJustice, security and biometrics: the EU's proximity paradox', *European Journal of Crime, Criminal Law and Criminal Justice* 13, no. 4 (2005), pp. 533–64.

282 European Council, Presidency Conclusions, CONCL3 1492/04.

283 COM(2006)332, p. 19.

284 Cf. Gallya Lahav, *Immigration and Politics in the New Europe: Reinventing Borders* (Cambridge: Cambridge University Press, 2004).

285 Council Regulation No (2725/2000); Jörg Monar, 'Justice and home affairs', *Journal of Common Market Studies* 42, s. 1 (2004), pp. 117–33; Jef Huysmans, 'The European Union and the securitization of migration', *Journal of Common Market Studies* 38, no. 5 (2000), pp. 751–77.

286 Cf. Jonathan P. Aus, 'Eurodac: a solution looking for a problem? *European Integration Online Papers* 10, no. 6 (2006); http://eiop.or.at/eiop/index.php/eiop/article/view/2006_006a; Jonathan P. Aus, 'Supranational governance in an "area of freedom, security and justice": Eurodac and the politics of biometric control', Paper presented at ARENA, University of Oslo, 18 November 2003.

287 Cf. Michael Levi and David S. Wall, 'Technologies, security and privacy in the post-9/11 European information society', *Journal of Law and Society* 31, no. 2 (2004), pp. 194–220; Angela Liberatore, 'Balancing security and democracy, and the role of expertise: biometric politics in the European Union', *European Journal on Criminal Policy and Research* 13, no.1–2 (2007), pp. 109–37.

288 Cf. Theodora Kostakopoulou, 'The protective Union: change and continuity in migration law and policy in post-Amsterdam Europe', *Journal of Common Market Studies* 38, no. 3 (2000), pp. 497–518. The network approach to surveillance and identity control is also visible in other EU surveillance systems. The council agreed in 2005 to establish the ICONET (Information and Coordination Network) as a secure web-based information network, which is supposed to connect the migration management services of the member states to confidentially exchange information on irregular entry and the return of illegal residents. This is expected to be supplemented by the FADO, which is a network-based image archiving system of False and Authentic Documents. The FADO is designed to provide the member states with information on the authenticity of travel documents, with the goal of preventing persons with forged documents from entering the EU. Cf. also Petra Bendel, 'Immigration policy in the European Union: still bringing up the walls for fortress Europe?', *Migration Letters* 2, no. 1 (2005), pp. 20–31.

289 Cf. Erika Feller, 'Carrier sanctions and international law', *International Journal of Refugee Law* 1, no. 1 (1989), pp. 48–66; Virginie Guiraudon and Gallya Lahav, 'A reappraisal of the state sovereignty debate: the case of migration control', *Comparative Political Studies* 33, no. 2 (2000), pp. 163–95.

290 Monica Svantesson, 'The EU and illegal immigration: an ascending (in)secure community?' in Arjen Boin, Magnus Ekenbergen and Mark Rhinard (eds), *Protecting the European Union: Policies, Sectors and Institutional Solutions* (University of Leiden: National Defence College, 2006), pp. 61–78, esp. p. 71.

291 Didier Bigo, 'Security and immigration: toward a governmentality of unease', *Alternatives* 27 (2002), pp. 63–92.

292 Cf. David Lyon, 'National ID cards: crime-control, citizenship and social sorting', *Policing* 1, no. 1 (2007), pp. 111–18.

293 Cf. Evelien Brouwer, 'Immigration, asylum and terrorism: a changing dynamic of legal and practical developments in the EU in response to the terrorist attacks of 11.09', *European Journal of Migration and Law* 4, no. 4 (2002), pp. 399–424.

294 Cf. Claudia Aradau and Rens Van Munster, 'Governing terrorism through risk: taking precautions, (un)knowing the future', *European Journal of International Relations* 13, no. 1 (2007), pp. 89–115.

295 Cf. Richard Jackson, 'Constructing enemies: Islamic terrorism in political and academic discourse', *Government and Opposition* 42, no. 3 (2007), pp. 394–426.

296 Conor Gearty, 'Terrorism and human rights', *Government and Opposition* 42, no. 3 (2007), pp. 340–62.

297 Bill Durodié, 'Fear and terror in a post-political age', *Government and Opposition* 42, no. 3 (2007), pp. 427–50.

298 Wolfgang Hetzer, 'Terrorist attacks: criminal prosecution or national defence?', *European Journal on Criminal Policy and Research* 13, no. 1–2 (2007), pp. 33–55.

299 Cf. Lucia Zedner, 'Securing liberty in the face of terror: reflections from criminal justice', *Journal of Law and Society* 32, no. 4 (2005), pp. 507–33; Anastassia Tsoukala, 'Democracy in the light of security: British and French political discourse on domestic counter-terrorism policies', *Political Studies* 54, no. 3 (2006), pp. 607–27.

300 Cf. Gerrard Quille, 'The European security strategy: a framework for EU security interests?', *International Peacekeeping* 11, no. 3 (2004), pp. 422–38.

301 Cf. IP/07/1064.

302 De Vries was followed in his office in 2007 by Gilles de Kerckhove.

303 Cf. Gijs de Vries, 'European strategy in the fight against terrorism and the co-operation with the United States', Speech at the CSIS European Dialogue Lunch, Washington, 13 May 2004.

304 Laurence Thieux, 'European security and global terrorism: the strategic aftermath of the Madrid bombings', *Perspectives* 22 (2004), pp. 59–74.

305 Susie Alegre and Marisa Leaf, 'Mutual recognition in european judicial cooperation: a step too far too soon? Case study – the European arrest warrant', *European Law Journal* 10, no. 2 (2004), pp. 200–217; Nikolaos Lavranos, 'Europol and the fight against terrorism', *European Foreign Affairs Review* 8, no. 2 (2003), pp. 259–75.

306 Cf. House of Lords, The EU/US Passenger Name Record (PNR) Agreement, 21st Report of Session 2006–7, London, 2007.

307 Commission, Communication from the Commission to the Council and the Parliament: Transfer of Air Passenger Name Record (PNR) Data – A Global EU Approach, Brussels 16 December 2003, COM(2003) 826.

308 European Parliament Resolution of 12 July 2007 on the PNR agreement with the USA, P6–TA-PROV(2007)0347.

309 *Ibid.*

310 European Parliament, 'Fighting terrorism can never be an excuse to violate human rights', Press Release, Brussels, 12 December 2007; cf. also María Verónica Pérez Asinari and Yves Poullet, 'Public security versus data privacy: airline passengers' data, adoption of an adequacy decision by the European Commission', *Computer Law & Security Report* 20, no. 5 (2004), pp. 370–76.

311 According to this proposal, the EU will collect personal data on air passengers coming into and leaving EU airspace, including phone number, email address, travel agent, full itinerary, billing data and baggage information. The information will be collected in analysis units that will make a 'risk assessment' of the traveller, which could lead to the questioning or even refusal of entry. The data is to be kept for five years and then another eight years in a 'dormant' database. Commission, Proposal for a Council Framework Decision on the use of Passenger Name Record (PNR) for law enforcement purposes, Brussels 6 November 2007, COM(2007) 654.

312 Commission, Communication from the Commission to the European Parliament and the Council: Stepping up the fight against terrorism, Brussels, 6 November 2007, COM(2007) 649; Franco Frattini, 'EU counter-terrorism strategy', Speech/07/505.

313 Commission, Green Paper on Bio-Preparedness, Brussels 11 July 2007, COM(2007) 399.

314 Claudia Aradau and Rens Van Munster, 'Governing terrorism through risk: taking precautions, (un)knowing the future', *European Journal of International Relations* 13, no. 1 (2007), pp. 89–115, esp. p. 104.

315 Cf. Elspeth Guild, 'The uses and abuses of counter-terrorism policies in Europe: the case of terrorist lists', *Journal of Common Market Studies* 46, no. 1 (2008), pp. 173–93.

316 Commission, Green Paper on detection technologies in the work of law enforcement, customs and other security authorities, Brussels, 1 September 2006, COM(2006) 474.

317 Franco Frattini, Closing speech on 'Public Security, Privacy and Technology', Speech/07/728, Brussels, 20 November 2007.

318 Commission, Annual Policy Strategy for 2008, Brussels 21 February 2007, COM(2007) 65.

319 *The Times*, 16 March 2007.

320 Directive 2006/24/EC of the European Parliament and of the Council of March 2006, Official *Journal of the European Union*, L 105/54.

321 European Parliament, Resolution on SWIFT, the PNR agreement and the transatlantic dialogue on these issues, P6–TA(2007)0039.

322 Council, Conclusions and Plan of Action of the Extraordinary European Council Meeting on 21 September 2001, SN (140/01).

323 Javier Solana, 'A secure Europe in a better world: European security strategy, the European Union Institute for Security Studies', Paris, December 2003.

324 Jörg Monar, 'Common threat and common response? The European Union's counter-terrorism strategy and its problems', *Government and Opposition* 42, no. 3 (2007), pp. 292–313.

325 Cf. Anne Deighton and Victor Mauer (eds), *Securing Europe? Implementing the European Security Strategy*, Zürcher Beiträge zur Sicherheitspolitik Nr. 77 (ETH: Zürich, 2006).

326 Cf. Jürgen Storbeck and Mascia Toussaint, 'Outline of a balanced and effective internal security strategy for the European Union', *European Journal of Crime, Criminal Law and Criminal Justice* 12, no.1 (2004), pp. 1–13.

327 Council, The European Union Counter-Terrorism Strategy, Brussels 30 November 2005, 14469/4/05 REV 4.

328 Gijs de Vries, ' The European Union's Role in the fight against terrorism', *Irish Studies in International Affairs* 16 (2005), pp. 3–9; Jan Wouters and Frederik Naert, 'Of arrest warrant, terrorist offences and extradition deals: an appraisal of the EU's main criminal law measures against terrorism after 11 September', Institute for International Law, Working Paper no. 56, University of Leuven, 2004; Paul Wilkinson, 'International terrorism: the changing threat and the EU's response', Chaillot Paper 84, Institute for International Studies, Paris, 2005.

329 Council, EU Plan of Action on Combating Terrorism, Brussels, 15 June 2004, 10586/04; Counter-Terrorism Coordinator, Implementation of the Action Plan to Combat Terrorism, Brussels 12 December 2005, (15704/05); Council, Implementation of the Action Plan to combat terrorism, 9809/1/05. Cf also Raphael Bossong, 'The action plan on combating terrorism: a flawed instrument of EU security governance', *Journal of Common Market Studies* 46, no. 1 (2008), pp. 27–48.

330 Cf. Annegret Benediek, 'Cross-pillar security regime building in the European Union: effects of the European Security Strategy of December 2003', *European Integration Online Papers* 10, no. 9 (2006), http://eiop.or.at/eiop/index.php/eiop/article/view/2006_009a; Monica Den Boer et al., 'Legitimacy under pressure: the European web of counter-terrorism networks', *Journal of Common Market Studies* 46, no. 1 (2008), pp. 101–24.

331 Cf. Marianne L. Wade, 'Fear vs. freedom post 9/11: a European debate', *European Journal on Criminal Policy and Research* 13, no.1 (2007), pp. 3–12.

332 Council Presidency, The Hague Programme, 14292//04 REV 1, Brussels 4–5 November 2004.

333 Cf. Daniel Keohane, 'The absent friend: EU foreign policy and counter-terrorism', *Journal of Common Market Studies* 46, no. 1 (2008), pp. 125–46.

334 Cf. Ian Loader, 'Policing, securitization and democratization in Europe', *Criminal Justice* 2, no. 2 (2002), pp. 125–53.

335 House of Lords, Behind Closed Doors: the meeting of the G6 Interior Ministers at Heiligendamm, 40th Report of Session 2005–6, 2006, London.

336 Cf. Antoni Podolski, 'European security after terrorist attacks in Madrid, reports and analyses 3/04/A', Centre for International Relations, Warsaw; Alexander Spencer, 'Counter-terrorism in new Europe: what have the new EU members done to combat terrorism after September 11th?', *International Public Policy Review* 2, no. 2 (2006), pp. 92–112.

337 Vertrag über die Vertiefung der grenzüberschreitenden Zusammenarbeit, insbesondere zur Bekämpfung des Terrorismus, der grenzüberschreitenden Kriminalität und der illegalen Migration, Prüm, 27 May 2005; House of Lords, 'Prüm: an effective weapon against terrorism and crime?', 18th Report of Session 2006–7, London, 2007.

338 Cf. Thierry Balzacq, 'The policy tools of securitization: information exchange, EU foreign and interior policies', *Journal of Common Market Studies* 46, no. 1 (2008), pp. 75–100.

339 Thierry Balzacq et al., 'Security and the two-level game: the Treaty of Prüm, the EU and the management of threats', CEPS Working Paper No. 234, Centre for European Policy Studies, Brussels, 2006.

340 Cf. Jef Huysmans, 'Minding exceptions: the politics of insecurity and liberal democracy', *Contemporary Political Theory* 3, no. 3 (2004), pp. 321–41.

341 John Benyon, 'The politics of police co-operation in the European Union', *International Journal of the Sociology of Law* 24, no. 4 (1996), pp. 353–79.

342 Cf. James I. Walsh, 'Intelligence-sharing in the European Union: institutions are not enough', *Journal of Common Market Studies* 44, no. 3 (2006), pp. 625–43; Björn Müller-Wille, 'The effect of international terrorism on EU intelligence co-operation', *Journal of Common Market Studies* 46, no. 1 (2008), pp. 49–73.

343 Daniel Keohane, 'The EU and counter-terrorism', Centre for European Reform, Working Paper, London, 2005.

344 Cf. Florian Geyer, 'Fruit of the poisonous tree: members states' indirect use of extraordinary rendition and the EU counter-terrorism strategy', CEPS Working Document No. 263/2007, Brussels, Centre for European Policy Studies; European Parliament, Decision to set up a Temporary Committee on extraordinary rendition, *Official Journal of the European Union*, 24 November 2006.

345 Cf. Alex J. Bellamy, 'Dirty hands and lesser evils in the war on terror', *British Journal of Politics and International Relations* 9, no. 3 (2007), pp. 509–26. For a legal analysis of rendition see Margaret L. Satterthwaite, 'Rendered meaningless: extraordinary rendition and the rule of law', New York University Public Law and Legal Theory Working Paper 43, 2006.

346 Alex Danchev, 'Accomplicity: Britain, torture and terror', *British Journal of Politics and International Relations* 8, no. 4 (2006), pp. 587–601; European Parliament, Report on the alleged use of European countries by the CIA for transportation and illegal detention of prisoners, 30 January 2007, A6–(0020/2007). In addition, Italy, Poland and Romania were named as either colluding with the United States in human rights abuses or not cooperating with the inquiry committee. The report also implicates nine other EU countries.

347 Cf. William Walters, 'The power of inscription: beyond social construction and deconstruction in European integration studies', *Millennium: Journal of International Studies* 31, no. 1 (2002), pp. 83–108; Alexandra Dobrowosky, '(In)Security and citizenship: security, im/migration and shrinking citizenship regimes', *Theoretical Inquiries in Law* 8, no. 2 (2007), pp. 629–62; Antje Wiener, 'European responses to international terrorism: diversity awareness as a new capability?', *Journal of Common Market Studies* 46, no. 1 (2008), pp. 195–218.

Index

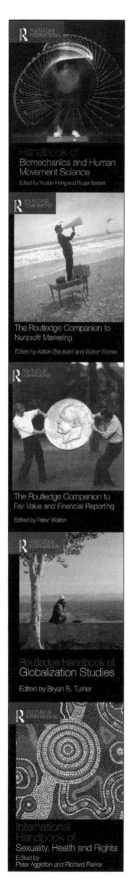

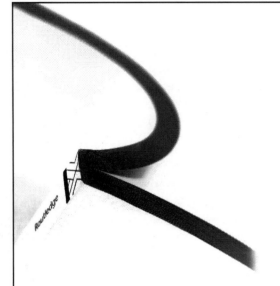

Made in the USA
Middletown, DE
24 February 2018